The Intermediary in the Criminal Justice System

This book undertakes a sociolegal examination of the intermediary role within the criminal justice system.

The intermediary special measure is one of the most innovative and controversial developments in the history of English criminal procedure. But what does the role actually involve? That is the central question explored in this book. Despite increased academic attention into this new criminal justice actor, the content of the intermediary role remains unclear. Based centrally on empirical data gathered in England and Wales and Northern Ireland, but also drawing upon comparative material from other jurisdictions, the book examines how those executing the intermediary role understand its work and how other criminal justice actors perceive it. The book then uses this as the basis for generating a theory of the intermediary role and its scope and content. It also considers the future of the role and its integration into the criminal justice system.

This book will appeal to those researching and studying in the areas of sociolegal studies, criminal law and criminology, as well as lawyers, judges, intermediaries and policy makers working in relevant areas.

John Taggart is Lecturer at QUB School of Law, Belfast, Northern Ireland, U.K. He is a qualified barrister in both Northern Ireland and England and Wales and has practised criminal law in both jurisdictions.

The Intermediary in the Criminal Justice System

John Taggart

Routledge
Taylor & Francis Group
a GlassHouse Book

First published 2026
by Routledge
4 Park Square, Milton Park, Abingdon, Oxon OX14 4RN

and by Routledge
605 Third Avenue, New York, NY 10158

Routledge is an imprint of the Taylor & Francis Group, an informa business

A GlassHouse book

British Library Cataloguing-in-Publication Data
A catalogue record for this book is available from the British Library

ISBN: 978-1-032-60934-8 (hbk)
ISBN: 978-1-032-60935-5 (pbk)
ISBN: 978-1-003-46116-6 (ebk)

DOI: 10.4324/9781003461166

Typeset in Sabon
by Apex CoVantage, LLC

Contents

Foreword: intermediaries and the second generation

Dr Taggart's expertise on *intermediaries in the criminal justice system* was apparent when I examined his PhD. Since then, we have collaborated on several occasions, most notably when developing materials for Australian intermediaries and policy makers. Reading this book took me back to when I led what turned out to be the first of many accredited training courses for intermediaries.

In 2003, in a law school in central London, the first cohort of trainee intermediaries prepared for a practical exercise in the mock-courtroom. The witness (a young girl played by an actress) sat ready to be questioned. A barrister colleague sat on the bench playing the judge. I had my carefully prepared cross-examination on hand. The first trainee intermediary walked forward, a little nervously it must be said. She took her seat next to the witness. My questioning began. The trainee raised her hand to intervene. 'Your Honour, that is a tag question'. I put the question again more simply. The trainee intervened again, 'Your Honour, could counsel please avoid using a tag question'. I called for a break because we, the two experienced barristers in the room, had no idea what a tag question was. The exchange and discussion that followed served to cement the realisation that intermediaries had an enormous mountain to climb; enabling the best evidence from vulnerable witnesses would require nothing short of a cultural revolution in the criminal justice system.

Dr Taggart offers us a detailed account of the dynamic, creative and influential role of the intermediary from its birth at a time of conflicting ideas about what and how it would be, to the internationally impactful profession it is today. The author's analysis demonstrates how intermediaries navigate a complex path with each case they take on. What emerges is a picture of steady, though at times painfully slow, progress for the profession.

This author delicately draws out the complexity of the role and shows us that despite all that the role has become and has overcome, there remain some very real challenges. Almost every intermediary the author interviewed as part of his research 'talked about feeling excluded by the archaic world of the criminal justice system'. That is clearly a difficult professional space for an intermediary to inhabit but, as in that classroom in 2003, from that uniquely entrusted outsider's viewpoint, the intermediary can enlighten those within the system.

Dr Taggart has met the need for up-to-date qualitative, empirical research on the content and scope of the intermediary role in the criminal justice system. This is an outstanding tome, providing indispensable reading for intermediaries and essential understanding for those who work with them, including police officers, solicitors, barristers and judges. Policy makers in England and Wales and Northern Ireland as well as those in the many countries now implementing similar models, need look no further than Dr Taggart's work for a goldmine of knowledge.

It is over 20 years since intermediaries began working in the criminal justice system in England and Wales; thus, a second generation of intermediaries is now taking on this unique and indispensable role. The author is in the second generation of academic researchers in this field; as one of the first generation, it gives me great pleasure to see that intermediary research is in such safe hands.

Dr Penny Cooper
Co-founder of The Advocate's Gateway

Cases

United Kingdom (U.K)

European Court of Human Rights (ECtHR)

New Zealand

Australia

Legislation

Australia

Australian Capital Territory

New South Wales

Queensland

South Australia

Tasmania

Victoria

Western Australia

Chile

Ireland

New Zealand

United Kingdom (U.K)

International instruments

Abbreviations

ABE	Achieving Best Evidence
ACT	Australian Capital Territory
CPD	Criminal Practice Directions
CPR	Criminal Procedure Rules
DoJ	Department of Justice (Northern Ireland)
ECHR	European Convention on Human Rights
ECtHR	European Court of Human Rights
GRH	Ground Rules Hearing
HAIS	HMCTS Court Appointed Intermediary Scheme
IPGAJ	International Principles and Guidelines on Access to Justice for Persons with Disabilities
MoJ	Ministry of Justice
NCA	National Crime Agency
RIS	Registered Intermediary Scheme
SALRI	South Australian Law Reform Institute
VLRC	Victorian Law Reform Commission
WIS	Witness Intermediary Scheme
YJCEA	Youth Justice and Criminal Evidence Act 1999

Chapter 1

Introduction

1.1 Introduction

Imagine a specialist police interview suite where it is proving difficult to elicit evidence from a child interviewee. But a breakthrough is imminent. The police have introduced a communication expert who contrives a game to secure the child's evidence. Requiring a mouth swab from the child for forensic analysis, the specialist child abuse police officer cuts an intimidating figure armed with blue latex medical gloves. The 2-year-old girl initially hides and refuses to cooperate with anyone. It is only when a game involving everyone pretending to brush their teeth is played that the child relaxes and provides a swab without complication. The defendant's subsequent guilty plea results in a minimum ten-year custodial sentence for a child sex offender whom prosecutors believe targeted very young victims believing they could never testify against him.[1] The outcome also ensures the child is spared the ordeal of testifying later in the trial process.

The communication expert in the preceding scenario is known as an intermediary – a 'special measure' introduced by s.29 of the Youth Justice and Criminal Evidence Act 1999 (YJCEA). The legislation introduced a range of special measures to facilitate the evidence gathering process in criminal courts in England and Wales for those considered vulnerable.[2] Collectively, the measures sought to maximise the quality of evidence and reduce the stress associated with the criminal justice process.[3] Other special measures include the use of a live link, enabling the witness to give evidence during the trial from outside the court through a visual link, the use of screens in court and

1 Owen Bowcott, 'Two Year-old Girl Gives Evidence in UK Abuse Case' *The Guardian* (Tuesday 10 October 2017).

2 ss. 23–30.

3 Ministry of Justice (MoJ), *Achieving Best Evidence in Criminal Proceedings: Guidance on Interviewing Victims and Witnesses, and Guidance on Using Special Measures* (January 2022) [1.22].

DOI: 10.4324/9781003461166-1

the removal of wigs and gowns from advocates.[4] This book focuses on the role of the intermediary – the only special measure that is imposed between the questioner (usually the judge or a lawyer) and the witness. The role's function is to communicate 'questions put to the witness' and 'to any person asking such questions, the answers given by the witness in reply to them'.[5] While all of the special measures contained within the YJCEA affect how criminal trials operate, the intermediary has been recognised as perhaps the most ambitious and controversial development.[6] Described as 'little short of revolutionary',[7] the role has been credited with effecting a 'culture change'[8] in the dynamics of traditional adversarial cross-examination. It has elsewhere been described as 'the single biggest improvement in the criminal justice system over the last thirty years'[9] which can enable 'the most vulnerable in the community [to] be heard when before they would have been forced to remain silent'.[10]

This chapter introduces the intermediary role and provides some context for issues examined in the book, namely what the intermediary role involves and how it is perceived by intermediaries themselves and other criminal justice actors. While revolutionary, the intermediary role is beset with problems about its scope and function. Although the role has been operational in the criminal justice system for over 20 years, various competing conceptualisations exist. This chapter outlines the current framework for intermediary provision in England and Wales and Northern Ireland and develops a basis for the interjurisdictional comparison that threads throughout the book. It will be explained how the two jurisdictions have previously been compared and how this work has been valuable and enlightening. As various intermediary-type models emerge internationally (see Chapter 3: The International Context), the United Kingdom (U.K) is an understandable reference point. Thus, it is increasingly useful to consider how the role was initially

4 Many of these measures, such as use of screens and removal of wigs and gowns, had developed through individual court practices, but the YJCEA gave them a statutory footing, see: Camilla MacPherson, 'The Youth Justice and Criminal Evidence Act 1999: Achieving Best Evidence?' (2001) 41(3) Medicine, Science and the Law 230.

5 YJCEA, s. 29.

6 Louise Ellison, *The Adversarial Process and the Vulnerable Witness* (OUP 2002) 6.

7 Emily Henderson, 'A Very Valuable Tool': Judges, Advocates and Intermediaries Discuss the Intermediary System in England and Wales' (2015) 19(3) International Journal of Evidence and Proof 154, 155.

8 Penny Cooper and David Wurtzel, 'Intermediaries' in Penny Cooper and Heather Norton (eds) *Vulnerable People and the Criminal Justice System – A Guide to Law and Practice* (OUP 2017) 364.

9 Victims' Commissioner, *Next Steps for Special Measures: A Review of the Provision of Special Measures to Vulnerable and Intimidated Witnesses* (May 2021) 27.

10 The Rt. Hon. The Lord Judge, Lord Chief Justice of England and Wales, *Vulnerable Witnesses in the Administration of Criminal Justice* (Australian Institute of Judicial Administration 7 September 2011) 15–16.

conceived in the U.K and has developed since. The overall methodological approach to the research underpinning the book will then be explained. Finally, the structure of the individual chapters will be laid out.

1.2 A role in need of clarification

> *'We fear that [the intermediary] may have misunderstood her role. If so, she may not be the only one to do so.'*[11]

The central motivation for the research project underpinning this book was the absence of qualitative, empirical research on the content and scope of the intermediary role in the criminal justice system. The increasing codification of the intermediary's functions in England and Wales through rules, directions and guidance necessitated a qualitative enquiry to examine potential differences in the role 'in the books' and 'in action'.[12] The preceding quote from Lord Thomas CJ in the case of *R v Grant-Murray* is an important starting point in understanding different conceptualisations of the intermediary role. Several interrelated questions flow from this judicial comment. Firstly, and most broadly, in what sense is the intermediary role 'misunderstood'? Does this suggest a judicial conceptualisation of the intermediary role from which intermediaries in practice deviate? How, then, do intermediaries experience the role and how do they conceptualise its content and parameters? These questions deserve attention and relate to aspects of the intermediary role that have hitherto not featured in the literature. As recognition of communication difficulties and demand for intermediary services increases, these questions become central to understanding the nature and scope of the role and its relative position within the criminal justice system.

While Lord Thomas CJ's comments in *Grant-Murray* point to a general discord between the judiciary and the intermediary, the case law relating to intermediaries raises several other issues. In recent years, there has been an increase in the number of cases before the appellate courts involving intermediaries and their role in criminal proceedings. Examined discretely, these decisions ostensibly provide important guidance on the intermediary role and reflect the growing influence of the intermediary as a criminal justice actor. However, when read together, these judgments seem to complicate an already poorly understood role.[13] Perhaps of even more concern is that these

11 *R v Grant-Murray & Anor* [2017] EWCA Crim 1228 [199] (Lord Thomas CJ).

12 Roscoe Pound, 'Law in Books and Law in Action' (1910) 44 American Law Review 12, 12–15.

13 Penny Cooper, 'Highs and Lows: The 4th Intermediary Survey' (Kingston University London, 13 October 2014) <http://eprints.kingston.ac.uk/28868/1/Cooper-P-28868.pdf> accessed 8 February 2019.

decisions reflect a glaring divide between the judicial conception of the intermediary role and that of intermediary practitioners themselves. More recent research, which postdates the empirical research underpinning this book, suggests an even more troubling discord between intermediaries and the legal profession.[14]

As will become clear throughout the book, there are critical questions around the distinction between intermediaries assisting witnesses and those assisting defendants. A number of the appeal cases concerning intermediaries have focused on the length of defendant intermediary appointment, i.e., whether appointments defendants should be made for 'evidence only' or for the full duration of the trial (see below for further discussion). The amendment to the Criminal Practice Directions (CPD) in April 2016 which outlines that 'Directions to appoint an intermediary for a defendant's evidence will thus be rare, but for the entire trial extremely rare'[15] suggested a serious curtailment to defendant intermediary appointments which was confirmed in the case of *R v Rashid*.[16] As Hoyano and Rafferty have pointed out, no equivalent Practice Direction exists for prosecution or defence witnesses and no reason is given for the specific focus on the defendant.[17] Subsequently, in the case of *R v Biddle*, the Court of Appeal reinforced the judicial discretion in deciding whether intermediaries should be appointed for the entire trial.[18] The court was firm in directing intermediaries to follow the trial judge's directions and not dictate the terms of their own appointment.[19] In *R v Thomas* the court largely echoed this but emphasised the need for intermediary applications to be 'addressed carefully, with sensitivity and with caution to ensure the defendant's effective participation'.[20] The more recent case of *TI v Bromley Youth Court*,[21] however, signals a potential change in judicial attitude to defendant intermediary appointments with the 'rarity' provision of the CPD directly questioned.[22] How these appellate decisions can be reconciled, and whether the number of defendant intermediary appointments will now increase, remains to be seen. In Northern Ireland, the restriction of defendant intermediary to the period of witness testimony only remains and has not been challenged in the courts.

14 Samantha Fairclough and John Taggart, 'Lost in Translation? Perceptions of Defendant Intermediaries in the Legal Profession (2023) 7 Criminal Law Review 440.

15 Criminal Practice Directions 2015 (April 2016 amendment) 3F.13.

16 [2017] 1 WLR 2449.

17 Laura Hoyano and Angela Rafferty QC, 'Rationing Defence Intermediaries under the April 2016 Criminal Practice Direction' (2017) Criminal Law Review 90, 99.

18 [2019] EWCA Crim 86.

19 [2019] EWCA Crim 86.

20 [2020] EWCA Crim 117 [38].

21 [2020] EWHC 1204 (Admin).

22 Hoyano and Rafferty (n 17). The updated Criminal Practice Directions (Criminal Practice Directions 2023 (CrimPRC(23)90(b))) (CPD) contain no reference to intermediary appointments for defendants being 'rare'.

The question of the 'role' of the intermediary is complex and goes beyond the duration of appointment by the judge. Even though much of intermediary practice in England and Wales is now governed by the CPD[23] and the Criminal Procedure Rules (CPR),[24] intermediaries have generally been regarded as a peripheral figure within the context of the adversarial criminal trial. This assumption was challenged in *R v Grant-Murray* as it was contended that an intermediary had been 'undermined and undervalued' and had been treated as an 'enemy of the court'.[25] The Court of Appeal recognised that intermediaries 'provide a very useful service to the court' but commented that they are 'not to dictate to anyone what is to happen' and that the role provides assistance 'as directed by the judge'.[26] In equally strong terms, the court stated that intermediaries 'should not interfere with the functions of others unless specifically directed to do so by the judge'.[27] Cooper has commented that these judicial statements should act as a reminder to defendant intermediaries who are not selected, trained or quality assured by the Ministry of Justice (MoJ). However, the force of the judgment must surely apply equally to all intermediaries.[28] The court clarified that while intermediaries are instrumental in the effort to achieve the effective participation of the defendant, ultimately the burden for discharging this burden is on the judge. This approach has subsequently been echoed in decisions of the Family Division of the High Court. For example, in the case of *Re X & Y (Intermediary: Practice and Procedure)*,[29] the court noted that that the need for intermediary involvement is case specific and that it is ultimately 'for the experienced family judges to determine what is required to make the process fair'.[30]

Considering the pivotal role of the judge in controlling criminal proceedings, the relationship between the judiciary and the intermediary requires closer examination. Intermediaries cannot be expected to operate effectively without the confidence of the judiciary, and it is the judge who ultimately decides the individual terms of intermediary appointments.[31] In their research focusing on young witnesses, Plotnikoff and Woolfson found it troubling that

23 CPD (n 22) [6.2].
24 Criminal Procedure Rules (October 2020) Pt 18, rules 18.27–18.32 (hereafter referred to as 'CPR'). Note that neither the CPD nor the CPR apply in Northern Ireland.
25 *Grant-Murray* (n 11) [196].
26 *Grant-Murray* (n 11) [199].
27 *Grant-Murray* (n 11) [199].
28 Penny Cooper, 'Joint Enterprise: R. v Grant-Murray (Janhelle); R. v McGill (Joseph) Court of Appeal (Criminal Division): Lord Thomas of Cwmgiedd CJ, Hallett LJ (VP CACD) and Goss J: 11 August 2017; [2017] EWCA Crim 1228' (2018) 1 Criminal Law Review 71, 74.
29 [2024] EWHC 906 (Fam).
30 [2024] EWHC 906 (Fam) [19].
31 Joyce Plotnikoff and Richard Woolfson, *Falling Short? A Snapshot of Young Witness Policy and Practice: A Report for the NSPCC, Revisiting 'Measuring Up? Evaluating Implementation of Government Commitments to Young Witnesses in Criminal Proceedings* (NSPCC, February 2019) 17.

many judges were unable to distinguish between intermediaries who assist witnesses and those who assist defendants. As will be developed further, 'Registered Intermediaries' who assist witnesses are recruited, trained and regulated by the MoJ while defendants fall outside this scheme and have no statutory entitlement to intermediary assistance.[32] This difference in treatment has resulted in what Henderson has termed a 'two-tier' system of intermediary provision.[33] Inconsistency among judges as to the scope of the intermediary role during witness examination (or indeed trial proceedings more generally) is also of concern. For example, the Victims' Commissioner found a striking difference in the perceived effectiveness of intermediaries among magistrates/District Judges (20%) compared to Crown Court judges (67%). These figures suggest that intermediary function may, in practice, differ not only between registered/non-registered intermediaries but also between those in lower and higher courts.[34]

Further, some reported appeal cases involving intermediaries suggest that the role's status within criminal proceedings is far from settled. For example, in both *R v Boxer*[35] and *R v Beards and Beards*,[36] intermediaries were asked to provide expert evidence on the communication needs of vulnerable individuals. As has been recognised by The Advocate's Gateway,[37] this is contrary to good practice if the intermediary is simultaneously acting in their intermediary role.[38] In the more recent case of *R v Pringle*, the Court of Appeal noted that the trial judge was open to the possibility of an intermediary acting as an expert witness and did not expressly reject the notion.[39] It is stark that all three of these cases came years after the Lord Chief Justice, speaking extrajudicially, stated categorically that intermediaries are neither expert witnesses nor supporters.[40] Elsewhere, the Equal Treatment Bench Book and the Registered Intermediary Procedural Guidance plainly state that

32 Plotnikoff and Woolfson (n 31) 17.

33 Henderson (n 7); Also see: Louise Tickle, '"Justice Must Be for All": Why Court Intermediaries Are Vital for Vulnerable' *The Guardian* (London, 28 October 2020) <https://www.theguardian.com/society/2020/oct/28/justice-for-all-court-intermediaries-vulnerable-people-england-wales> accessed 5 June 2021.

34 Victims' Commissioner (n 9) 1.

35 [2015] EWCA Crim 1684.

36 [2016] EW Misc B14 (CC).

37 The Advocate's Gateway, 'Intermediaries: Step by Step' (Toolkit 16, 2 September 2019) <https://www.theadvocatesgateway.org/images/toolkits/16-intermediaries-step-by-step-2019.pdf> accessed 7 April 2019.

38 The Advocate's Gateway, 'Cases' <https://www.theadvocatesgateway.org/cases> accessed 18 April 2019.

39 [2019] EWCA Crim 1722.

40 The Rt. Hon. The Lord Judge, Lord Chief Justice of England and Wales (n 10).

the intermediary is not to be treated as an expert witness.[41] The practice of judges asking intermediaries to effectively act as expert witnesses has been well documented empirically and must be recognised as inappropriate.[42]

The literature on intermediaries provides insight into the role's historical development, organisation and legal provision. Plotnikoff and Woolfson's book, *Intermediaries in the Criminal Justice System*, narrates the emergence of the role and documents some of the earliest experiences of those working at the coalface. Cooper has also written extensively about the use of intermediaries in England and Wales and Northern Ireland as well as similar schemes internationally with several co-authors.[43] These publications are crucial to understanding how the role operates, from the police station to the courtroom, and how it has become integrated into the criminal justice process. O'Mahony et al.'s research is also crucial to understand the practical challenges intermediaries encounter in their work and how the role could be better utilised.[44] The operation of the 'two-tier' intermediary system in England and Wales has been the subject of more recent academic critique, with Hoyano and Rafferty lamenting the 'inequality of arms' between witnesses and defendants in terms of intermediary access.[45] This followed the Law Commission's conclusion a year earlier that statutory entitlement to intermediaries should be extended to defendants to ensure the right to a fair trial is upheld.

However, there has been less research into the scope and content of the intermediary role. Shortly after the YJCEA was implemented, Birch noted that flesh would have to be put on the 'bare bones' of s.29 YJCEA due to

41 Judicial College, *Equal Treatment Bench Book* (February 2018 edn, revised March 2020) 58 <www.judiciary.uk/wp-content/uploads/2018/02/ETBB-February-2018-amendedMarch-2020.pdf> accessed 7 November 2020; MoJ, Registered Intermediary Procedural Guidance Manual 36.

42 Joyce Plotnikoff and Richard Woolfson, *Intermediaries in the Criminal Justice System* (Policy Press 2015) 258–60; Law Commission, 'Unfitness to Plead, Volume 1: Report Law' (2016 Com No. 364) 117–18.

43 Penny Cooper and David Wurtzel, 'Better the Second Time around? Department of Justice Registered Intermediaries Schemes and Lessons from England and Wales' (2014) 65(1) Northern Ireland Legal Quarterly 39; Penny Cooper and David Wurtzel, 'A Day Late and a Dollar Short: In Search of an Intermediary Scheme for Vulnerable Defendants in England and Wales' (2013) 1 Criminal Law Review 4; Penny Cooper, Paula Backen and Ruth Marchant, 'Getting to Grips with Ground Rules Hearings – a Checklist for Judges, Advocates and Intermediaries' (2015) 6 Criminal Law Review 420; Penny Cooper and David Wurtzel, 'Intermediaries' in Cooper and Norton (n 8); Penny Cooper, Michelle Mattison and Heather Norton, 'Looking Ahead' in Cooper and Norton (n 8).

44 Brendan O'Mahony and others, 'Developing a Professional Identity in a New Work Environment: The Views of Defendant Intermediaries Working in the Criminal Courts' (2016) 18(2) Journal of Forensic Practice 155.

45 Hoyano and Rafferty (n 17) 97.

the legislation's vagueness.[46] While the literature has contributed to a better understanding of intermediary provision, scant empirical research has examined how the role is performed. Cooper and Mattison have identified a 'pressing need for further research into . . . the role in practice' and found it 'striking how little research has been conducted into the completeness, accuracy and coherence of the evidence that intermediaries facilitate'.[47]

Based on the aforementioned, no distinctive 'models' or 'ideal types' of intermediary practice have been theorised in any depth. In the case of *OP*, however, the Court of Appeal sought to outline the core functions of the intermediary, as well as clarify what the role does *not* involve.[48] The court discerned two distinct forms of support which witnesses with communication difficulties may require during a trial. The first involves 'general support, reassurance and calm interpretation of unfolding events',[49] which need not necessarily be provided by an intermediary but is 'readily achievable by an adult with experience of life'.[50] The second requires 'skilled support and interpretation' of questions which often only an intermediary will be qualified to perform.[51] Clearly, the court felt that the intermediary executes a fundamentally different role during testimony than is required for the remainder of the trial. This approach has been criticised by Hoyano, who argues that 'sympathy and compassion cannot compensate for the cognitive defects of defendants with comprehension as well as communication difficulties'.[52] In other words, a vulnerable defendant with communication difficulties needs assistance not just during evidence but also in attempting to follow and understand the whole trial. Perhaps most significant about *OP* is that this task does not necessarily require a professional communication expert, such as an intermediary, but rather involves helping the vulnerable individual to cope with understandable human emotions, such as 'uncertainty . . . nervousness and agitation'.[53] Any support the intermediary provides may therefore only occur in the witness box under the supervision of the judge who decides on the propriety of intervention.

Academic commentators have advanced differing views on the breadth of the intermediary role. Cooper and Wurtzel advocate a broad communicative role with the intermediary advising on appropriate vocabulary and other

46 Diane Birch, 'A Better Deal for Vulnerable Witnesses?' (2000) Criminal Law Review 223, 249.

47 Penny Cooper and Michelle Mattison, 'Intermediaries, Vulnerable People and the Quality of Evidence: An International Comparison of Three Versions of the English Intermediary Model' (2017) 21(4) International Journal of Evidence and Proof 351.

48 *OP v Secretary of State for Justice* [2014] EWHC 1944 (Admin).

49 *OP v Secretary of State for Justice* (n 48) [35].

50 *OP v Secretary of State for Justice* (n 48) [35].

51 *OP v Secretary of State for Justice* (n 48) [34].

52 Laura Hoyano, 'Commentary on *R (on the application of OP) v Secretary of State for* Justice' (2015) 1 Criminal Law Review 79, 82.

53 *OP* (n 48) [35].

linguistic difficulties, but also intervening when they consider breaks would be useful or to allow the witness time to remain calm and attentive.[54] In a similar vein, Backen suggests that 'the remit of an intermediary is greater than just the questions to be asked during cross-examination. It encompasses anything which may affect communication and understanding in the widest sense'.[55] These views contrast sharply with Ellison's prediction that the role would 'perform a relatively passive translator function "reinterpreting" lawyers' complex language into a more developmentally appropriate and therefore accessible form'.[56]

Returning to a theme mentioned earlier, it is also significant that no research to date has compared the roles of intermediaries working with witnesses and defendants. Indeed, much of the research which has touched on the use of intermediaries has done so as part of a wider focus on witness policy and practice and has not considered the use of defendant intermediaries at all.[57] While there have been calls for the extension of Registered Intermediaries to vulnerable defendants in England and Wales, there has been insufficient regard given to how intermediary work might differ between witnesses and defendants.[58] The continuation of the 'two-tier' provision of intermediaries in England and Wales through the establishment of His Majesty's Courts and Tribunal Service (HMCTS) Appointed Intermediary Service (HAIS), which is discussed further later, is significant in this regard. Intermediary appointments for witnesses and defendants in England and Wales are still administered and processed separately. There has been no research of any kind into how this bifurcation of intermediary provision impacts the work of intermediaries themselves or the quality of communication assistance received by vulnerable witnesses and defendants.

Finally, the internationalisation of the intermediary role, particularly in the last four to five years, offers an opportunity to assess how expert communication assistance operates in different contexts and settings. As will be explored in Chapter 3 (The International Context), developments in countries such as Australia, New Zealand and Chile should cause us to critically reflect on the normative function of the intermediary role. At the very least, some of the diverging practices that are emerging in different jurisdictions can inform how we conceptualise the role and its relative status within the criminal process.

54 Penny Cooper and David Wurtzel, 'Intermediaries' in Cooper and Norton (n 8) 367.

55 Paula Backen, *They Just Don't Get It: Communication and the Work of an Intermediary with Vulnerable People in the Justice System* (independently published 2017) 117.

56 Ellison (n 6).

57 Victims' Commissioner, *A Voice for the Voiceless: The Victims' Commissioner's Review into the Provision of Registered Intermediaries for Children and Vulnerable Victims and Witnesses* (January 2018).

58 Law Commission (n 42); Victims' Commissioner (n 9).

1.3 Legal framework

Considering that England and Wales and Northern Ireland share broadly similar legal systems, there is obvious scope for comparison between the jurisdictions. More importantly for the purposes of intermediary provision, the Northern Irish model established by the Department of Justice (Northern Ireland) (DoJ) in 2013 was largely based on the experience of the Witness Intermediary Scheme (WIS) in England and Wales since 2004. Shortly after the launch of the DoJ's pilot project, Cooper and Wurtzel compared the respective schemes 'which, though similar, are distinct and significantly different in respect of defendants'.[59] Cooper and Wurtzel's work also provided a useful analysis of the challenges the DoJ was likely to face in implementing the Registered Intermediary Scheme (RIS) and lessons that could be learned from nearly a decade of intermediary provision in England and Wales. As such, there are similarities in how intermediaries are organised in both jurisdictions but sufficient divergence for a useful research enquiry.

i) England and Wales

The intermediary role is a creature of statute. S.29 of the YJCEA contains the intermediary special measure and outlines the role's functions as follows:

(2) The function of an intermediary is to communicate –

- (a) to the witness, questions put to the witness, and
- (b) to any person asking such questions, the answers given by the witness in reply to them,

and to explain such questions or answers so far as necessary to enable them to be understood by the witness or person in question.

The eligibility criteria for an intermediary for non-defendant witnesses are contained within s.16(1)(a).[60] This sets out that a witness may be granted an intermediary:

- '(a) if under the age of [18] at the time of the hearing; or
- (b) if the court considers that the quality of evidence given by the witness is likely to be diminished by reason of any circumstances falling within subsection (2).

59 Cooper and Wurtzel (n 43).

60 The YJCEA, as amended in June 2011 by s.98 of the Coroners and Justice Act 2009 (CJA) increases the age limit from 17.

(2) The circumstances falling within this subsection are –

(a) that the witness –

(i) suffers from mental disorder within the meaning of the Mental Health Act 1983, or
(ii) otherwise has a significant impairment of intelligence and social functioning;

(b) that the witness has a physical disability or is suffering from a physical disorder'.

After the YJCEA was implemented, it was not clear how any resulting intermediary scheme would be rolled out, what profile of individual would carry out the role or how it would operate in practice.[61] Birch raised similar questions and noted that s.29 provided only a 'briefest description of the intermediary's function'.[62] The intermediary special measure was first piloted in 2004 in six police force areas (pathfinder areas) in England.[63] The Home Office recruited a cadre of intermediaries, mostly trained as speech and language therapists, deemed to possess the 'relevant professional skills' who were required to undergo a specific training course.[64] These first intermediaries were trained on criminal procedure and writing court reports based on their assessment of communication needs. Based largely on a poor understanding of the extent of miscommunication in the criminal justice process, recognition of eligibility was initially a major obstacle.[65] The pilot scheme was relaunched in 2005 with clearer guidance and the rates of requests increased.[66] The resulting evaluation report recommended the national rollout of the intermediary scheme which occurred in 2007. This involved delegating the cost of the scheme to local police forces and the Crown Prosecution Service (CPS) areas, which helped further improve awareness of the scheme and the number of vulnerable individuals matched with intermediaries.[67] The Witness Intermediary Scheme (WIS), now managed by the National Crime Agency (NCA), was fully implemented nationally in 2008. The key operational element of

61 Home Office, *Measures to Assist Vulnerable Or Intimidated Witnesses in the Criminal Justice System: Implementing the Speaking Up for Justice Report* (Home Office Communication Directorate 2002). Chapter 2 of this book outlines the 'emergence' of the intermediary role in a historical context.
62 Birch (n 46) 249.
63 Joyce Plotnikoff and Richard Woolfson, *The Go-between: Evaluation of Intermediary Pathfinder Projects* (Lexicon 2007).
64 Plotnikoff and Woolfson (n 42) 11.
65 Plotnikoff and Woolfson (n 42) 10–11.
66 Plotnikoff and Woolfson (n 42) 13.
67 Cooper and Wurtzel (n 43) 45.

the scheme became known as the 'Matching Service', which is the mechanism by which Registered Intermediaries are matched to the requirements of witnesses at the request of the end-user.[68] The service is run by the Witness Intermediary Team (WIT) which is responsible for matching requests from the police and the CPS using a centrally held register of qualified 'Registered Intermediaries'.[69] While the vast majority of intermediaries initially recruited to the register were speech and language therapists, in recent years there has been an increase in individuals from other backgrounds, such as teaching, nursing and social work.[70]

Registered Intermediaries operating within the WIS are available only to non-defendant witnesses.[71] As a result, any application for intermediary assistance for a vulnerable defendant must be dealt with under common law, applying the court's inherent jurisdiction.[72] Intermediaries who assist suspects and defendants through this route are termed 'non-registered intermediaries'.[73] As Cooper and Wurtzel note, in the absence of in-force legislation, judges in England and Wales have 'stepped in to fill the gap and permit defendant intermediaries where they are necessary for a fair trial'.[74] Exercise of the court's inherent powers in this way has been viewed as an attempt to 'redress the imbalance between witnesses and defendants'.[75] Non-registered intermediary appointments are decided on a case-by-case basis. The difference in treatment between witnesses and defendants in terms of intermediary

68 MoJ, 'The Witness Intermediary Scheme: Annual Report 2023' <https://assets.publishing.service.gov.uk/media/664487d0993111924d9d3504/Witness_Intermediary_Scheme_Annual_Report_2023.pdf> 9.

69 For a full outline of the governance of the Witness Intermediary Scheme (WIS) see: MoJ, 'Registered Intermediary Procedural Guidance Manual 2024' <https://assets.publishing.service.gov.uk/media/671b819bfc28a840abc6d26d/Registered_Intermediary_Procedural_Guidance_Manual_2024__Official_.pdf>.

70 52.3% of Registered Intermediaries in England and Wales list their profession as 'Speech and Language Therapist', 25.1% list 'Education', 4.1% 'Psychologist', 4.1% 'Nurse', 2.5% 'Social Worker', 2.9% list their profession as 'Therapist', and the remaining 9.1% list a range of other professional backgrounds, for example, ex-police officer, Independent Sexual Violence Advisor, counsellor, accredited mediator or registered case manager (Response to a Freedom of Information Request from Dr John Taggart to the Ministry of Justice, 25 February 2025).

71 Penny Cooper and David Wurtzel, 'A day late and a dollar short: In search of an intermediary scheme for vulnerable defendants in England and Wales' (2013) 1 Criminal Law Review 4, 7. Section 33A of the Youth Justice and Criminal Act 1999 (YJCEA) now provides that the court can allow a defendant to give evidence by live link.

72 Section 33BA of the Coroners and Justice Act 2009 (CJA) amended the YJCEA to provide a statutory basis for defendant access to intermediaries; however, this has not been implemented.

73 Cooper and Wurtzel note that there is no standard way of finding an appropriate defendant intermediary and funding arrangements differ for pre-trial and trial. See Cooper and Wurtzel (n 43) 18.

74 Cooper and Wurtzel (n 43) 18.

75 Plotnikoff and Woolfson (n 42) 248.

provision has been described as 'puzzling' by the Divisional Court.[76] As Plotnikoff and Woolfson highlight, many defendants would meet the criteria governing intermediary assistance, which makes the discrepancy even more difficult to justify.[77]

In practice, the work of intermediaries extends beyond assisting at police interview and facilitating communication at trial as originally envisaged by the YJCEA.[78] Registered Intermediaries in England and Wales routinely attend police stations, as well as other locations, such as schools or homes, to assess vulnerable witnesses.[79] The purpose of the communication assessment is for the intermediary to ascertain the witness's communication abilities and specific needs.[80] This includes language, attention span, understanding of temporal and spatial concepts, abstract terms, and the extent of suggestibility and compliance. After the assessment, the Registered Intermediary is required to prepare a preliminary report, setting out their findings and recommendations for the Achieving Best Evidence (ABE) interview. ABE interviews are investigative interviews with witnesses which aim to obtain 'an accurate and reliable account in a way that is fair, is in the witness's interests and is acceptable to the court'.[81] Once the intermediary has assessed and established a rapport with the witness, they will have a planning meeting for the ABE interview with the police officer. This may include a discussion of communication needs, room layout, potential use of communication aids or props, vocabulary and how to ensure that the witness remains engaged and calm.[82] The police officer conducts and manages the ABE interview, and while the intermediary may intervene when communication breaks down, their role does not amount to 'a second interviewer'.[83] Intermediaries rarely attend suspects at the police station, although when they do, it is on an ad hoc basis. Official guidance on questioning vulnerable suspects at the police interview stage provides only for the involvement of an appropriate adult.[84] Appropriate adults aim to support, assist and advise vulnerable suspects in custody, ensure that the police act fairly and enable the suspect to understand their

76 *OP* (n 48).

77 Plotnikoff and Woolfson (n 42) 247; communication difficulties and disorders are even higher among defendants than the general population, see: Laura Farrugia and Fiona Gabbert, 'Vulnerable Suspects in Police Interviews: Exploring Current Practice in England and Wales' (2020) 17(1) Journal of Investigative Psychology and Offender Profiling 17.

78 Plotnikoff and Woolfson (n 42) 18.

79 The Advocate's Gateway (2019) 'Intermediaries' <www.theadvocatesgateway.org/intermediaries> accessed 4 March 2021.

80 MoJ (n 69) 13.

81 MoJ (n 3) [3.00].

82 MoJ (n 3) [4.52].

83 MoJ (n 3) [2.200].

84 Home Office, 'Code C: Revised Code of Practice for the Detention, Treatment and Questioning of Persons by Police Officers' (Police and Criminal Evidence Act (PACE) 1984) [1.4].

rights and entitlements.[85] While both appropriate adults and intermediaries facilitate communication, appropriate adults are not ordinarily communication experts like intermediaries and operate mostly in a volunteer capacity.[86] The role can be performed by various individuals, including parents or family members, friends, carers or social workers.[87]

If a case proceeds to court, the intermediary is required to prepare a written report explaining their own experience and skills and how communication assistance may be given. For Registered Intermediaries, comprehensive guidance on the court report, its structure and what it should include are contained within the MoJ's Procedural Guidance Manual.[88] Unsurprisingly, no such guidance exists for non-registered intermediaries. However, since many non-registered intermediaries also work with witnesses under the WIS, there tends to be a degree of uniformity in how recommendations are presented.[89] The period of communication assistance provided to vulnerable individuals often differs between witnesses and defendants. Registered Intermediaries facilitate communication during the period of oral testimony. While non-registered intermediaries may be appointed to assist a defendant throughout the duration of a trial, the CPD and subsequent case law make clear that even when the appointment of an intermediary has the potential to improve the trial process, 'appointment is not mandatory'.[90] As such, there is no presumption that a defendant will be assisted by an intermediary and the terms of any appointment are entirely a matter for the court.[91] Without any formalised guidance or equivalent procedural manual, the involvement of intermediaries for defendants is more varied and potentially flexible. As will be developed later in the book, the different participatory roles of witnesses and defendants invariably mirror intermediary involvement at all stages of the criminal process.[92]

ii) Northern Ireland

The DoJ in 2013 developed a model for the provision of intermediaries for vulnerable complainants and witnesses in the criminal justice system. This

85 Home Office (n 84).
86 For further discussion on how the appropriate adult role is framed, see: Roxanna Dehaghani, 'Defining the "Appropriate" in "Appropriate Adult": Restrictions and Opportunities for Reform' (2020) 12 Criminal Law Review 1137.
87 National Appropriate Adult Network, 'About Appropriate Adults' (NAAN, 2018) <https://www.appropriateadult.org.uk/information/what-is-an-appropriate-adult#act> accessed 8 December 2017.
88 MoJ (n 69) 31–39.
89 Plotnikoff and Woolfson (n 42) 250.
90 CPD (n 22) [6.2.4].
91 CPD (n 22) [6.2.6].
92 For further discussion of 'effective participation', see: Chapter 7 (Witness work, defendant work and participatory role).

was based on the provisions of the Criminal Evidence (Northern Ireland) Order 1999,[93] which mirror the provisions of s.29 YJCEA. These provide that an application for an intermediary may be made where their use is likely to improve the quality (completeness, coherence and accuracy) of the evidence given by a witness. For defendants, an intermediary may be appointed to enable effective participation during oral evidence in court and to help ensure a fair trial.[94] Intermediaries in Northern Ireland are trained, registered and regulated by the DoJ. The DoJ concluded that respect for the principle of equality of arms demanded that all vulnerable individuals – including defendants – be eligible for intermediary assistance.[95] Therefore, what Henderson has termed the 'two tier' intermediary provision in England and Wales does not exist in Northern Ireland.[96] The DoJ initially sought to recruit candidates 'from a wide background of professional roles and occupations, including speech and language therapy, occupational therapy, psychology, social work, the mental health professions, counselling, teaching and nursing'.[97] It advertised for 'professionals with specialist skills in communication' from fields such as 'speech and language therapy and social work'.[98] Like England and Wales, the vast majority of those on the RIS register are speech and language therapists with a number hailing from a social work background.[99] The RIS was subsequently established to allow end users, i.e. police, prosecutors and defence solicitors, to access intermediary services. The first batch of Registered Intermediaries underwent an intensive training and assessment course covering legal procedures, report writing, the role and responsibilities of the intermediary and court work with a witness.[100]

Registered Intermediaries in Northern Ireland can support both witnesses and suspects at the police station, assist with the planning of interviews and, indeed, attend interviews to help facilitate communication.[101] Their involvement at this stage mirrors the WIS in England and Wales and is comprehensively set out in the DoJ Procedural Guidance Manual. The demand for intermediary assistance at the investigative stage in Northern Ireland is significant. For example, in 2021/2022 there were 384 requests for intermediary assessment for a suspect at the police station, which constituted 34% of the total referrals across all witness types for the year. The number of suspect

93 Arts 17 and 21BA.

94 DoJ, *Northern Ireland Registered Intermediaries Schemes Pilot Project: Post-Project Review* (January 2015) 6.

95 DoJ (n 94).

96 Henderson (n 7).

97 DoJ, *Application Information Pack* (August 2012) 7.

98 DoJ (n 97) 5.

99 E-mail from DoJ to author (August 21, 2020).

100 Cooper and Wurtzel (n 43) 40.

101 DoJ (n 94) 3.

Table 1.1 Age of Northern Ireland Registered Intermediary Scheme (RIS) service users

Age range	*2019/20*	*2020/21*	*2021/22*	*2022/23*	*2023/24*	*Total*
0–7	378	279	320	304	292	1,573 (29%)
8–11	109	70	121	128	118	546 (10%)
12–17	179	232	283	321	329	1,344 (24%)
Adult 18+	253	257	383	434	476	1,803 (33%)
60+	28	30	48	62	49	217 (4%)
Total	947	868	1,155	1,249	1,264	**5,483**

(Table compiled by the Department of Justice (Northern Ireland) and reproduced with permission).

referrals in 2022/2023 was 383 (which represented 31% of all referrals), and this figure increased to 392 in 2023/2024 (which represented 31% of all referrals).[102] This is in stark contrast to England and Wales, where no comparable provision of intermediary services for suspects exists.

The majority of vulnerable individuals appointed an intermediary in Northern Ireland are children, as shown in **Table 1.1**. **Table 1.2** shows a breakdown the vulnerabilities of RIS service users in Northern Ireland. Although comparison is difficult due to variations in matching procedure and definitions, these broadly correspond with figures collected by the MoJ in England and Wales.[103]

At trial, Registered Intermediaries in Northern Ireland are appointed on an 'evidence only' basis, i.e. they are restricted to assisting during the period of testimony.[104] The court can, however, appoint a 'court defendant supporter', who typically also works as an appropriate adult, to provide emotional and general support to the defendant when an intermediary is not present.[105] After an initial pilot in May 2013, the scheme was extended and now operates in criminal cases in all Crown, magistrates' and youth courts. In both jurisdictions, intermediaries are involved in pre-trial case management hearings known as 'Ground Rules Hearings' (GRH). The GRH affords the intermediary the opportunity to discuss with the advocates and the judge any adjustments to questioning and any other recommendations contained within the court report. The GRH should establish the rules relating to the

102 Figures provided to the author by the Department of Justice (Northern Ireland) (Email, 1 May 2024).

103 MoJ (n 69) 22.

104 This has also been set out in a recent Crown Court Practice Direction: Practice Direction No. 2/2019, Case Management in the Crown Court Including Protocols for Vulnerable Witnesses and Defendants, A5.4.

105 DoJ (n 94) 21.

Table 1.2 Breakdown of vulnerabilities of RIS service users of the Northern Ireland RIS

Vulnerabilities	*2020/21*	*2021/22*	*2022/23*	*2023/24*
ADD/ADHD	94	123	132	133
Asperger's	4	16	23	15
Aphasia	4	3	5	1
ASD	131	144	169	175
Brain/head injury	27	32	29	28
Cerebral palsy	3	4	6	2
Deafness/hearing impairment	7	14	10	12
Dementia	5	8	17	18
Down syndrome	3	7	4	5
Dysarthria/dyspraxia	1	3	2	1
Fluency difficulties	1	5	4	5
Language delay disorder	14	17	17	12
Mental health	47	91	123	145
Mild/moderate learning disabilities	233	307	271	280
Neurological	5	3	4	2
Physical disability	4	3	6	4
Severe learning disabilities	47	50	67	69
Young age	238	324	358	355
Voice disorders	0	1	2	2
Total	**868**	**1155**	**1249**	**1264**

(Table compiled by the Department of Justice (Northern Ireland) and reproduced with permission).

manner and duration of questioning, how the intermediary may intervene if necessary and generally how the intermediary will assist the advocates and judge.[106] The judge may also order that the intermediary reviews the advocate's questions and provide advice on their suitability considering the witness's communication needs. The judge makes the necessary directions to set the parameters for fair treatment of the witness.[107] GRHs are integral to ensuring the proper questioning of a vulnerable witness or defendant.[108]

The available empirical research relating to GRHs suggests that intermediaries consider that their participation is best achieved through informal means. This is evidenced by a preference for 'open, collegial discussion'[109] and 'discussion rather than formality',[110] emphasising a collective responsibility for effective communication. Intermediaries consider that their recommendations

106 MoJ (n 69) 35; DoJ, *The Registered Intermediaries Procedural Guidance Manual (Northern Ireland)* (April 2024) 45–46.
107 Cooper, Backen and Marchant (n 43) 431.
108 Penny Cooper, 'Ticketing Talk Gets Serious' *Counsel Magazine* (November 2014) 11–12.
109 Plotnikoff and Woolfson (n 42) 113.
110 Penny Cooper, 'Highs and Lows: The 4th Intermediary Survey' (Kingston University London, 13 October 2014) [14].

are better understood when the shackles of formal court proceedings are discarded and they can communicate on their terms.[111] Flexibility from judges allows the intermediary to tailor their recommendations and focus on bespoke communication strategies.[112] Good practice guidelines produced by The Advocate's Gateway describe the GRH as a 'discussion' and further stipulate that the intermediary ought not enter the witness box or make any sort of declaration.[113] Cooper and Farrugia and Plotnikoff and Woolfson all found a mixed response from intermediaries, advocates and lawyers regarding their experience of GRHs.[114] However, one common thread in the findings was that the intermediary's ability to execute their communication function is significantly impacted by the willingness of advocates to engage and judges to enforce agreed rules.

The differing intermediary regimes in England and Wales and Northern Ireland are set out in **Table 1.3**.

While the preceding information relates to England and Wales and Northern Ireland, the legal provision and organisation of intermediaries in other jurisdictions will be discussed in further detail in Chapter 3.

1.4 Research methods and methodology

This book employs a socio-legal approach in seeking to better understand the work of intermediaries in the criminal justice system. A socio-legal approach applies social theories and methods to the study of law and its institutions in their social, cultural and historical contexts. This allows for an assessment of their effectiveness, but also whether actors in their own legal settings are accomplishing what the law prescribes.[115] By examining the role of the intermediary, this book examines 'law's reality' through empirical research and contextualises law in the social and political conditions as experienced by those performing the role.[116]

The relative lack of academic attention given to the intermediary role makes a qualitative form of investigation appropriate. Qualitative inquiry is useful when seeking to develop knowledge in an under-researched area.[117] Intermediaries, as relative newcomers to the criminal justice system, have

111 Plotnikoff and Woolfson (n 42) 114; Backen (n 55) 51.

112 Penny Cooper and Laura Farrugia, 'Ground Rules Hearings' in Cooper and Norton (n 8) 412

113 The Advocate's Gateway, 'Ground Rules Hearings and the Fair Treatment of Vulnerable People in Court: Toolkit 1' (1 December 2016) <https://www.theadvocatesgateway.org/news/toolkit-1%3A-ground-rules-hearings> accessed 5 May 2020.

114 Cooper and Farrugia (n 112).

115 Reza Banaker and Max Travers, *Law and Social Theory* (Hart Publishing 2013).

116 Keith Hawkins, 'Prologue: Donald Harris and the Early Years of the Oxford Centre' in Keith Hawkins (ed), *The Human Face of Law: Essays in Honour of Donald Harris* (Clarendon Press 1997) 4.

117 Uwe Flick, Ernst von Kardoff and Ines Steinke, *A Companion to Qualitative Research* (SAGE Publishing 2004) 21.

Table 1.3 Intermediary provision in Northern Ireland and England and Wales compared

	Northern Ireland	*England and Wales*
Coverage	Witnesses and defendants eligible for Registered Intermediaries (RIs).	Only witnesses are eligible for Registered Intermediaries (RIs). Defendant intermediaries are appointed using the court's inherent jurisdiction.
Duration of appointment	Evidence only.	Generally evidence only, although courts can exercise their inherent powers to allow longer appointments for defendants.
Use for suspects	RIs routinely attend police station to assist suspects at interview.	Defendant intermediaries rarely attend for suspect interview.
Funding	DoJ provides funding for RI appointments at set rates.	MoJ provides funding for RI work at set rates. Fees for defendant appointments are unregulated with the Legal Aid Agency covering pre-trial work and HMCTS funding work at court.
Training and accreditation	All RIs are trained, overseen and regulated by the DoJ and must adhere to a Code of Ethics and a Code of Practice. RIs must update their knowledge and skills through continuing professional development.	All RIs are trained, overseen and regulated by the MoJ and must adhere to a Code of Ethics and a Code of Practice. RIs must update their knowledge and skills through continuing professional development. Defendant intermediaries are unregulated with no equivalent oversight.

often found their voices neglected. Given this, it is appropriate that a project seeking to gain some preliminary insights into an under-researched actor should be qualitative in nature. Taking this further, the procedures that underpin qualitative research are characterised as inductive and emerging.[118]

118 John Creswell, *Qualitative Inquiry and Research Design: Choosing among Five Approaches* (SAGE Publishing 2012) 22.

This links with the fact that my data collection was not theory-driven nor trying to prove or disprove a particular claim or set of claims.

The data underpinning this research project were collected and analysed utilising a grounded theory approach. Grounded theory seeks to 'close the gap between theory and method' and allows for the conceptualisation of emergent social patterns from research data.[119] The methodology was initially designed to create theories which are empirically derived from real-world situations and are intended to be applicable to 'real work settings'.[120] Resulting theories are thus *constructed* through past and present involvements and interactions with people, perspectives and research practices.[121] From an epistemological perspective, constructivism propounds the view that reality is constructed by individuals by assigning meaning to their environment.[122] The outcome is that the researcher never reveals an exact picture of the phenomena being studied, but rather an interpretative portrayal of the studied world.[123]

Grounded theory, as a methodological process, involves the progressive identification, re-working, re-interpretation and integration of categories of meaning from data. Underpinning these elements of the methodology is that it involves both the process of category identification and integration (as method) and its product (as theory). Firstly, as a *method* the researcher is provided with coding guidelines on how categories can be identified and how to uncover links between categories and relationships between them. Secondly, *theory* can be considered the end-product of this process; it provides an explanatory framework with which to understand the phenomenon under investigation.[124]

1.4.1 Sampling

From the outset, I was interested in collecting data from intermediaries working in the criminal justice system (as opposed to family courts, employment tribunals or civil courts). When familiarising myself with the extant literature, in particular the relevant case law, it became clear that focusing solely on the voice of the intermediary could produce a limited, or even potentially

119 Barney Glaser, 'The Grounded Theory Perspective: Its Origins and Growth' (2016) 15(1) Grounded Theory Review 4.

120 Julianne Oktay, *Grounded Theory* (OUP 2012) 5.

121 Kathy Charmaz, *Constructing Grounded Theory. A Practical Guide through Qualitative Analysis* (SAGE Publishing 2006) 10.

122 Jenna Breckenbridge and others, 'Choosing a Methodological Path: Reflections on the Constructivist Turn' (2012) 11(1) Grounded Theory Review 64, 65.

123 Kathy Charmaz, 'Grounded Theory' in Jonathan Smith, Rom Harré and Luk Langenhove (eds), *Rethinking Methods in Psychology* (SAGE Publishing 1995) 27–49.

124 Charmaz (n 123) 24–49.

skewed picture of the role. I decided that as well as speaking to intermediaries, judges could provide valuable insights. In terms of the intermediary's court-based role, the literature and case law suggested that the bench wields considerable influence over the intermediary's involvement during the questioning of witnesses.[125] In December 2019, towards the end of my interview schedule with intermediaries and judges, I also decided that it was important to try and speak to some police officers. This is because intermediaries can be appointed to facilitate communication with vulnerable witnesses in ABE interview and suspects at police interview – although the latter is extremely rare in England and Wales. I was able to interview two police officers in January 2020 with the help of a contact in the Ministry of Justice. Unfortunately, the beginning of the Covid-19 pandemic in March 2020 meant that I was unable to continue with these interviews.

Access to the intermediary population was secured in several ways. The first of these was through 'Intermediaries for Justice (IFJ)' which describes itself as 'the professional body for intermediaries who work in the justice system'.[126] IFJ represents intermediaries working with all categories of witness (including defendants) and so was able to disseminate information about my research to its members. Further requests were sent via the 'Registered Intermediaries Online' portal which is operated by the NCA and is an information-sharing platform for those who work in a registered capacity. In Northern Ireland, interviews were arranged in collaboration with the Intermediaries Schemes Secretariat (ISS), which disseminated information to all Registered Intermediaries. In Northern Ireland, four judges were interviewed (two District Judges from the magistrates' court and two Crown Court judges) through the Lord Chief Justice's Office. These judges were selected based on their experiences of working with intermediaries in the criminal justice system. Accessing judges in England and Wales proved unsuccessful.

Of the 27 intermediaries I interviewed, 20 were based in England and Wales and seven in Northern Ireland. In terms of the sample's representativeness, over one third of the total intermediary cohort in Northern Ireland were interviewed.[127] In England and Wales, it is more difficult to ascertain precise numbers, since I sought to interview intermediaries who had worked in both a registered and a non-registered capacity. It is difficult to be sure how many practising intermediaries fall into this category. When interviews commenced in November 2018, there were 115 intermediaries on the MoJ

125 For example, the MoJ Intermediary Guidance (n 69) makes clear that '[i]t is the decision of the judge whether or not to take any action following the RI's intervention'. Also see: Grant-Murray (n 11), Plotnikoff and Woolfson (n 42) and Backen (n 55).

126 Intermediaries for Justice, 'About IFJ' <https://www.intermediaries-for-justice.org/vision-and-aims> accessed 12 March 2020.

127 DoJ (n 94) 11.

register actively taking cases.[128] Based on anecdotal evidence from the field, it is estimated that less than half of those intermediaries would be able to comment on working in a registered and non-registered capacity. Therefore, one can say with reasonable confidence that the 20 interviews conducted amounted to a significant percentage of the target population. Interviews in England were conducted in all nine administrative regions. No intermediary resident in Wales replied to any interview requests, but several interviewees had attended court in Wales. Interviewees had a mixture of experience, with some working in the role for over 11 years and others qualifying less than a year prior to interview. One feature of the intermediary population is that the majority come from a speech and language therapy background. While taking account of this, intermediaries from other backgrounds, such as social work, nursing and psychiatry, were included to get as broad a view of experiences as possible. Of the 27 intermediaries interviewed, 15 came from a speech and language therapy background, three from social work, three from nursing, two from occupational therapy, two from psychology, one from teaching and one worked as a sign language interpreter.

1.4.2 Interviews

The use of in-depth interviews suited the fact that I could formulate some initial research questions around the topic of intermediaries and identify potential interviewees, but not much more.[129] One important consideration was which location for interview would ensure confidentiality and a relaxed atmosphere to develop rapport.[130] One difficulty that arose was that intermediaries do not have an obvious space or work setting – something that would later contribute to my conceptualisation of the role as an 'outsider' to the world of criminal justice. Intermediaries are often required to carry out assessments in people's homes or hang around courthouses and, even then, there is scant provision for them compared to lawyers, judges and witnesses. As with the venue, the timing of the interview needed to be chosen carefully. I was aware that intermediaries do not work standard hours, so planning interviews in advance would pose some problems. Three interviews took place around the LSE campus which was convenient for some intermediaries who had a case in London or had other reasons to be in London. Two interviews took place at a court location due to intermediary preference. For the remainder of the interviews, I travelled to the hometown of

128 E-mail correspondence from IFJ to author (26 April 2018).

129 Greg Guest, Emily Namey and Marilyn Mitchell, 'In-depth Interviews' in Greg Guest, Emily Namey and Marilyn Mitchell (eds), *Collecting Qualitative Data: A Field Manual for Applied Research* (SAGE Publishing 2013) 117.

130 Judith Green and Nicki Thorogood, *Qualitative Methods for Health Research* (2nd edn, SAGE Publishing 2009) 111.

each intermediary and mostly met in people's homes or a quiet place where confidentiality could be maintained. The four judicial interviews took place in chambers, which provided a private, quiet environment.

During transcription of interview data, I removed any references to specific courts or police stations, colleagues, and names of clients or witnesses to keep the identities of the respondents and those involved in their cases confidential. All interviewees were provided with an information sheet prior to interview and signed a consent form agreeing to their participation in the research. I anonymised each interviewee and have used the prefix 'NI-' to identify interviewees in Northern Ireland and 'E&W-' for those based in England and Wales. I used 'CCJ-' to denote Crown Court judges and 'MCJ-' to denote judges in the magistrates' court. This anonymisation helps ensure that it is not possible to identify a participant from the information provided during interview.

Finally, a brief note on gender. Most intermediaries are female, which is not surprising since the professions from which they are drawn tend to be female dominated, e.g. speech and language therapy and social work. When in the field, I was made aware that only a handful of male intermediaries are in practice. Although I interviewed three male intermediaries (one in Northern Ireland and two in England and Wales) I have decided to refer to all interviewees with a female pronoun. This is to protect the identities of male participants who may be more easily identified.

1.4.3 Data analysis

According to grounded theory, the data needed to be coded, analysed, re-coded and reanalysed.[131] I adopted an inductive approach when identifying themes and generating codes. This means that the coding was data-driven, with the codes emerging within the data itself.[132] I began the coding process with open coding which occurs when 'conceptual labels are placed on discrete happenings' and reflects a 'process of breaking down, examining, comparing, conceptualising and categorising the data'.[133] Some of my early open codes were: 'importance of partnership with police', 'lack of support for defendants', 'broad role of communication', 'misunderstanding of role by professionals', 'need for individualised assistance' and 'struggling with court environment'. The coding then became more focused as the codes took shape and the theory began to emerge. I established links between codes where relationships

131 Barney Glaser and Anselm Strauss, *The Discovery of Grounded Theory: Strategies for Qualitative Research* (Aldine 1967).

132 Svend Brinkman and Steiner Kvale, *Interviews: Learning the Craft of Qualitative Research Interviewing* (3rd edn, SAGE Publishing 2015) 228.

133 Anselm Strauss and Juliet Corbin, *Basics of Qualitative Research* (SAGE Publishing 1990) 61.

became apparent, and some codes were consolidated or merged with others. I also continued collecting data during the analysis and re-analysed my data as codes and themes emerged. I eventually distilled all codes into four core codes of: i) neutrality, ii) professionalism, iii) participation and iv) communication. After revising all the codes again, I realised 'communication' threaded into the other three remaining core codes and could be incorporated within them. As such, the three codes of i) neutrality, ii) professionalism and iii) participation were selected and are explored further in the analysis chapters.

1.5 Book structure

The first part of the book (Chapters 1–4) provides important context for the remainder of the book. It sets the scene for later chapters by examining the emergence of the intermediary role, developments at the international level, and how the role fits within the existing trial structure and theories of the criminal trial. The second part of the book (Chapters 5–7) engages with the empirical data collected and explores some of the key themes, i.e. neutrality, professional work and participatory roles. Chapter 8 offers a conclusion and discusses the future of the intermediary role.

Chapter 2 sets out the story of how the intermediary role first emerged. While the YJCEA outlines the intermediary's function in straightforward terms, the role was the subject of much disagreement for the preceding 30 years. The intermediary role did not merely appear with the passing of the YJCEA but had been in embryonic form for quite some time. This chapter considers the historical record of the parliamentary debates, government committees and surrounding academic literature, which paints a picture of a confused and ill-understood role. It reveals how diverging representations of the intermediary role have contributed to questions about the role's scope and underscores the importance of this research project.

Chapter 3 explores the international context and is divided into two parts. The first considers the intermediary role with reference to two key international legal instruments: firstly, the UN Convention on the Rights of the Child (UNCRC) and, secondly, the Convention on the Rights of Persons with Disabilities (CRPD). The second part of the chapter examines various other intermediary schemes which have developed internationally, with a particular focus on Australia. Although the book focuses primarily on the intermediary model first developed in England and Wales, developments internationally should prompt critical reflection on how and why aspects of the role are approached differently in different settings.

Chapter 4 locates the intermediary role within the structure of the English criminal trial. This chapter considers some of the main theoretical accounts of the trial and asks how the intermediary role impacts the core aims underpinning the trial. This sets the scene for a more nuanced discussion of the values intrinsic to the trial and how they relate to the intermediary role.

This acts as an important foundation for subsequent chapters, which explore the ambiguities around the role's parameters. This chapter also serves as an important reference point for the analysis chapters wherein a grounded theory of the role and its content emerge.

Chapter 5 focuses on the contested status of the intermediary as a 'professional' in the criminal justice system. The analysis contained within the chapter focuses on two key theoretical constructs. The first is Abbott's work on inter-professional jurisdictional disputes, which details how professions operate in dynamic social settings which shape and define individual professional roles and their content.[134] The second is Gieryn's conception of 'boundary work',[135] which outlines how professionals demarcate the boundaries representing status, autonomy and claims over professional resources. This chapter concludes by reflecting on the various conflicts which the intermediary faces in trying to secure and maintain jurisdiction. It asks if the role's jurisdictional conflicts will result in a 'jurisdictional settlement' whereby intermediaries accept a more limited role with the distribution of some of their work tasks among other criminal justice actors.[136]

Chapter 6 posits that intermediaries are embroiled in an ongoing struggle about how the principle of neutrality is conceptualised and negotiated within their work. It argues that the normative expectation of neutrality underpinning the role requires reassessment based on the realities of the role at the coalface. This inherent tension allows for an analysis utilising the Bourdieusian concept of 'illusio'. Illusio relates to a collective belief among members of a 'field' in the value of taking part in collective struggles.[137] Reflecting on the strength (or weakness) of the illusio generated by intermediaries helps locate the intermediary within the social world of the criminal justice system. Furthermore, examining the intermediary role through the prism of neutrality reinforces a key theme emerging from my data: the roles of Registered Intermediaries and non-registered intermediaries are qualitatively different. I term these concepts 'witness work' and 'defendant work' respectively.

Chapter 7 focuses on the relationship between intermediaries and the criminal justice value of participation. It examines how the performance of the intermediary role is inextricably tied to the different ways in which vulnerable individuals participate within the criminal justice process. The chapter further develops the concepts of 'witness work' and 'defendant work' through a focused analysis of participatory roles. This includes an analysis

134 Andrew Abbott, *The System of Professions: An Essay on the Division of Expert Labor* (Chicago UP 1988).

135 Thomas Gieryn, 'Boundary-Work and the Demarcation of Science from Non-Science: Strains and Interests in Professional Ideologies of Scientists' (1983) 48 American Sociological Review 781–795.

136 Abbott (n 134) 72.

137 Pierre Bourdieu, *Pascalian Meditations* (CUP 2000) 187.

of how intermediaries work to ensure the defendant's right to effective participation. This chapter seeks neither to rank witness/defendant participatory rights nor strike a conceptual balance between the two groups. Instead, it attempts to analyse the meaning and experience of participation and how this can relate to the nature and scope of the intermediary's role.

Chapter 8 returns to consider some of the central questions underpinning the book and assesses some future directions for the intermediary role. It also discusses recent developments with the introduction of the new HMCTS Court Appointed Intermediary Services (HAIS) and makes recommendations regarding intermediary provision.

Chapter 2

Emergence of the intermediary role

2.1 Introduction

The following quote from Dr Penny Cooper recognises that the intermediary role has evolved since its inception:

> Since the first RIs were trained in 2003 and the scheme became operational in 2004 the nature and scope of the role has continued to evolve. Intermediaries are a precious resource and the role has 'highs', namely the reward of making a positive and significant difference in the lives of the vulnerable, but too often there are 'lows'. The 'lows' occur when the role is not well understood and other professionals do not adequately engage with them and consider their advice.[1]

Later chapters in this book reveal how the intermediary role is highly relational and its status in the professionalised world of criminal justice continues to be contested. Before these issues are explored, a key question must first be addressed: how did the intermediary role first emerge? In the U.K the role is a creature of statute and was formally introduced on 23 February 2004 when s.29 of the Youth Justice and Criminal Evidence Act 1999 (YJCEA) came into force. The legislation provides for the 'examination of a witness through an intermediary' and outlines that this individual will be 'an interpreter or other person approved by the court for the purposes of this section'.[2] While the intermediary is one of a broad range of special measures, there has been little focus on the background to s.29 YJCEA and the developments that led to its inclusion within the legislation. Tracing the legislative and policy background to s.29 can help us understand how the intermediary role was originally envisaged and how it was expected to operate within the criminal

1 Penny Cooper, 'Highs and Lows: The 4th Intermediary Survey' (Kingston University London, 13 October 2014) <http://eprints.kingston.ac.uk/28868/1/Cooper-P-28868.pdf>.
2 Youth Justice and Criminal Evidence Act 1999 (YJCEA), s.29.

DOI: 10.4324/9781003461166-2

justice system. This is an important prerequisite to understanding the scope and nature of the intermediary role.

The discussion in this chapter sets the scene for two fundamental questions which thread throughout the book: i) who are intermediaries? and ii) what does the role involve? This chapter firstly considers the development of accommodations for the child as the archetypal vulnerable individual and how momentum developed for the extension of assistance to a wider cohort of vulnerable witnesses. It then explores the workings and recommendations of the Pigot Committee, which was established to examine a 'growing body of support for a change in the law' relating to the treatment of vulnerable witnesses.[3] The Committee's recommendation of an 'interlocutor' was a forerunner to the intermediary role and is an instructive reference for the remainder of the book. This chapter then examines the Speaking up for Justice report which recommended the establishment of a scheme for the accreditation of the intermediary role. Finally, the chapter considers the legislative passage of the YJCEA and the discussions, debates and concerns that were raised about the prospective operation of the intermediary role.

2.2 Children as archetypal vulnerable individuals

The momentum for change regarding special measures began with a focus on children and the challenges associated with their testimony. Children providing evidence to police at interview and later at trial has not always been the norm. Children were viewed as different from adults because their developmental immaturity was thought to render their evidence intrinsically unreliable.[4] Under the common law, children under 14 could only testify if they were sworn and possessed sufficient knowledge of the nature and consequences of an oath.[5] Legislative provision in The Children and Young Persons Act of 1933 then provided for the allowance of the unsworn evidence of children who did not understand the oath. However, the Court of Appeal decision of *R v Wallwork* in 1958 diminished the value of child witnesses, branding any suggestion that a jury could treat unsworn evidence seriously as 'ridiculous'.[6]

While children have historically been depicted as unreliable witnesses, they have also been portrayed as archetypal vulnerable victims and witnesses.[7] Yet, other categories of witness have also been recognised as vulnerable. For

3 Home Office, 'Report of the Advisory Group on Video Evidence' (London 1989) (hereafter referred to as the 'Pigot Report').

4 Jessica Jacobson and Jenny Talbot, *Vulnerable Defendants in the Criminal Courts: A Review of Provision for Adults and Children* (Prison Reform Trust 2009, ISBN: 0 946209 96 0) 8.

5 Pigot Report (n 3).

6 [1958] 42 Cr App R 153 [160].

7 Paul Rock, *Constructing Victims' Rights: The Home Office, New Labour and Victims* (OUP 2004) 377.

example, the plight of victims of sexual offences, who often feel stigmatised by their ordeals being ventilated in public, has also been well documented. In response, the Sexual Offences (Amendment Act) 1976 was introduced to prevent the questioning of victims that 'does not advance the cause of justice but in effect puts the woman on trial'.[8] While bespoke procedures were introduced to ensure child witnesses understood the oath and the importance of telling the truth, they were still expected to cope with the other associated pressures of the court process. Despite children being recognised as vulnerable, the primary concern of the criminal process continued to be reliability of their evidence rather than their subjective experience of testifying.[9]

Since the 1970s, there has been a growing acceptance that the adversarial model of criminal justice poses particular problems for victims and witnesses.[10] For example, the establishment of 'Victim Support' signified a growing realisation that achieving reliable evidence must be balanced with the better treatment of witnesses and victims.[11] Through the Criminal Justice Bill 1987, the government outlined its plans for live video-link evidence and the possibility of video recordings of investigative interviews in child abuse prosecutions.[12] Despite an attempt in the Commons to revive an amendment allowing for video-recorded interviews, the government rejected it, stating that the proposal raised 'complex issues which need careful consideration'.[13] The government continued to resist introducing pre-recorded testimony but agreed to modest reforms in the Criminal Justice Act 1988, most significantly, the use of a live link for the evidence of a witness.

Around the same time, the first prototype of the intermediary role was proposed by Glanville Williams in the form of a 'child examiner' who would relay questions from lawyers to young witnesses.[14] The proposal sought to remove the child from the courtroom environment entirely, with all evidence being video-recorded and later relayed to the full trial.[15] However, the government rejected the proposal based on concerns that it could 'dilute the interaction between counsel and child'.[16] It continued that such interaction is a 'key

8 Dame Rose Heilbron, *Report of the Advisory Group on the Law of Rape* (HMSO 1975).
9 Mandy Burton, Roger Evans, and Andrew Sanders, *Are Special Measures for Vulnerable and Intimidated Witnesses Working? Evidence from the Criminal Justice Agencies* (Home Office Online Report 01/06, 2016) 2.
10 Burton, Evans and Sanders (n 9). For further critique of the adversarial model, see: Chapter 4 (Locating the intermediary within theories of the criminal trial).
11 Burton, Evans and Sanders (n 9) 2.
12 Carolyn Yates, 'The Pigot Committee Report: Children, Evidence and Video-tape' (1990) 2 Journal of Child Law 96.
13 HL Deb 27 April 1987, cols 1266–347.
14 Glanville Williams, 'Videotaping Children's Evidence' (1987) New Law Journal 108.
15 Kate Warner, 'Child Witnesses: Evidentiary Reforms' in Julia Vernon (ed), *No 8: Children as Witnesses: Conference Proceedings* (Australian Institute of Criminology 1988).
16 HL Deb 22 October 1987, vol 120, cols 266–267.

part of protecting the right of the accused person who, we must remember, is innocent until proven guilty'.[17] It is noteworthy that other jurisdictions had introduced an intermediary-type role much earlier. For example, in Israel, the 'youth examiner' role has existed since 1955. However, this role assumes investigatory powers ordinarily held only by the police and thus is much broader in scope.[18] In Western Australia, legislation has been in force since 1906, affording a court discretion to appoint a 'communicator' for a child. As noted later in this chapter, much about this role in Western Australia was unexplored when the intermediary role was proposed in England and Wales.

2.3 The Pigot Committee

The government's commitment to investigate further reforms led to the establishment of the 'Report of the Advisory Group on Video Evidence'. The exploratory mandate given to the Advisory Group reflected the caution of some of the final speeches made in the Commons during the debates on the Criminal Justice Act 1988. These speeches urged restraint from rushing into the introduction of radical changes to evidence-giving procedures. Nonetheless, it was apparent that conflicting arguments existed, and the responsibility of evaluating all viewpoints was offloaded to an independent committee. Subsequently described as an attempt to 'deflect' the proposed amendments to the Criminal Justice Act 1988, the move was postulated as an opportunity to thoroughly examine the merits and drawbacks of the greater use of video technology in courts.[19]

Immediately before the Advisory Group's establishment, the government was unclear about the sort of conclusions it may have welcomed. In justifying the limitations of the 1988 Act and its decision to establish the Advisory Group, the government was ambivalent about the benefits of widening measures for children in courts. Whilst noting the immediate attractiveness of the proposals, Home Secretary Douglas Hurd cautioned that 'we have had some doubts as to whether it would actually have the effect of making things easier for the child victim, and can see grounds for fearing that it might make matters worse'.[20] These differing opinions and the government's preference for a comprehensive, independent evaluation were explicitly recognised by the Advisory Committee in its report.[21]

17 HL Deb 22 October 1987, vol 120, cols 266–267.
18 Solomon Eaglestin and Yuval Karniel, 'The Youth Examiner: An Israeli Socio-legal Experiment' (1991) 5(4) Children and Society 317.
19 Laura Hoyano, 'Variations on a Theme by Pigot: Special Measures Directions for Child Witnesses' (2000) Criminal Law Review 250.
20 Pigot Report (n 3).
21 Pigot Report (n 3) 7.

The Committee, chaired by HHJ Thomas Pigot QC, was given malleable terms of reference: 'to look in greater depth than has so far been possible that video recordings of interviews of child witnesses (and possibly other victims of crime) should be readily admissible as evidence in criminal trials'.[22] While children had hitherto monopolised discussion relating to court adaptations, the Pigot Committee broadened the scope of concern. The fact that certain groups of adults could also come within the Pigot Committee's remit must have been surprising at the time. Prior to the establishment of the Committee, it had not been recognised that certain adults might also require assistance when giving evidence.[23] Indeed, the only mention of adult witnesses throughout the House of Lord's debate on the CJA 1988, for example, was the government's view that a court appearance placed more of a strain on children than adults.[24]

2.4 Pigot's vision of the 'interlocutor'

Contrary to the previously cautious attitude of the government, the Pigot Committee recommended that 'quite radical changes are now required if the courts are to treat children in a humane and acceptable way'.[25] Using the Committee's own terminology, one of these more 'radical' changes came in the form of the recommendation that a child could be examined through 'an interlocutor'. The report clarified that this would involve:

> the relaying of questions from counsel through a paediatrician, child psychiatrist, social worker or person who enjoys the child's confidence. In these circumstances nobody except for the trusted party would be visible to the child although everyone with an interest would be able to communicate, indirectly, through the interlocutor.[26]

Of the Committee's 24 recommendations, this was the only one not to receive unanimous support from its members. The unease at the prospect of interposing a third party between the advocate and the witness was noted, and the expected opposition of the legal profession was pre-emptively addressed. The fact that an advocate may have to sacrifice some 'forensic skills, timing, intonation and the rest' was recognised but not seen as an automatic barrier to introducing the interlocutor measure.[27] Committee member Anne Rafferty, a practising barrister, dissented and argued that the interlocutor would 'hinder

22 Pigot Report (n 3) 1.
23 Jonathan Herring, *Vulnerable Adults and the* Law (OUP 2015) 38.
24 HL Deb 27 April 1987, vol 120, cols 1266–347.
25 Pigot Report (n 3) [2.9].
26 Pigot Report (n 3) [2.33].
27 Pigot Report (n 3) [2.33].

rather than assist counsel conducting the case'[28] and instead proposed that more opportunity could be given to counsel to 'establish a rapport with a child witness before the hearing takes place'.[29]

Pigot's vision of the interlocutor raises some important points when considering how the role of the intermediary emerged and subsequently developed. The first relates to who the Committee envisioned would perform the interlocutory role. As noted earlier, the sole dissenting voice on this recommendation rejected the proposal in its entirety instead of advocating a less obstructive measure. It may be asked: why did the Committee identify paediatricians, child psychologists and social workers as suitable for the role? A similar question arose in relation to the Criminal Justice Bill 1987 and, specifically, amendments on the use of video-recorded interviews and questioning of child witnesses. The amendment included a provision that a 'prescribed officer of the court' would help to relay questions put to child witnesses by lawyers.[30] The amendment specified that the prescribed officer should be a 'qualified social worker, child psychologist or probation officer'.[31] While the amendment was withdrawn, it was announced by the government that the Pigot Committee would be established to consider the specific issues in more detail.[32]

The Committee also considered '[a] person who enjoys the child's confidence' as a potentially suitable interlocutor.[33] It noted that 'nobody except for the trusted party would be visible to the child, although everyone with an interest would be able to *communicate*, indirectly, through the interlocutor' [emphasis added].[34] One can imagine how this label could apply to a relatively large pool of individuals, including, for example, a parent or close relative. How this aspect of the role aligns with the bespoke interlocutor role to be executed by a paediatrician, child psychiatrist or social worker is puzzling. The Committee did not explain whether, for example, these professions might fulfil different roles depending on the type or severity of communication difficulty.

In attempting to rationalise its interlocutor recommendation, the Committee compared it with the court interpreter. It noted that there would be 'no great difference of principle' between the use of someone who can help a child to communicate and 'the employment of an interpreter where a witness cannot speak English'.[35] It was suggested that both roles can prevent the

28 Pigot Report (n 3)
29 Pigot Report (n 3) [2.34].
30 HC Deb 20 June 1988, vol 135, col 846.
31 HC Deb 20 June 1988, vol 135, col 846.
32 HC Deb 20 June 1988, vol 135, col 879.
33 Pigot Report (n 3) [2.34].
34 Pigot Report (n 3) [2.34].
35 Pigot Report (n 3) [2.33].

loss of crucial evidence without which the court cannot dispense justice. The comparison with the court interpreter is interesting as it appears to be the first time an analogous position or role is identified. Five years previously, the Police and Criminal Evidence Act 1984 (PACE) introduced the new role of the 'Appropriate Adult' who could assist juveniles or mentally vulnerable persons to understand the custody procedures and their own rights.[36] While the interlocutor and the Appropriate Adult are both involved in assisting communication, the latter role was limited to the police station.[37] The Pigot Committee's terms of reference, however, were limited to the court stage. For this reason, it seems that more was not made of the potential overlap between both roles.

The rationale for comparing the interlocutor and the interpreter is not tenuous. As the Committee recognised, the non-involvement of either actor, when required, will likely diminish the quality of evidence. However, there are two clear differences between the roles that the Committee did not address. The first relates to the 'rapport', 'trust' and 'confidence' underpinning the interlocutor role. Interpreters, while possessing their own qualifications and no doubt able to form trusting relationships, are not typically required to do so in order to execute the role.[38] Indeed, the impartiality that characterises the work of an interpreter is incongruous with the profile of a 'trusted individual' who has been appointed because they are known to the witness.[39] Secondly, the Committee envisaged a complete removal of the child from the courtroom when assisted by an interlocutor. This was later described as an attempt to 'shield [the child] from direct contact with anyone participating in the trial, including the judge'.[40] Interpreters, conversely, are ordinarily visible to the courtroom and the suggestion that their role may involve 'shielding' the witness has been criticised both judicially and academically.[41]

36 Home Office, *Code C: Revised Code of Practice for the Detention, Treatment and Questioning of Persons by Police Officers* (Police and Criminal Evidence Act (PACE) 1984).

37 Home Office, *Guidance for Appropriate Adults* (19 April 2011).

38 Whilst the demonstration of understanding and compassion are often encouraged, the 'detachment' and avoidance of personal dependency of an interpreter from their client has been stressed, see: Joan Colin and Ruth Morris, *Interpreters and the Legal Process* (Waterside Press 1996) 144–145; Ruth Morris, 'The Gum Syndrome: Predicaments in Court Interpreting (1999) Forensic Linguistics 6.

39 National Register of Public Service Interpreters (NRPSI), 'Code of Professional Conduct' <https://www.nrpsi.org.uk/for-clients-of-interpreters/code-of-professional-conduct.html> [3.12] accessed 18 June 2020.

40 Home Office, *Speaking Up for Justice: Report of the Interdepartmental Working Group on the Treatment of Vulnerable or Intimidated Witnesses in the Criminal Justice System* (1998) 58.

41 William Wells, *An Introduction to the Law of Evidence* (AB Caudell Adelaide 1991) quoting a former Australian Supreme Court judge at [329]: 'It cannot be overemphasised that an interpreter should interpret every single word that the witness utters, exactly as it is said, whether it makes sense or whether it is obviously nonsense; whether the witness has plainly

Finally, while the Pigot Report recognised the position of vulnerable adults and the range of available special measures, the interlocutory role was restricted to children.[42] The trial judge would have the power to make special arrangements 'for the examination of very young or very disturbed children . . . if he thinks appropriate'.[43] Children, however, were not to be automatically eligible because of their age, and the measure was to be available only 'exceptionally'.[44] Furthermore, there was no acknowledgement that children could be considered vulnerable for reasons other than their age and the meaning of 'very disturbed' was not elaborated. The Committee adopted a narrow understanding of children's inherent vulnerability rather than an individual assessment – a position which has changed significantly in more recent research.[45] Nonetheless, it is apparent that the interlocutor was to be an exclusively child-focused special measure. The possibility of vulnerable adult witnesses, for example, requiring similar communication assistance does not feature in the recommendation nor its accompanying explanatory notes.

The Committee recognised that once their recommendations had been implemented, they could be extended to vulnerable adult witnesses at the court's discretion.[46] Considering the subsequent legislative developments discussed later in this chapter, the Pigot Committee's recommendations may be regarded as a harbinger of later campaigns that sought to better accommodate vulnerable adults within the criminal justice system. Building on the small steps taken by the Criminal Justice Act 1988, the Pigot Report delineated the parameters for future reform and gave impetus to the campaign for more wide-ranging modifications of evidence-giving procedures.[47]

2.5 Speaking up for Justice

Shortly after its election victory in 1997, the Labour government committed to providing a greater amount of support to victims of sexual offences

not heard or whether, if he has heard, he has not understood. The interpreter should look upon himself as an electronic transformer; whatever is fed into him is to be fed again, duly transformed'; Sandra Beatriz Hale, *The Discourse of Court Interpreting: Discourse Practices of the Law, the Witness and the Interpreter* (John Benjamins Publishing Co. 2004) 8.

42 Diane Birch, 'A Better Deal for Vulnerable Witnesses?' (2000) Criminal Law Review 223, 229.

43 Pigot Report (n 3) [2.32].

44 Pigot Report (n 3) [2.32].

45 Ruth Marchant and Marcus Page, 'The Memorandum and Disabled Children' in Helen Westcott and Jocelyn Jones (eds), *Perspectives on the Memorandum* (Arena 1997); Helen Westcott, 'The Memorandum of Good Practice and Children with Disabilities' (1994) 3(2) Journal of Law and Practice 21; Law Commission, *Evidence in Criminal Proceedings: Previous Misconduct of a Defendant* (Law Com No 141, 1996).

46 Jacki Pritchard, *Good Practice in the Law and Safeguarding Adults* (Jessica Kingsley Publishing 2008) 72.

47 Hoyano (n 19) 251.

and for vulnerable and intimidated witnesses generally.[48] The first effort towards securing this pledge was the establishment of the 'Working Group on the Cross-Examination of Rape Victims by Unrepresented Defendants'. Much like other government committees, it acquired what Rock terms a 'sponge-like capacity to absorb new tasks' and assumed a broad agenda which considered the difficulties faced by victims generally.[49] The group's focus shifted towards vulnerable or intimidated witnesses and although it remained a working group, it was renamed the 'Vulnerable Witness Group' in April 1997. A significant reason for the enlargement of the group's remit related to the research findings of Andrew Sanders one year previously.[50] Sanders argued that legislative reforms relating to children could equally apply to other vulnerable individuals and suggested a focus on individual assessment of a person's needs.[51]

The Vulnerable Witness Group enjoyed wide terms of reference to consider measures that would improve the treatment of vulnerable witnesses and, additionally, measures that may encourage such witnesses to give evidence in court.[52] The narrow perspective that children, or even victims of sexual abuse, were the only witnesses deserving of special attention was dispensed with.[53] The Vulnerable Witness Group published its report titled Speaking up for Justice in June 1998.[54] It contained 78 recommendations which sought to improve the treatment of vulnerable and intimidated witnesses within the criminal justice system and to enable them to give their 'best evidence'.[55] It should be remembered that the Working Group accepted the constraints of existing trial procedure. While recognising that many of the difficulties faced by vulnerable witnesses emerge directly from the adversarial nature of the trial process, the format of the process itself was not questioned.[56] A series of recommendations involving modifications to the traditional trial process were proposed and became known as 'special measures'.[57] These included the provision of screens to shield a witness from the accused and CCTV links for witnesses to give live evidence in a separate room.[58]

48 Burton, Evans and Sanders (n 9).
49 Rock (n 7) 352.
50 Andrew Sanders and others, *Witnesses with Learning Disabilities: Research Findings No. 44* (Home Office Research and Statistics Directorate December 1996).
51 Sanders and others (n 50) 3.
52 Sanders and others (n 50) 35.
53 Sanders and others (n 50) 35.
54 Home Office (n 40).
55 Burton, Evans and Sanders (n 9) 4.
56 Louise Ellison, 'The Protection of Vulnerable Witnesses in Court: An Anglo-Dutch Comparison' (1999) 3(1) The International Journal of Evidence of Proof 29.
57 Home Office (n 40) 43.
58 Home Office (n 40) 44.

2.6 Communicator/Intermediary

Although the Pigot Report nine years earlier had recommended the introduction of an 'interlocutor', nothing was done legislatively to realise that ambition. Significantly, recommendations 47 and 48 of Speaking up for Justice revived the issue and envisaged a special measure referred to as a 'communicator or intermediary'.[59] Building on the Pigot Report's recommendation that measures relating to children should be extended to vulnerable adults, the communicator/intermediary measure was to be of dual application. In support of this recommendation, the report cited 'The Western Australia Experience' and the use of a 'communicator' for a child under 16.[60] Through the Evidence Act 1906 (Western Australia),[61] courts were afforded the discretion to appoint a communicator who could explain questions to the child as well as explain the child's responses. While impressed by the Australian model, the report recognised that much was 'unexplored' about the role of the communicator.[62]

Like the Pigot Committee, Speaking up for Justice drew parallels with the court interpreter and submitted that the new role might 'involve the intermediary/communicator putting supplementary questions to the witness'.[63] More broadly, the function of the role was to 'assist the witness communicate' with a particular focus on the complexity of language used in courts.[64] This would involve the intermediary/communicator explaining questions asked of the child to ensure comprehension and avoid the child feeling unfairly treated.[65] It is worth remembering that the Pigot Committee had identified that both 'very young children' and 'very disturbed children' might be eligible for interlocutory assistance. Despite discussing the plight of young witnesses in some detail, these particular categories were not developed by Speaking up for Justice.

The concerns underpinning Anne Rafferty's dissent from the Pigot Committee's interlocutor recommendation also re-emerged. The danger that the role's boundaries could become blurred was acknowledged, as well as the risk that the communicator/intermediary may provide their own interpretation of the witnesses' evidence.[66] The report recognised the 'fine line' between the witness being assisted in giving evidence and the communicator/intermediary

59 Home Office (n 40) 59.

60 Penny Cooper and Michelle Mattison, 'Intermediaries, Vulnerable People and the Quality of Evidence: An International Comparison of Three Versions of the English Intermediary Model' (2017) 21(4) International Journal of Evidence and Proof 351, 352.

61 s.106(f)(1).

62 Home Office (n 40) 58.

63 Home Office (n 40).

64 Home Office (n 40) 58.

65 Home Office (n 40) 58.

66 Home Office (n 40) 58.

essentially distorting the evidence produced.[67] Another concern noted was the divide among the Western Australian Judiciary where exactly half of those surveyed were strongly opposed to the child communicator provision.[68] Even those judges who supported the introduction of the role voiced concerns that it was untested.[69] As will be explored in Chapter 4 (Locating the intermediary within theories of the criminal trial), a range of concerns has been raised that such an intermediary/communicator role undermines the principle of orality underpinning the criminal trial.

Despite providing more detail than Pigot about the rationale behind its recommendation, Speaking up for Justice made no mention of the occupational profile of the communicator/intermediary. As noted earlier, Pigot suggested several professions that might perform the role, although the Committee's reasoning behind its choices was unclear. It is arguable that the recommendations within Speaking up for Justice were general in nature and that the goal was to alert the government to the need for a communicator-type role. This view is buttressed by the report's lack of guidelines or criteria for judges to consider when making an appointment. Further, there was an explicit expectation that an accreditation scheme would later be established.[70] Perhaps the 'novel nature' of the role,[71] as described by the report, meant that it would have been premature to identify potential candidates when the parameters of the role were not yet established.

The fact that Speaking up for Justice precipitated a legislative response demonstrates how it maintained the momentum of Pigot.[72] However, much about the intermediary role was unclear at the time of its publication, and as noted earlier, it even rowed back from some of the specificities of Pigot nine years earlier. The recommendation that vulnerable adults might also benefit from intermediary assistance went further than Pigot but did not clarify the role's intended scope or function. If anything, this broadened eligibility raised difficult questions about whether an adult should be treated differently from a child and whether the intermediary might be expected to perform a different role.[73] By 1998, the intermediary role was at an embryonic stage of development with a need for delineation of its scope and function.

67 Home Office (n 40) 59.
68 Celia O'Grady, *Child Witnesses and Jury Trials: An Evaluation of the Use of Closed Circuit Television and Removable Screens in Western Australia* (Ministry of Justice 1996).
69 O'Grady (n 68).
70 Home Office (n 40) 59.
71 Home Office (n 40) 59.
72 Jo Goodey, *Victims and Victimology: Research, Policy and Practice* (Longman 2004) 132.
73 Note that Jonathan Herring argues that all humans should be deemed inherently vulnerable by virtue of being a member of the human race and thus prima facie vulnerable adults and vulnerable children share many common traits: Herring (n 23).

2.7 The Youth Justice and Criminal Evidence Act 1999

Speaking up for Justice and its 78 recommendations were accepted by the government, which indicated its intention to implement its findings via legislation. In contrast to the 'half hearted' attempt to implement the Pigot Report in 1991, most of the recommendations were included in Part II of the Youth Justice and Criminal Evidence Bill 1999.[74] Speaking up for Justice had concluded that 7–10% of all witnesses fall into the 'vulnerable or intimated' category. Thus, the legislation's endorsement of its findings recognised that such individuals form a small, but significant, distinct minority of witnesses.[75]

Part II of the Bill outlined what were termed 'special measures directions' aimed at the vulnerable and intimated witnesses that Speaking up for Justice had identified. A raft of 'specific measures' was included in the Bill, including the use of screens to shield witnesses from the accused, removal of wigs and gowns, clearing the court to allow evidence to be heard in private and measures concerning video-taped evidence. In addition, the Bill contained provisions to prevent the cross-examination of witnesses by unrepresented defendants, measures relating to the use of sexual history evidence in trials involving rape and other sexual offences and changes to the restrictions on press reporting of criminal cases.[76]

2.8 Passage through Parliament

Speaking up for Justice identified that vulnerable witnesses may need help to give their 'best evidence' in court.[77] It further recognised that many might encounter communication difficulties as a part of the evidence-giving experience.[78] During the Bill's passage through Parliament, it was also recognised by the House of Lords that special measures were an important step for 'the determination of the truth' in the criminal trial.[79] Yet the initial House of Lords debate revealed scepticism about whether the Bill was as

74 Jonathan Doak, *Victim's Rights, Human Rights and Criminal Justice: Reconceiving the Role of Third Parties* (Hart Publishing 2008) 78.

75 Burton, Evans and Sanders (n 9) 5.

76 Mary Barber, 'The Youth Justice and Criminal Evidence Bill [HL]' (HOC Research Paper 99/40, Bill 74 of 1998–1999) 7.

77 Home Office (n 40) 5. For further discussion of the meaning of 'best evidence', see: Samantha Fairclough, 'The Lost Leg of the Youth Justice and Criminal Evidence Act (1999): Special Measures and Humane Treatment' (2021) 41(4) Oxford Journal of Legal Studies 1066.

78 Home Office, *Action for Justice: Achieving Best Evidence in Criminal Proceedings: Guidance for Vulnerable or Intimidated Witnesses, Including Children: Implementing the Speaking Up for Justice Report* (Home Office 2000).

79 HL Deb 15 December 1998, vol 595, cols 1266–307.

transformational as had been suggested. The speech of Viscount Colville of Culross questioned the need for a statutory basis for special measures when certain measures were already in operation in criminal courts. He argued:

> We already use screens on suitable occasions in the Crown Court, we already use the television link and there are many cases where the video recording of the evidence-in-chief of a child is played in court to the jury in the course of the trial. I am not absolutely certain why it is necessary to put these procedures on a statutory basis.[80]

Lord Thomas of Gresford agreed and questioned why Parliament was required to legislate for what appeared to already exist:

> There is nothing new in the special measures proposed in the Bill, as the noble Viscount, Lord Colville of Culross, pointed out in his speech. I have personal experience of screens being erected in court. Indeed, it is now so commonplace in the Old Bailey that in some courts, there are permanent frameworks in place so that screens can readily be put up. Similarly, I have personal experience of video links, of private hearings, of video questioning, even of removing my wig and gown in an appropriate case.[81]

However, the Bill amounted to more than a mere codification of existing evidence-giving procedures. Clause 27 of the Bill, relating to the cross-examination and re-examination of witnesses on video, was indeed new. The findings of a Home Office Police Research Group from 1996 were cited, which found judicial reluctance to allow video evidence.[82] It was noted that various members strongly supported early recording of the evidence of distressed witnesses.[83] Ensuring that children could avoid physically attending court was cited in support of Clause 27, and calls were made for full pre-trial evidence recording to be piloted before being phased in.[84] Conversely, the potential pitfalls of Clause 27 were raised, and Lord Thomas strongly opposed its enactment, arguing that giving evidence in court is unlikely to be worse than being videoed remotely.[85]

80 HL Deb 15 December 1998, vol 595, 1266–307.
81 HL Deb 15 December 1998, vol 595 [1297].
82 Despite being cited in the House of Lords, this report has been described as 'apparently unpublished and untraceable', see: Rock (n 7) 379.
83 HL Deb 15 December 1998, vol 595, cols 1266–307.
84 HL Deb 15 December 1998, vol 595, cols 1266–307.
85 HL Deb 15 December 1998, vol 595, cols 1266–307.

2.9 Clause 28 – the intermediary

Clause 28 of the Bill provided for the examination of a witness through an intermediary in what has since been described as 'perhaps the most witness-centred of all of the reforms introduced in the 1999 Act'.[86] The precursor to its inclusion in the Bill was the recommendation in Speaking up for Justice providing for the introduction of a 'communicator/intermediary'. While an extremely significant development and one that built on the 'interlocutory' as envisaged by Pigot, there were still many questions about what the role of the communicator/intermediary might entail. The House of Commons Research Paper, providing background on the Youth Justice and Criminal Evidence Bill after it had passed the House of Lords, made no reference at all to what the role involved.[87] This was in stark contrast to the detailed explanations of the measures concerning video-recorded evidence, which cited various historical reference points, including the Pigot and legislation such as the Criminal Justice Act 1988 and the Criminal Justice Act 1991.[88]

It is perhaps unsurprising that the parliamentary debates on the intermediary provision were limited in scope and detail. During the House of Lords debate, it was considered by some that the intermediary role would be similar to that of the foreign language interpreter, particularly since the intermediary must not represent the intent or the particulars of a question or answer.[89] At a later sitting, Lord Williams of Mostyn, recounting his experiences as a defence barrister, noted that the communication needs of witnesses vary considerably and that any intermediary scheme must be flexible.[90] Beyond these comments, the rest of the debates emphasised that intermediaries must have sufficient qualifications and undergo appropriate training.[91] The imperative that 'intermediaries understand their function clearly' was highlighted in the debates, yet at that stage the title of 'intermediary' had barely been decided and no specific role had been clarified.[92]

Once the legislation had passed through Parliament, ensuring that intermediaries were trained, organised and competent was regarded by Lord Williams as imperative:

> it is vital that the scheme is implemented carefully so that both the intermediary and the court can be assured that they are performing to standards consistent with the production of good evidence. This will take some very innovative thinking on the part of the Home Office.[93]

86 Anthony Beech and Graham Davies, *Forensic Psychology: Crime, Justice, Law Interventions* (Wiley-Blackwell 2017) 413.
87 Barber (n 76).
88 Barber (n 76).
89 HL Deb 1 February 1999, vol 596, cols 1363–410, 1383.
90 HL Deb 2 March 1999, vol 597, cols 1633–54, 1648.
91 HL Deb 1 February 1999, vol 596, cols 1363–410, 1383.
92 HL Deb 1 February 1999, vol 596, cols 1363–410, 1383.
93 HL Deb 1 February 1999, vol 596, cols 1363–410.

This fear was shared by other members of the Lords who urged caution in implementing what was considered one of the most controversial measures in the whole Bill. It was remarked that unless the intermediary schemes could be systematically implemented, then the whole concept 'could be jettisoned on the grounds that they are likely to inhibit the production of quality evidence'.[94]

The Bill's passage through the committee stage revealed many of the same concerns. Foremost among these related to the need for formal training which, it was argued, would ensure 'confidence in the intermediary'.[95] At committee stage in the Lords, training was noted as necessary to ensure 'standards consistent with the production of good evidence'.[96] No specific details were outlined in either chamber about what this training should involve, and the aspirations were framed in general terms, i.e. that intermediaries should provide safe, reliable service to vulnerable witnesses.[97] Despite this, a consensus maintained that some form of accreditation should be established to ensure that intermediaries possess the required skill set. A scheme for interpreters, which aimed to standardise arrangements and utilised a 'directory' from which interpreters could be selected, was cited as an already existing working model.[98]

The concern raised in the Lords that intermediaries might act 'ultra vires' also featured at the Commons Standing Committee and formed the basis of a tabled amendment. Amendment no. 57 sought to clarify the ambit of the role and ensure that the intermediary 'understands the need for him to confine himself to explaining the questions to the witness and the answers given by the witness'.[99] The amendment's proposer, John Greenaway MP, worried that intermediaries might advance their own interpretation of the witness's words rather than merely reflecting them.[100] The government rejected this amendment, arguing instead that such statutory language was no substitute for relevant training that intermediaries would be obliged to undertake. In addition, the government sought to assuage fears that the intermediary role would disrupt the trial process by highlighting that each appointment would be judicially approved.[101] This echoes the recommendation in Speaking up for Justice that it would be within the court's purview whether to appoint an intermediary. The Minister of State clarified that the intermediary's function would be 'purely to communicate and, if necessary, to explain'[102] and that

94 HL Deb 2 March 1999, col 1647.
95 Youth Justice and Criminal Evidence Bill Deb 22 June 1999, col (Ms Angela Smith).
96 Youth Justice and Criminal Evidence Bill Deb (HL) 1 February 1999, col 1383.
97 Youth Justice and Criminal Evidence Bill Deb (HL) 1 February 1999, col 1383.
98 HL Deb 2 March 1999, col 1647.
99 Youth Justice and Criminal Evidence Bill [Lords] Clause 28 (22 June 1999).
100 Youth Justice and Criminal Evidence Bill [Lords] Clause 28 (22 June 1999).
101 Youth Justice and Criminal Evidence Bill [Lords] Clause 28 (22 June 1999) (Mr Paul Boateng).
102 Youth Justice and Criminal Evidence Bill [Lords] Clause 28 (22 June 1999) (Mr Paul Boateng).

matters relating to training and guidance would subsequently be considered by a Steering Group.

While the introduction of the intermediary was described at committee stage as 'unprecedented' and representing a 'radical shift in courtroom practice', the government's initial conceptualisation of the role did not appear so maverick.[103] The Minister for State stressed that those assuming the role must ensure victims and witnesses are comfortable, should have the capacity to empathise and have a familiarity with disabilities or vulnerability in the case of youths.[104] It was further explained that intermediaries need not possess a degree, and their ability to display the aforementioned qualities would be 'more important than any formal qualification'.[105] This notion of the intermediary as a non-professional was also a feature of the Lords Standing Committee when Lord Swinfen remarked:

> the intermediary who could be appointed to help someone with a mental disability may have no idea of a courtroom, or how the courts operate, or the proper procedure. They may not be all that well educated, and it would be helpful to the court if they had some training to enable the proceedings to proceed smoothly.[106]

It is clear that at this early stage of the Bill there was no identifiable category of individual or profession from which the intermediary was expected to be drawn. The expectation that the intermediary would be an 'outsider' and not part of the 'court workgroup' resonates with this position.[107] Lord Williams made a brief reference to the expertise of speech therapists but equally recognised that a relative could perform the role without explaining in what circumstances this may be appropriate.[108]

The committee debates envisaged a completely new and distinct criminal justice role which would require a skill set not readily identifiable within one profession. The focus on the need for specialist training and the development of an accreditation programme supports this contention. Indeed, the entire committee discussion about intermediaries related to the court environment, suggesting that this was to be their primary place of work. This understanding is, however, difficult to reconcile with the position of Lord Williams, who noted that some individuals, such as speech therapists, may be called to act as

103 Youth Justice and Criminal Evidence Bill [Lords] Clause 28 (22 June 1999) (Mr Bob Russell).
104 Youth Justice and Criminal Evidence Bill [Lords] Clause 28 (22 June 1999) (Mr Paul Boateng).
105 Youth Justice and Criminal Evidence Bill [Lords] Clause 28 (22 June 1999) (Mr Paul Boateng).
106 Youth Justice and Criminal Evidence Bill Deb (HL) (n 96) col 1384.
107 For further discussion of the intermediary's status as an outsider from the 'court workgroup', see: Chapter 5 (Professional work – jurisdictions and boundary work).
108 Youth Justice and Criminal Evidence Bill Deb (HL) (n 96) col 1384.

intermediaries regularly.[109] While he identified this profession as an example, it nonetheless suggests that such professionals would not be expected to work as intermediaries on an exclusive basis. Earlier comments in the House of Lords that a relative may also act as an intermediary reinforces this point.[110]

The discussion of the intermediary at committee stage provided little information beyond identifying the general communicative nature of the role and the need for training and accreditation. The government eschewed attempts to provide guarantees on aspects of the role's function. In rejecting the tabled amendments, the government noted that the role 'must be tightly restricted to communicating questions and answers between court and witness'.[111] Mirroring the debates in the House of Commons and the House of Lords, there was no discussion of the intermediary role beyond the courtroom. Issues relating to pre-court involvement, contact with the witness/complainant outside of the court, or even post-trial support or assistance feature nowhere on the record.

The passage of the Youth Justice and Criminal Evidence Bill through Parliament demonstrated that confusion about many aspects of the intermediary role endured. Anyone hoping that the debates would build on Pigot's 'interlocutor', and the 'communicator/intermediary' role outlined in Speaking up for Justice would have been disappointed. The same concerns that troubled Pigot Committee member Anne Rafferty, and which remerged years later in Speaking up for Justice, were also noted in Parliament. One explanation for the scarcity of detail about the intermediary role in the parliamentary debates is that such matters were expected to be clarified later by the Home Office. As highlighted earlier, the need for training and accreditation featured heavily in the parliamentary debates and any ancillary matters were to be 'tackled through guidance'.[112]

2.10 s.29 – The intermediary provision

The intermediary provision was eventually introduced through s.29 of the YJCEA, and its wording remains unchanged from the original bill. Section 29(2) reads:

(2) The function of an intermediary is to communicate –

  (a) to the witness, questions put to the witness, and
  (b) to any person asking such questions, the answers given by the witness in reply to them,

109 Youth Justice and Criminal Evidence Bill Deb (HL) (n 96) col 1384.
110 Youth Justice and Criminal Evidence Bill Deb (HL) (n 96) col 1384.
111 Youth Justice and Criminal Evidence Bill Deb (HC Standing Committee E (5th sitting)),17 June 1999 (Mr Paul Boateng).
112 Youth Justice and Criminal Evidence Bill Deb (HC Standing Committee E (5th sitting)),17 June 1999 (Mr Paul Boateng).

and to explain such questions or answers so far as necessary to enable them to be understood by the witness or person in question.

The enactment of s.29 did not immediately clarify the various questions surrounding the intermediary provision. As the parliamentary debates demonstrated, the legislation would require some form of accompanying guidance or accreditation scheme to give substance to its wording. Writing after the YJCEA's enactment but before intermediaries were officially rolled out in courts, Birch echoed earlier views that much remained unresolved about the intermediary role. Arguing that the impact of the intermediary was difficult to predict due to the 'bare bones' of s.29, she considered that Rules of Court would ultimately fill in the apparent gaps.[113] Birch recognised that the YJCEA provided only the 'briefest description of the intermediary's function' and that the judiciary would put flesh on the proverbial legislative bones.[114]

S.29 of the YJCEA did not include a profile of who would perform the intermediary role. Hoyano considered it 'remarkable' that nothing in the legislation hinted at whether an intermediary was expected to have formal qualifications or be examined by the trial judge prior to appointment.[115] While Pigot had identified specific occupations suited to the analogous 'interlocutor' role, it also implied that those closest to a child witness and who enjoyed their confidence could be eligible. Hoyano later argued that in the case of young children, it was unlikely that anyone other than a parent could be confident of fully understanding the child's meaning.[116] This echoed Lord Williams' statement in the House of Lords that the intermediary could occasionally be a family member 'who will probably never be called upon again in his or her lifetime to be an intermediary'.[117] In contrast, McEwan considered that the formality of the court process would rule out any possibility that the witness would know the intermediary well.[118] McEwan also noted that although the government had acknowledged that specific intermediary training would be required, it had not clarified who would provide it.[119] The government accepted that these issues would need to be explored by a Steering Group which would complement the statutory framework.[120] The result was that when the YJCEA received royal assent on 27 July 1999, an incomplete

113 Birch (n 42) 249.
114 Birch (n 42) 249.
115 Hoyano (n 19) 271.
116 Hoyano (n 19) 272.
117 HL Deb 1 February 1999, vol 596, cols 1363–4101, 1384.
118 HL Deb 1 February 1999, vol 596, cols 1363–4101, 1384.
119 Jenny McEwan, 'In Defence of Vulnerable Witnesses: The Youth Justice and Criminal Evidence Act 1999' (2000) International Journal of Evidence and Proof 1, 11.
120 Youth Justice and Criminal Evidence Bill [Lords] Clause 28 (22 June 1999).

picture of the intermediary role existed and little could be gleaned from reading s.29 in isolation.

In Northern Ireland, the intermediary model was introduced based on the provisions of the Criminal Evidence (Northern Ireland) Order 1999, which mirror those in the YJCEA. As such, the key debates and discussions around the scope of the role took place in England and Wales. However, as will be discussed in later chapters, Northern Ireland's implementation and regulation of the intermediary has diverged from England and Wales in several key areas.

2.11 Conclusion

This chapter has traced the emergence of the intermediary role from the recognition of challenges associated with child testimony, the development of the Pigot Committee and the later Speaking Up for Justice Report which led to the enactment of s.29 YJCEA. Although the legislation provided a statutory basis for the intermediary special measure, its scope remained underdeveloped. It was unclear who would perform the role, how it would be regulated and, crucially, how it would be integrated into the criminal justice system. As practice has developed, we are clearer about the profile of intermediaries and much of the role's work is now provided in Practice Directions and the Criminal Procedure Rules.[121] Nevertheless, as will be discussed in later chapters, there is a need to better understand the scope of the role in practice, its relationships with other criminal justice professionals and how intermediaries conceptualise their work in different contexts.

This chapter is an important reference point for later chapters regarding how the intermediary role was initially conceptualised and the challenges the role was expected to face. It also provides important historical context for some of the ambiguities of the role that persist today, more than 20 years after the first cohort of intermediaries was rolled out. As other jurisdictions increasingly adopt intermediary-type roles, it is instructive to consider the historical backdrop to the intermediary's introduction in the U.K and consider how the role has evolved from its earliest designs.

121 Criminal Procedure Rules (October 2020) Pt 3, rules 3.8–2.9; The Criminal Procedure Rules apply to England and Wales only.

Chapter 3

The international context

3.1 Introduction

This book focuses primarily on the intermediary special measure within the U.K – the first country to legislate for, and provide specific procedural guidance on, the intermediary role in its criminal justice system. However, locating the intermediary role within the broader, international context is instructive. While justice models can vary widely, for example, in terms of their approach to adjudication and the structure of judicial authority,[1] comparative legal analysis can yield deeper understanding of a jurisdiction's legal order.[2] This chapter examines how other countries have implemented their own model of expert communication assistance based on the intermediary special measure, with a particular focus on Australia. Before doing that, the provision of intermediary assistance will be considered with reference to two core international legal instruments. The first relates to the status of the child as deserving of 'special safeguards and care, including appropriate legal protection' as per the UN Convention on the Rights of the Child (CRC).[3] The second relates to the need for legal protection for persons who encounter 'social . . . attitudinal and environmental barriers' under the UN Convention on the Rights of Persons with Disabilities (CRPD).[4] Intermediary assistance may impact the participatory role of defendants in proceedings as protected by Article 6 of the European Convention on Human Rights (ECHR), which will be discussed further throughout the book.

1 Mirjan Damaška, *The Faces of Justice and State Authority: A Comparative Approach to the Legal Process* (Yale UP 1986).
2 Edward J Eberle, 'The Methodology of Comparative Law' (2011) 16(1) Roger Williams University Law Review 51, 52.
3 Convention on the Rights of the Child (CRC) (adopted 20 November 1989, entered into force 2 September 1990) 1577 UNTS 3, Preamble.
4 Ilias Bantekas, Michael Ashley Stein and Dimitris Anastasiou, *The UN Convention on the Rights of Persons with Disabilities: A Commentary* (OUP 2018) 67.

DOI: 10.4324/9781003461166-3

3.2 UN Convention on the Rights of the Child (CRC)

A significant number of intermediary appointments are made for children deemed vulnerable because of their age. For example, in Northern Ireland, where intermediaries have been operational since 2013, the Department of Justice (DoJ) has identified 'Young Age' as the most common type of referral (28% of the total).[5] Of the total intermediary requests for suspects made by the Police Service of Northern Ireland in 2023/2024, 49% were for individuals up to 17 years of age. Although the data in England and Wales are collected differently, vulnerability due to age was the most common reason for an intermediary request to the Witness Intermediary Scheme (WIS) in 2023.[6]

As was discussed in the previous chapter, the first intermediary/interlocutor role was conceived by the Pigot Committee in England and Wales which considered the admissibility of video-recorded evidence, specifically for 'child witnesses'.[7] Momentum for establishing the committee developed amidst increased recognition of the particular difficulties children face when giving evidence in court.[8] As Tobin has noted, the concept of the 'child' was well known in international human rights law prior to 1989 when the UN Convention on the Rights of the Child (CRC) was signed.[9] International documents such as The Universal Declaration on Human Rights ('UDHR') and the International Covenants on Economic Social and Cultural Rights and Civil and Political Rights both previously conferred a right of special protection for children. Nonetheless, the CRC represents the first international human rights instrument to provide a definition of a child. Article 1 states, 'For the purposes of the present Convention, a child means every human being below the age of eighteen years unless under the law applicable to the child, majority is attained earlier'.[10] The convention is underpinned by the rule that the best interests of the child shall be a primary consideration in all actions concerning children, both in the public and private sphere.[11] Article 3 of the CRC, taken as a whole, requires states to introduce measures for the

5 Email correspondence between the Department of Justice of Northern Ireland (DoJ) and author (24 July 2024).

6 Ministry of Justice (MoJ), The Witness Intermediary Scheme: Annual Report 2023' <https://assets.publishing.service.gov.uk/media/664487d0993111924d9d3504/Witness_Intermediary_Scheme_Annual_Report_2023.pdf> accessed 3 February 2025.

7 Home Office, *Report of the Advisory Group on Video Evidence* (1989) (hereafter referred to as the 'Pigot Report').

8 See Chapter 2 (Emergence of the intermediary role) section 2.1.

9 John Tobin, *The UN Convention on the Rights of the Child: A Commentary* (OUP 2019) 21.

10 CRC Committee, (2019) General Comment No. 24, Children's rights in juvenile justice (CRC/C/GC/24).

11 CRC (n 3) Art. 3.

full implementation of the right when adopting or reviewing laws, policies, guidelines and even when devising governmental strategies and budgets.[12]

When examining the contents of the CRC concerning the intermediary role, Article 12 is arguably the most relevant provision. Paragraph 2 of Article 12 states that:

> the child shall in particular be provided the opportunity to be heard in any judicial and administrative proceedings affecting the child, either directly, or through a representative or an appropriate body, in a manner consistent with the procedural rules of national law.

The UN Committee on the Rights of the Child (CRC Committee) has noted that Article 12 should be viewed as a general principle with which all Convention provisions must be read.[13] Lundy and McEvoy contend that this right should be read in conjunction with two other articles of the CRC: Article 5, which states that children have a right to be assisted by adults in claiming and upholding their rights, and Article 13, which states that children have a right to 'seek, receive and impart' information.[14] Article 13 and Article 17 have been described as 'crucial pre-requisites for the effective exercise of the right to be heard' as provided for by Article 12.[15]

The CRC Committee has advocated a broad understanding of the term 'judicial and administrative proceedings' contained within Article 12, noting that it 'applies for all relevant judicial proceedings affecting the child without limitation, including for example, separation of parents, custody, case and adoption, children in conflict with the law'.[16] As Lundy et al. point out, the Committee has adopted an expansive approach in other general comments by suggesting that the term 'courts' is sufficiently broad to cover 'all judicial

12 Wouter Vandenhole, Gamze Erdem Türkelli and Sara Lembrechts, *Children's Rights: A Commentary on the Convention on the Rights of the Child and Its Protocols* (Edward Elgar 2019) 60.

13 CRC Committee, General Guidelines regarding the form and contents of Periodic Reports to be submitted by States Parties under Article 44, paragraph 1(b) of the Convention (UN Doc No CRC/C/58, 1996).

14 Laura Lundy and Lesley McEvoy, 'Children's Rights and Research Processes: Assisting Children to (in)Formed Views' (2012) 19 Childhood 129. For further analysis of how children's rights can be operationalised, see the 'Lundy Model' of child participation: Laura Lundy, '"Voice" Is Not Enough: Conceptualising Article 12 of the United Nations Convention on the Child' (2007) 33(6) British Educational Research Journal 927.

15 CRC Committee, (2009) General Comment No. 12, The Right of the Child to be Heard (CRC/C/GC/12) [80].

16 CRC Committee, (2009) General Comment No. 12, The Right of the Child to be Heard (CRC/C/GC/12) [32].

proceedings . . . whether staffed by professional judges or lay persons'.[17] This must cover criminal proceedings, including preparatory hearings such as Ground Rules Hearings (GRH). In terms of the CRC's relevance to the pre-court stage, it has been recognised that in addition to protections under domestic law, decisions relating to the arrest and detention of children in police custody require the child's best interests to be a primary consideration.[18] Furthermore, the CRC Committee has understood that Convention rights should be engaged 'from the earliest contact with the criminal justice system', including 'the stopping, warning or arrest stage, while in custody of police or other law enforcement agencies'.[19]

Returning to the central pillar of the CRC – the best interests of the child – Henegan argues that any best interests analysis must be underpinned by a focus on 'the particular child and his or her way of seeing the world'.[20] It is useful to consider the emphasis Article 12 places on the different modes through which a child might be 'heard'. Article 12(2) is not prescriptive in terms of how children's views are advanced in judicial and administrative proceedings – they may be conveyed either directly by the child or indirectly through a representative or an 'appropriate body'.[21] Somewhat confusingly, some authors have used the term 'adult intermediary' to describe someone 'representing' the interests of the child, whether that be a lawyer, parent, legal guardian or other representative.[22] The intermediary operating as a communication specialist in the criminal process, however, does not cover 'representation' and is focused squarely on facilitating communication. This point underscores the value of neutrality which characterises the role. However, as will be explored in Chapter 6 (The neutrality paradox), tensions can exist between the normative attachment to neutrality and the realities of the role's execution. An intermediary may operate to facilitate communication of a child's views regardless of whether the child is heard directly or indirectly. Importantly, whether the child should be heard directly or indirectly should prioritise the wishes and views of the child.[23] As such, it is feasible that an

17 CRC Committee, (2013) General Comment No. 14, The Right of the Child to Have His or Her Best Interests Taken as a Primary Consideration (CRC/C/GC/14) [27] (interpreting the phrase 'courts of law' as it appears in art 3 of the Convention).

18 House of Commons Library, *Rights of Children in Police Custody (Number CDP 2022/0122)* (21 June 2022).

19 CRC Committee (n 10) [40].

20 Mark Henegan, 'Final Appeal Courts and Article 3 of the UN CRC: What Do the Best Interests of the Particular Child Have to Do with It?' in Elaine E Sutherland and Lesley-Anne Barnes Macfarlane (eds), *Implementing Article 3 of the United Nations CRC* (CUP) 81.

21 For an in-depth discussion about what constitutes a 'representative' and an 'appropriate body', see: Laura Lundy, John Tobin and Aisling Parkes, 'Article 12: The Right to Respect for the Views of the Child' in Tobin (n 9) 423.

22 Vandenhole and others (n 12) [12.27].

23 Lundy (n 14) 927.

intermediary could facilitate communication to allow a child's preference to be heard, regardless of whether a representative or an appropriate body is ultimately involved.

When locating the intermediary role within the Article 12 framework, it is important to consider the underpinning principle of 'accessibility'. In the context of legal processes, this recognises that traditional 'adult-centric methods' to facilitate participation will not always be appropriate for children.[24] The CRC Committee has stressed that '[p]roceedings must be both accessible and child appropriate' with particular attention being given to 'the provision and delivery of child friendly information . . . appropriately trained staff, design of court rooms, clothing of judges and lawyers, sight screens and separate waiting rooms'.[25] As Lundy et al. argue, states are obligated to 'create inclusive communication systems' which include special measures such as the intermediary.[26] The nature of the adversarial model of adjudication, which dominates common law legal systems, should be noted here. The CRC Committee has acknowledged that children cannot be heard effectively when the 'environment is intimidating, hostile, insensitive or inappropriate for his or her age'.[27] As will be explored further in Chapter 4 (Locating the intermediary within theories of the criminal trial), the special measures regime in England and Wales, which included the intermediary role, was introduced to deal with the limitations of the adversarial model. As such, parallels can be drawn between the drive to promote the participation of children as envisaged by the CRC and the introduction of the intermediary special measure. Invariably, parallels can also be identified in the challenges which exist in effecting this kind of cultural change in the legal system. The CRC Committee conceded that the implementation of Article 12 'continues to be impeded by many long-standing practices and attitudes, as well as political and economic barriers'.[28] As will be discussed throughout the book, resistance to the intermediary role is often embedded in an attachment to traditional legal practices and an unease at the entrance of an 'outsider' to the professional world of the criminal justice system.

3.3 Social model of disability and access to justice

Many individuals who are appointed an intermediary suffer from disabilities, including physical disabilities and intellectual and learning disabilities. There is an increasing recognition globally that disabled people require additional

24 Lundy, Tobin and Parkes (n 21) 433.
25 CRC Committee (n 15) [34].
26 Lundy, Tobin and Parkes (n 21) 433.
27 CRC Committee (n 15) [34].
28 CRC Committee (n 15) [4].

consideration and specific accommodation in a variety of settings.[29] In this regard, there has been a 'paradigm shift' in approaches to the rights of disabled people.[30] Growing recognition of these rights has occurred against the backdrop of the emergence of the 'social model of disability' in which disability is viewed as a socially produced injustice, able to be challenged through radical social change.[31] The social model recognises 'impairment as part of human diversity',[32] which is important for many of the issues and themes addressed in this book. While intermediaries work with a range of disabilities, including physical disability, learning disability and intellectual disability, they also work with people deemed 'vulnerable' due to their age, i.e. children. While the terms disabled and vulnerable are not interchangeable,[33] many individuals in both groups will have 'a shared experience of disablement through exclusionary societal structures, attitudes and practices'.[34] As will be discussed throughout the book, the criminal justice process contains several barriers to effective communication which the intermediary role operates, at least partially, to counteract.

Perhaps the most important right of disabled persons in the context of the intermediary role is the right of access to justice. Access to justice is a fundamental right in itself and is a precondition for the protection and promotion of all other human rights.[35] While the right has no universal definition, conceptually it can be said to focus on two fundamentals: firstly, that justice systems are equally accessible to all, and secondly, that they produce results which are individually and socially just.[36] It is well recognised that disabled

29 UN High Commissioner on Human Rights, 'Right to Access to Justice under Article 13 of the Convention on the Rights of Persons with Disabilities: Report of the Office of the United Nations High Commissioner for Human Rights' (A/HRC/37/25) (27 December 2017).

30 Arlene Kanter, *The Development of Disability Rights under International Law: From Charity to Human Rights* (Routledge 2014) 46.

31 Anna Lawson and Angharad Beckett, 'The Social and Human Rights Models of Disability: Towards a Complementarity Thesis' (2021) 25 The International Journal of Human Rights 348.

32 Lawson and Beckett (n 31) 361.

33 As is recognised by the Crown Prosecution Service (CPS) in England and Wales: 'Special Measures | The Crown Prosecution Service' <https://www.cps.gov.uk/legal-guidance/special-measures> accessed 5 October 2024.

34 Lawson and Beckett (n 31) 367. For an insightful discussion around the use of the terms 'vulnerable' and 'disabled', see: Angharad Beckett, *Citizenship and Vulnerability: Disability and Issues of Social and Political Engagement* (Springer 2006).

35 UN High Commissioner for Human Rights, 'Access to Justice for Children' (16 December 2013) A/HRC/25/35 [3].

36 Mauro Cappelletti and Bryant Garth, 'Access to Justice: The Newest Wave in the Worldwide Movement to Make Rights Effective' (1978) 27(2) Buffalo Law Review 181; Jacobson and Cooper also point out that access to justice is closely interrelated to the broader principle of participation, see: Jessica Jacobson and Penny Cooper, *Participation in Courts and Tribunals: Concepts, Realities and Aspirations* (Bristol UP 2020).

persons face a range of barriers which can obstruct access to justice, not only because of legal rules but also due to legal traditions, practices and even the physical environment of the justice system.[37] Access to justice also encompasses other factors, including access to legal aid, access to legal representation and the use of technology, which 'has the capacity to enhance, empower and automate, but it also has the potential to exclude vulnerable members of society'.[38]

For present purposes, one prevailing barrier to ensuring access to justice when considering the intermediary role at various points in the criminal process is the failure to provide reasonable adjustments. For example, in the U.K, police have a duty under the Equality Act 2010 to take positive steps to ensure that disabled people are not substantially disadvantaged compared to non-disabled people when interacting with the police.[39] While there can be no claim under the Equality Act against a court or tribunal for failing to make reasonable adjustments to accommodate a disability, courts and tribunals have a duty to ensure the effective participation of disabled persons in its proceedings.[40] The Equal Treatment Benchbook in the U.K contains specific guidance for judges on 'the duty to make reasonable adjustment for witnesses, defendants and jurors with disabilities'[41] to 'remove any unnecessary barriers to participation'.[42] It also notes that intermediaries may advise courts on the kind of adjustments that might be necessary.[43] While intermediary provision has a legislative basis in the U.K, the special measure can be seen as an 'adjustment' or 'accommodation' to the traditional adversarial model (see Chapter 4: Locating the intermediary within theories of the criminal trial). As Lawson notes, the prevention of access to justice can arise from a failure to provide reasonable adjustments or accommodations before, during and after formal legal proceedings.[44] As will be discussed throughout this book, there are ongoing academic and policy debates about the extent of intermediary involvement at different stages of the criminal process. Intermediaries will often be instrumental to the participation of vulnerable individuals in the criminal process and, as a result, enable access to justice.

37 Anna Lawson, 'Disabled People and Access to Justice: From Disablement to Enablement?' in Eilionóir Flynn (ed), *Routledge Handbook of Disability Law and Human Rights* (Routledge 2016).

38 The Bach Commission, *The Right to Justice: The Final Report of the Bach Commission* (Fabian Policy Report, September 2017).

39 Independent Police Complaints Commission, 'IPCC Guidelines for Handling Allegations of Discrimination' (2015) <https://www.policeconduct.gov.uk/sites/default/files/documents/guidelines_for_handling_allegations_of_discrimination_updated.pdf> accessed 3 November 2024.

40 *Rackham v NHS Professionals Ltd* [2015] UKEAT 0110_15_1612.

41 Judicial College, *Equal Treatment Bench Book February 2024 Edition* (July 2024) 63.

42 Judicial College (n 41) 80.

43 Judicial College (n 41) 48.

44 Lawson (n 37).

3.4 The Convention on the Rights of Persons with Disabilities (CRPD)

The CRPD contains the first expression of a stand-alone right of access to justice in international human rights law.[45] It is also the first international legislative instrument to describe disability in terms of the interaction between persons with impairments and attitudinal and environmental barriers that hinder their 'full and effective participation' in society on an equal basis with others.[46] The phrase 'full and effective participation' appears at several points throughout the full text of the CRPD and is cited as one of the 'General Principles' in Article 3. The term is significant in the context of the intermediary, given that the legislative basis for defendant intermediary provision in England and Wales is to ensure the 'effective participation' of the accused in legal proceedings.[47] However, as Jacobson and Cooper point out, the right of access to justice closely relates to the principle of participation.[48] Developing this further, McKeever argues that an ability to participate in legal proceedings is a basic facet of access to justice and normative perceptions of fairness.[49] This entitlement is sufficiently broad to cover all categories of vulnerable individuals who may require intermediary assistance. Chapter 4 (Locating the intermediary within theories of the criminal trial) will discuss the court's requirement to take 'every reasonable step' to facilitate the participation of *all* individuals within proceedings, including witnesses.[50] Chapter 7 (Witness work, defendant work and participatory roles) further unpacks the understanding of the term participation in the context of the intermediary role.

The provision within the CRPD which most obviously relates to the intermediary role is Article 9 (Accessibility). It requires state parties to identify and eliminate barriers to facilities or services open or provided to the public.[51] Article 9 obligates state parties to take appropriate measures to provide forms of 'live assistance and intermediaries, including guides, readers and professional sign language interpreters'. Although this Article does not provide further information on the occupational profile of these individuals, it equally does not prescribe any required qualifications, nor does it rule

45 Eilionóir Flynn, 'Art.13 Access to Justice' in Ilias Bantekas, Michael Ashley Stein and Dimitris Anastasiou (eds), *Oxford Public International Law* (OUP 2018).

46 Anne-Marie Callus and Ruth Farrugia, *The Disabled Child's Participation Rights* (Routledge 2016) 3; Stephanie Ortoleva, 'Inaccessible Justice: Human Rights, Persons with Disabilities and the Legal System' (2011) 17(2) ILSA Journal of International and Comparative Law 281.

47 Coroners and Justice Act 2009, s.104.

48 Jacobson and Cooper (n 36).

49 Grainne McKeever, 'Comparing Courts and Tribunals through the Lens of Legal Participation' (2020) 39 Civil Justice Quarterly 217.

50 Criminal Procedure Rules (October 2020) Pt 3, rule 3.8(3)(b).

51 CRPD Committee, (2014) General Comment No. 1, Article 12: Equal Recognition before the Law (CRPD/C/GC/1) [37].

out certain professions from performing the role. Article 9 should be read in light of a later General Comment from the Committee on the Rights of Persons with Disabilities that stresses the importance of continuing professional development and training for professionals working with disabled persons.[52] The language employed by the Convention can be contrasted with the Pigot Committee in the U.K, which identified a range of occupations it considered best-placed to execute the 'interlocutor' role (see: Chapter 2: Emergence of the intermediary role). The 'professional' profile of the intermediary is explored further in Chapter 5 (Professional work – jurisdictions and boundary work).

Returning to the concept of access to justice, Article 13 of the CRPD is significant as it represents the first time any international treaty explicitly uses the phrase 'access to justice' as a separate, substantive right. It is also important to briefly mention Article 12, as it addresses barriers faced by those with disabilities in legal contexts, which may impede access to justice. Article 12 outlines the right to equal recognition before the law and the right to exercise legal capacity.[53] The right of access to justice contained in Article 13 is more widely framed than the ECHR Article 6 right to a fair trial; it obligates states to eliminate barriers faced by disabled persons in accessing justice on an equal basis.[54] Article 13 also imposes an obligation on states to implement appropriate training on disability issues for those working within the administration of justice, including police and prison staff.[55] It also requires state parties to adapt procedures, where appropriate and reasonable, so as to ensure the 'effective participation' of disabled persons within the legal process.[56] Returning to the importance of accommodations and adjustments to justice systems, Article 13 outlines that:

> Parties shall ensure effective access to justice for persons with disabilities on an equal basis with others, including through the provision of procedural and age-appropriate accommodations, in order to facilitate their effective role as direct and indirect participants, including as witnesses, in all legal proceedings, including at investigative and other preliminary stages.

52 CRPD Committee, (2016) General Comment No. 4, Article 24 – the Right to Inclusive Education (CRPD/C/GC/4).

53 For further discussion of Article 12, see: Lucy Series and Anna Nilsson, 'Article 12 CRPD: Equal Recognition before the Law' in Ilias Bantekas, Michael Ashley Stein, Dimitris Anastasiou (eds), *The UN Convention on the Rights of Persons with Disabilities: A Commentary* (OUP 2018).

54 UN High Commissioner on Human Rights (n 29).

55 CRPD, Article 13, section 2. Also, see: Louise Ellison, 'Responding to the Needs of Victims with Psychosocial Disabilities: Challenges to Equality of Access to Justice' (2015) 1 Criminal Law Review 28.

56 Anna Lawson, 'People with Psychosocial Impairments or Conditions, Reasonable Accommodation and the Disabilities Convention' (2008) 26 Law in Context 62.

The general accessibility obligations entrenched in Article 9 reinforce the obligations placed on states contained within Article 13.[57] In its General Comment on Article 9, the Committee on the Rights of Persons with Disabilities drew a link between Article 9 and Article 13 by noting that:

> There can be no effective access to justice if the buildings in which law-enforcement agencies and the judiciary are located are not physically accessible, or if the services, information and communication they provide are not accessible to persons with disabilities.
>
> (art. 13)

While Article 13 makes no specific link between access to justice and communication needs, it is noteworthy that the 'List of illustrative indicators on access to justice' compiled by the Office of the United Nations High Commissioner for Human Rights (OHCHR) uses the term at several points.[58] For example, it notes that a key measure in gauging compliance with the CRPD is the extent to which members of the legal profession and law enforcement are trained on 'the obligation to ensure procedural accommodations, and on communication with persons with disabilities, including on alternative means and modes of communication'.[59] The indicators also provide that contracting states must ensure that 'information and communications are accessible' for those with a range of disabilities and impairments and that 'multiple means of communication' must be accommodated in 'all judicial and administrative proceedings'.[60] Although there is no explicit mention of an intermediary-type role in these indicators, the intermediary measure, as it is broadly conceived and operates in various jurisdictions, aligns with the language employed in the Convention.

3.5 International Principles and Guidelines on Access to Justice for Persons with Disabilities (IPGAJ)

In 2020, the International Principles and Guidelines on Access to Justice for Persons with Disabilities clarified how the various rights contained within the CRPD might apply more practically to vulnerable court users.[61] The IPGAJ

57 Andrea Broderick and Delia Ferri, *European Disability Law and Policy: Text, Cases and Materials* (CUP 2019) 194.

58 OHCHR, *Article 13: List of Illustrative Indicators on Access to Justice* (UN 2020); For further examination of the utility of indicators in assessing performance and compliance with human rights protections, see: The Danish Institute for Human Rights, *Human Rights Indicators at Programme and Project Level* (2006, ISBN: 87-91836-06-9).

59 OHCHR (n 58) 1.

60 OHCHR (n 58) 4.

61 The Special Rapporteur on the rights of persons with disabilities, *International Principles and Guidelines on Access to Justice for Persons with Disabilities* (Office of the High Commissioner for Human Rights, August 2020).

were the product of work carried out by the Special Rapporteur on the rights of persons with disabilities, the Committee on the Rights of Persons with Disabilities and the Special Envoy of the Secretary-General on Disability and Accessibility. The IPGAJ developed the provisions and interpretations of the CRPD, affirming ten principles of access to justice for people with disabilities and setting out detailed guidelines on how to implement each.[62] Shortly after their publication, the Principles were described as a 'practical handbook on how to design and implement justice systems that provide equal access to justice for people with disabilities'.[63] Further, they constitute a 'framework for the inclusion and participation of persons with disabilities in diverse roles within the administration of justice (e.g. judge, juror and witness) as a democratic imperative'.[64]

The role of the intermediary is explicitly recognised in the Principles. In its glossary, the document defines the role of intermediaries (which it uses interchangeably with the term 'facilitator') as follows:

> persons who work, as required, with justice system personnel and persons with disabilities to ensure effective communication during legal proceedings. They support persons with disabilities to understand and make informed choices, making sure that things are explained and talked about in ways that they can understand and that appropriate accommodations and support are provided. Intermediaries are neutral and they do not speak for persons with disabilities or for the justice system, nor do they lead or influence decisions or outcomes.

The most significant submission to the Special Rapporteur relating to the intermediary role was from the 'Access to Justice Knowledge Hub for Fair Participation'.[65] This group of academics and practitioners 'aggregates approaches, expertise, practice, and tools from around the world, to advance the evolution of justice systems so that they enable full and fair participation

62 International Commission of Jurists, 'Groundbreaking New UN Guidance on Access to Justice for Persons with Disabilities' (28 August 2020) <https://www.icj.org/a2jpwd/> accessed 5 February 2025.

63 Special Envoy of the Secretary-General on Disability and Accessibility, 'UN Experts Launch Ground-breaking Guidance on Access to Justice for People with Disabilities' (28 August 2020) <https://www.ohchr.org/en/press-releases/2020/08/un-experts-launch-ground-breaking-guidance-access-justice-people> accessed 2 May 2024.

64 The Special Rapporteur on the Rights of Persons with Disabilities (n 61) 2.

65 The Access to Justice Knowledge Hub, 'Research on Good Practices to Ensure Effective Access to Justice for Persons with Disabilities' (15 August 2009) <https://www.ohchr.org/sites/default/files/Documents/Issues/Disability/SR_Disability/GoodPractices/Access_to_Justice_Knowledge_Hub.docx.> accessed 12 September 2024.

of persons with disabilities in the justice system'.[66] In their submission, the group extolled the 'valuable and positive experiences' of intermediaries in several countries and recommended that the measure should be 'widely replicated'.[67] However, the group also acknowledged that the definition of the role contained within the IPGAJ was relatively 'loose' due to variations in how the role is configured in different jurisdictions.[68] The definition employs generic language and is sufficiently silent on specific functions of the role so that it pertains neither to the adversarial nor inquisitorial tradition. Perhaps deliberately, the definition gives no insight into how the role might be appointed – an important factor considering wide variation in the role of the judge across different legal traditions.

Further questions may be asked about the scope of the intermediary role based on the definition contained within the IPGAJ. For example: who counts as 'justice system personnel'? While this would plainly seem to cover judges and lawyers, would it also extend to probation officers, social workers and police officers? The term 'legal proceedings' would surely cover court hearings, but would consultations with legal representatives and parole hearings post-conviction be covered? As discussed earlier, the importance of ensuring access to justice for disabled persons beyond the courtroom has been recognised by the CRC Committee and by other civil society actors.[69] It is instructive to reflect on such questions when considering the normative profile of the intermediary role – especially in the context of jurisdictions which have not yet implemented such a measure and are prospectively considering its operation.

3.6 International intermediary models

The intermediary model introduced in England and Wales through the YJCEA 1999 has been exported internationally. While the most obvious analogue to the Witness Intermediary Scheme (WIS) in England and Wales is the Registered Intermediary Scheme (RIS) in Northern Ireland, both models emerge from the same legislative framework. Cooper and Wurtzel wrote that Northern Ireland 'went second' by implementing the measure after England and Wales, but the wording of the Criminal Evidence (NI) Order 1999

66 Justice Intermediary, 'Access to Justice Knowledge Hub' <https://justiceintermediary.org/> accessed 12 September 2024.

67 Justice Intermediary (n 66).

68 Access to Justice Knowledge Hub for Fair Participation, 'Report on Intermediaries for Justice around the Globe' (November 2020) <https://justiceintermediary.org/wp-content/uploads/report-on-intermediaries-for-justice.pdf> accessed 29 April 2024.

69 Julinda Beqiraj, Lawrence McNamara and Victoria Wicks, *Access to Justice for Persons with Disabilities: From International Principles to Practice* (International Bar Association, October 2017).

essentially replicates that of the YJCEA 1999.[70] As such, references to the 'U.K model' of intermediary provision in this section broadly relate to the WIS and the RIS.

Different adaptations of the intermediary special measure are evident in the experiences of Australia, New Zealand and, more recently, Ireland.[71] These jurisdictions have introduced an intermediary-type role that shares many core commonalities with the England and Wales progenitor but has developed some distinct features. Other jurisdictions, such as Chile, Spain and South Africa, have employed a form of communication assistance that is analogous to the intermediary but differs in some key features.[72] The normative attachment to neutrality which is a feature of the intermediary role in the U.K is approached differently in other jurisdictions, as discussed later. Similarly, the professional profile of some intermediaries, e.g. judges in Chile, quite clearly diverges from the WIS model in England and Wales. Nonetheless, how other jurisdictions have interpreted, and in some cases diverged from, the original intermediary model in England and Wales is instructive to understanding the parameters of the role and the content of its work. The following section outlines some of these models and highlights salient features of each that are relevant to the research underpinning this book.

3.7 Australia

Awareness of the prevalence of vulnerability in the criminal justice system has increased in Australia over the past ten to 15 years. In 2013, the Australian Human Rights Commission recognised that many people with 'complex and multiple support needs are not having their rights protected, and are not being treated equally, in the criminal justice system'.[73] The Commission highlighted the need for what it termed 'communication support' and recognised

70 Penny Cooper and David Wurtzel, 'Better the Second Time around? Department of Justice Registered Intermediaries Schemes and lessons from England and Wales' (2014) 65(1) Northern Ireland Legal Quarterly 39.

71 In Ireland, the Evidence Act 1992 (s.14) allows for evidence to be given via an intermediary in a court setting. From April 2024, a Register of Intermediaries has been established, although no significant research has been undertaken into the operation of the role in practice. However, there is likely to be significant development in this area as the University of Limerick has established the world's first 'Professional Diploma in Intermediary Studies' which is an 'inter-faculty programme delivered across the School of Allied Health and the School of Law', see: <https://www.ul.ie/gps/courses/intermediary-studies-professional-diploma> accessed 20 December 2024).

72 For a comprehensive overview of all intermediary-type roles international, see: Justice Intermediary (n 66).

73 Australian Human Rights Commission, 'Access to Justice in the Criminal Justice System for People with Disability' (Issues Paper: April 2013, ABN 47 996 232 602) 3.

various barriers to implementing any potential change.[74] The Commission used the CRPD as a benchmark for assessing the adequacy of legal protections for disabled individuals.

Australia has had the most experience with an intermediary-type role outside of the U.K Currently, South Australia, Western Australia, Victoria, New South Wales, Tasmania, Queensland and the Australian Capital Territory (ACT) have some legal provision for intermediaries – only the Northern Territory fails to provide any common law or legislative basis for the role.[75] Awareness of the need for a specialist communication role has been heightened in Australia since the establishment of the Royal Commission into the Institutional Responses to Child Sexual Abuse, which ran from 2013–2017. In its list of recommendations, the Royal Commission included that:

> State and territory governments should establish intermediary schemes similar to the Registered Intermediary Scheme in England and Wales which are available to any prosecution witness with a communication difficulty in a child sexual abuse prosecution. Governments should ensure that the scheme:
>
> a. requires intermediaries to have relevant professional qualifications to assist in communicating with vulnerable witnesses
> b. provides intermediaries with training on their role and in understanding that their duty is to assist the court to communicate with the witness and to be impartial
> c. makes intermediaries available at both the police interview stage and trial stage
> d. enables intermediaries to provide recommendations to police and the court on how best to communicate with the witness and to intervene in an interview or examination where they observe a communication breakdown.[76]

Given its terms of reference, the Royal Commission did not make any specific recommendation about intermediary provision for suspects or defendants. Nonetheless, in recommending an intermediary scheme for witnesses, it recognised 'the inherent fairness' in the notion of provision of intermediaries

74 Australian Human Rights Commission (n 73) 6.

75 The Northern Territory Department of Justice briefly considered the use of intermediaries/communication assistants but concluded 'that there are other steps that can be taken to improve the way that special sittings are conducted at this time'. See: Northern Territory Government Department of Justice, *Review of Vulnerable Witness Legislation* (Northern Territory Legal Policy Division, June 2011) 13.

76 Royal Commission into Institutional Responses to Child Sex Abuse, *Final Report Recommendations* (Commonwealth of Australia 2017) 108.

to defendants.[77] The Royal Commission inquiry and its subsequent report acted as a catalyst for several Australian jurisdictions, which had not already done so, to introduce intermediaries into their criminal justice processes.[78] The next section examines the content and organisation of various schemes within the different Australian states and Territories.

3.7.1 *Western Australia*

Although there is a lack of available research into its operation, Western Australia is recognised as having the longest-established practice of witness intermediaries in any common law jurisdiction. In 1992, this practice was given a legislative basis via an amendment to the Evidence Act 1906 and the introduction of a role described as a 'communicator'.[79] The communicator's role was to explain to the child the questions asked of them, and then, to the court, answers given by the child in reply.[80] Due to the broad terms of the legislative wording, the provision could apply to witnesses and defendants. No restriction was placed on who could perform the role, and no limitation was placed on the type of proceedings in which it could be appointed. As such, the court could determine eligibility on a case-by-case basis, guided primarily by the individual needs of the person for whom communication assistance was required.[81] Despite the patent ambiguity surrounding the role, one aspect of its function was clear – it was only available to children.[82] Another section of the legislation, s.106R(4)(b), recognised that individuals declared to be 'special witnesses' may also benefit from the assistance of the communicator. The legislation outlines that a special witness would be treated 'as if [they] were an affected child', and it has been suggested that physical disability, mental impairment, age or cultural background would be relevant factors in determining whether a witness would be eligible.[83]

As discussed in Chapter 2 (Emergence of the intermediary role), the Pigot Committee in England and Wales was clearly influenced by what it termed 'The Western Australian Experience', despite conceding that much of the

77 Royal Commission into Institutional Responses to Child Sex Abuse (n 76) Pts VII-X; Jacqueline Giuffrida and Anita Mackay, 'Extending Witness Intermediary Schemes to Vulnerable Defendants' (2021) 33(4) Current Issues in Criminal Justice 498, 513.

78 Raymond Arthur, 'The Use of Intermediaries for Young Defendants: Overcoming Barriers to Young People's Participation in Criminal Proceedings' (2022) 34(2) Child and Family Law Quarterly 149, 161.

79 s.106(F)(1).

80 s.106(F)(1).

81 Tasmania Law Reform Institute, 'Facilitating Equal Access to Justice: An Intermediary Communication Assistant Scheme for Tasmania?' (Final Report No. 23) 61.

82 Tasmania Law Reform Institute (n 81).

83 s.106R(4b).

scheme's operation was 'unexplored'.[84] Later iterations of the intermediary role in Western Australia appear to diverge more starkly from what is now recognised as the neutral communicator-facilitator model. In its 1990 Discussion Paper, the Law Reform Commission of Western Australia envisaged the intermediary role as a quasi-advocate who would 'put to the child questions formulated by the accused' in cases where an unrepresented accused could not directly confront a child witness.[85] It is later discussed in the report whether the intermediary 'must necessarily be a legal practitioner'.[86] While the term 'intermediary' is used in this context, such a role is qualitatively different from how it has developed in most other common law jurisdictions. It appears that communicators were used sparingly in Western Australia, owing mainly to a lack of available infrastructure and an associated lack of suitable training.[87]

Despite lagging behind other Australian states and territories for many years, since September 2024 Western Australia has operated the newest intermediary-type role in the country. The 'Communication Partner Program' was introduced by the Criminal Law (Mental Impairment) Act 2023. Under the new legislation, Western Australian courts have the authority to appoint a communication partner to help facilitate communication for accused and 'supervised persons' with mental impairments.[88] The Western Australia Department of Justice has produced a 'Procedural Guidance Manual',[89] which is closely modelled on that used in the Australian Capital Territory (ACT) – see further in the following. The function of the role, as outlined in the legislation, mirrors the language used in the YJCEA in England and Wales and in the relevant ACT legislation almost verbatim.[90] The legislation notes that the required qualifications and experience required for the role are to be provided for in regulations.[91]

The Communication Partner Program is different from other communication assistance models in Australia as it does not cover witnesses, only accused persons. As will be examined later, most of the other models utilised

84 Home Office, *Speaking Up for Justice: Report of the Interdepartmental Working Group on the Treatment of Vulnerable or Intimidated Witnesses in the Criminal Justice System* (1998) 58.
85 The Law Reform Commission of Western Australia, 'Project No. 87: The Evidence of Children and Other Vulnerable Witnesses – Discussion Paper' (April 1990) [4.61].
86 The Law Reform Commission of Western Australia (n 85) [6.4].
87 Hal Jackson, 'Children's Evidence in Legal Proceedings – The Position in Western Australia' in John R Spencer and Michael E Lamb (eds), *Children and Cross-Examination: Time to Change the Rules?* (Hart Publishing 2012) 81.
88 Criminal Law (Mental Impairment) Act 2023 (WA), s.21.
89 Western Australia Department of Justice, 'Communication Partners: Procedural Guidance Manual' (Version 1: September 2024).
90 Criminal Law (Mental Impairment) Act 2023, s.21.
91 Criminal Law (Mental Impairment) Act 2023, s.21(6).

in Australia focus on vulnerable witnesses, with provision for accused persons being the exception. This restriction of eligibility raises obvious access to justice concerns. The Procedural Guidance Manual states that 'communication facilitation increases access to justice and . . . assists people who struggle to communicate, thereby assisting the functioning of criminal justice processes'.[92] However, vulnerable witnesses, whether young children or those with intellectual and learning disabilities, are unable to access communication partners. The current inequality of access to communication partners in Western Australia goes against the Australian Law Reform Commission's position that that law should not limit communication assistance 'to particular categories of witness needing support'.[93]

Western Australia could, however, soon match the ACT in terms of its progressive intermediary coverage. In 2024, the 'Evidence Amendment Bill' was introduced to establish a witness intermediary service and the legislation contained several other operational provisions and requirements regarding accreditation and training.[94] If the Bill passes and the scheme is implemented, Western Australia will become one of the few jurisdictions globally to provide communication assistance on a statutory basis to eligible defendants and witnesses.

3.7.2 *South Australia*

In late 2015, the Department of Attorney-General of South Australia launched the state's Disability Justice Plan, which recognised the lack of support for vulnerable witnesses in the criminal justice system.[95] The Plan noted that vulnerable witnesses can provide comprehensive and reliable testimony but can also face various barriers relating to misconceptions about their capability or credibility, on top of a lack of support.[96] The South Australian Disability Inclusion Act 2018 was subsequently enacted to support equal access and inclusion for disabled people based on the principles contained within the CRPD.[97]

One of the initiatives proposed in the Disability Justice Plan was the introduction of a 'specifically trained Communication Assistant' to assist vulnerable individuals during 'any contact with the criminal justice system'.[98]

92 Communication Partners: Procedural Guidance Manual (n 89) 6.
93 Australian Law Reform Commission, 'Chapter 7: Access to Justice' <https://www.alrc.gov.au/wp-content/uploads/2019/08/fr124._chapter_7_access_to_justice.pdf> accessed 9 February 2025 [7.176].
94 Evidence Amendment Bill 2024 (WA), s.23B.
95 Attorney-General (South Australia), Disability Justice Plan 2014–2017 (June 2014).
96 Attorney-General (South Australia), Disability Justice Plan 2014–2017 (June 2014) 9.
97 Attorney-General (South Australia), Disability Justice Plan 2014–2017 (June 2014) 6.
98 Attorney-General (South Australia), Disability Justice Plan 2014–2017 (June 2014) 6.

This eventually led to the amendment of an existing piece of legislation, the Evidence Act 1929 (South Australia), by the Statutes Amendment (Vulnerable Witnesses) Act 2015. S.14A of the now-amended Evidence Act provides communication assistance for both witnesses and defendant. It also enables courts to modify court processes and/or other measures that may facilitate communication between the witness and the court, enabling them to give their best possible evidence. Importantly, a distinction is made between 'communication partners' who are approved by the Minister 'for the purposes of providing assistance in proceedings to a witness with complex communication needs'[99] and 'communication assistants', which covers 'any other suitable person to be appointed by a court to act as a communication assistant in court'.[100] A communication assistant essentially provides communication assistance but is untrained as a communication partner. The law was further amended shortly after to cover the use of communication partners outside of court. As such, the law now provides that, if practicable, a communication partner should be present for vulnerable witnesses or suspects when interviewed by police.[101] For present purposes, the communication partner role (as opposed to communication assistant) is treated as most closely analogous to the intermediary role operating in England and Wales and Northern Ireland.

The communication partner model in South Australia is noteworthy for its eligibility inclusivity. The legislation that provides for its establishment made the special measure available to anyone with 'complex communication needs', whether that need arises from disability, illness, injury 'or some other cause'.[102] As the South Australian Law Reform Institute (SALRI) highlights, this aspect of the scheme complies with the CRPD and the need to ensure 'equalisation of opportunities'.[103] Another hallmark of the model is that communication partners were rolled out on a voluntary basis. The South Australian government contracted a not-for-profit organisation to operate the communication partner service. Volunteers were chosen from applicants with suitable professional backgrounds, including retired teachers, social workers and psychologists who had demonstrated relevant knowledge, skills and experience working with people with disability and/or working in the legal sector.[104]

99 Evidence Act 1929 (SA), s.4(1).

100 Summary Offences Regulations 2016 (SA) s.22(1)(b).

101 Summary Offences Regulations 2016 (SA) s.19 and s.23.

102 Evidence Act 1929 (SA), s.14A.

103 South Australian Law Reform Institute (SALRI), 'Review of the Use of Communication Partners in South Australia' (University of Adelaide, 9 March 2021).

104 Sarah Hoff, Martine Powell and David Plater, 'When Good Intentions Are Not Enough: Professionals' Perceptions of the South Australian Communication Partner Scheme' (2022) 57(4) Australian Journal of Social Sciences 970.

Ultimately, however, the volunteer model largely failed in South Australia. Funding for the scheme was discontinued, and on 1 March 2020, the volunteer scheme ceased operation. As Plater et al.'s research shows, the scheme was seldom used in the courts and communication partners were appointed on only four occasions in the principal trial court over three years.[105] Further, the police rarely requested the assistance of communication partners when interviewing suspects with complex communication needs. However, it appears that specialist police officers did request assistance when interviewing vulnerable witnesses and victims.[106] Hoff et al. have argued that 'mistrust of the volunteer model' was a significant contributory factor to the failure of the communication partner scheme.[107] More specifically, many criminal justice professionals felt that volunteer communication partners lacked the necessary level of expertise and that their knowledge 'did not go beyond' that of the lawyers instructed in the case.[108] This is a significant finding which reverberates throughout parts of this book. Indeed, it goes to the core reason for the introduction of the intermediary as a communication expert into the criminal justice system. As will be argued in Chapter 5 (Professional work – jurisdictions and boundary work), the scope of the intermediary role is intimately connected with the work of other criminal justice professionals and, importantly, how these other professionals perceive and engage with intermediary work.

In the wake of the failure of the volunteer model in South Australia, a new 'fee-for-service' model was introduced whereby the court may now appoint paid professionals. These communication partners are privately funded by the individual, agency and/or the party requiring communication assistance.[109] The profile of a communication partner is now defined as a person or class of persons approved by the Attorney-General.[110] Only a restricted group of professionals, including certified speech pathologists, occupational therapists, psychologists, social workers and developmental educators, are eligible to carry out the role.[111] In addition to the relevant qualifications,

105 David Plater and others, 'Providing a Voice to the Vulnerable: A Study of Communication Assistance in South Australia' (SALRI Report 16, September 2021).

106 Jennifer Jacobs, *Communication Partner Service Final Report: 1 July 2016–29 February 2020* (Uniting Communities 2020). A new 'fee-for-service' model of intermediary provision has now replaced the volunteer model, but there has been no focused research on its operation to date.

107 Hoff and others (n 104) 981.

108 Hoff and others (n 104) 981.

109 Hoff and others (n 104) 973.

110 Hoff and others (n 104) 973.

111 Government of South Australia, 'A Guide for Communication Partners' (2020) <https://www.sa.gov.au/__data/assets/pdf_file/0009/599337/Guide-for-communication-partners.pdf> accessed 11 November 2024.

there is a minimum requirement to have five years' relevant experience working with people with complex communication needs.[112]

Unlike many other jurisdictions, professionals who work as communication partners are not considered officers of the court but must agree in writing to adhere to the Code of Conduct.[113] Like analogous communication roles in Australia, and the intermediary in the U.K, the communication partner Code of Conduct emphasises the importance of the role's impartiality and states that it must not assume the role of an advocate or support person.[114] Similarly, the guidance explicitly states that communication partners are not translators or interpreters.[115] Unlike other jurisdictions, for example the Australian Capital Territory (ACT), there are currently no training programs for lawyers or judicial officers that informs them of the existence of the communication partner service.[116]

Despite initial widespread support for the communication partner scheme, its limited uptake means that there is little scope for analysis of its operation. As a result of the poor utilisation of the service:

> no clear practice has been established as to the boundaries or expectations of the role and whether the courts would allow the role to extend beyond the function of a quasi-interpreter.[117]

Research into the operation of the new 'fee-for-service' model in South Australia is sorely needed. As other Australian states and territories continue to develop their respective intermediary models, South Australia could benefit from analogous experiences and the development of best-practice guidance. There must be a concern that if the new service is tainted by the poor outcomes of the previous one, then there may be a lack of interest in it from both a policy and research perspective. Mackay and Giuffrida suggest that the private 'fee-for-service' nature of the South Australia model may result in 'less quality control and oversight' compared to other jurisdictions.[118] SALRI notes in its Review of the South Australia model, the absence of communication assistance for an eligible vulnerable court user arguably contravenes Article 5(3) of the CPRD, which requires state parties to 'take all appropriate

112 Government of South Australia (n 111) 3.
113 Government of South Australia (n 111) 8.
114 Government of South Australia (n 111) 8.
115 Government of South Australia (n 111) 6.
116 SALRI (n 103) 10.
117 SALRI, 'Review of the Use of Communication Partners in South Australia' (University of Adelaide, 9 March 2021).
118 Anita Mackay and Jacqueline Giuffrida, 'Ensuing the Right to a Fair Criminal Trial Using Communication Assistance' (2022) 10(1) Griffith Journal of Law and Human Dignity 1, 14.

steps to ensure that reasonable accommodation is provided'.[119] Even if a communication partner scheme technically exists, limiting access to those who can afford its services may impose a de facto barrier to justice.[120]

3.7.3 New South Wales (NSW)

Since 1986, NSW has had a statutory basis allowing a support person to assist vulnerable persons when giving evidence. The Criminal Procedure Act 1986 is broadly framed and states that a 'parent, guardian, relative, friend or support person' may carry out the support role.[121] Hanna and Henderson note that the legislation covers those who 'ordinarily require assistance to communicate . . . due to impairment or disability'.[122] Regarding the role's scope, practice guidelines state that the supporter must remain silent, meaning the role is geared more towards emotional support than serving a more typical communicative purpose.[123] Much like Western Australia, however, there has been a lack of documented usage of the provision with no meaningful research into its operation. Bowden et al. note that the role has been interpreted as providing nothing more than emotional support and does not extend to assisting comprehension and communication of evidence.[124]

The first recognisable cohort of intermediaries (also initially known as 'children's champions') was rolled out in April 2016. The impetus for the role's introduction came from the NSW Joint Select Committee on Sentencing of Child Sexual Assault Offenders, 'Every Sentence Tells a Story: Report on Sentencing of Child Sexual Assault Offenders', which made recommendations about introducing pre-recorded hearings.[125] Alongside this, the NSW government made a commitment to introduce a 'child champion' to help child witnesses through the trial process, reduce their trauma as well as preserve the right of the accused to a fair trial.[126]

119 SALRI (n 103) 203.

120 Vienna Declaration and Programme of Action, UN Doc A/ CONF 157/ 23 (25 June 1993) [63].

121 s.306.

122 Kirsten Hanna and Emily Henderson, 'Child Witnesses in the Criminal Courts' in Antje Deckert and Rick Sarr (eds), *The Palgrave Handbook of Australian and New Zealand Criminology, Crime and Justice* (Palgrave Macmillan 2017) 428.

123 Hanna and Henderson (n 122) 428.

124 Phoebe Bowden, Terese Henning and David Plater, 'Balancing Fairness to Victims, Society and Defendants in the Cross-Examination of Vulnerable Witnesses: An Impossible Triangulation' (2014) 37 Melbourne University Law Review 539, 574.

125 Joint Select Committee on Sentencing of Child Sexual Assault Offenders (NSW), 'Every Sentence Tells a Story: Report on Sentencing of Child Sexual Assault Offenders' (Report No. 1/55, October 2014).

126 Penny Cooper and Michelle Mattison, 'Intermediaries, Vulnerable People and the Quality of Evidence: An International Comparison of Three Versions of the English Intermediary Model' (2017) 21(4) International Journal of Evidence and Proof 351.

The child champion/witness intermediary role introduced in NSW is firmly based on the intermediary model introduced in England and Wales. Cooper and Mattison noted that the terminology used in the role description is 'virtually identical' to that introduced by the Youth Justice and Criminal Evidence Act 1999.[127] Section 88 of the Criminal Procedure Amendment (Child Sexual Offence Evidence Pilot) Act 2015 sets out the framework for the role in NSW. The Department of Justice established a three-year pilot of an accredited 'children's champion' scheme for child complainants in sexual assault cases. The pilot was initially limited to two court venues within the state. What began as the 'Child Sexual Offence Evidence Pilot' became the Child Sexual Offence Evidence Program (CSOEP).[128] In October 2023, the NSW Parliament passed legislation extending the CSOEP to all District Courts in the state.[129] The new legislation contains a subtle reformulation of the intermediary role by clarifying that the intermediary does not 'communicate and explain' directly to the witness but rather carries out these functions directly to the court and questioner.[130] More specifically, the intermediary communicates to the court whether the witness can understand the questions and then may explain to the court and the oral examiner how the question may be asked differently. This change emphasises the intermediary's advisory role and the court's power to determine its scope. It is significant that, after consultation in 2018, the decision was taken to replace all references to 'children's champion' with 'witness intermediaries'. The NSW Department of Justice considered this change to be 'urgent in order not to prejudice acceptance and further implementation of the special measures'.[131]

Despite the expansion of intermediary services in NSW, witness intermediaries remain available only to children in sexual offence matters. As Stein and Goodman-Delahunty argue, this has led to a 'critical gap' in the legal framework, which means that NSW is failing to comply with protections guaranteed under the CRC and the CRPD.[132] There have, however, been examples of courts using their broad trial management powers to permit intermediary

127 Cooper and Mattison (n 126) 357 (citing the NSW Commissioner of Victims Rights, Mahashini Krishna in 2016).

128 The Criminal Procedure Amendment (Child Sexual Offence Evidence Pilot) Act 2015 amended the Criminal Procedure Act 1986.

129 NSW Government, 'Expansion of Child Sexual Evidence Program Statewide to Reduce Trauma for Children' (12 October 2023) <https://www.nsw.gov.au/media-releases/child-sexual-evidence-program-reduce-trauma> accessed 19 December 2023.

130 Criminal Procedure Amendment (Child Sexual Offence Evidence) Act 2023 No 32, 294L, 1(b).

131 Judy Cashmore and Rita Shackel, 'Evaluation of the Child Sexual Offence Evidence Pilot Final Outcome Evaluation Report, Prepared for: Victims Services, NSW Department of Justice' (August 2018) 9.

132 Rukiya Stein and Jane Goodman-Delahunty, 'Bridging the Justice Gap: Inequity in Provision of Intermediary Assistance for Adults with Disabilities' (2024) Alternative Law Journal (online first, 22 December 2024).

assistants for accused persons. In the case of *R v MR, JB and CS (young persons)* (No 4), the Supreme Court of NSW held that s.26 of the Evidence Act 1995 enabled a judge to appoint an intermediary to ensure the best evidence of a defendant, should they choose to testify.[133] The court clarified that the intermediary role was simply to 'assist with communication' and that the ultimate control over questioning rested with the court.[134] It remains to be seen how common such 'out of program' appointments for defendants become and the extent of intermediary assistance beyond the period of oral testimony (e.g. during consultations with lawyers, during evidence of other witnesses, etc).

The NSW legislation does not specifically cover intermediary provision at the police investigation, although the process of conducting an assessment and planning alongside police has been described as 'fluid and changing with experience'.[135] In terms of the role's operation, ground rules hearings are becoming increasingly common and there is growing acceptance of intermediary presence and contribution to them.[136] Intermediaries must undergo a specific training programme in communication assessment during a five-day compulsory course. This includes a written exam, a mock written assessment report and a mock oral assessment.[137] The NSW Department of Justice has compiled a Witness Intermediary Handbook covering much of what is expected of the intermediary role.

The professional profile of intermediaries in NSW also closely follows experience in other jurisdictions. Intermediaries must have 'a tertiary qualification in Psychology, Social Work, Speech Pathology, Teaching or Occupational Therapy or such other qualifications, training, experience or skills as may be prescribed by the regulations (or both)'.[138] An evaluation of the operation of the intermediary scheme has recommended expanding the number of intermediaries to meet growing demand and recruiting intermediaries from a wider professional pool 'with skills in mental health and complex trauma'.[139]

3.7.4 Tasmania

The introduction of intermediaries in Tasmania must be viewed against the backdrop of various special measures employed to assist both children and 'special witnesses' to give evidence in proceedings. These measures were

133 [2024] NSWSC 909.
134 [2024] NSWSC 909 [6].
135 Cashmore and Shackel (n 131) 48.
136 Judy Cashmore and others, 'Evaluation of the Child Sexual Offence Evidence Pilot: Process Evaluation Report' (NSW Government Department of Justice Report No. SPRC Report 16/17, October 2017) 7.
137 Cashmore and Shackel (n 131).
138 Criminal Procedure Amendment (Child Sexual Offence Evidence) Act 2023 No 32, 294M, 2(a).
139 Cashmore and Shackel (n 131) 15.

predominantly aimed at reducing the stress associated with providing testimony and reducing the risk of ongoing trauma.[140] Despite these developments, none of the measures specifically addressed issues experienced by individuals with communication needs. Despite the relevant legislation enabling judges to disallow 'improper questioning', Tasmanian courts often failed to accommodate witnesses because of attachment to the adversarial model.[141]

In its 2018 report, which considered the potential introduction of an intermediary/communication assistant scheme, the Tasmania Law Reform Institute (TLRI) identified a 'missing link' in the legislative regime 'for achieving the optimal participation of people with communication needs in trials and hearings'.[142] As a 'remedy' to this problem, it recommended that:

> an expert intermediary/communication scheme should be established by legislation and should operate across the entire criminal process including during the pre-trial interactions of people with communication needs with police officers and members of the legal profession and during court hearings and trials.[143]

The TLRI clarified that the underpinning purpose of such a role would be to 'maximise the opportunity for people with communication needs to participate in the criminal justice process by optimising their communication and comprehension capacities'.[144] It further explained that the role should be distinguished from advocates and support persons. This was an attempt to clarify and emphasise the new role's neutrality.[145] The TLRI was concerned that the intermediary role could become 'conflated and confused with [that] of a support person'.[146]

On 20 June 2018, the Tasmanian government committed to implementing a Witness Intermediary Scheme Pilot. The pilot program was introduced via the Evidence (Children and Special Witnesses) Amendment Act 2020 and commenced on 1 March 2021, operating for three years. According to the Minister's explanatory statement when the Bill was first introduced, the legislative changes delivered on the 'Tasmania Government's commitment to implement the recommendations of the Royal Commission into Institutional Responses to Child Sexual Abuse', in particular the recommendation

140 Evidence (Children and Special Witnesses) Act 2001.
141 Tasmania Law Reform Institute, 'Facilitating Equal Access to Justice: An Intermediary/Communication Assistant Scheme for Tasmania?' (Final Report No. 23) (2018) 5.
142 Tasmania Law Reform Institute (n 141) 10.
143 Tasmania Law Reform Institute (n 141) 15.
144 Tasmania Law Reform Institute (n 141) 7.
145 Tasmania Law Reform Institute (n 141) 7.
146 Tasmania Law Reform Institute (n 141) 85.

to establish a 'Pilot Witness Intermediary Scheme'.[147] Despite the recommendations of the TLRI, suspects and defendants were not covered by the legislation. In addition, eligibility was restricted to children under 18 years who were victims or witnesses in sexual offence matters and homicide-related matters and adults with a communication need who were victims or witnesses in sexual offence matters and homicide related matters.[148] Intermediaries who took part in the pilot had a professional background in areas such as psychology, speech pathology, occupational therapy, mental health nursing and working with vulnerable adults and children.[149]

Shortly after the pilot scheme was launched in Tasmania, the Commission of Inquiry into the Tasmanian Government's Responses to Child Sexual Abuse in Institutional Settings was established. In August 2023, the Commission delivered its findings.[150] It commended the Tasmanian government and the Tasmanian criminal justice agencies for their efforts but noted that 'further stakeholder engagement and marketing' would be required to 'clarify the unique role' of intermediaries.[151] Further, it noted widespread support for extending the use of intermediaries to other vulnerable groups.[152] The Commission made two recommendations relevant to the Witness Intermediary Scheme review. Firstly, it recommended extending the Scheme to include children under investigation for, or who have been charged with, sexual offences.[153] Secondly, it recommended legislation requiring police to use intermediaries in police interviews of children and young people and adults with communication needs (including defendants) relating to sexual offences.[154] These findings echo the conclusions of a 'Process Evaluation' of the pilot scheme published in December 2022.[155] A final review of the Witness Intermediary Scheme Pilot was recently conducted by Dr Penny Cooper, although at time of writing the report had not been released.

147 Evidence (Children and Special Witnesses) Amendment Bill 2020 (31 of 2020) (Tas), second reading speech and explanatory statement.
148 Evidence (Children and Special Witnesses) Act 2001 (Tas).
149 Dr Miriam Vandenberg, *Process Evaluation of the Witness Intermediary Scheme Pilot* (Sprout Labs, December 2022) 3.
150 Commission of Inquiry into the Tasmanian Government's Responses to Child Sexual Abuse in Institutional Settings, *Who Was Looking after Me? Prioritising the Safety of Tasmanian Children, Volume 1: Summary, Recommendations and Findings* (2023).
151 Commission of Inquiry into the Tasmanian Government's Responses to Child Sexual Abuse in Institutional Settings (n 150) 67.
152 Commission of Inquiry into the Tasmanian Government's Responses to Child Sexual Abuse in Institutional Settings (n 150) 67.
153 Commission of Inquiry into the Tasmanian Government's Responses to Child Sexual Abuse in Institutional Settings (n 150) 68.
154 Commission of Inquiry into the Tasmanian Government's Responses to Child Sexual Abuse in Institutional Settings (n 150) 68.
155 Vandenberg (n 149).

3.7.5 *Victoria*

In 2018, the state of Victoria introduced an Intermediary Pilot Program which was recommended as part of the 2016 Victorian Law Reform Commission (VLRC) Report titled 'The Roles of Victims of Crime in the Criminal Trial Process'.[156] The recommendation of the VLRC was endorsed shortly after by the Victoria Supreme Court in the case of *R v Ward (a pseudonym)*.[157] The proposal advanced by the VLRC received almost universal support from various stakeholders, including the Office of Public Prosecutions, and it was noted that the scheme would increase 'access to the justice system'.[158] The VLRC recommended that the intermediary scheme should be modelled closely on the WIS in England and Wales, with the role amounting to a 'professional and impartial facilitator'.[159] However, rather than advocating for the establishment of a new service, it suggested that the Child Witness Service and a 'volunteer independent third person service' coordinated by the Office of Public Prosecutions could assume the responsibility for intermediary provision.[160] The VLRC also addressed fair trial concerns by noting that 'equal participation' required intermediary provision to be extended to assist accused persons and witnesses.[161] While this was technically beyond its terms of reference, the VLRC noted that it supported equal access to intermediary services 'in principle' without exploring specific details.[162]

The pilot programme was legislated through the Justice Legislation Amendment (Victims) Act 2018 (Vic), which amended the Criminal Procedure Act 2009 (Vic). It was also accompanied by a Practice Direction (No. 6 of 2018), which outlined, inter alia, how an intermediary should be requested, the requirements for a GRH and the format and contents of the GRH.[163] The pilot commenced in July 2018 and applied to criminal proceedings relating to a sexual offence (as defined in s 4(1) Criminal Procedure Act 2009) or a homicide offence. It was also geographically limited to courts in Melbourne and four police sexual offence and child investigation team sites. When intermediaries are involved with the video and audio recorded statement (VARE), i.e. at the investigative stage, all children and young people are eligible.[164]

156 Victorian Law Reform Commission (VLRC), *The Role of Victims of Crime in the Criminal Trial Process* (August 2016, ISBN: 9780994372369).
157 [2017] VSCA 37.
158 VLRC (n 156) 169.
159 VLRC (n 156) 170.
160 VLRC (n 156) 172.
161 VLRC (n 156) 173.
162 VLRC (n 156) 173.
163 Magistrates' Court of Victoria, *Practice Direction, No. 6 of 2018: Intermediary Pilot Program at Melbourne Magistrates' Court* (20 July 2018).
164 County Court of Victoria, *Multi-jurisdictional Court Guide for Ground Rules and the Intermediary Program* (28 July 2023).

For court hearings, a child is eligible for assistance if they were under 18 when the charges were laid. Adults with a cognitive impairment are also eligible.[165] Similar to NSW, intermediaries must have a tertiary qualification in psychology, social work, speech pathology, occupational therapy or other prescribed qualifications, training, experience or skills. Intermediaries are impartial officers of the court and have a responsibility to promote justice and uphold the law.[166]

In terms of the scope of the intermediary role in Victoria, its primary function is to enhance the quality of evidence and facilitate communication between the court, legal professionals and the witness.[167] As per the legislation, intermediaries may advise 'on the formulation of questions so as to avoid misunderstanding and they may actively assist and intervene during questioning'.[168] The breadth of the role's scope was recently addressed in a decision of the High Court of Australia, which held that it was permissible for an intermediary to attend a private meeting in a judge's chambers to facilitate communication between the judge, a young complainant and the lawyers in the case.[169]

Despite the VLRC's recommendation, accused persons were excluded from the Program from the outset. Antolak-Saper and MacPherson point out that the failure to extend intermediary provision to the vulnerable accused violates international human rights standards.[170] The exclusion of defendants is difficult to justify, considering that the Victorian Charter of Human Rights and Responsibilities Act 2006 contains the right of accused persons to 'free assistance of assistants and specialised communication tools and technology if he or she has communication or speech difficulties that require such assistance'.[171] Further, the explanatory memorandum for the Victorian Charter of Human Rights and Responsibilities Bill 2006 outlines that these 'communication tools' should assist the accused to properly 'understand the nature and the reason for the criminal charge and to participate in the

165 Victoria Government, 'Intermediary Programme: About the Programme' <https://www.justice.vic.gov.au/node/3/courts-and-tribunals/intermediary-program/about-the-intermediary-program#about-intermediaries> accessed 3 November 2024.

166 Victoria Government (n 165).

167 Magistrates' Court of Victoria, 'Multi-Jurisdictional Court Guide for the Intermediary Pilot Program: Intermediaries and Ground Rules' <https://www.mcv.vic.gov.au/sites/default/files/2023–08/multi-jurisdictional%20court%20guide%20intermediary%20pilot%20program%20intermediaries%20ground%20rules%20hearings.pdf> accessed 6 February 2025.

168 Criminal Procedure Act 2009 (Vic), s.389I.

169 *Director of Public Prosecutions v Smith* [2024] HCA 32.

170 Natalia Antolak-Saper and Hannah MacPherson, 'Vulnerable Witnesses and Victoria's Intermediary Pilot Program' (2019) 43 Criminal Law Journal 325, 336.

171 Charter of Human Rights and Responsibilities Act 2006(Vic), s.25(2)(j).

judicial process'.[172] As discussed earlier regarding South Australia, the lack of access to intermediary services for suspects and defendants may impinge on the right of access to justice. Echoing this, the Special Rapporteur on the rights of persons with disabilities has highlighted that a 'lack of information and understanding' by persons with disabilities undermines access to justice and its associated rights.[173]

The Victoria Intermediary Program is still in its infancy; no full evaluation report or study has been conducted. Resistance to the scheme has emerged mainly from the legal profession. However, it is not clear yet to what extent intermediaries have effected a 'culture shift' in the questioning and treatment of vulnerable witnesses.[174] In particular, assessing the extent to which the intermediary has become an 'active role' – as initially envisaged by the VLRC – regarding intermediary involvement pre-trial and at the court stage will be interesting. In its report, the VLRC highlighted potential concerns that the role may 'undermine the principle of party control over the presentation of evidence to the court and the ability of the accused to test the prosecution evidence'.[175] Such concerns are not unique to Victoria and were raised as early as 1989 in England and Wales via the Pigot Report (see Chapter 2: Emergence of the intermediary role). A comprehensive evaluation of intermediary provision in Victoria is essential to better understand the scope of the role in practice. This evaluation should consider how the intermediary role can be utilised across the criminal justice system and, importantly, how it can gain legitimacy among other criminal justice professionals.

3.7.6 Australian Capital Territory (ACT)

The first intermediary services were rolled out in the ACT in January 2020. In response to the findings of the Royal Commission's Report, the ACT government allocated funding in its 2019–2020 budget to establish an Intermediary Program within the ACT Human Rights Commission. The Intermediary Program facilitates the provision of intermediary services to relevant criminal justice system stakeholders, in accordance with relevant provisions of the Evidence (Miscellaneous Provisions) Amendment Act 2019 (ACT). This legislation amends the Evidence (Miscellaneous Provisions) Act 1991 (ACT) and the Evidence (Miscellaneous Provisions) Regulation 2009 (ACT) to allow for the introduction of intermediaries. Regarding the scheme's organisation, the Intermediary Program Team in Canberra centrally manages case referrals

172 Vandenberg (n 149) 3.
173 International Principles and Guidelines on Access to Justice for Persons with Disabilities (n 61) 7.
174 Antolak-Saper and MacPherson (n 170) 352.
175 VLRC (n 156) 173.

and is the first point of contact for stakeholders and intermediaries.[176] There are several employed 'in-house' intermediaries embedded within the Intermediary Program Team, while most intermediaries are members of a 'panel' who may be contacted to take on cases as required. Eligibility for intermediary assistance is based on the witness having a 'communication difficulty', defined as 'a mental or physical disability that impedes speech'.[177]

The intermediary 'Procedural Guidance Manual' produced by the ACT Human Rights Commission provides a comprehensive overview of the role's governance, organisation and scope.[178] It outlines the procedure for intermediary referral (whether by the police or the court) and the expected content and form of the intermediary communication assessment. It also outlines the format and procedure relating to Ground Rules Hearings (which are legislated in Chapter 1A of the Evidence (Miscellaneous Provisions) Amendment Act 2019 (ACT)). The Procedural Guidance Manual contains other practical information, including a Code of Conduct[179] and a template for the Communication Assessment Report.[180] It also contains a list of professional obligations that intermediaries are expected to meet, including a professional qualification in speech pathology, social work, psychology, occupational therapy or another relevant qualification approved by the Intermediary Program.[181]

The function of the intermediary in the ACT is outlined in the legislation and mirrors almost identically the wording of the legislation in England and Wales and Northern Ireland.[182] The only additional element of the intermediary's function compared to the U.K is that it provides explicitly that the role will 'otherwise assist the court, and any lawyer in the proceeding, to communicate to the witness'.[183] This additional wording adds nothing substantive to the role as legislated in the U.K. As such, the ACT and the U.K are closely aligned in terms of the intermediary role's normative function. The Procedural Guidance Manual supplements the legislation by summarising that intermediaries operate to 'effectively facilitate communication between witnesses and police and during the trial process'.[184] The legislative framework[185] and the Procedural Guidance Manual also highlight the role's

176 ACT Human Rights Commission, 'ACT Intermediary Program' <https://www.hrc.act.gov.au/intermediaries#:~:text=Intermediaries%20are%20officers%20of%20the,during%20the%20criminal%20trial%20process> accessed 9 September 2024.
177 Evidence (Miscellaneous Provisions) Act 1991 (ACT), s.4AJ.
178 ACT Human Rights Commission, 'Procedural Guidance Manual' (August 2024).
179 ACT Human Rights Commission (n 178) 7.
180 ACT Human Rights Commission (n 178) 37.
181 ACT Human Rights Commission (n 178) 10.
182 Evidence (Miscellaneous Provisions) Act 1991 (ACT), s.4AI.
183 Evidence (Miscellaneous Provisions) Act 1991 (ACT), s.4AI(1)(b)(iii).
184 ACT Procedural Guidance Manual (n 178) 5.
185 Evidence (Miscellaneous Provisions) Act 1991 (ACT), s.4AI(2).

impartiality and status as an officer of the court.[186] In this regard, intermediaries in the ACT do not discuss case merits and are not informed of case outcomes, as such information is irrelevant to their role. The role's impartiality is repeated and emphasised again in the Procedural Guidance Manual's 'Courtroom Etiquette and Dress Code' section.[187]

The ACT Intermediary Program is relatively broad in that eligibility extends beyond cognitive impairment to cover communication needs and covers suspects/defendants as well as witnesses. While the initial pilot restricted intermediary access to certain witnesses since 2023, the ACT Intermediary Program has begun allocating intermediaries to eligible suspects and defendants in certain cases.[188] As such, the ACT became the first Australian jurisdiction to expand intermediary services to accused persons. This development is significant in terms of both the CRPD and the CRC. Extending intermediary services to vulnerable accused persons in addition to witnesses invariably promotes the right of access to justice. Article 12 of the CRC, which ensures that children have the opportunity to be heard, is relevant here as child suspects and defendants are enabled to access intermediary services. Prior to the official rollout of the suspect/defendant intermediary provision, significant effort was made by the Intermediary Program to develop an understanding of the role of intermediaries among police, legal professionals and the judiciary. These efforts have involved various outreach events and training to build confidence in the role and reassure criminal justice professionals about the role's operation in practice.[189]

3.7.7 *Queensland*

Similar to other states and territories in Australia, Queensland launched its intermediary provision in response to the findings of the Royal Commission. The Department of Justice and the Attorney General initiated a pilot study to operate in Brisbane and Cairns in July 2021, which was funded until the end of the 2024/2025 financial year.[190] The underpinning aim of the Queensland Intermediary Scheme (QIS) is to 'create a more accessible justice system

186 ACT Procedural Guidance Manual (n 178) 4.

187 ACT Procedural Guidance Manual (n 178) 21–22.

188 ACT Human Rights Commission, 'Australian First as ACT Intermediary Program Expands to Support Communication Needs of Vulnerable Accused' (13 March 2024) <https://www.hrc.act.gov.au/news-and-events/news/australian-first-as-act-intermediary-program-expands,-supporting-communication-needs-of-vulnerable-accused> accessed 10 October 2024.

189 The author was engaged in several outreach events on the role of intermediaries organised by the ACT HRC in July 2023 which involved presentations to ACT judiciary, ACT police and the ACT Law Society.

190 Queensland Courts, 'Queensland Intermediary Scheme' (18 November 2024) <https://www.courts.qld.gov.au/services/queensland-intermediary-scheme> accessed 21 November 2024. A full evaluation of the QIS was carried out by an external evaluation team, but publication of the report has not been approved.

by facilitating the communication of evidence that may not otherwise be heard'.[191] A 'Procedural Manual', very similar to procedural guidance manuals used in other jurisdictions, operates to ensure 'best practice' among intermediaries in Queensland.[192] The manual includes detailed information about the intermediary role, how intermediaries services can be accessed, the role's scope at different stages of the criminal process and templates for intermediaries to use when drafting their reports.[193]

The establishment of the QIS required amendments to the Evidence Act 1977 (Qld). This was achieved by the introduction of the Criminal Code (Child Sexual Offences Reform) and Other Legislation Amendment Act 2020. At the time of its introduction, it was envisaged that the pilot would see intermediaries engaged 'from police investigation through to court hearing'.[194] As per the legislation, eligibility for intermediary assistance in Queensland is restricted. An intermediary may be appointed – on the court's initiative or by application of a party – for witnesses in child sexual offence matters, where the witness is under 16 or has an impairment of the mind or difficulty communicating.[195] A 'child sexual offence' refers to any offence of a sexual nature committed in relation to a child, including offences contained in Chapter 22 (Offences against morality) and Chapter 32 (Rape and sexual assault) of the Criminal Code Act 1899 (Qld).[196] It is notable that there is no provision in the legislation for intermediary assistance for an accused individual, vulnerable or not. As such, the same concerns about limiting the right of access to justice discussed earlier apply to Queensland.

The role and function of the intermediary role in Queensland are set out comprehensively in the amended Evidence Act 1977 (Qld). Closely following the wording of the YJCEA in England and Wales, the function of intermediaries working within the QIS is to 'communicate or explain' both the questions put to the witness and answers given in reply.[197] Both functions must be done 'to the extent necessary' to enable understanding.[198] Further detail on the role's functions was provided by the Department of Justice and the Attorney General's tender for the scheme's first recruitment in which the role was outlined as: i) assessing witness communication and describing any specific

191 Queensland Courts (n 190).

192 QIS, 'Procedural Manual' (Version 6: September 2024).

193 QIS, 'Procedural Manual' (Version 6: September 2024).

194 Queensland Government, 'Intermediaries to Assist Vulnerable Witnesses to Give Their Best Evidence' (December 2020) <https://www.justice.qld.gov.au/community-engagement/news/2020/intermediaries-to-assist-vulnerable-witnesses-to-give-their-best-evidence> accessed 2 November 2024.

195 Evidence Act 1977, Division 4C, 21AZL(1).

196 Queensland Courts (n 190).

197 Evidence Act 1977, Division 4C, 21AZM.

198 Evidence Act 1977, Division 4C, 21AZM.

communication assistance required; ii) providing practical strategies on how to best communicate with the witness and how to pose a question to get the most reliable evidence; iii) informing directions hearings, where applicable, to establish court communication guidelines for a vulnerable witness; and iv) writing court reports on an individual's communication needs.[199]

Resembling the role of intermediaries in the U.K, the legislation makes clear that intermediaries must operate impartially and as officers of the court.[200] As the explanatory notes to the amended law spell out, intermediaries must 'act impartially to facilitate communication between witness and police, and a witness and courts'.[201] The QIS relies on a professional model whereby individuals with qualifications in speech pathology, psychology, occupational therapy or social work execute the role.[202] The QIS currently has four internal, 'staff' intermediaries as well as 18 'contracted' intermediaries who are selected through a rigorous procurement process.[203] The legislation also contains a list of 'excluded persons' who are prohibited from carrying out the intermediary role. This list includes 'relatives, friends or acquaintances' of the witness or defendant, a potential party or witness in the relevant proceedings and anyone who has, other than in the capacity of an intermediary, assisted the witness or defendant in a professional capacity.[204] This is a relatively novel aspect of the law relating to intermediaries compared to the original legislative framework in the U.K, which contains no such specific exclusion. It is assumed that the restrictions contained within the Evidence Act 1977 on who may be appointed as an intermediary were added to reinforce the impartiality of the role – an issue developed in detail in Chapter 6 (The neutrality paradox).

The operation of the QIS is also supported by a Practice Direction (No. 7 of 2021), which outlines the procedure for applying for an intermediary and the format of a 'directions hearing'.[205] At this hearing, the intermediary explains their recommendations to the court.[206] The Practice Direction outlines that the court may make formal directions 'about how the intermediary

199 Queensland Government, 'Witness Intermediary Scheme for Qualified Communication Specialists' (QTenders, November 27t 2020) <https://qtenders.epw.qld.gov.au//qtenders/tender/display/tender-details.do?action=display-tender-details&id=31852&CSRFNONCE=A04926D4A19509364C0B447CBBF7735C> accessed 4 August 2024.

200 Evidence Act 1977, Division 4C, 21AZM(3).

201 Evidence (Intermediaries) Amendment Regulation 2021 (Explanatory notes for SL 2021 No. 41).

202 Evidence (Intermediaries) Amendment Regulation 2021 (Explanatory notes for SL 2021 No. 41).

203 Email from the QIS to author (5 September 2024).

204 Evidence Act 1977, Division 4C, 21AZL(5).

205 Queensland Magistrate's Courts, 'Practice Direction No.4 of 2021' (25 November 2021).

206 Queensland Courts, 'Queensland Intermediary Scheme: Information for Lawyers' (Version 4.00, September 2023) <https://www.courts.qld.gov.au/__data/assets/pdf_file/0011/679574/factsheet-info-for-lawyers.pdf> accessed 8 October 2024.

is to participate . . . including the appropriate way to intervene'.[207] This addition to the Practice Direction emphasises that, ultimately, the intermediary role operates at the judge's discretion. This touches on a key theme explored throughout this book – the boundaries of the intermediary role are negotiated by those who perform and by other criminal justice professionals who engage with it.

3.8 New Zealand

In New Zealand, an early form of the intermediary role existed pursuant to the Evidence Act 1908. Section 23E(4) of the legislation permitted questions to be put to certain witnesses through an 'approved person' and was aimed at accommodating the needs of children or those who were 'mentally handicapped'.[208] The New Zealand Law Commission in 1996 proposed expanding the role, but these plans did not materialise – mainly due to opposition from the legal profession.[209] Although plans were announced in 2011 to introduce witness intermediaries over two years, this decision was withdrawn for the following reasons: i) an intermediary role would be better suited to an inquisitorial system, ii) the accused's right to cross-examine witnesses could be adversely impacted, iii) there was a lack of suitably qualified professionals to fill the role and iv) there was no satisfactory framework for the role's establishment.[210]

Intermediaries (or 'communication assistants') have been operating in the criminal justice system in New Zealand since 2012. However, numbers have increased significantly since 2015/2016.[211] These appointments have been based on s.4 of the Evidence Act 2006, which defines communication assistance broadly as:

> any assistance (for example, oral or written interpretation of a language, written assistance, or technological assistance) that enables or facilitates communication with a person who for any reason (for example, insufficient proficiency in the English language, age, or a disability) requires assistance to – (a) understand court proceedings; or (b) give evidence.

207 Queensland Courts (n 206).

208 Evidence Act (New Zealand) 1908, s.23C(b)(II).

209 New Zealand Law Commission, 'The Evidence of Children and Other Vulnerable Witnesses' (NZLC PP26, 1996).

210 Cabinet Social Policy Committee, 'Amendment to the Evidence Act 2006' (Obtained under Official Information Act 1982: Request to the Ministry of Justice, Wellington, New Zealand, 2013).

211 Email from Sally Kedge (coordinator and director of 'Talking Trouble Aotearoa/New Zealand) (12 February 2025).

A witness or defendant is eligible for communication assistance if they lack proficiency in English or have a communication disability. What amounts to 'sufficient ability to give evidence' and/or 'understand proceedings' is left to the judge's discretion based on the circumstances of the case.[212] Experience in New Zealand has been that 'communication disability' is broadly interpreted. Individuals who benefit from a communication assistant often have a language and communication profile which is quite different from what is expected in the courtroom. As such, these individuals may have 'needs' that must be accommodated, but the framing of 'disability' isn't always used.[213]

The scope of the communication assistant role in New Zealand is wider than merely assisting the witness when giving evidence.[214] Rather, experience in New Zealand suggests that communication assistance centres on facilitating understanding and participation more broadly – both inside and outside the courtroom. Further, communication assistants have advocated communication strategies and educated other professionals.[215] Communication assistance is also available for witnesses and defendants, regardless of their age or the type of crime. As discussed earlier, this contributes positively to the ability of vulnerable individuals to access justice under the CRPD. The available research into the practice of communication assistants in New Zealand has focused on the youth justice system and young offenders.[216] Encouragingly, research in New Zealand points to a broadly positive reception of the communication assistant role among criminal justice professionals and that communication assistants have prompted a 'critical reflection' on the experiences of young persons in justice processes.[217]

In New Zealand, in the youth context, some communication assistant work focuses on facilitating communication outside the court, in meetings with lawyers, and in 'family group conferences', which act as a collaborative

212 New Zealand Law Commission, 'Evidence: Reform of the Law' (NZLV, 1999, Report 55, vol 1).

213 Email from Sally Kedge (coordinator and director of 'Talking Trouble Aotearoa/New Zealand) (12 February 2025).

214 Kelly Howard, Clare McCann and Margaret Dudley, "It's Really Good . . . Why Hasn't It Happened Earlier?' Professionals' Perspectives on the Benefits of Communication Assistance in the New Zealand Youth Justice System' (2020) 53(2) Journal of Criminology 265.

215 Howard, McCann and Dudley (n 214).

216 Laura Makker, Sally Clendon and Elizabeth Doell, 'Speech-language Pathologists' Perspectives of Communication Strategies for Young People in the New Zealand Youth Justice System' (2022) 24 International Journal of Speech-Language Pathology 585; Sally Kedge, 'Language and Communication Difficulties: Children and Young People Involved with the Legal System' (2024) 66 The Youth Court of New Zealand 7.

217 Howard, McCann and Dudley (n 214) 280.

forum involving the young defendant, their family and often the victim.[218] This model is based on restorative justice principles – a diversionary measure endorsed by the CRC committee.[219] Although some concerns have been raised about conferencing as a diversionary measure, the involvement of communication assistants in New Zealand appears to address many of them directly. Tobin raises concerns about the suitability of conferencing for children with communication difficulties and potential limited support.[220] However, communication assistants can enable the 'voice of the child' to be heard at youth conferences and to help foster an 'inclusive communication' environment which respects the young offender's rights under the CRC.[221] The contributions of communication assistants to upholding rights contained under the CRC and the CRPD have been recognised in several Youth Court decisions in New Zealand.[222] In one judgment, the Youth Court noted the following:

> This case illustrates the vitally important role that communication assistants now play in the New Zealand Youth Justice System by identifying communication difficulties for young people that had previously gone unrecognised and often misinterpreted, and also by enabling the meaningful participation of young people with communication disorders who enter the Youth Justice system.

The provision of communication assistance in New Zealand is organised by two commercial providers and is funded by the Ministry of Justice. These two specialist organisations ('Talking Trouble' and 'Moretalk') are contracted by the Ministry of Justice to provide communication assistants and create and deliver their own training appropriate to the role. In terms of regulation, communication assistants in New Zealand operate under the 'Communication Assistance Quality Framework', which covers qualifications and training, service delivery guidance, performance monitoring and ongoing quality improvement.[223] The Framework outlines relatively strict requirements on who can perform the role. Currently, only speech-language

218 Kelly Howard, Clare McCann and Margaret Dudley, 'What Is Communication Assistance? Describing a New and Emerging Profession in the New Zealand Youth Justice System' (2020) 27(2) Psychiatry, Psychology and Law 300.

219 CRC Committee, (2007) General Comment No. 10, Children's rights in juvenile justice (CRC/C/GC/10) [27].

220 Tobin (n 9) 1656.

221 Lundy, Tobin and Parkes (n 21) 433.

222 *New Zealand Police (Prosecutor) v HH (Young Person)* [2021] NZYC 583; *New Zealand Police (Prosecutor) v FG (Young Person)* [2020] NZYC 328.

223 Ministry of Justice (New Zealand), 'Communication Assistance Quality Framework' (July 2021) <https://www.justice.govt.nz/about/lawyers-and-service-providers/service-providers/communication-assistance/communication-assistance-quality-framework> accessed 8 August 2024.

therapists, psychologists, occupational therapists, mental health specialist nurses and specialist teachers are qualified to work as communication assistants, provided they meet certain requirements.[224] Communication assistants increasingly facilitate communication in non-criminal legal settings, e.g. Family Court and some Tribunals and Inquiries, and also in some court-adjacent processes, e.g. Parole Board, Family Group Conferences and occasionally in police interviews.[225]

There is ample scope for further research into the operation of communication assistants in New Zealand – particularly the scope of the role across different stages of the criminal process. While early indications suggest that communication assistants are highly valued among criminal justice professionals, a better understanding of how the role operates in the court setting and during witness examination is needed. Anecdotal evidence suggests that communication assistants are already working in this environment – as such, there is fertile ground for further empirical research into how the role is experienced both by communication assistants themselves and the other criminal justice professionals they engage with.[226]

3.9 Chile

As is evident from the preceding discussion, intermediary-type roles have primarily emerged in countries steeped in a historically adversarial English model of criminal adjudication. Although Australia and New Zealand have developed their own distinctive legal cultures and criminal processes, intermediaries in these jurisdictions have faced similar challenges of accommodating vulnerable individuals in systems that are wedded to the principle of orality.[227] While countries such as South Africa, Spain and Israel have developed similar intermediary-type roles to promote the participation of such vulnerable court users, the case of Chile is particularly noteworthy when considering the intermediary role from a comparative perspective. This emergence of intermediaries (or 'intermediarios') has occurred against the backdrop of Chile's transition from an inquisitorial to an adversarial legal system and as the country has sought to incorporate 'respect of human rights and international standards'.[228] The movement from a largely 'written' form of

224 Ministry of Justice (New Zealand) (n 223).
225 Email from Sally Kedge (coordinator and director of 'Talking Trouble Aotearoa/New Zealand) (12 February 2025).
226 Email from Sally Kedge (coordinator and director of 'Talking Trouble Aotearoa/New Zealand) (12 February 2025).
227 Louise Ellison, *The Adversarial Process and the Vulnerable Witness* (OUP 2002).
228 Sergio Endress Gómez, 'Update: Essential Issues of the Chilean Legal System' (Hauser Global Law School Program, February 2019) <www.nyulawglobal.org/globalex/Chile1.html#_Regarding_the_Criminal_Procedure%20Re> accessed 8 October 2024.

litigation to a 'system of oral argument' in Chile has been tied to the need for judicial reform and to improve efficiency in justice procedures.[229]

Although there have been efforts to make the justice system in Chile more accommodating for vulnerable court users, there has historically been a lack of expertise and adequate training about communicative, emotional, cultural or social needs.[230] The introduction of intermediaries via Law 21.057 in 2018 was a significant development in this regard as it sought to enable child witnesses to give their best evidence through a range of measures, including the provision of pre-recorded investigative interviews. The law was also underpinned by a desire to prevent secondary victimisation and delays. More specifically, the law was influenced by research from the Ministry of Justice, which found that criminal justice professionals lacked the competencies to engage with child victims or witnesses with special communication or emotional needs.[231]

The intermediary role was formally introduced in January 2018 and rolled out nationwide in 2022. Intermediaries must be certified and accredited by the Ministry of Justice to ensure confidence and legitimacy.[232] In terms of the role's ambit, the legislation covers communication assistance for child victims or witnesses of sexual and other serious crimes at trial.[233] The intermediary's role is to provide specialised assistance to the court and facilitate communication with the child while monitoring their mental and physical condition.[234] The cross-examination of a child when an intermediary is involved is described by Cooper and Jacobson as follows:

> The parties, their lawyers and the presiding judges remain in a traditional courtroom linked by closed-circuit television to the witness. The lawyer states a question, the judge repeats it in a form that they are content with and the intermediary hears the question (as conveyed by the judge) through an earpiece and repeats it to the witness. The witness will neither see nor hear what is happening in the courtroom. However, the court can see and hear the intermediary via the TV link.[235]

229 Rafael Blanco, Richard Hutt and Hugo Rojas, 'Reform to the Criminal Justice System in Chile: Evaluation and Challenges' (2004) 2(2) Loyola University Chicago International Law Review 253, 256.

230 Valentina Ulloa and Rocio Acosta, 'Taking Oral Evidence in Chile from Child Victims in Priority Groups: Challenges for the Practice and Training of Justice Professionals' (2023) 27 Journal of Police and Criminal Psychology 1.

231 Valentina Ulloa and Rocio Acosta (n 230); Nora Rosatti and Carlos Iturra, *Ley de entrevistas videograbadas. Un cambio procesal y sistémico* (Monografías 2011) 12.

232 Law 21.057, Arts 6 &15.

233 Law 21.057, Arts 6 &15. Arts 20–21.

234 Valentina Ulloa, Nicolás Pietrasanta and Rocío Acosta,'Intermediaries in Chile: Facilitating the Right of Child Victims and Witnesses to Participate and Be Heard in Criminal Trials' (2022) 26(3) The International Journal of Evidence & Proof 223.

235 Jacobson and Cooper (n 36) 145.

A few salient features of the Chilean intermediary model deserve elaboration. Firstly, the intermediary is alone with the child in a separate room, except for cases requiring an interpreter, translator or accompanying animal.[236] The examining lawyer does not pose questions directly to the child. Instead, questions are asked 'through' the supervisory judge, who transmits them to the intermediary through an earpiece.[237] The intermediary then asks the child questions, taking consideration of the child's age, maturity, mental condition and the procedural standards for adversarial proceedings.[238] It is possible, therefore, for the intermediary to modify the question to ensure it is comprehensible. This aspect of the intermediary role in Chile contrasts starkly with experience in England and Wales, where the ambit of the intermediary role does not extend to reformulating questions in such a manner.

One unique aspect of Chile's intermediary scheme is that the only persons eligible to perform the role are public prosecutors, police, judges and members of the Ministry of Interior and Public Security.[239] This contrasts markedly from the professional profile of intermediaries in other jurisdictions, where most are drawn from speech and language therapy, social work, psychology and other related Allied Health backgrounds. Anecdotally, most intermediary appointments in Chile so far have been judges.[240] The prevailing reason for this trend relates to matters of efficiency as it is easier to coordinate.[241] Further, the limited research on the role suggests that judges are perceived as particularly adept at the role, understanding how to facilitate communication in particularly difficult trials. However, the same research points to a potential conflict between the overlapping professional roles, questioning the ability of judge intermediaries to extricate themselves from their judicial mindset.[242] This peculiarity of the Chilean intermediary system is difficult to reconcile with the movement away from the inquisitorial model towards adversarialism. Traditionally, it is in inquisitorial systems that the judge plays a 'dominant part in the management and control of proceedings'[243] – yet the judicial control over the intermediary's functions in Chile appears a vestige of the old model of judicial case management.

Finally, it is worth noting that the intermediary scheme in Chile has been criticised for its lack of a 'balanced approach' between protecting witnesses

236 Ulloa, Pietrasanta and Acosta (n 234) 227.
237 Ulloa, Pietrasanta and Acosta (n 234) 229.
238 Ley 21.057 (Law 21.057) Regula Entrevistas Grabadas En Video y, Otras Medidas de Resguardo a Menores de Edad, Víctimas de Delitos Sexuales (Regulates Recorded Video Interviews, and Other Protection Measures for Minors, Victims of Sexual Crimes) Art. 17.
239 Ulloa, Pietrasanta and Acosta (n 234) 224.
240 Email correspondence between 'Fundacíon Amparo y Justicia' and author (22 December 2024).
241 Email correspondence between 'Fundacíon Amparo y Justicia' and author (22 December 2024).
242 Ulloa, Pietrasanta and Acosta (n 234).
243 John Langbein, *The Origins of Adversary Criminal Trial* (OUP 2005).

and accommodating the rights of defendants.[244] Maureira centres his concern on the legislation's diminution of the right of the accused to 'confront' the witness and that the use of intermediaries for children and adolescents is mandatory.[245] As such, Law 21.057 has been described as removing the court's 'discretion and latitude' and preventing judges from assessing competing 'values or interests'.[246] Importantly, the law appears to prevent judges from deciding that, in some cases, an intermediary may be inappropriate. There is some merit in this observation. For example, imagine a child witness who made it clear that they would prefer to provide live testimony. Under Law 21.057, the judge would have no scope to accede to the child's wishes and would be required to appoint an intermediary (albeit it would likely be the judge themselves). It may reasonably be argued that such a system is irreconcilable with Article 12 CRC, which requires the child to be 'heard' in judicial proceedings. Going further, the nature of the intermediary model in Chile appears to contain what Lundy describes as a 'predetermination' by adults concerning matters affecting children.[247]

3.10 Conclusion

As awareness of the needs of vulnerable witnesses improves across justice systems internationally, there is increased interest in specialist communication roles such as the intermediary. While the jurisdictions discussed in this chapter operate (or have adopted) an adversarial model of adjudication, it is equally the case that individual practices and idiosyncrasies have emerged. The English intermediary model is understandably treated as the progenitor to other international models. Still, this chapter highlights how other countries have developed their own systems and processes to provide specialist communication assistance. For example, the extension of intermediary provision to the accused in ACT and the practice of judges executing the role in Chile are developments independent of policy and practice in England and Wales. In 2014, Cooper and Wurtzel suggested that Northern Ireland could capitalise on 'going second' after England and Wales in terms of developing its own intermediary model.[248] This chapter has revealed how subsequent attempts to implement similar schemes have enjoyed varying success – some enjoying broad support and continuing to expand (e.g. ACT and New

244 Claudio Alfonso Fuentes Maureira, 'Vulnerable Witnesses in Chilean Criminal Proceedings: New Developments' (2024) 28(1) International Journal of Evidence and Proof 65.
245 Fuentes Maureira (n 244).
246 Fuentes Maureira (n 244).
247 Laura Lundy, 'Voice' Is Not Enough: Conceptualising Article 12 of the United Nations Convention on the Rights of the Child' (2007) 33 (6) British Educational Research Journal 927.
248 Cooper and Wurtzel (n 70).

Zealand) while others have faced significant hurdles (e.g. South Australia). Others are still in their relative infancy and require proper evaluation before similar assessments can be made.

This chapter also examines the intermediary role in the context of the CRC and the CRPD. While the remainder of the book focuses mainly on the operation of intermediaries in a U.K context, it has been instructive to 'zoom out' to consider how the rights enshrined in these sources of international law relate to the role. Indeed, in the U.K context, there has been a lack of focus on how these rights might be realised domestically to secure intermediary access for some of the most vulnerable individuals.[249] This contrasts with practice in some other jurisdictions, such as New Zealand, where access to specialist communication assistance has been granted with reference to both the CRC and the CRPD.[250] While this chapter's discussion on the conventions is relatively brief, it serves to highlight how the intermediary role relates to several of the core protections afforded to children and to persons with disabilities. Much more research is needed to better understand how these sources of international law can be harnessed to ensure access to justice through intermediary assistance.

249 Some authorities focus more on the broad duty of the court to deal with a case flexibly and 'justly' without specifically linking intermediary provision with any convention rights: Civil Justice Council, 'Vulnerable Witnesses and Parties Within Civil Proceedings: Current Position and Recommendations for Change' (August 2019).

250 [2021] NZYC 583 [85].

Chapter 4

Locating the intermediary within theories of the criminal trial

4.1 Introduction

Criminal justice is often conceptualised as a process in which interdependent parts operate around central themes.[1] This chapter explores various theories of one component of the criminal process: the trial. The criminal trial is, at least in the English common law tradition, the focal point of criminal procedure and has been termed the 'make or break point' of the broader criminal process.[2] This chapter focuses on the trial for two main reasons. Firstly, as argued by Duff et al., the norms that govern the trial have implications for the remainder of the criminal process and the trial provides a fundamental background for how the other stages operate.[3] It is through the operation of the trial that criminal responsibility is formally assigned and the doctrines that comprise the substantive criminal law are articulated and applied.[4] Secondly, the intermediary is commonly depicted as a trial-focused role. Although the involvement of intermediaries at the investigatory stage is – for good reason – increasingly recognised, my empirical data suggest that, as a 'scene of conflicting aims and interests', the trial contours the intermediary role significantly.[5] The role's professional identity, neutrality and its impact on

1 Nicola Padfield and Jonathan Bild, *Text and Materials on the Criminal Process* (5th edn, Routledge 2016) 8; Stephanos Bibas, *The Machinery of Justice* (OUP 2015) 111.

2 Hock Lai Ho, 'Liberalism and the Criminal Trial' (2010) 32 Sydney Law Review 269; Andrew Ashworth and Mike Redmayne, *The Criminal Process* (4th edn, OUP 2010) 321. For a discussion of the 'crime control' vs 'due process' models and where the trial fits within both, see: Herbert Packer, 'Two Models of the Criminal Process' (1964) 113(1) University of Pennsylvania Law Review 1.

3 Antony Duff and others, 'Introduction: Towards a Normative Theory of the Criminal Trial' in Antony Duff and others (eds), *The Trial on Trial 1: Truth and Due Process* (Hart Publishing 2004) 11.

4 Antony Duff, 'Theories of Criminal Law' (The Stanford Encyclopedia of Philosophy, Summer 2013 edn) <https://plato.stanford.edu/archives/sum2013/entries/criminal-law/> accessed 13 January 2021.

5 Andrew Ashworth, *The Criminal Process: An Evaluative Study* (2nd edn, OUP 1998) 30.

DOI: 10.4324/9781003461166-4

participation are profoundly affected by intermediaries' experiences in and around the trial (see Chapters 5–7). This chapter provides a foundation for subsequent chapters, which explore the ambiguities and confusion around the role's parameters.

The chapter begins by considering the nature of the English criminal trial and the movement towards what is loosely termed 'modified adversarialism'. This is followed by an examination of how the intermediary has shaped, and indeed is shaped by, a trial system that is increasingly dominated by managerialist concerns and prioritises obtaining 'best evidence'.[6] The chapter then considers several aims and values of the trial, which are considered together as they overlap. This discussion provides an important reference point for subsequent chapters where I will present a grounded theory of the role and its content.

4.2 The intermediary and 'modified adversarialism'

The rationale underpinning the adversarial trial, at least in theory, is the pursuit of the truth through a 'sharp clash of proofs'.[7] However, because the adversarial trial is commonly understood as the opportunity for the defence to put the prosecution to proof on the evidence, the search for objective truth may be relegated to secondary importance, with the primary concern being that the case brought against the defendant is sufficiently robust to warrant a conviction.[8] It is intrinsic to the adversarial trial that the two parties, prosecution and defence, are partisan and are expected to substantiate their own case while discrediting their opponent.[9] Within this 'competitive battle between foes and contestants',[10] the judge fulfils a 'passive umpire' role and the bulk of evidence is presented orally.[11]

A shift away from adversarialism in English criminal justice is widely recognised and is closely related to the rise of managerialism. Managerialism, which broadly refers to services and facilities being run as streamlined, technocratic systems, suggests that judges have assumed an increased managerial role underpinned by the aim of improving the efficiency of the adjudication

6 For a discussion of the conflict between 'best evidence' and 'best interests', see: Emily Henderson, 'Best Evidence or Best Interests? What Does the Case Law Say about the Function of Criminal Cross-examination' (2016) 20(3) Journal of International Evidence and Proof 183.

7 Stephen Landsman, *Readings on Adversarial Justice: The American Approach to Adjudication* (West Publishing 1988) 2.

8 Jonathan Doak and Claire McGourlay, *Evidence in Context* (3rd edn, Routledge 2012) 39.

9 Doak and McGourlay (n 8) 20.

10 Australian Law Reform Commission, 'Review of the Adversarial System of Litigation: Rethinking the Federal Civil Litigation System (Issues paper No. 20, Canberra, Australia Government Publishing Service 1997) [2.29].

11 Peter Duff, 'Changing Conceptions of the Scottish Criminal Trial: The Duty to Agree Uncontroversial Evidence' in Duff and others (n 3) 29.

process.[12] Although judicial case management has promoted efficiency for decades,[13] the Criminal Procedure Rules (CPR) provided impetus for the 'emergence of a managerialist system of criminal justice'.[14] The increased judicial power to timetable, require written rather than oral arguments and impose sanctions for failure to comply with directions, all represent a transfer of power from the parties to the court.[15] The CPR encourage agreement where possible and to ensure that trials begin promptly, that they are as narrowly focused as possible and do not last longer than necessary.[16] This is accompanied by an increased emphasis on accurate fact-finding and efficiency.[17] As such, it may be more accurate to describe the English trial as operating under a modified adversarial tradition and one that contains elements of both the adversarial and inquisitorial models.[18] This chapter is not concerned with drawing clear distinctions or ascribing strict labels to the system of criminal adjudication. Instead, it is important to recognise that the intermediary role operates in a system which contains aspects of both traditions and is informed by concerns which are not central to either, for example efficiency and managerialism.[19]

Even before its introduction through the Youth Justice and Criminal Evidence Act 1999 (YJCEA), the position of the intermediary within the adversarial trial was heavily scrutinised. As the only recommendation of the Pigot Committee which was not unanimously agreed upon, the introduction of what was termed the 'interlocutor' caused concern for several reasons. The committee raised issues about the imposition of a third party between advocate and witness, and expressed concerns that intermediaries may 'hinder rather than assist counsel conducting the case'.[20] During the YJCEA's legislative passage, several parliamentarians sought reassurance that the intermediary role would not impinge on the role of counsel.[21] Fears were later raised that advocacy techniques would require radical reassessment and that an

12 Darryl Brown and others, *The Oxford Handbook of Criminal Process* (OUP 2019); Jennifer Ward, *Transforming Summary Justice: Modernisation in the Lower Criminal Courts* (Routledge 2017) 6.

13 Penny Darbyshire, 'Judicial Case Management in Ten Crown Courts' (2014) 1 Criminal Law Review 30.

14 Jacqueline Hodgson, *The Metamorphosis of Criminal Justice* (OUP 2020) 68.

15 Hodgson (n 14).

16 Jenny McEwan, 'From Adversarialism to Managerialism: Criminal Justice in Transition' (2011) 31(4) Legal Studies 519, 527; Frank Belloni and Jacqueline Hodgson, *Criminal Injustice: An Evaluation of the Criminal Justice Process in Britain* (Palgrave Macmillan 2000) 203.

17 McEwan (n 16) 520.

18 Mirjan Damaska, *The Faces of Justice and State Authority: A Comparative Approach to the Legal Process* (Yale UP 1986).

19 Abenaa Owusu-Bempah, *Defendant Participation in the Criminal Process* (Routledge 2016) 32.

20 Home Office, 'Report of the Advisory Group on Video Evidence' (December 1989, London) [2.34].

21 Youth Justice and Criminal Evidence Bill [Lords] Clause 28 (22 June 1999).

enhanced judicial role would inevitably settle disputes between questioner and intermediary over content and tone of questioning.[22]

Based on Doak and McGourlay's view that the intermediary special measure was 'the most innovative' reform contained within the YJCEA, it is not surprising that the role is viewed as a threat to the adversarial trial.[23] The mere presence of an intermediary with a witness represents a 'radical departure from the archetypal adversarial duel'.[24] In the traditional adversarial trial, the judge assumes a passive role while counsel largely conduct proceedings.[25] As Langbein explains, the principle of orality cherished by the adversarial trial orientated the process on the lawyers.[26] The interposition of the intermediary between the advocate and witness (or more accurately, alongside the witness) does not fundamentally undermine a commitment to orality, but it constrains the advocate in how they conduct their questioning. The loosely defined modified adversarialism which this chapter recognises has been shaped by the YJCEA more generally. The legislation did not represent a full-scale overhaul of orthodox adversarial trial procedures but amounted to an 'accommodation approach' in which special measures operate within the constraints of the established procedure.[27] The principle of orality and the insistence on direct oral evidence remains, but with an acknowledgement of the need to reduce the associated stress level.[28]

The adversarial tradition protects the advocate's control of their case through the ability to pursue arguments in their client's favour, including through cross-examination.[29] The intermediary challenges this norm in several ways. Firstly, the intermediary's ability to intervene during witness examination represents a departure from the 'near complete autonomy' advocates enjoy in the adversarial model.[30] It should be recognised that judges have always enjoyed considerable power to intervene during witness examination, but the modified adversarial model positively *requires* judges to intervene proactively in the management of criminal cases before and during trial.[31]

22 Laura Hoyano, 'Variations on a Theme by Pigot: Special Measures Directions for Child Witnesses' (2000) Criminal Law Review 250, 272.
23 Doak and McGourlay (n 8) 106.
24 Jonathan Doak and Lauran Doak, 'Non-verbal Victims in the Adversarial Criminal Process: Communication, Competency, and Credibility' (2017) 68(4) Northern Ireland Legal Quarterly 451, 457.
25 William David Evans, 'On the Law of Evidence' in Robert J Pothier (ed), *A Treatise on the Law of Obligations* (W. D. Evans trans.) (London 1806).
26 John Langbein, *The Origins of the Adversary Criminal Trial* (OUP 2003) 110.
27 Louise Ellison, *The Adversarial Process and the Vulnerable Witness* (OUP 2002) 7.
28 Ellison (n 27) 7.
29 Emily Henderson, 'Theoretically Speaking: English Judges and Advocates Discuss the Changing Theory of Cross-examination' (2015) 12 Criminal Law Review 927; Doak and Doak (n 24) 457.
30 Doak and McGourlay (n 8) 113.
31 McEwan (n 16) 527.

This is now also reflected in the Criminal Practice Directions (CPD).[32] In the case of *Lubemba*, Lady Justice Hallett emphasised the duty of judges to intervene during the examination of vulnerable witnesses or defendants to avoid misapprehension or confusion.[33]

The intermediary role is innovative in that it may pivot between counsel and the judge.[34] The Court of Appeal in *OP* identified the intermediary role as including 'the potential for intervention and on occasion suggestion to the Bench'.[35] Further, judges must take 'every reasonable step'[36] to ensure vulnerable individuals can give best evidence (which can include the appointment of an intermediary) and prevent 'over-rigorous' cross examination.[37] The introduction of the intermediary may be seen as contributing to a more interventionist approach and a shift in the approach/understanding of the purpose of cross-examination from an opportunity to advocate to a more communicative exercise. Yet while Hoyano feared that intermediary involvement would require an enhanced judicial role during witness examination, there is no empirical evidence to suggest that this is the case in practice.[38] As will be discussed later, the relationship between the intermediary and advocates prior to court examination is often key to how often interventions occur.

The intermediary is responsible for questioning if, in their view, a communication issue arises.[39] Understandably, this involves a degree of discretion and depends significantly on the profile of the vulnerable witness and the nature of their communication difficulties.[40] As recognised by Plotnikoff and Woolfson, the responsibility of the intermediary to intervene at trial requires the role to 'navigate a landscape of grey areas'.[41] The authors also note that intermediaries may be constrained as some lines of questioning

32 Criminal Practice Directions 2023 (CPD) (CrimPRC(23)90(b)) [6.1.6].

33 *R v Lubemba* [2014] EWCA Crim 2064; *R v JP* [2014] EWCA Crim 2064 [44]–[45].

34 Henderson (n 29) 944.

35 [2014] EWHC 1944 (Admin) [34].

36 Criminal Procedure Rules (CPR) (October 2020) Pt 3, Rule 3.8(3).

37 CPD (n 32) [6.1.6].

38 In their interviews with judges, Plotnikoff and Woolfson found markedly different views about the extent to which the involvement of intermediaries reduced the need for judicial intervention. See: Joyce Plotnikoff and Richard Woolfson, *Falling Short? A Snapshot of Young Witness Policy and Practice* (NSPCC, February 2019) 102; Also see: Emily Henderson, 'Theoretically Speaking: English Judges and Advocates Discuss the Changing Theory of Cross-examination' (2015) 12 Criminal Law Review 927.

39 Ministry of Justice, 'Registered Intermediary Procedural Guidance Manual 2024' <https://assets.publishing.service.gov.uk/media/671b819bfc28a840abc6d26d/Registered_Intermediary_Procedural_Guidance_Manual_2024__Official_.pdf> accessed 8 February 2025.

40 Writing shortly after the introduction of the YJCEA, Ellison suggested that intermediaries would have 'limited influence over the basic tenor of cross examination . . . there is, for example, no suggestion that the intermediary will be at liberty to intervene actively during cross-examination to challenge the use of interrogatory devices which are potentially misleading or suggestive and liable to elicit unreliable', see: Louise Ellison, 'The mosaic art?: cross-examination and the vulnerable witness' (2001) 21(3) Legal Studies 353, 366.

41 Joyce Plotnikoff and Richard Woolfson, *Intermediaries in the Criminal Justice System* (Policy Press 2015) 188.

which impede communication 'go beyond the boundaries of the [intermediary] function'.[42] For example, a child witness may be visibly upset by robust cross-examination but the intermediary feels their intervention risks demonstrating sympathy and partiality.[43] This indicates that some elements of traditional cross-examination remain ingrained despite efforts to reform. Henderson suggests that this is reflected in practice with judicial reluctance to enforce interventions and lawyers taking advantage of this beyond the intermediary's authority.[44] Even more alarming is Plotnikoff and Woolfson's finding that poor questioning from advocates persisted in several cases despite judicial intervention.[45] Intermediaries may be able to modify the culture of cross-examination to a degree, but their impact is limited if their practices are not legitimised by the bench.[46] Since the judge decides the nature and scope of the intermediary role in each case, judicial understanding of the role and its parameters is crucial to the impact the role can have.

A second way intermediaries challenge the adversarial tradition relates to the intricacies of witness examination in terms of question content, style and delivery. In their court report, the intermediary is expected to 'give detailed and specific instructions on how questions may best be put to the witness' and make suggestions regarding the 'pace of questioning'.[47] Perhaps the most significant development in this area is the practice of the intermediary 'reviewing' or 'vetting' counsel's questions before examination which is now increasingly common in practice (see further later in this chapter). This has helped to 'fuel cultural change regarding cross-examination of vulnerable witnesses'.[48] Amendments to questions are to be agreed at the Ground Rules Hearing (GRH) at the judge's direction as noted by the Court of Appeal in *R v Lubemba*:[49]

> The ground rules hearing should cover, amongst other matters, the general care of the witness. . . . So as to avoid any unfortunate misunderstanding at trial, it would be an entirely reasonable step for a judge at the ground rules hearing to invite defence advocates to reduce their questions to writing in advance.

42 Plotnikoff and Woolfson (n 41).
43 This is based on a real example cited by NI-1 in interview.
44 Emily Henderson, 'A Very Valuable Tool': Judges, Advocates and Intermediaries Discuss the Intermediary System in England and Wales' (2015) 19(3) International Journal of Evidence and Proof 154.
45 Plotnikoff and Woolfson (n 41) 119.
46 John Spencer and Michael Lamb, *Children and Cross-Examination: Time to Change the Rules?* (Bloomsbury 2012). This also links in with the role's struggle for 'professional jurisdiction' as discussed in Chapter 5 (Professional work – jurisdictions and boundary work).
47 MoJ (n 39) [4.31].
48 Plotnikoff and Woolfson (n 41) 219.
49 [2014] EWCA Crim 2064; Henderson has noted that the Court of Appeal has effectively been rewriting the rules of cross examination of witnesses since 2010: Emily Henderson, 'All the proper protections – the Court of Appeal rewrites the rules for the cross-examination of vulnerable witnesses' (2014) Criminal Law Review 93.

The practice of a third party reviewing questions is anathema to many advocates. It jars with the freedom of the questioner to formulate questions loaded with presuppositions, make declaratory statements and use coercive forms of enquiry.[50] In my early days of practice at the Criminal Bar, one defence barrister was scathing about intermediaries generally and told me that the insistence that questions be reviewed has led to intermediaries being despised.[51] Plotnikoff and Woolfson also found strong resistance among some older barristers who saw the practice of reviewing questions as completely at odds with traditional oral advocacy.[52] Other authors suggest that acceptance of the role is growing and with it a greater willingness among advocates to cooperate with the reviewing of questions.[53] Attitudes may, slowly at least, be changing. However, these findings must be considered alongside the rules and underpinning rationale of cross-examination of vulnerable individuals, including children. In *R v Barker*, the Court of Appeal held that advocates must 'adapt . . . cross-examination . . . to enable the child to give the *best evidence* of which he or she is capable'.[54] If judges are expected to approach the admissibility of cross-examination questions with concern for the completeness and accuracy of the evidence, then this inevitably impacts the normative function of the intermediary during question vetting. While vetting encroaches on party control and autonomy, it may also be viewed as aiding the best evidence of the witness – something explicitly recognised as a core intermediary function in the relevant procedural guidance manual.[55] Henderson argues that the best evidence account is consistent with the wider purposes and functions of the accusatorial trial as a fact-finding exercise.[56] If so, the intermediary role may be viewed as assisting one aspect of traditional adversarialism.

The vetting of questions as a practice has now been formalised to a degree through the CPD and the CPR.[57] In line with *R v Lubemba*, judges should

50 Sarah Lowndes, 'Comprehension and Misapprehension in Courtroom Discourse (2007) 14(2) International Journal of Speech Language and the law 305.

51 This conversation took place with a barrister in Northern Ireland circa 2016.

52 Plotnikoff and Woolfson (n 41) 221–224.

53 Penny Cooper and Michelle Mattison, 'Intermediaries, Vulnerable People and the Quality of Evidence: An International Comparison of Three Versions of the English Intermediary Model' (2017) 21(4) International Journal of Evidence and Proof 351.

54 [2010] EWCA Crim 4.

55 MoJ (n 39).

56 Henderson (n 44).

57 For example, the CPD explain that the outcome of a GRH hearing should be recorded in a document which should 'record any arrangements made for the editing and judicial approval of questions to be asked in cross-examination, where appropriate. Where questions are to be committed to writing and subject to judicial editing, with or without input from an intermediary, then, as a general rule, the proposed questions must be shared with the other parties to the trial' (CPD (n 32)) [6.1.5]; Criminal Procedure Rules (CPR) (n 36) rule 3.9(5)(a).

use the GRH to check that the advocates have consulted with the intermediary to ensure questions are framed in a manner that is likely to achieve the best quality evidence from the vulnerable person.[58] It is interesting to examine this aspect of intermediary practice against the rise of managerialism. The judicial responsibility to 'set the parameters' of questioning at the GRH will often be imperative for the intermediary to be able to perform its role.[59] However, while good practice positions the judge at the centre of this vetting process, it seems that advocates rarely submit questions before the GRH.[60] Also concerning is that defendant intermediaries are even less likely to have the opportunity to review counsel's questions prior to trial.[61] This situation has two significant consequences. Firstly, it removes the judge from the reviewing process and leaves questions to be agreed upon between the intermediary and the advocate.[62] Secondly, it means that intermediaries are likely to review questions closer to witness examination, thus leaving less time for preparation and increasing the need for judicial/intermediary intervention at trial. The first point undermines a central pillar of managerialist theory, which holds that criminal justice reforms have produced a 'transfer of power from parties to the court'.[63] This generates a risk that without judicial oversight, advocates have less incentive to collaborate with intermediaries to tailor their questions (although this does mean that a core element of adversarialism, i.e. party control, is retained). In this regard, intermediaries rely on coercive judicial power to enforce their recommendations and legitimise their position. The adversarial tradition of party control depicts advocates zealously protecting their questions, particularly defence counsel who may view the sharing of their questions as being at odds with the duty to advance their client's interests. While the vetting of questions is one example of this, the intermediary is heavily reliant on the direction of the judge for the execution of *all* its functions. As the Court of Appeal noted in *R v Grant Murray*:

> [Intermediaries] are instructed to provide advice and guidance to the judge (and to the advocates), not to dictate to anyone what is to happen. Their role is to provide a report and, if required by the court, to provide

58 Penny Cooper, Paula Backen and Ruth Marchant, 'Getting to Grips with Ground Rules Hearings – a Checklist for Judges, Advocates and Intermediaries' (2015) 6 Criminal Law Review 420, 427.

59 Cooper, Backen and Marchant (n 58) 420–435.

60 Plotnikoff and Woolfson (n 41) 30.

61 Plotnikoff and Woolfson (n 41) 106.

62 However, there is evidence of good practice in this regard. In the case of *R v FA* [2015] EWCA Crim 209, the intermediary worked with both prosecution and defence counsel in a collaborative way to make 'sensible expert suggestions' ([13]) which were adopted at trial.

63 McEwan (n 16) 544.

> assistance to a witness or defendant *as directed by the judge* (emphasis in original).[64]

This judicial statement indicates the uneven power relations within the trial and the intermediary's status as an outsider to the inner group of court professionals (as will be discussed in more detail in Chapter 5: Professional work – jurisdictions and boundary work).[65] It also suggests that the capacity for the intermediary role to shape the nature of the trial depends on judicial management and activism, which are already at odds with elements of adversarialism. In this context, it is worth returning to consider Henderson's claim that the intermediary is the 'first new, active role to be introduced into the criminal trial in two centuries'.[66] Despite the role's distinctive character, it shares the same underpinning rationale as all the special measures contained within the YJCEA, i.e. to enable witnesses to give their 'best evidence'.[67] Section 16(5) of the legislation emphasises the importance of evidence quality with special measures granted to improve the 'completeness, coherence and accuracy' of testimony.[68] Fairclough argues that these aims would also be furthered by assisting defendants to give their best evidence should they wish to testify.[69] Yet the special measures regime specifically excludes defendants and has taken inherent judicial powers for defendant intermediaries to be granted at trial.[70] The exercise of inherent jurisdiction to fill the breach created by the legislation resonates with the concept of judicial managerialism and the view that every court of law has wide inherent powers to 'control its own procedure'.[71]

Finally, what does all this mean for the defendant and their procedural rights? Dilution of the adversarial model has produced concern for defendant rights, including the accused's right to participate in their own defence.[72]

64 *R v Grant-Murray & Anor* [2017] EWCA Crim 1228 [199].
65 Paul Rock, *The Social World of an English Crown Court* (Clarendon Press 1993).
66 Henderson (n 44) 155.
67 MoJ (n 39).
68 There is some, albeit limited, empirical evidence to support the claim that intermediary involvement with witnesses leads to a higher quality evidence output, see: Kimberley Collins, Natalie Harker and Georgios Antonopoulos, 'The Impact of Registered Intermediary Presence on Adults' Perceptions of Child Witnesses: Evidence from a Mock Cross Examination' (2016) 23 European Journal on Criminal Policy and Research 211.
69 Samantha Fairclough, 'The Role of Equality in the Provision of Special Measures to Vulnerable and/or Intimidated Court Users Giving Evidence in Crown Court Trials' (PhD thesis, University of Birmingham 2017) 90.
70 I am grateful to Robert Craig for alerting me to the potential problems of judicial use of their inherent powers to 'circumvent gaps in statutory language'.
71 *Attorney General v Leveller Magazine Ltd* [1979] AC 440 [464].
72 John Jackson, 'Autonomy and Accuracy in the Development of Fair Trial Rights' (2009) University College Dublin Law Research Paper (No 09/2009) <http://papers.ssrn.com/sol3/papers.cfm?abstract_id=1407968> accessed 5 January 2021; McEwan (n 16) 525.

As Owusu-Bempah notes, the shift away from adversarialism in England and Wales has affected, and has been affected by, changes to the defendant's role.[73] While this is true, there is nothing intrinsic about the intermediary special measure or its normative function which necessarily diminishes defendant rights.[74] In fact, the *raison d'etre* of defendant intermediaries is ensuring vulnerable defendants can effectively participate in proceedings. Thus, while some changes to the adversarial model can impede certain defence rights, others (such as the introduction of intermediaries) have the potential to enhance them. In theory, at least, in a modified adversarial system, in which judges enable intermediaries to facilitate communication, the defendant's participatory rights are protected.[75] As will be discussed in later chapters, the accused may effectively participate even if they decide not to testify but receive intermediary assistance to understand other aspects of proceedings. Of course, rights are useless if they exist purely in abstraction and Chapter 7 (Witness work, defendant work and participatory roles) will examine whether defendants who need intermediaries are in practice able to access them. For now, the introduction of intermediaries has contributed to, and been a consequence of, a shift from adversarialism to a modified adversarial system concerned with efficient fact-finding. The following sections of this chapter explore several aims and values of the trial in more depth and examine the potential impact of the intermediary role on how the trial is conceptualised.

4.3 Theories of the criminal trial

Characterising the criminal trial as an example of modified adversarialism does not suggest that it is fundamentally flawed or that, as Ellison argues, a shift away from orality towards inquisitorial is urgently needed.[76] Rather, the objective has been to better understand where the intermediary can be located within the existing system of criminal adjudication. It is necessary to develop the analysis further and examine the trial's function and what values underpin it.[77] When considering the criminal trial from a theoretical perspective, the complexity of the issues involved soon becomes apparent. One may ask, what distinguishes the trial from other kinds of social institution or institutions of the criminal justice system? How are the limits of state authority

73 Owusu-Bempah (n 19) 35.
74 McEwan (n 16) 535.
75 Prior to the invocation of inherent powers of the court to appoint defendant intermediaries, Hoyano argued that the 'withholding' of special measures (including the intermediary) from defendants risked their fair trial rights: Laura Hoyano, 'Striking a Balance between the Rights of Defendants and Vulnerable Witnesses: Will Special Measures Directions Contravene Guarantees of a Fair Trial?' (2001) Criminal Law Review 948, 968.
76 Ellison (n 27) 70.
77 Duff and others (n 3) 18.

within the trial process established, and is the criminal trial as it is currently structured an appropriate response to alleged wrongdoing? These are some of the issues that emerge when reflecting on the trial and its wider significance and status.[78] They are, of course, not exhaustive, and many other features of the trial could form the subject of theoretical examination.

Seeking to theorise the criminal trial presents another difficulty: do we need to develop a theory that articulates the principles and ideals against which empirical reality can be assessed? As Redmayne noted when reflecting on the enormity of the task: 'where does one start?'.[79] The main reason for this concern is that the *type* of theory sought is often vexed. Redmayne noted a problematic commitment among many theorists to 'explanatory unification' and considered attempts to reconcile the trial's overarching aim(s) with other competing, and often divergent values into a 'rich theory' as misguided.[80] Duff et al. suggest that attempts to theorise the trial often fragment into consideration of various evidential and procedural questions and that 'no general theory of the trial but rather theories of different aspects of trials' have emerged.[81] Others have argued against a theory of the trial that seeks to balance primary aims with other principles or goals which are deemed secondary and incommensurable.[82]

This section does not advance a normative theory of the criminal trial nor dwell on whether a single theory is attainable or desirable.[83] Instead, I first survey some potential trial aims and values to demonstrate how they impact the role of the intermediary as well as how the intermediary can shape the trial itself. It is recognised throughout that no hard line exists between what may amount to a trial aim or value and that a degree of overlap is inevitable.

4.4 Aims and values of the trial

We turn, then, to consider the aims and values of the criminal trial. Aims can be described as the desired outcomes of criminal adjudication with values underpinning and informing how these aims are achieved.[84] There is,

78 Andrew Ashworth and Lucia Zedner, *Preventative Justice* (OUP 2014).

79 Mike Redmayne, 'Theorizing the Criminal Trial' (2009) 12(2) New Criminal Law Review 287, 289.

80 Redmayne (n 79) 313.

81 Antony Duff and others, *The Trial on Trial 3: Towards a Normative Theory of the Criminal Trial* (Hart Publishing 2007) 5.

82 Ian Dennis, 'Reconstructing the Law of Criminal Evidence' (1989) 42(1) Current Legal Problems 21, 31.

83 Andrew Ashworth, *Sentencing and Criminal Justice* (5th edn, CUP 2010) 71.

84 Andrew Ashworth, Liz Campbell and Mike Redmayne, *The Criminal Process* (5th edn, OUP 2019) 346.

however, considerable overlap and intertwining between these aims and values.[85] For example, it may be thought that the right of participation at trial facilitates the aim of truth-finding but participation is in itself a value that is considered desirable.[86] Equally, Owusu-Bempah[87] argues that commitment to some values can act as a 'constraint' on achieving broader aims, whereas Ashworth et al. suggest that values mould how these ends may be achieved.[88] Examining these aims and values can help us more broadly locate the intermediary within the criminal trial and the criminal justice system. They can also shape our understanding of the trial for witnesses and defendants, even though their substance may differ.[89]

It is possible to view the trial as a purely instrumental process that identifies offenders and offers a range of measures to reduce the risk of further damage to society.[90] This position regards the trial as serving the state's punitive aims by identifying those liable for punishment.[91] A system that encourages guilty pleas, for example, could be viewed as serving the purpose of the trial as culpable individuals are identified and rendered liable to punishment.[92] From another instrumentalist viewpoint, the trial is concerned solely with accurate fact-finding, with other values being unable to outweigh the strong emphasis on a search for the truth.[93] However, there is broad agreement that the criminal trial is not reducible to a mere instrumental process and has intrinsic values.[94] As Redmayne contends, the more difficult question, on which there is less agreement, relates to other, perhaps less instrumental, aims of the criminal trial.[95] This could include moral engagement with the defendant or even the cathartic effect of contested issues being resolved.[96] The aims and values in this section are not presented as exhaustive – but provide an opportunity to examine how the intermediary impacts and is impacted by different conceptions of the trial.

85 Masha Fedorova, *The Principle of Equality of Arms in International Criminal Proceedings* (Intersentia 2012) 70.
86 Fedorova (n 85) 72.
87 Owusu-Bempah (n 19) 22.
88 Ashworth and others (n 84) 28.
89 Home Office, *Rebalancing the Criminal Justice System in Favour of the Law Abiding Majority* (2006).
90 Antony Duff, *Trials and Punishments* (CUP 1986).
91 Antony Duff, *The Realm of Criminal Law* (OUP 2018) 31.
92 Duff (n 91) 31.
93 Larry Lauden, *Truth, Error and Criminal Law: An Essay in Legal Epistemology* (CUP 2006).
94 Ashworth and others (n 84) 322; Duff and others (n 3) 94.
95 Redmayne (n 79) 322.
96 Duff and others (n 3) 53.

4.4.1 Calling the accused to account

Duff et al. view the trial as a 'communicative process' in which the accused is 'called to account' by the state for the public to answer allegations of wrongdoing.[97] The trial must communicate and justify that judgment – to demonstrate its justice – to the defendant and others.[98] At first sight, there is obvious resonance between the intermediary function of communication facilitation and the centrality of communication in Duff et al.'s trial account. In practice, however, the 'rationing' of intermediaries (see Chapter 1: Introduction) for defendants may prevent the accused from addressing the allegations against them and being responsive to a communicative dialogue.[99] There are other challenges within the communicative account. As Lacey notes, the communicative theory places so much store on shared membership of a political community and some individuals will fall outside its scope.[100] This is a valid criticism, and those who require intermediary assistance are invariably vulnerable and often unlikely to be responsive to a communicative dialogue.[101] How the intermediary role may contribute towards this communicative process, or may even prompt a reconsideration of it, informs the analysis which develops later in the book.

4.4.2 Accurate fact-finding

Ashworth et al. advocate a theory of criminal procedure that is trial-centred.[102] Their account is underpinned by the twin goals of 'regulating the processes for bringing suspected offenders to trial to produce accurate determinations, and . . . ensuring that fundamental rights are protected in those processes'.[103] The authors caution against an overly simplistic, diagnostic conception of the trial; they view accurate determinations as a key aspiration of the trial process.[104] Importantly, they view the preparation of cases for *possible* trial as the principal objective of the investigative and pre-trial stages. The aims of the trial, according to Ashworth et al., cannot be examined in isolation. Their account interweaves these aims with the trial's underpinning values seamlessly so that the two must be considered together. For example, a court may reach an accurate verdict (accuracy being a potential trial aim), but all

97 Duff and others (n 3) 53.
98 Duff (n 90) 115.
99 Laura Hoyano and Angela Rafferty QC, 'Rationing Defence Intermediaries under the April 2016 Criminal Practice Direction' (2017) Criminal Law Review 90.
100 Nicola Lacey, 'Punishment, Communication and Community' (2002) 111(442) Mind: A Quarterly Review of Philosophy 392, 395.
101 Antony Duff, *Punishment, Communication and Community* (OUP 2001) 110.
102 Ashworth and others (n 84) 345.
103 Ashworth and others (n 84) 49.
104 Ashworth and others (n 84) 345.

actors involved must be treated with dignity and respect (these both being potential trial values). Another example is the overlap between the potential aim of accuracy and the value of participation. As noted earlier, courts are required to take 'every reasonable step' to facilitate the participation of any person, including the defendant.[105] It intuitively follows that the participation of both witnesses and defendants within the trial incorporates the ability to provide good quality evidence which can contribute towards the accuracy of verdicts.[106] As will be discussed throughout the book, and focused on in Chapter 7 (Witness work, defendant work and participatory roles), intermediaries are often central to the participation of vulnerable individuals throughout the criminal process but perhaps most visibly at the trial. Further, an application for a Registered Intermediary may be made where it is considered that their use is likely to improve the quality (completeness, coherence and accuracy) of the evidence given by the witness.[107] These examples suggest that there need not be a trade-off between the aims and values of the trial and indeed the intermediary can be instrumental to both. Although McEwan laments the possibility of a 'contest' between fair trial rights of the accused and accurate fact-finding, it is not obvious that the intermediary represents a threat to either of these.[108]

4.4.3 Conflict resolution

A third potential trial aim/value is conflict resolution. This may be linked to accurate fact-finding, in that one way that a conflict can be resolved is through a determination of facts.[109] Even so, conflict resolution may be considered a trial aim/value in its own right. When the conflict arising from the alleged commission of a criminal offence is resolved, finality and closure can be achieved.[110] The intermediary role, whether working with witnesses or defendants, plays no direct role in resolving conflicts between the state and the accused. For example, the neutrality of the intermediary means it ought not to have any direct input into the decision of an accused to plead guilty. Chapter 6 (The neutrality paradox) explores how intermediaries sometimes tread a fine line between the facilitation of communication and upholding their neutral stance. However, there are ways in which the role may contribute to conflict resolution. The intermediary aids the vulnerable individual to provide testimony which is often vital to the operation and conclusion of the

105 CPD (n 32) and CPR (n 36).
106 Abenaa Owusu-Bempah, 'The Interpretation and Application of the Right to Effective Participation' (2018) 22(4) International Journal of Evidence and Proof 321, 327.
107 YJCEA, s.16(5) and Criminal Evidence (Northern Ireland) Order 1999, art 17.
108 McEwan (n 16).
109 Owusu-Bempah (n 73) 20.
110 Owusu-Bempah (n 73) 20.

trial process. As will be explored further in Chapter 7 (Witness work, defendant work and participatory roles), intermediaries sometimes play a key role in ensuring that an accused understands the evidence against them prior to trial. Occasionally, this can dispense with the need for a trial if there is a resulting guilty plea which assists the resolution of proceedings.[111] The practice of plea bargaining is recognised as a form of dispute resolution within trial proceedings, notwithstanding concerns that there is a fundamental asymmetry between the parties involved.[112] Conversely, an intermediary may slow the progress of a trial if there is a judicial direction to review counsel's questions, recommendations for a slower pace of questioning and/or interventions during witness examination. However, if the intermediary's input assists the production of the witness' best evidence, then any delays to conflict resolution are arguably justified as a more legitimate trial outcome can be reached.[113]

4.4.4 *Legitimacy*

The concept of legitimacy lies at the heart of the criminal justice system.[114] For criminal justice institutions to operate effectively they must hold legitimate authority in the eyes of those they serve.[115] Although the scope of the term is complex and contested, there is general agreement that institutions must be perceived as legitimate by citizens in order to maintain a valid claim on authority.[116] Legitimacy may also be conceptualised as a trial aim with instrumental value, i.e. the need to produce legitimate outcomes and have acceptable processes. This is linked to procedural justice theory and the imperative that the trial commands legitimacy in the eyes of the public.[117] The value of legitimacy is useful for the present enquiry for several reasons. Firstly, because the legitimacy of criminal justice is so intrinsically connected to the perceptions of individuals who engage with it, it is suitable for empirical enquiry.[118] How intermediaries experience the social world of the criminal justice system, and understand the nature and value of their role,

111 As is made clear in Chapter 7 (Witness work, defendant work and participatory roles), this should be a free choice informed by proper legal advice.

112 Michael O'Hear, 'Dispute Resolution in Criminal Law' (2007) 91(1) Marquette Law Review 1.

113 Ian Dennis, *The Law of Evidence* (5th edn, Sweet & Maxwell 2013) 51–56.

114 Adam Crawford and Anthea Hucklesby, *Legitimacy and Compliance in Criminal Justice* (Routledge 2013) 1.

115 Anthony Bottoms and Justice Tankebe, 'Beyond Procedural Justice: A Dialogic Approach to Legitimacy in Criminal Justice' (2013) 102(1) Journal of Criminal Law and Criminology 119.

116 Bottoms and Tankebe (n 115).

117 Mike Hough and others, 'Procedural Justice, Trust and Institutional Legitimacy' (2010) 4(3) Policing: A Journal of Policy and Practice 203.

118 Crawford and Hucklesby (n 114).

is pivotal to answering the research underpinning this book. A second reason is that legitimacy is generated and sustained at the interactional level by criminal justice actors, and the intermediary has a role to play in maintaining legitimacy through their everyday practices.[119] Roberts and Plesničar suggest that perceptions of legitimacy are shaped by contact with criminal justice professionals which 'colour perceptions of the whole system'.[120] Legitimacy, therefore, is continually 'cultivated' through the actions of these actors in how they present themselves, communicate and engage with others.[121]

How does the intermediary cultivate legitimacy? One might question the ability of the intermediary – an outsider to the professionalised world of the criminal justice system – to impact the legitimacy of the trial process. Based on Becker's 'hierarchy of credibility', it may be assumed that intermediaries are poorly positioned to do so.[122] The recent work of Jacobson et al., which investigates perceptions of legitimacy among Crown Court users, suggests the opposite. The authors identify five inter-related dimensions which affect legitimacy: moral alignment, positive outcomes, fair decisions, respectful treatment and passive acceptance.[123] While there are broad differences between court users regarding how legitimacy is perceived, the intermediary may positively impact each dimension to varying degrees. Jacobson et al. found that court users had a stronger belief in the legitimacy of the court process when it was viewed as a 'fair process' and they were individually 'treated with humanity . . . consideration and respect'.[124] In relation to witnesses and complainants, the intermediary's status as one of the YJCEA's special measures is key.[125] The special measures were implemented with the twin concern of enabling the production of best evidence and reducing the stress associated with live testimony, but they have also 'increase[d] the standing of victims and witnesses within the court process'.[126]

In more concrete terms, there is ample evidence that intermediaries contribute to improved experiences for vulnerable witnesses. Plotnikoff and Woolfson's empirical work has documented countless examples of Registered

119 Sharyn Roach Anleu and Kathy Mack, *Performing Judicial Authority in the Lower Courts* (Palgrave Macmillan 2017) 155.
120 Julian Roberts and Mojca Plesničar, 'Sentencing, Legitimacy, and Public Opinion' in Justice Tankebe and Gorazd Meško (eds), *Trust and Legitimacy* in *Criminal Justice: European Perspectives* (Springer 2015) 33.
121 Roach Anleu and Mack (n 119) 164.
122 Howard Becker, 'Whose Side Are We On?' (1967) 14(3) Social Problems 239, 242.
123 Jessica Jacobson, Gillian Hunter and Amy Kirby, *Inside Crown Court: Personal Experiences and Questions of Legitimacy* (Policy Press 2016) 166.
124 Jacobson, Hunter and Kirby (n 123) 184.
125 Carolyn Hoyle and Lucia Zedner, 'Victims, Victimisation and Criminal Justice' in Mike Maguire, Rod Morgan and Robert Reiner (eds), *Oxford Handbook of Criminology* (4th edn, OUP 2007) 468–70.
126 Jacobson, Hunter and Kirby (n 123) 36.

Intermediaries enabling witnesses to make informed choices, helping to familiarise witnesses with the court environment and improving interactions with court professionals.[127] While a rich discussion of legitimacy is beyond the scope of this section, we can make a simple yet important observation at this stage: intermediaries are demonstrably effective in making the criminal justice system more accessible and navigable for many vulnerable individuals. Considering that disengagement and dissatisfaction with criminal justice processes are symptoms of illegitimacy, intermediaries have the potential to act as a legitimising tool at the coalface of the criminal process.[128]

The legitimacy of the trial depends not only on concern for the welfare of court users – it must also involve granting proper access to proceedings and ensuring individuals are, as far as possible, treated as valued participants.[129] The trend towards bureaucratic efficiency in criminal justice raises questions about access to justice and may undermine due process principles.[130] The fair treatment of the accused seems central to this debate, and Carlen and McBarnet have written about the marginalisation of the defendant throughout criminal proceedings.[131] When considering Jacobson et al.'s framework, the dimensions of 'moral alignment' and 'passive acceptance' are primarily concerned with the position of the accused. The authors use the term 'passive acceptance' to describe a general malaise among defendants regarding their situation, their disengagement with the court process and also a 'profound sense of powerlessness'.[132] This resonates with Carlen's concept of the defendant as a 'dummy player', and Jacobson et al. link the silencing of the defendant with a diminishing perception of legitimacy.[133] Returning to potential trial aims, the manner in which a dispute is resolved through the trial reflects the importance attached to its underpinning values. Therefore, the trial as a mechanism for conflict resolution is more legitimate when the accused is treated as an autonomous, right-bearing subject (see later in this chapter for further discussion of autonomy and participation as trial values).

As will be developed in subsequent chapters, intermediaries often view themselves as enabling the accused to engage with proceedings and offering

127 Plotnikoff and Woolfson (n 41).

128 Tom R Tyler and others, 'Legitimacy and Criminal Justice: International Perspective' in *Legitimacy and Criminal Justice: International Perspectives* (Russell Sage Foundation) 9.

129 Nina Peršak, 'Procedural Justice Elements of Judicial Legitimacy and Their Contemporary Challenges' (2016) 6(3) Oñati Socio-legal Series 749, 757.

130 Jennifer Ward, *Transforming Summary Justice: Modernisation in the Lower Criminal Courts* (Routledge 2017) 7.

131 Pat Carlen, *Magistrates Justice* (Wiley-Blackwell 1976); Doreen McBarnet, *Conviction: Law, the State and the Construction of Justice* (Macmillan 1981).

132 Jacobson, Hunter and Kirby (n 123) 196.

133 Carlen (n 131).

them a voice. By doing so, intermediaries can empower the accused to participate and, consequently, help foster a belief in the legitimacy of a process which may ultimately impose coercive sanctions.[134] This is closely linked to the assumption that legitimate criminal procedures offer a fair adjudicative forum.[135] Backen has noted that vulnerable defendants tend to view proceedings as broadly fairer when an intermediary is present to facilitate communication – procedural fairness being a crucial element in building trust in the trial process.[136] The dimension of moral alignment, whilst multifaceted, is concerned with understanding the authority of the trial and believing this authority is justified.[137] It is important to stress that the normative parameters of the intermediary role do not extend to ensuring defendants are invested in concepts of justice or morality. However, the intermediary will often prove crucial to a defendant understanding the charges and what consequences may flow from a finding of guilt. Any prospect of a defendant feeling morally aligned with the values of the criminal trial are surely predicated on a basic understanding of the process which threatens censure.

To conclude, we should reconsider the rationale for the introduction of the intermediary into the criminal trial. As Ellison notes, the limited approach of the adversarial trial in merely 'accommodating' vulnerable witnesses was deemed inadequate and ultimately led to the special measures contained within the YJCEA.[138] While the special measures regime is underpinned by the twin aims of securing best evidence and reducing the stress of testimony, its introduction can be seen as part of a broader attempt to address a legitimacy deficit within the trial. Legislative intervention was deemed necessary 'to maintain public confidence in the administration of justice' and the adversarial model not only had a welfare problem, but also one of legitimacy.[139] Whether the YJCEA satisfactorily addresses the needs, aspirations, expectations, interests, rights and emotions of vulnerable individuals is arguably less important than recognition of these values and steps taken to accommodate

134 Jacobson, Hunter and Kirby (n 123) 199; Kenneth Einar Himma, *Coercion and the Nature of Law* (OUP 2020) 68.

135 Kate Leader, 'The Trial's the Thing: Performance and Legitimacy in International Criminal Trials' (2020) 24(2) Theoretical Criminology 241 (2020).

136 Paula Backen, *They Just Don't Get It: Communication and the Work of an Intermediary with Vulnerable People in the Justice System* (independently published 2017) 181; Crawford and Hucklesby (n 114) 23.

137 Mike Hough, Jonathan Jackson and Ben Bradford, 'Trust in Justice and the Legitimacy of Legal Authorities: Topline Findings from a European Comparative Study' in Sophie Body-Gendrot and others (eds), *The Routledge Handbook of European Criminology* (Routledge 2013) 243.

138 Ellison (n 27) 60.

139 Diane Birch, 'A Better Deal for Vulnerable Witnesses?' (2000) Criminal Law Review 223, 226.

them.[140] The intermediary thus represents a desire to ameliorate systemic communication deficiencies and, consequently, foster legitimacy. When the criminal process struggles to generate legitimacy, it may delegate to other actors to do so. As a new criminal justice actor, the intermediary has been delegated the task of facilitating communication by a system that has historically struggled to accommodate vulnerable court users. The trial only amounts to a legitimate communicative enterprise if it seeks to individually engage citizens rather than treat them as a monolith. This reiterates the centrality of communication within the trial, since a procedure that does not adequately communicate *with* and allow communication *from* the accused generates legal uncertainty.[141]

4.4.5 Autonomy

The concept of autonomy is difficult to define and is presented differently depending on the context. Duff et al. contend that the term has been 'put to such diverse uses, with such vague or varying meanings . . . that its utility must now be in doubt'.[142] For example, in American jurisprudence the term has often been used in relation to the accused's control of their own case.[143] Duff's 'moral good' theory justifies offender punishment based on respect for individual rationality and autonomy. Most accounts of the criminal process recognise that respect for the individual requires criminal procedure to respect the autonomy, dignity and liberty of the human person. These values are closely linked and, as such, are often considered complementary. Thus, we can say that *dignity* requires a recognition of the intrinsic worth of every individual, that this includes being treated as a self-governing *autonomous* individual who should be at liberty to make choices, *free* of external interference.[144]

At first sight, the role of the intermediary in giving effect to values such as dignity and autonomy seems straightforward. Better treatment of vulnerable individuals lies at the heart of the special measures regime and is recognised as 'a barometer of our moral worth as a society'.[145] Explaining the introduction of the special measures regime to the House of Commons, then

140 Jean-Marc Coicaud, 'Crime, Justice and Legitimacy: A Brief Theoretical Inquiry' in Justice Tankebe and Alison Liebling (eds), *Legitimacy and Criminal Justice: An International Exploration* (OUP 2013) 37.

141 Mireille Hildebrandt, 'Trial and 'Fair Trial': From Peer to Subject to Citizen' in Antony Duff and others (eds), *The Trial on Trial 2: Truth and Due Process* (Hart Publishing 2006) 225.

142 Duff et al. (n 81) 130.

143 Erica Hashimoto, 'Resurrecting Autonomy: The Criminal Defendant's Right to Control the Case' (2010) 90 Boston University Law Review 1147.

144 Owusu-Bempah (n 73) 10.

145 Jacqueline Wheatcroft, 'Witness Assistance and Familiarisation in England and Wales: The Right to Challenge' (2017) 21(1/2) International Journal of Evidence and Proof 158.

Home Secretary Jack Straw spoke of the need to re-establish 'proper dignity and respect' for vulnerable witnesses.[146] By acting as a communication facilitator, the intermediary provides a voice to individuals who otherwise may not be able to participate in proceedings. Furthermore, an intermediary's involvement in assessing the vulnerable person and creating individualised recommendations to the court is recognition of the human condition. It also recognises the person as capable of autonomy and personhood.[147] The utility of autonomy as a value in the present enquiry is twofold: firstly, we can examine how the intermediary role operates to ensure individuals are treated as autonomous agents within the trial, and secondly, we can better understand the nature and scope of the intermediary role itself.

It is useful to reconsider the basis of intermediary involvement with both witnesses and defendants. When assessing a vulnerable witness, a Registered Intermediary is principally concerned with whether their involvement is 'likely to improve the completeness, coherence and accuracy of the witness's evidence'.[148] However, another important element of the intermediary role involves first assessing whether the vulnerable individual is *capable* of communicating their evidence to the court.[149] The language employed here relates to witness competency and the intermediary will often be central to facilitating an otherwise incompetent witness to give evidence.[150] In *R v Watts*, the Court of Appeal held that the competency test is satisfied if the witness is able to 'understand the question put to him (or her) and give answers to them which can be understood'.[151] This definition mirrors the statutory definition of the intermediary's function almost word for word.[152]

Although the term autonomy rarely appears in the literature relating to intermediaries or special measures more generally, there is scope for consideration of its use and potential overlap with competency. For example, Christman and Anderson consider autonomy to focus on *competent* self-direction or, in other words, self-governance.[153] Dubber considers the ability to understand and answer questions as an example of 'active autonomy' exercised by a free, autonomous citizen.[154] He claims that autonomy and competency are not mere synonyms, but rather that competency is a

146 Youth Justice and Criminal Evidence Bill, 15 April 1999, Col 385.

147 Markus Dirk Dubber, 'The Criminal Trial and the Legitimation of Punishment' in Duff and others (n 3) 85.

148 MoJ (n 39).

149 MoJ (n 39).

150 Judicial College, *Equal Treatment Bench Book February 2024 Edition* (July 2024) 35.

151 [2010] EWCA Crim 1824 [18]. This is also set out in s.53 of the YJCEA.

152 YCJEA, s.29.

153 John Christman and Joel Anderson, *Autonomy and the Challenges to Liberalism* (CUP 2009) 110.

154 Dubber (n 147). Dubber goes on to discuss 'active' and 'passive' autonomy with specific relevance to the defendant, but the ability to understand and respond to questions applies to both witnesses and defendants.

pre-requisite to recognising autonomy. An incompetent witness, he argues, cannot exercise autonomy at all.[155] Despite their close association with the concept of competency, intermediaries are prohibited from commenting on whether a witness is competent to give evidence, which is determined by the court.[156] Since this restriction is based on concerns for the role's impartiality, the lack of definitional precision surrounding the term autonomy also raises potential issues. For example, if witness autonomy includes concerns for welfare and emotional wellbeing, then the boundaries of the intermediary's neutrality may become blurred.

The significant proportion of intermediary cases involving child witnesses deserves attention when considering the value of autonomy. Hollingsworth notes that the legal system does not consider children fully autonomous rights holders.[157] She argues for a relational approach which highlights the importance of childhood experiences and relationships and is consistent with respect for individual agency. Reflecting on this, we may ask whether, and to what extent, intermediaries consider issues of autonomy when assessing young witnesses and how the role impacts autonomy through the facilitation of communication. The potential for blurred lines between competence and autonomy becomes apparent here and raises issues relating to the intermediary's neutrality. The conceptualisation of the role as an objective communication conduit resonates with the requirement that it takes no position on witness competency. However, this presupposes that the intermediary assesses communication mechanically, without regard for context or circumstances. In other words, the ability of the child to understand questions and give coherent answers is of sole importance. As will be explored later in the book, the notion of intermediaries assessing communication in such a vacuum is a fallacy. Intermediaries are encouraged to gain some understanding of the evidential matrix in a case, particularly involving child witnesses and sexual abuse allegations, to avoid mentioning potential suspects during assessment. In such examples, how is the intermediary expected to assess a child without consideration of their welfare, emotional wellbeing and potential for re-traumatisation? If the child is competent to provide testimony, but court examination may adversely affect him, should the child's entitlement to be treated as an autonomous agent be denied? These issues implicate a broad range of considerations, including the dignity and autonomy of the child, and go beyond the characterisation of competence as a mere 'gateway' to

155 Dubber (n 147).

156 YJCEA, s.53; The Advocate's Gateway, 'Intermediaries: Step by Step' (Toolkit 16, 2 September 2019) <https://www.theadvocatesgateway.org/_files/ugd/1074f0_5ceb5d236c6b488e97d2cbbfbdd3cf06.pdf> accessed 12 February 2025.

157 Katherine Hollingsworth, 'Theorising Children's Rights in Youth Justice: The Significance of Autonomy and Foundational Rights' (2013) 76(6) Modern Law Review 1046.

autonomy.[158] In reality, the two are intrinsically linked and should inform a broader discussion about the normative expectations of the role.

We now consider the autonomy of the accused. Many authors view respect for the accused's autonomy as central to a fair, just and legitimate criminal trial. For example, Owusu-Bempah argues that if defendants are to be treated as free, autonomous and dignified citizens of a liberal democracy, they must be able to choose whether or not to actively participate in criminal proceedings.[159] McEwan and Dubber argue that the defendant must be treated as self-governing with autonomy operating as a fundamental trial value.[160] Other authors consider the focus on the value of autonomy as misguided. Toone doubts the trial's ability to recognise the accused as an autonomous agent and describes the sustained academic attention on autonomy as 'a rhetorical flourish that sidesteps more difficult questions about inequality and injustice in the criminal justice system'.[161] Similarly, Duff et al. eschew the use of the term and prefer to focus on the concept of 'responsible citizenship' to explain their normative theory.[162]

In line with Kantian principles, the defendant deserves to be treated as an autonomous, right-bearing subject within the criminal trial.[163] But what is the intermediary's role in upholding these values? Just as with witnesses, the intermediary will often enable a vulnerable accused to give evidence when they may otherwise be unable to. The basis of defendant intermediary appointments and how they differ from witnesses is key: vulnerable defendants may benefit from intermediary assistance to enable their *effective participation* in proceedings. This reflects the position that defendants enjoy procedural rights which have not been extended to complainants and witnesses.[164] Developing a more nuanced understanding of trial values, it becomes clear that autonomy is closely aligned with the value of participation. Within the criminal trial, respect for the accused as an autonomous agent rests primarily on their freedom to choose whether to actively respond to allegations. The principles of dignity, autonomy and freedom dictate that the defendant should, at least,

158 Aoife Daly, 'Assessing Children's Capacity: Reconceptualising our Understanding through the UN Convention on the Rights of the Child' (2020) 28(3) International Journal of Children's Rights 471, 482.

159 Daly (n 158) 55.

160 McEwan (n 16); Dubber (n 147).

161 Robert Toone, 'The Incoherence of Defendant Autonomy' (2005) 83(3) North Carolina Law Review 621, 623.

162 Duff and others (n 81) 130.

163 Immanuel Kant, *Groundwork of the Metaphysics of Morals* (CUP 1996).

164 Owusu-Bempah (n 73) 28; Ernestine Henriëtte Hoegen and Marion Eleonora Ingeborg Brienen, *Victims of Crime in 22 European Criminal Justice Systems: The Implementation of Recommendation (85) 11 of the Council of Europe on the Position of the Victim in the Framework of Criminal Law and Procedure* (Wolf Legal Productions 2000); Toone (n 161).

be able to choose whether to actively participate and how to conduct their defence and be enabled to do so effectively.[165]

Even where the accused exercises their autonomy or freedom to *not* actively participate, the trial aims may still be achieved. For example, conflict resolution can be achieved through either the participation of the accused's legal representatives or by putting the prosecution to proof.[166] It is also important to recognise that autonomy is not simply a matter of comprehension but also relates to the ability to make evaluative judgements. As Arthur argues, this includes making decisions and engaging in practical reasoning.[167] This requires the combination of cognitive ability (to understand the nature and likely consequences of an action) and the evaluative ability to appraise the action and consequences considering the decision-maker's own preferences, desires, goals, values and standards.[168] As such, the defendant's enhanced participatory role in the criminal trial illuminates our understanding of autonomy. The following section, which focuses on the value of participation, develops this discussion further.

4.4.6 Participation

Participation is regarded as a 'core element of procedural and substantive justice and of legal values embedded in legal rules'.[169] Participation impacts legitimacy – a transparent and participatory model of criminal justice can foster trust in criminal justice procedures and bridge the gulf between perceived 'insiders' of the system and the general public.[170] By asking what it means to participate, we can begin to conceptualise the different participatory roles that exist within the trial. For example, the term 'lay participation' has been commonly used to mean lay adjudication in the form of the

165 Owusu-Bempah (n 19) 182.
166 Owusu-Bempah (n 19) 21.
167 Raymond Arthur, 'Giving Effect to Young People's Right to Effectively Participate in Criminal Proceedings' (2016) 28(3) Child and Family Law Quarterly 223.
168 Arthur (n 167).
169 Grainne McKeever, 'Comparing Courts and Tribunals through the Lens of Participation' (2020) 38(3) Civil Justice Quarterly 217, 228; Jessica Jacobson and Penny Cooper, *Participation in Courts and Tribunals* (Bristol UP 2020) 1. It is also worth noting that participation is emerging as an international trial norm irrespective of procedural tradition, see: John Jackson and Sarah Summers, *The Internationalisation of Criminal Evidence: Beyond the Common Law and Civil Law Traditions* (CUP 2012).
170 Stephanos Bibas, 'Transparency and Participation in Criminal Procedure' (2006) 81(3) New York University Law Review 911; Abenaa Owusu-Bempah, 'Understanding the Barriers to Defendant Participation in Criminal Proceedings in England and Wales' (2020) 40(4) Legal Studies 69; Duff and others (n 3) 21.

jury as a decision-making body.[171] There is, however, growing recognition that lay participation also includes complainants, witnesses and defendants. It is widely accepted that complainants and witnesses should be supported, informed and treated with respect and dignity. Still, reforms in England and Wales have not yet granted them a set of procedural rights, including participatory rights, along the same lines as the defendant.[172] For example, neither witnesses nor complainants enjoy a right to be present during the trial, to question witnesses, present evidence or to legal representation.[173] Chapter 7 (Witness work, defendant work and participatory roles) examines the different participatory entitlements of defendants and non-defendants and demonstrates how these are reflected through the work of registered and non-registered intermediaries.

The question of non-defendant participation goes to the heart of how we conceptualise the trial as an institution.[174] On the face of it, vulnerable witnesses are not eligible for intermediary assistance based on concerns about their participation. Instead, they are solely eligible for assistance by virtue of being under 18 or if the court considers that the quality of their evidence will likely be diminished.[175] It is striking that in the Registered Intermediary Procedural Guidance Manual there is zero reference to the participation of a vulnerable witness. This contrasts with the use of intermediaries in the family courts where the role's value as an 'enabler' of participation has been acknowledged.[176] As per the CPD, courts must take 'every reasonable step' to facilitate the participation of *all* individuals within proceedings, including witnesses.[177] This can, of course, include the appointment of an intermediary for a vulnerable witness.

Plotnikoff and Woolfson found that the 'every reasonable step' requirement often allows intermediaries to make innovative recommendations to enable vulnerable witnesses to participate.[178] This enables a broader degree of intermediary involvement to ensure the vulnerable individual's communication

171 Anthony Musson, 'Lay Participation: The Paradox of the Jury' (2015) 3(2) Comparative Legal History 245.

172 Owusu Bempah (n 19) 28; Hoegen and Ingeborg Brienen (n 164).

173 Jonathan Doak, *Victim's Rights, Human Rights and Criminal Justice: Reconceiving the Role of Third Parties* (Hart Publishing 2008).

174 Duff and others (n 81) 214.

175 YJCEA, s.16(a)(b).

176 *Newcastle City Council v WM and Others* [2015] EWFC 42; Penny Cooper, 'Like Ducks to Water? Intermediaries for Vulnerable Witnesses and Parties' (2016) Family Law 374.

177 CPD (n 32) [6.1.1].

178 Lexicon, 'Every Reasonable Step': A More Flexible Approach to Vulnerable Witnesses and Defendants Consolidated List of Intermediary Examples (November 2017) <https://www.intermediaries-for-justice.org/sites/default/files/consolidated-list-of-a-more-flexible-approach-november-2017.pdf> accessed 9 February 2025).

requirements are met.[179] As such, participation seems less of an outcome of the intermediary role and more of an instrument through which intermediaries can justify aspects of their work. While the legislation and procedural guidance avoid directly connecting the intermediary with the participatory role of the witness, this is unconvincing. Indeed, since a consistent definition of participation across all criminal justice actors is elusive, there is force in the argument that the intermediary should be central to its conceptualisation and application. While it is ultimately the judge's responsibility to manage proceedings and balance conflicting rights and principles, the intermediary will often play a key role in advising the court on the vulnerable individual's participatory capabilities. The extent to which this is the case and its impact on the intermediary role will be explored in later chapters.

Understandably, the defendant assumes a more central role when considering the value of participation within the trial. Questions around how the accused answers the charges brought and whether they elect to provide testimony force us to consider what participation means, why it might be normatively desirable and what instrumental value it may have for the trial's aims. As mentioned earlier, the participatory rights of defendants are much more firmly established than those of non-defendants. Fundamentally, the accused enjoys the right to be present at their own trial as well as the right of confrontation.[180] However, these rights are of limited value to the defendant if they cannot participate effectively.[181] It is a long-standing principle in criminal law that defendants must be able to understand and participate effectively in the criminal proceedings of which they are a part.[182] In *SC v U.K*, the ECtHR explained that the right 'includes, inter alia, not only the right to be present, but also to hear and follow the proceedings' and 'presupposes that the accused has a broad understanding of the nature of the trial process and of what is at stake for him or her, including the significance of any penalty which may be imposed'.[183] Chapter 7 (Witness work, defendant work and participatory roles), which focuses on participatory roles, explores how intermediaries are often central to ensuring the effective participation of the accused and how this is qualitatively different from what is termed

179 Victims' Commissioner, *A Voice for the Voiceless: The Victims' Commissioner's Review into the Provision of Registered Intermediaries for Children and Vulnerable Victims and Witnesses* (January 2018) 14.

180 The right of confrontation under Art.6 of the Convention includes the defendant's right to 'examine or have examined witnesses against him'. Also see: Elmar Widder, 'The Right to Challenge Witnesses – an Application of Strasbourg's Flexible 'Sole and Decisive' Rule to other Human Rights' (2014) 3(4) Cambridge Journal of International and Comparative Law 1084.

181 Owusu-Bempah (n 19) 609.

182 Jessica Jacobson and Jenny Talbot, *Vulnerable Defendants in the Criminal Courts: A Review of Provision for Adults and Children* (Prison Reform Trust 2009, ISBN: 0 946209 96 0) 8.

183 *SC v U.K* (2005) 40 EHRR 10 [29].

'witness work'. While it is not claimed that intermediaries unilaterally ensure the effective participation of defendants, it is clear that they can make a significant contribution through the facilitation of communication.

Returning to some of the main accounts of the trial, the value of the accused's participation is prominent. Duff recognises that while a purely instrumental trial enquiry might benefit from the defendant's engagement, their participation is valued as more than a means to an accurate verdict – it is essential to justice.[184] This resonates with the communicative account of the trial, which conceptualises it as calling the accused to account for their wrongdoing and seeks to justify the judgment to them. According to this account, not only is the defendant to be treated as an autonomous, rational moral agent deserving of a participatory role, but he owes an *obligation* to communicate and explain his conduct.[185] This has profound implications for the value of participation and its conceptualisation. Hodgson defends this account of the trial by suggesting that it respects the accused as a responsible citizen.[186] Such a suggestion is challenging, especially considering the accused's participation at the sentencing stage. Requiring an offender to offer an apology to express remorse involves expecting him to represent his own actions as wrong or morally blameworthy. As Duff admits, there is a risk that such coercion fails to respect the offender as an autonomous member of a liberal polity.[187] There are surely questions over whether the defendant's participation attains the same value if the state coerces it. At the very least, the state should *facilitate* communication between parties and the court to enable an apology to be offered.

The main difficulty with the communicative theory of the trial is that it struggles to accommodate the accused who chooses not to participate.[188] As noted earlier, a communicative dialogue is underpinned by a degree of reciprocity which is lacking when the defendant is either incapable or unwilling to engage. Conceptualising the trial as a mechanism for calling the state (rather than the defendant) to account arguably better accommodates the vulnerable defendant. Owusu-Bempah argues that if defendants are to be treated as free and dignified citizens of a liberal democracy, they must be able to choose whether to actively participate in criminal proceedings.[189] This account focuses on 'active' participation which involves 'mental effort or voluntary physical movement on the part of the defendant'.[190] A relevant consideration within this discussion is the role of the defence counsel, who

184 Duff (n 101) 115.
185 Duff and others (n 81) 207.
186 Jacqueline Hodgson, *French Criminal Justice* (Hart Publishing 2005) 21.
187 Duff (n 90) 110.
188 Owusu-Bempah (n 19) 54.
189 Owusu-Bempah (n 19) 55.
190 Owusu-Bempah (n 19) 2.

Duff argues may help 'secure' the defendant's participation.[191] Duff suggests that in some circumstances, participation by the defendant might be *more* effectively secured by communicating through counsel rather than in his own voice.[192] It is interesting to consider how Duff would envisage the intermediary fitting into this model and whether the role may also be capable of 'securing' the defendant's participation. Of course, central to Duff's position is that defence counsel represents the accused and scrutinises the prosecution case on their behalf. Thus, a defendant who is incapable of following proceedings may effectively participate if their legal representation has tested the prosecution evidence and satisfactorily represented the accused's position. The intermediary's position is different for two main reasons. Firstly, the intermediary is not a representative of the vulnerable accused. Depending on the terms of the appointment, the intermediary may only assist for the period of testimony which may be too peripheral to 'secure' participation in Duff's terms. Secondly, unlike the lawyer in Duff's account, the intermediary cannot prioritise participation over communication. While effectively facilitating communication will often lead to enhanced defendant participation, the end does not necessarily justify the means. However, this reveals a paradox within the intermediary role's praxis: while judges may only appoint a defendant intermediary to ensure effective participation, the role itself is not principally concerned with this right unlike the accused's lawyer who may exercise it by proxy.

We should consider the defendant's participation in trial proceedings based on his position as a self-governing, autonomous agent. This view is represented by Owusu-Bempah's normative account of the criminal process, which calls for recognising the accused's right to follow proceedings based on respect for individual autonomy.[193] Intermediaries will often be central to this value being protected. In Northern Ireland, the role of the court defendant supporter plainly aids participation since the accused can better understand and follow proceedings. There are legitimate questions about whether a defendant with complex communication needs can effectively participate without intermediary assistance for the duration of his trial. The decision of the Divisional Court in *OP* is disappointing as it expressly prioritises the defendant's participation during oral examination.[194] The upshot of this is that the mental effort required to follow the trial and understand proceedings from the dock is treated as a lesser form of participation. By holding that 'an adult with experience of life and the cast of mind apt to facilitate

191 Duff and others (n 81) 211.
192 Duff and others (n 81) 211.
193 Owusu-Bempah (n 19) 182.
194 *OP v Secretary of State for Justice* [2014] EWHC 1944 (Admin) [41].

comprehension' can essentially substitute for the intermediary when the defendant is not giving evidence, the Divisional Court tacitly recognised as much.[195]

Finally, it must be desirable that the defendant's right to hear and follow proceedings cannot be exercised by proxy through an intermediary. Such an instrumental conception of the intermediary role risks prioritising the achievement of trial aims, such as accurate fact-finding and conflict resolution, over respect for the accused's autonomy. Unfortunately, the right to effective participation does not require that the accused should understand or be capable of understanding every point of law or evidential detail, given the right to legal representation.[196] While this may be impossible to realise in practice, the courts have gone too far in suggesting that the defendant does not need to hear/follow proceedings if a lawyer can do it for them.[197] Where autonomy and participation of defendants (and other laypeople) are valued, legal representation cannot be viewed as a panacea to participation issues. As will be explored in Chapter 7 (Witness work, defendant work and participatory roles), the scope of intermediary involvement with vulnerable defendants suggests that defence legal representatives are poorly equipped to unilaterally 'secure' the right to effective participation. A key question, which is explored in later chapters, is where the intermediary fits into this participation equation and how a multifaceted conception of participation accommodates the role.

4.5 Conclusion

This chapter has examined the intermediary role alongside some of the potential aims and values of the criminal trial. The trial acts as a useful point of reference for examining the intermediary's work and its relationships with other criminal justice actors. As the 'focal point of the criminal process', the trial invariably reflects the criminal justice system's overarching aims and underpinning values.[198] This should not, however, diminish the importance of intermediary work at other stages, such as the police station and locations where assessments take place. Indeed, later chapters argue strongly for extending intermediary provision to earlier stages of the criminal process as well as the sentencing stage.

Theorisation of the trial must be viewed against the shifting emphasis towards what has been termed 'modified adversarialism' and the intermediary as a special measure is symptomatic of this shift. Regarding the various

195 *OP v Secretary of State for Justice* (n 194) [35].
196 Owusu-Bempah (n 19) 71.
197 As suggested in *Stanford v U.K* App no 16757/90 (ECHR, 23 February 1994).
198 Ashworth and others (n 84) 345.

normative accounts of the trial, it is too simplistic to assume that one neatly accommodates the intermediary role. Instead, it is more accurate to say that aspects of different accounts resonate with the role and its work. We have seen how legitimacy, autonomy and participation intertwine with the objectives of ensuring accurate verdicts are reached, conflicts are resolved and the defendant is held accountable.[199] It seems clear that the intermediary role has the potential to positively impact these aims and values when working with both witnesses and defendants. The legitimacy of the trial as an institution is strengthened if individuals are treated with dignity, as autonomous agents, whether they choose to participate. Since the intermediary role operates entirely at the direction of the judge and is more broadly constrained by resource limitations, there is a risk that its full utility is not realised. These themes, which thread throughout the book, are important since they impact the scope and nature of the intermediary role and its ability to generate legitimacy and professional recognition.

Finally, an important issue, which is beyond the scope of this research, is how respect for the values discussed in this chapter is apportioned between witnesses and defendants and how this impacts our broader view of the trial as an institution. This can only be adequately achieved by the development of a normative framework which clearly articulates the relationship between trial aims and values.[200] The present chapter does preparatory work for further theorising of the trial by casting the intermediary in a role which can (potentially) further its broad aims and values. While a grounded theory of the intermediary role is generated and explained in later chapters, the present chapter lays some theoretical foundation and informs the analysis of the empirical evidence.

199 Ashworth and others (n 84) 346.
200 Duff and others (n 3) 7.

Chapter 5

Professional work – jurisdictions and boundary work

5.1 Introduction

Twenty-five years after their introduction through the Youth Justice and Criminal Evidence Act 1999 (YJCEA), intermediaries are increasingly visible throughout the criminal justice system in England and Wales and Northern Ireland.[1] The nature of intermediary work involves interaction with numerous actors, including the police, lawyers and the judiciary. Despite the differences between these established actors, in terms of responsibilities and status, they share one commonality: all are traditionally considered to be 'professionals'. Definitions of what constitutes a 'professional' vary widely but have tended to centre on traits such as high levels of skill, a recognised body of knowledge and the existence of an organising body.[2] Scholars have tended to view the 'professionalisation' of the criminal justice system as an incremental process with various roles identified by government as requiring greater accountability, modernisation and improved efficiency.[3] Individual criminal justice roles have taken steps towards professionalisation at different points and to varying degrees.[4] For example, the push towards professionalisation of the police has been well documented[5] and lawyers are frequently depicted

1 Since 2010, there has been a 66% increase in requests for Registered Intermediaries through the WIS. See: Ministry of Justice, 'The Witness Intermediary Scheme: Annual Report 2023' <https://assets.publishing.service.gov.uk/media/664487d0993111924d9d3504/Witness_Intermediary_Scheme_Annual_Report_2023.pdf> 6.

2 Ackroyd provides an instructive summary of the 'historically important and theoretically distinct' approaches to the professions. See: Stephen Ackroyd, 'Sociological and Organisational Theories of Professions and Professionalism' in Mike Dent and others (eds), *The Routledge Companion to the Professions and Professionalism* (Routledge 2016) 15.

3 Paula Brough, Jennifer Brown and Amanda Biggs, *Improving Criminal Justice Workspaces: Translating theory and research into evidence-based practice* (Routledge 2016) 66–67.

4 Brough (n 3) 66–67.

5 Robert Mark, *Policing a Perplex Society* (George, Allen and Unwin 1977); Tracey Green and Alison Gates, 'Understanding the Process of Professionalisation in the Police Organisation' (2014) 87(2) The Police Journal: Theory, Practice and Principles 75.

DOI: 10.4324/9781003461166-5

as one of the 'traditional' professions.[6] Indeed, the 'court workgroup' articulated by Eistenstein and Jacob is a theoretical construct made up exclusively of legal professionals, namely lawyers and judges.[7]

This chapter examines intermediary work in context and focuses on how the role's status is impacted by its working relationships. After addressing the professional status of the intermediary, this chapter then focuses on the work tasks of the intermediary and how control over that work is established and maintained. This discussion begins by recognising the intermediary as an 'outsider' to the world of criminal justice and explains the relevance of this label to the role's work and content. The substantive discussion which follows focuses on two main theoretical constructs. The first is Abbott's work on inter-professional jurisdictional disputes, which details how professions operate in dynamic social settings which shape and define individual professional roles and their content. Abbott describes this concept of jurisdiction as 'the link between a profession and its work'[8] and the 'central phenomenon of professional life'.[9] This approach considers how jurisdictions are expanded and defended and how professionals stake claims to certain bodies of expert knowledge within an 'interacting system, an ecology'.[10] Jurisdictional conflicts characterise social processes, but how these jurisdictional boundaries are created, maintained and are liable to shift can be examined using Gieryn's conception of 'boundary work'.[11] Boundary work outlines how professionals demarcate the boundaries representing status, autonomy and claims over professional resources. Acting as a resource to legitimise actions and status, boundary work occurs through strategies to impose order and stability around the professional work.[12] The chapter concludes by reflecting on the various conflicts the intermediary faces in trying to secure and maintain jurisdiction. It asks if the role's jurisdictional conflicts will result in a 'jurisdictional settlement' whereby intermediaries accept a more limited role with the distribution of some of their work tasks among other criminal justice actors.[13]

6 Christopher Brooks, *Lawyers, Litigation and English Society since 1450* (The Hambledon Press 1998) 149.
7 James Eisenstein and Herbert Jacob, *Felony Justice: An Organizational Analysis of Criminal Courts* (Little, Brown 1977).
8 Andrew Abbott, *The System of Professions: An Essay on the Division of Expert Labor* (Chicago UP 1988) 20.
9 Abbott (n 8) 20.
10 Abbott (n 8) 33.
11 Thomas Gieryn, 'Boundary-Work and the Demarcation of Science from Non-Science: Strains and Interests in Professional Ideologies of Scientists' (1983) 48 American Sociological Review 781.
12 Hauke Riesch, 'Theorizing Boundary Work as Representation and Identity' (2010) 40(4) Journal for the Theory of Social Behaviour 452.
13 Abbott (n 8) 72; Andrew Abbott, 'Jurisdictional Conflicts: A New Approach to the Development of the Legal Professions' (1986) 11 (2) American Bar Foundation Research Journal 187.

5.2 The question of 'professional' status

The professional status of the intermediary, and what that label may entail, is not clear. The terms 'professional' and 'professionalism' are used by both the Department of Justice (Northern Ireland) (DoJ) and the Ministry of Justice (MoJ) when describing the organisation of intermediaries and the standards expected of their work.[14] The penultimate chapter of Plotnikoff and Woolfson's seminal book on intermediaries is titled 'A new profession', with the opening line noting that intermediaries 'have emerged as a new professional identity'.[15] Indeed, the most recent academic research into the fledgling Irish intermediary scheme has identified 'establishing mechanisms of professional development and support' as a key priority.[16] Many, therefore, seem to take for granted that the intermediary is a professional role. However, this is not necessarily an uncontentious position. A rich literature on the 'sociology of the professions' analyses professions as modes of social organisation and as the locus for other social processes and dynamics, allowing scope for an enquiry into the professional status of the intermediary. Nonetheless, while an understanding of professional identity is a key component of this body of work, the present chapter focuses on mapping what an intermediary does rather than what they are.[17] Seeking to define a 'profession' and analysing the intermediary against the resulting definition is potentially 'unnecessary and dangerous', since it distracts from the content of the role's work and how intermediaries think about, act towards and ultimately justify their work.[18] As a result, it is accepted that the intermediary can be viewed as a professional without enquiring too deeply into what that means.

Relevant to the professional status of the intermediary is the variety of occupational backgrounds of those who perform the role. Many intermediaries that I interviewed spoke about their previous professional roles and the

14 Department of Justice (Northern Ireland) (DoJ), 'The Registered Intermediaries Procedural Guidance Manual' (April 2024); Ministry of Justice, 'Registered Intermediary Procedural Guidance Manual 2024' <https://assets.publishing.service.gov.uk/media/671b819bfc28a840abc6d26d/Registered_Intermediary_Procedural_Guidance_Manual_2024__Official_.pdf> accessed 8 February 2025.

15 Joyce Plotnikoff and Richard Woolfson, *Intermediaries in the Criminal Justice System* (Policy Press 2015) 281; The Victims' Commissioner has also stated that the intermediary has gone from a 'new role to a new profession in the CJS', see: Victims' Commissioner, *A Voice for the Voiceless: The Victims' Commissioner's Review into the Provision of Registered Intermediaries for Children and Vulnerable Victims and Witnesses* (January 2018) 19.

16 Aoife Gallagher and others, 'Establishing Stakeholder Priorities for Advancing the Role of the Intermediary in the Justice System: Findings from a Consensus Study' (2024) The International Journal of Evidence & Proof (online first).

17 See, for example Evett's view that 'to most researchers in the field it no longer seems important to draw a hard and fast line between professions and occupations but, instead, to regard both as similar social forms that share many common characteristics': Julia Evetts, 'Short Note: The Sociology of Professional Groups' (2006) 54(1) Current Sociology 133.

18 Abbott (n 8) 58.

experience of bringing their existing skill set to a new work environment. How these diverse backgrounds may shape, or even hinder, the emergence of a new professional status is complicated by the fact that many practitioners execute their role as an intermediary 'on the side', in addition to their main professional role. Indeed, several intermediaries spoke passionately about the importance of being recognised as professionals and felt aggrieved when this did not happen:

> [Judges] have started to expect a psychologist or psychiatrist to recommend us. That's another problem we have, they are wasting money on a psychological report because they want a 'professional' to decide whether we're needed or not. They're not recognising *us* as professionals.
>
> (E&W-17) [emphasis added]

It does not seem that this view is widely held amongst judges. For instance, one magistrate I interviewed indicated that the intermediary's status as a professional had been secured:

> Now, everybody is clear they are professional experts who are providing an independent role within the trial.
>
> (MCJ-2)

This book is centred around an inquiry into the *role* of the intermediary as opposed to the profession, its structure, organisation and even any 'collective ideological persuasion'.[19] This book is concerned with understanding the parameters of the intermediary role, how other key criminal justice actors perceive it as well as, crucially, how intermediaries experience their role. These questions require an analysis of the intermediary's work within a dynamic social context rather than treating any intermediary 'profession' as a static entity or a fixed social structure.[20]

While this chapter does not question the intermediary's status as a professional, it is concerned with whether intermediaries are engaged in what Abbott calls 'professional work'. The conduct of this work determines the parameters of inter-professional jurisdiction between the intermediary and the police, lawyers, judges and others.[21] By drawing on concepts such as 'jurisdiction' and 'boundary work' we can examine the content and context of intermediary work, the expertise which underpins it and the interdependent nature of the network of actors in the criminal justice system. Merely

19 Abbott (n 8) 54.

20 Roy Suddaby and Daniel Muzio, 'Theoretical Perspectives on The Professions' in Laura Empson and others (eds), *The Oxford Handbook of Professional Service Firms* (OUP 2015) 30.

21 Abbott (n 8) 58.

labelling the intermediary as a professional tells us little about how its practitioners are involved in a negotiation process, conflict and exchange with other criminal justice actors. Examining these processes is fundamental to understanding the complexity of the role and how its content and character are dependent on relational work processes.

5.3 Jurisdictions and boundary work

5.3.1 *Jurisdictions*

Abbott views professions as operating in a complex system of interdependence and evaluates the link – which he terms 'jurisdiction' – between occupations and their work. The notion of jurisdiction relates to the 'control' occupations assert over certain task areas. In the case of the intermediary, this concerns how practitioners assert control over tasks, such as assessment, interview planning and formulation of recommendations in the court report.[22] Later in the chapter, we will see how this control is effected through the components of 'diagnosis, 'inference' and 'treatment'. The importance of the control or 'jurisdiction' claimed over work tasks is hard to overstate. If, when and how intermediaries may be said to carry out 'professional work' is defined by the jurisdiction they assert over this work.[23]

The focus on jurisdiction is conceptually useful as intermediaries operate in dynamic social settings in the criminal justice system with potential overlaps between respective work tasks. For example, Jackson highlights the expanding role of prosecutors into pre-trial investigatory functions and notes more generally how 'quasi' roles can emerge when jurisdictions overlap.[24] With specific reference to the criminal court, Young explains that the jurisdictional boundaries of the 'court workgroup' are closely guarded by its members as threats to its work tasks emerge.[25] Familiarity and physical proximity between actors facilitate 'informal communication" and therefore, opportunities for what has been described as 'creative solutions' in cases.[26] This portrayal of the criminal court as being controlled by this exclusive workgroup understandably creates difficulties for integrating other 'peripheral' actors.[27]

22 See Chapter 1 (Introduction) for an overview of the intermediary's main tasks.
23 Abbott (n 8) 2–9.
24 John Jackson, 'The Effect of Legal Culture and Proof in Decisions to Prosecute' (2004) 3 Law, Probability and Risk 109.
25 Richard Young, 'Exploring the Boundaries of the Criminal Courtroom Workgroup' (2013) 42 Common Law World Review 203.
26 Elizabeth Webster and others, '"Court Can Happen Anywhere": Courtroom Workgroup Members' Perceptions of the Challenges and Opportunities of a Transformed Workplace' (2023) 50(11) Criminal Justice and Behavior 1737.
27 Marcia Lipetz, *Routine Justice: Processing Cases in Women's Court* (Transaction Publishers 1984) 6.

Are the work tasks of the intermediary susceptible to encroachment from others, and does the intermediary similarly engage in encroachment when staking claims to jurisdiction? This question is key to understanding the nature of intermediary work and whether the role enjoys 'jurisdiction' or 'control' over it. Abbott's 'systems model' acts as a cogent framework for examining how respective jurisdictions are both expanded and defended. Asserting that these jurisdictional boundaries are perpetually disputed, Abbott argues that this conflict occurs because professions are in constant competition for control over work tasks.[28]

Two main reasons underpin the decision to focus on Abbott's systems model. Firstly, it is concerned primarily with the content of the work carried out by occupational groups. This aspect of Abbott's model resonates with the rich data I gathered about the intermediary role and the 'common work' of its practitioners.[29] Abbott's theory is also relational at its core. My interview data tell a story of a new actor in the hierarchical, ritualistic criminal justice system and explore how resulting conflicts with other actors are constitutive of the role. Secondly, Abbott explains that his model extends beyond analysis of the professions and 'offers a way of thinking about divisions of labour in general'.[30] This allows for an examination of intermediary work without the need to explore the role's professional status. Abbott ignores addressing the issue of *when* groups can be said to have coalesced into professions and instead focuses on *why* new groups may arise and how they disturb the system.[31] The systems model, therefore, allows a focus on 'the contents of professional activity [and] the larger situation in which that activity occurs'.[32]

5.3.2 Boundary work

The conceptualisation of 'boundaries' spans a range of disciplines and is recognised as an integral part of social theorising.[33] Beyond consideration of how boundaries merely demarcate, Klein urges a more inward focus on how boundaries are maintained and may be permeated and deconstructed.[34] An understanding that boundaries are not stable, but inherently contingent and relational, acts as a useful point of departure when considering professional

28 Abbott (n 8) 2.
29 Abbott (n 8) 187.
30 Abbott (n 8) 317.
31 Pamela Tolbert, 'Review of the Book: The System of Professions: An Essay on the Division of Labor' (1990) 35(2) Administrative Science Quarterly 410.
32 Abbott (n 8) 2.
33 Michèle Lamont and Virag Molnar, 'The Study of Boundaries in the Social Sciences' (2002) 28 Annual Review of Sociology 167.
34 Julie Thompson Klein, *Crossing Boundaries:* Knowledge, *Disciplinarities, and Interdisciplinarities* (UV Press 1996) 1.

work. Concepts such as 'boundary negotiation' and 'boundary crossing' have been utilised in theorisations of workplace relations and are useful in mapping how the jurisdiction of the intermediary is contested.[35]

If Abbott's concept of jurisdictions explicates conflicts over inter-professional domains, then 'boundary work' is the activity performed in constructing and negotiating the boundaries that mediate interaction. Changes between professional work tasks (for example, prosecutors assuming some investigatory functions as explained earlier) tend to occur most often at the 'edge of professional jurisdictions'.[36] Examining these boundaries, their edges and how they are crossed, aids understanding of inter-professional jurisdiction and how it is secured and maintained. Gieryn explains how boundary work is widely applicable as boundary demarcation 'is routinely accomplished in practical, everyday settings'.[37] It has proven particularly useful when researching emerging groups seeking to 'communicate their subject [and] establish their own credibility to talk authoritatively about their subject'.[38] This description fits well with the position of intermediaries as an occupational group. Building on this, we can examine how the intermediary uses boundary work as 'strategic practical action' to monopolise professional authority and expertise.[39]

Both concepts of jurisdiction and boundary work are complemented by 'knowledge claims': claims through which professionals control knowledge and skill which act as 'important currencies of competition'.[40] Knowledge claims are key in achieving jurisdictional control and 'represent an important vehicle through which professions can rhetorically play out their professional struggles'.[41] Such knowledge claims, and how they are demonstrated, thread throughout the three components of professional work discussed later (diagnosis, inference and treatment). How intermediaries perform boundary work and assert knowledge claims within the criminal justice system is fundamental to securing what Abbott terms 'exclusive jurisdiction'. This involves occupational groups that aspire to achieve full control over work tasks which they justify based on expertise and exclusive knowledge.[42] Why is this concept of exclusive jurisdiction important? First, the use of the word exclusive

35 Jo Angouri, Meredith Marra and Janet Holmes, 'Introduction: Negotiating Boundaries at Work' in Jo Angouri, Meredith Marra and Janet Holmes (eds), *Negotiating Boundaries at Work: Talking and Transitions* (Edinburgh UP 2017) 1–18; Andrew Abbott, 'Things of Boundaries' (1995) 62(4) Social Research 857.

36 Abbott (n 8).

37 Gieryn (n 11) 781.

38 Riesch (n 12) 454.

39 Gieryn (n 11) 23.

40 Abbott (n 8) 102.

41 Kristine Hirschkorn, 'Exclusive versus Everyday Forms of Professional Knowledge: Legitimacy Claims in Conventional and Alternative Medicine' (2006) 28 Sociology of Health & Illness 28 533.

42 Abbott (n 8) 192.

suggests legitimacy – i.e. that the intermediary has been able to control its tasks through successfully persuading other actors of the role's expertise.[43] Further, since jurisdiction is exclusive, movement in the jurisdiction of one profession invariably affects those of others. Therefore, by securing exclusive jurisdiction over its work tasks, the intermediary causes disturbances in inter-professional jurisdictional relations. This 'chain of effects' is critical to understand the nature of the jurisdictional settlement that the intermediary achieves with other criminal justice actors, which is addressed in section 5.7 of this chapter.[44]

5.4 Intermediaries as outsiders

The criminal justice system, with the courthouse and the criminal trial at its centre, has been described as 'hidden from outsiders' view'.[45] Despite most hearings being technically open to the public, much case preparation and inter-professional dialogue occurs in conference rooms, judicial chambers and via private phone calls and emails.[46] The spatial configuration of the court building and the arcane rituals and language employed by its inhabitants tend to exclude rather than include.[47] Perhaps unsurprisingly, almost every intermediary interviewed identified in one way or another as an 'outsider' in this work environment. Feelings of detachment from proceedings and hostility from others were common and very often recounted with genuine dissatisfaction:

> It is really hard . . . and you often feel like a spare part. . . . But where do we belong? We don't. I feel really uncomfortable sometimes.
>
> (E&W-7)

Intermediaries gave various reasons for identifying as outsiders, including a lack of understanding of established rules of procedure as well as the functions of criminal justice personnel:

> Weird, mind blowing. It is very intimidating and it's a bit like church, there are rules where you sit, stand up at a certain time, who you can speak to. I had never been in a court before, didn't know the difference between

43 Abbott (n 8) 188.
44 Abbott (n 8) 192.
45 Stephanos Bibas, *The Machinery of Justice* (OUP 2015) 34.
46 Bibas (n 45); Paul Rock, *The Social World of an English Crown Court* (Clarendon Press 1993) 261.
47 Linda Mulcahy and Emma Rowden, *The Democratic Courthouse* (Routledge 2020) 18; Pat Carlen, *Magistrates Justice* (Wiley-Blackwell 1976) 111; Jessica Jacobson, Gillian Hunter and Amy Kirby, *Inside Crown Court: Personal Experiences and Questions of Legitimacy* (Policy Press 2016) 65.

> the magistrates' court and Crown Court. You know, stuff that now I just take for granted. I remember those pennies dropping and thinking 'blimey, I didn't know that'.
>
> (E&W-2)

> At the beginning I didn't know the difference between prosecution and defence, so that gives you an idea of my understanding of the legal world. There was a lot of reading to do before we had any training. It didn't make a lot of sense at the time to be honest . . . I didn't have any knowledge, I don't have any family members working as lawyers or anything. . . . We had to read the Equal Treatment Benchbook, the Criminal Order Act, the Justice Act. And I certainly had no understanding of the police process either, I don't know anyone in the police so it was a really steep learning curve.
>
> (NI-3)

Some intermediaries spoke about feeling detached from proceedings despite their involvement being agreed at the Ground Rules Hearing (GRH). This included feeling more like a spectator than an active participant and often feeling their presence was unappreciated or resented. These sentiments were strong among those who tend to work primarily with defendants.[48] E&W-3, one of the few intermediaries who initially worked exclusively with defendants and then later became a Registered Intermediary, spoke passionately about how negative attitudes towards defendants transmitted to the defendant intermediary:

> There's a lot more resistance for intermediaries for defendants than for witnesses . . . I feel like because there is such a push to minimise how involved intermediaries are with defendants, you feel you are almost analysed and under the spotlight to demonstrate exactly the worth of the role. . . . There is open hostility sometimes, which you don't get when you work with witnesses.
>
> (E&W-3)

Outsiders to criminal justice 'see the system quite differently' and often have different interests, knowledge and relative power.[49] As the preceding quote illustrates, intermediaries can feel alienated by the 'theatre' (NI-4) and 'pomp and circumstance' (E&W-7) of their new work environment. Recognising

48 This chimes with Abbott's work examining social work as a profession and his conclusion that association with 'politically controversial' clients such as 'criminals, the poor and the mentally ill' damages the group's standing. See: Andrew Abbott, 'Boundaries of Social Work or Social Work of Boundaries?' (1995) 69 (4) *Social Service Review* 545, 561.

49 Bibas (n 45) 34.

Table 5.1 Occupational background of intermediary interviewees

Occupation	*Number*
Speech and language therapist	15
Social worker	3
Nursing	3
Occupational therapist	2
Psychologist	2
Teaching	1
Sign language interpreter	1

that the intermediary initially entered the criminal justice system as an outsider is an important starting point for the following analysis in this chapter. Whether intermediaries continue to warrant this label is at least partially dependent on how their work is perceived and how they stake claims in the competitive field of the criminal justice system. The varied occupational backgrounds of the intermediaries I interviewed are reflected in **Table 5.1**.

Using the terminology of Abbott, intermediaries entered the criminal justice system to address a 'problem' for which criminal justice insiders lacked 'effective treatment'.[50] Abbott explains that when a 'problem has bewildered a profession for some time . . . it tends to become fair game for outsiders'.[51] In terms of the intermediary, this 'problem' is related to the difficulties vulnerable individuals face when giving oral testimony. Chapter 4 (Locating the intermediary within theories of the criminal trial) explained how the adversarial system and the professions that work within it long struggled to accommodate the needs of vulnerable witnesses.[52] Thus, the court experience was 'confusing, intimidating and demeaning' for many.[53] In broad terms, the special measures introduced by the YJCEA sought to help vulnerable and intimidated witnesses give the best possible evidence in criminal proceedings.[54] As further explained in Chapter 4, the special measures regime may also be seen as part of a broader attempt to address a legitimacy deficit within the criminal trial. As one of these measures, the intermediary was well positioned to capitalise on this opening and convert it into a 'professional problem'.[55] Did this problem have to be solved by an external agent such as the intermediary?

50 Abbott (n 8) 50.
51 Abbott (n 8) 50.
52 Home Office, *Report of the Advisory Group on Video Evidence* (1989).
53 Penny Cooper and Linda Hunting, *Access to Justice for Vulnerable People* (Wildy, Simmonds and Hill Publishing 2018); Kate Brown, *Vulnerability and Young People: Care and Social Control in Policy and Practice* (Policy Press 2015) 10.
54 Camilla MacPherson, 'The Youth Justice and Criminal Evidence Act 1999: Achieving Best Evidence' (2001) 41(3) Medicine, Science and the Law 230.
55 Abbott (n 8) 59.

This is an important question when considering the interdependence of criminal justice actors. Outsiders can only be impugned for their lack of knowledge if insiders can be said to possess such a knowledge base already.[56] It was recognised as early as 1987, during the passage of the Criminal Justice Bill, that the specialist skills required to help elicit evidence from children must be sourced from outside the criminal justice system.[57] The 'lack of skills among lawyers' meant that whoever was chosen to fulfil this role would almost certainly be an 'outsider' to the criminal justice system.[58]

It is worth considering briefly how the intermediaries that I interviewed talked about the premise for the role's introduction. Many viewed what Mulcahy and Rowden term the 'remote, foreign and elite' elements of the criminal justice system as reified in the difficulties vulnerable people face.[59] Given their occupational backgrounds, all intermediary interviewees were acutely aware of the types of communication problems people face, although many were shocked by the inaccessibility of the language used in court. Some intermediaries admitted to being impressed by the arcane world of the criminal court with one being 'enamoured with the romance of it all' (E&W-7). Responses of this kind suggest a degree of paradoxical reasoning – on one hand the antiquated world of wigs and gowns was alluring; on the other it was sorely in need of modernisation. Despite some nostalgic sentiments, there was a consensus among interviewees that the criminal justice system had failed to adapt to the vicissitudes of courtroom testimony.

With the preceding in mind, we can now ask: what impact has the introduction of this outsider had on the pre-existing social structures of the criminal justice system? Abbott contends that when a new entrant enters such a field there is inevitably 'jostling and readjustment'.[60] Indeed, the system must necessarily react when a new actor such as the intermediary appears 'requiring professional judgement or a new technique for old professional work'.[61] The next section considers how the existing boundaries of the criminal justice system have been disturbed by the introduction of the intermediary and how the network of actors has responded accordingly.

5.5 Boundary disturbance

The previous section gave a brief insight into the feelings and perceptions of the intermediary as an 'outsider'. This section develops this analysis and recognises that the introduction of an outsider into a new work setting causes

56 Abbott (n 8) 254.
57 See Chapter 2 (Emergence of the intermediary role) for further discussion.
58 HC Deb 20 June 1988, vol 135, col 871.
59 Mulcahy and Rowden (n 47) 8; Jacobson, Hunter and Kirby (n 47).
60 Abbott (n 8) 33.
61 Abbott (n 8) 89.

disruption, upheaval and uncertainty. In the case of the intermediary, its new 'task area' threatened to weaken existing jurisdictions throughout the criminal justice system. In the words of Abbott, jurisdictional boundaries are perpetually in dispute and the system must 'absorb' the disturbance(s) in seeking to regain balance.[62]

The existence of boundaries in the criminal justice system helps regulate inter-professional relationships and allows individuals to perform their roles within 'procedurally correct boundaries'.[63] It is a complex social world where physical and non-physical boundaries dictate who sits where, who speaks to whom and how much involvement individuals will have in proceedings.[64] To understand the effects of external influences on the role, it is important to return to the point that intermediaries identify (and are identified) as outsiders. These perceptions are fundamental to understanding how both intermediary roles have adapted and continue to adapt to a world with firmly established rules and traditions. But when changes are introduced that upset cultural norms, resistance from established criminal justice actors normally follows. Young describes how these established actors 'patrol and defend' established boundaries.[65] This mirrors Abbott's notion of competitive struggles for jurisdiction, and we can examine how the intermediary as an outsider acts to disrupt existing jurisdictional arrangements. These themes are germane to how intermediaries construct and maintain boundaries to demarcate their own 'independent . . . self-contained area of knowledge' and how they seek recognition in claiming jurisdiction over it.[66]

As sites of contestation, boundaries demarcate distinctive bodies of knowledge and expertise.[67] The criminal justice system contains complex social networks in which professionals with claims to specialist knowledge exchange not only with each other but also with clients and the public. The stability of professional role boundaries within the criminal justice system (particularly within the court) has been well rehearsed. Eisenstein and Jacob describe the 'common task environment' of the 'courtroom workgroup' where specialised functions are orientated towards shared goals.[68] Boundaries are collectively drawn which ensures that 'everyone quickly fits into his accustomed place and in which the principals readily understand each other's work. Even

62 Abbott (n 8) 215.
63 Stina Bergman Blix and Åsa Wettergren, *Professional Emotions in Court: A Sociological Perspective* (Routledge 2018) 86.
64 Sida Liu, 'Boundaries and Professions: Toward a Processual Theory of Action' (2018) 5(1) Journal of Professions and Organization 45, 47.
65 Young (n 25) 218.
66 Valérie Fournier, 'Boundary Work and the (Un)making of the Professions' in Nigel Malin (ed), *Professionalism, Boundaries and the Workplace* (Routledge 2000) 69; Abbott (n 8) 59.
67 Liu (n 64) 49.
68 Eisenstein and Jacob (n 7) 10.

novices readily fit into the work routine of a courtroom'.[69] The pre-court environment, particularly the evidence gathering-procedures, is also carved up primarily between the police and prosecution in a way McConville et al. argue amounts to the collaborative venture of 'case construction'.[70] Similarly, Sanders highlighted how the prosecution prepare cases 'hand in glove' with the police where boundaries inevitably overlap and intertwine.[71] The boundaries demarcating the work of individual actors give rise to jurisdictional claims which, at least according to the workgroup, are mutually recognised in pursuance of collective goals.

To construct boundaries, intermediaries must stake jurisdictional claims. Abbott defines this as a claim for 'the legitimate control of a particular type of work' which entails 'first and foremost a right to perform the work as professionals see fit'.[72] However, several intermediaries discussed being unsure where the role seemed to fit among the established practices and routines of the criminal justice system. Equally from the other side, the lack of understanding of the intermediary role and its function among other criminal justice actors has been a consistent theme in the research carried out to date.[73] It became clear in my interviews that this made identification and performance of what might crudely be called 'intermediary work' very difficult:

> It was awkward because the barristers I worked with didn't have any idea what my role is, I was not totally convinced by my role, and similarly with police, you were requested but that officer might not think they need you. (E&W-6)

> It was almost like I have landed in this box and nobody has a clue what to do. It was like someone had dropped me in. . . . There was no lead from the prosecution or from the bench and I was standing there thinking: 'how long will I be standing here . . .' and that was really bizarre . . . I came away thinking: 'did they know what my role was and why I was there?' (E&W-20)

69 Eisenstein and Jacob (n 7) 29–30.

70 Mike McConville, Andrew Sanders and Roger Leng, *The Case for The Prosecution* (Routledge 1991) 11.

71 Andrew Sanders, *A Community Justice. Modernising the Magistracy in England and Wales* (Institute of Public Policy Research, 2000); Andrew Sanders, 'Core Values, the Magistracy, and the Auld Report' (2002) 29(2) Journal of Law and Society 324.

72 Abbott (n 8) 60.

73 Victims' Commissioner (n 15) 27; Joyce Plotnikoff and Richard Woolfson, *Registered Intermediaries in Action: Messages for the CJS from the Witness Intermediary Scheme Smartsite* (NSPCC and Ministry of Justice 2011) 5; Letter from National Police Chiefs' Council, National Crime Agency and CPS Lead for Victims and Witnesses to Dr Philip Lee, Justice Minister (5 March 2018).

Interactions between legal practitioners and intermediaries in the early stages of both schemes in Northern Ireland and England and Wales reflected an even greater lack of understanding. Despite the Registered Intermediary Scheme (RIS) covering both witnesses and defendants from the outset in Northern Ireland, interviewees found that solicitors were sometimes completely unaware of what an intermediary was or what the role entailed:

> I think there was a definite lack of awareness of what we do from solicitors. One solicitor didn't know about RIS and asked me 'What is it you do again?' He then said a few weeks later: 'I definitely need a Registered Intermediary' so he made an application.
>
> (NI-6)

Defendant intermediaries in England and Wales found the boundaries of the role particularly difficult to gauge when dealing with solicitors. In the absence of any specific guidance on the point, many intermediaries working in a non-registered capacity felt that solicitors struggled with one particular question: how much information about the case does the intermediary need to know prior to an assessment? Initially, many defendant intermediaries were swamped with mountains of medical evidence with little idea of their relative ethical position or how much reliance they could place on the provided material:

> I have had whole bundles arrive at the office for somebody in a trial in 3 weeks' time and I have never met them, never said I can do it, and the trial is in Bristol. I am not going to Bristol for a fortnight. And there is highly confidential information that just rocks up, so I think 'GDPR hasn't reached the legal world. . . . It's unnecessary . . . some solicitors seem unable to distinguish or differentiate what I might need.
>
> (E&W-2)

These examples demonstrate how the construction of boundaries posed a challenge as the content of the intermediary role had yet to be developed, shaped and tested through practice. As 'new players' in the criminal justice world, the lack of precedent for the role provided scope for testing its parameters.[74] Similar experiences have been found among interpreters, for example, who often encounter 'attitudinal resistance'[75] to their practices and challenges in managing expectations of their role.[76] The autonomous nature

74 Plotnikoff and Woolfson (n 15) 3.

75 Sandra Hale, *Interpreter Policies, Practices and Protocols in Australian Courts and Tribunals: A National Survey* (Australasian Institute of Judicial Administration 2011) 3.

76 Helen Colley and Frédérique Guéry, 'Understanding New Hybrid Professions: Bourdieu, *illusio* and the Case of Public Service Interpreters' (2015) 45 Cambridge Journal of Education 113.

of interpreting and lack of prior knowledge of the subject of their assignment also draws parallels with intermediary work.[77] At its heart, boundary construction is about distinguishing from other professionals, but intermediaries were initially constrained from doing so in an unfamiliar environment.[78] This contrasts with the norms, attitudes and common understandings that accumulate and are inculcated in the courtroom workgroup over a long period.[79] However, it was not just intermediaries who initially struggled with the parameters of the role's professional boundaries. Other actors appeared unsure about how the role might encroach upon or challenge their jurisdictional domains. One magistrate commented:

> When it first came out, I can remember a complaint, or an issue being raised in the Crown Court where a Registered Intermediary had felt they had got a particularly hard time and there was clearly a lack of understanding of the role from everybody. Everybody had felt that when they looked at it there was a lack of understanding of the role.
>
> (MCJ-2)

E&W-6, E&W-20 and MCJ-2 were reflecting on the encroachment of a new actor into a system with well-defined work tasks and boundaries. As Rock explains, there is an 'abiding preoccupation with the conflict, danger and threat to confidentiality represented by outsiders'.[80] As a member of the 'courtroom workgroup', MCJ-2's remarks signal an appreciation of the 'conflict, uncertainty and inefficiency' that introducing a new actor can engender.[81] These comments point to concerns about how the introduction of the intermediary role may impact interjurisdictional competition over tasks. Timmermans terms this an instance of a 'conflictual jurisdictional relationship' when traditional actors are 'confronted with the incursions of an emerging profession on its jurisdiction'.[82] Blok et al. offer a variant notion of the 'proto-jurisdiction' to explicate how professions navigate 'emerging task arenas' by renegotiating work routines among themselves.[83]

But is the intermediary seeking to make a claim on an entirely new jurisdictional task? Abbott explains, 'Professions develop when jurisdictions become

77 Colley and Guéry (n 76) 121.
78 Liu (n 64) 48.
79 Young (n 25).
80 Rock (n 46) 261.
81 Young (n 25) 220.
82 Stefan Timmermans, 'The Cause of Death vs. the Gift of Life: Boundary Maintenance and the Politics of Expertise in Death Investigation' (2002) 25(5) Sociology of Health & Illness 550, 570.
83 Anders Blok and others, 'Ecologies of Boundaries: Modes of Boundary Work in Professional Work Boundaries (2019) 42(4) Symbolic Interaction 588.

vacant' and such vacancy can arise through creation or abandonment by others.[84] It is not apparent that the intermediary has filled a jurisdictional vacuum because others have left to 'improve their status' as McKenna suggests.[85] For example, when elite British solicitors moved increasingly away from property-conveyancing, other professional groups sought to claim that vacant jurisdiction.[86] As noted earlier, recognising the need to improve the experience of vulnerable witnesses led to the YJCEA and the intermediary was just one of a panoply of special measures introduced. Police, lawyers and judges have always 'communicated' with vulnerable individuals, but none have abandoned any discrete jurisdictional task which made way for the intermediary role. But the sort of 'emerging tasks' that Lindstrom describes are distributed among locally situated actors who are often collectively concerned with implementing 'organizational strategies'.[87] This was not the case with the introduction of the intermediary. Instead, the inability of traditional criminal justice actors to perform a function satisfactorily meant that it was either inappropriate or impossible for them to distribute the task among themselves. The introduction of the intermediary was premised on the expectation that this new role would possess a skill set that had hitherto not been utilised in the criminal justice system. As such, the new jurisdictional tasks which the intermediary performs came about not through abandonment but through an opening created by legislative reform.

Despite the creation of new jurisdictional tasks for the intermediary, my interview data suggests that the role has a disruptive influence on existing jurisdictions. The intermediary can stake its own jurisdictional claims, but how other actors perceive these claims is central to their legitimacy. As discussed later, the 'vacancy' which was created for the intermediary was sometimes contested by others who question and scrutinise the nature of the jurisdictional claims the intermediary makes. What must now be considered is *how* such claims emerge. Jurisdictional claims are staked by demonstrating 'independent and self-contained field of knowledge'.[88] This serves to legitimise the work and sustain the jurisdiction claimed.[89] Just as the judges and lawyers in Eisenstein and Jacob's 'court workgroup' identified specialist tasks to be executed, the intermediary role has sought to carve out control

84 Abbott (n 8) 3.
85 Christopher McKenna, 'The System of Professions: An Essay on the Division of Expert Labor' (Book Review) (2006) 80(1) Business History Review 141, 142.
86 McKenna (n 85).
87 Matthew Kraatz and Emily Block, 'Organizational Implications of Institutional Pluralism' in Royston Greenwood and others (eds), *Sage Handbook of Organizational Institutionalism* (SAGE Publishing 2008) 243.
88 Nigel Malin, *Professionalism, Boundaries and the Workplace* (Routledge 1999) 69.
89 Abbott (n 8) 52–57.

over certain work.[90] An examination of how the intermediary claims or holds jurisdiction over its tasks requires consideration of the content of the role's 'professional work'.[91] The 'problem' which the intermediary was introduced to remedy, i.e. the criminal justice system's failure to adequately accommodate the needs of vulnerable witnesses, is shaped into coherent jurisdictions and resulting claims.[92] These claims are underpinned by three acts of professional practice which frequently overlap and intermesh: diagnosis, inference and treatment.[93] The following section discusses each of these in turn.

5.6 Professional work

What is it that intermediaries 'do' as professionals, and on what basis can they justify their control over it? We can refine this question and ask it more abstractly: how does intermediary work constitute a professional field of expertise which amounts to a legitimate area of knowledge?[94] Whether or not intermediaries operate autonomously in a field which is independent and self-contained is central to understanding how claims of jurisdiction can be made.[95] The three 'parts' of professional tasks identified by Abbott are i) diagnosis, ii) inference and iii) treatment. Together, these embody the essential cultural logic of professional practice and constitute the tangible work professionals engage in.[96]

5.6.1 Diagnosis

Diagnosis is a 'mediating act' whereby information is taken into the professional knowledge system and assembled into a picture that can then be classified.[97] For intermediaries, the act of diagnosis takes place at the assessment stage. The assessment has been described as what 'underpins intermediary recommendations about adapting questioning techniques and procedures at the police station and at court'.[98] The assessment tends to occur 'backstage' in more informal environments. A surprising discovery from my interviews was that Registered Intermediaries in both jurisdictions spoke of a complete lack of formal training on assessment techniques. This contrasts, for example, with the newly introduced Professional Diploma in Intermediary Studies

90 Abbott (n 8) 62.
91 Abbott (n 8) 59.
92 Abbott (n 8).
93 Abbott (n 8) 40.
94 Fournier (n 66) 69.
95 Fournier (n 66) 70.
96 Abbott (n 8) 40.
97 Abbott (n 8) 40.
98 Plotnikoff and Woolfson (n 15) 39.

in Ireland which trains prospective intermediaries on communication techniques and methods over a year-long course.[99]

In the U.K, the four official Registered Intermediary Surveys conducted by Cooper since 2009 detail the use of intermediaries in court, and their interaction with lawyers, judges and court staff, with almost no mention of communication assessment. Training initially focused on preparing intermediaries for entrance into the legal world rather than the practical reality of assessment techniques.[100] Whether this was the intention or not, familiarising recruits with the procedures of the criminal justice system was tacit recognition of their outsider status and the inevitable challenges this label would bring.

The scope of the intermediary's diagnostic role is recognised in the official procedural guidance manuals. The relevant MoJ guidance requires Registered Intermediaries to identify whether their involvement is likely to 'improve the completeness, coherence and accuracy of the witness's evidence'.[101] The DoJ in Northern Ireland adopts an almost identical requirement.[102] This phraseology allows for a mix of individuals from different backgrounds to perform the role without having to make a formal medical diagnosis. For many, this contrasts with the requirements of their other professional positions where such a diagnostic role is crucial. As noted earlier, the eligibility criteria are different for a defendant intermediary than a Registered Intermediary. For defendants, an appointment can be made to ensure that 'every reasonable step is taken to facilitate the defendant's participation' in proceedings.[103]

How then is diagnosis conducted? While intermediaries perform their own individual assessment, the 'end user' who has requested their services is often unsure of the nature or scope of the individual's vulnerability. The police officer or the instructing solicitor will have flagged a potential vulnerability – albeit based on limited professional knowledge or expertise of communicative disorders.[104] Therefore, when a referral reaches an intermediary, an informal diagnosis has already occurred. It was concerning how little the intermediaries that I interviewed knew about this process since their

99 For further information, see: University of Limerick, 'Intermediary Studies – Professional Diploma' <https://www.ul.ie/gps/courses/intermediary-studies-professional-diploma> accessed 6 November 2024.

100 Penny Cooper and David Wurtzel, 'A Day Late and a Dollar Short: In Search of an Intermediary Scheme for Vulnerable Defendants in England and Wales' (2013) 1 Criminal Law Review 4.

101 MoJ (n 14) 13.

102 DoJ (n 14) 12.

103 Criminal Practice Directions 2023 (CrimPRC(23)90(b)) [6.2.7].

104 John Pearse, 'Police Interviewing: The identification of vulnerabilities' (1995) 5(3) Journal of Community and Applied Social Psychology) 147; Roxanna Dehaghani, *Vulnerability in Police Custody: Police Decision Making and the Appropriate Adult Safeguard* (Routledge 2019); Iain McKinnon, Julie Thorp and Don Grubin, 'Improving the Detection of Detainees with Suspected Intellectual Disability in Police Custody' (2015) 9(4) Advances in Mental Health and Intellectual Disabilities 174.

involvement officially begins when they are 'matched' to a case. Despite evidence of ad-hoc training organised by some regional police forces, there seems to be no nationally coordinated effort to determine how training of police by intermediaries could improve the effective screening of individuals with communication problems. A 'triage' system, whereby intermediaries provide telephone advice to police when screening, has been suggested by Pettitt et al., but has not been adopted.[105] Unfortunately, even if police flag an issue, there is often such poor understanding of the intermediary's function among criminal justice professionals that vulnerable individuals are not given suitable support.[106] One of the most problematic examples of this is police officers not knowing what the intermediary role involves and not requesting their services, even in cases involving very young children.[107] The MoJ Procedural Guidance Manual for Registered Intermediaries explicitly recognises that 'no set procedure' for assessments exists and that 'the form and content . . . will depend on the witness's communication needs and the Registered Intermediary's skill set'.[108] This guidance reflects the reality that intermediaries come from a wide variety of backgrounds, and the differences in approach to 'diagnosis' were evident in my data:

> It's broader than most people initially think . . . it's the conversations you have with the professionals who know that witness, that will inform the needs they have and what strategies might help them outside the police interview and outside the courtroom, where they are at with their education . . . you're looking at how they're interacting with whoever has come with them, what means they are communicating by, how their body language appears, how anxious they are feeling.
>
> (E&W-15)

> I have kind of devised my own assessment over the years which is very functional based. So I start quite big and look at the environment that the person is communicating in now, how are they coping with distractions, what have they done to manage that environment, what is the impact of that and if I do it well then my assessment will feel like a chat but I know that I am asking certain types of questions, there's a lot of fact finding at the beginning and I will use that information later in the assessment to

105 Bridget Pettitt and others, 'At Risk, Yet Dismissed: The Criminal Victimisation of People with Mental Health Problems' (Victim Support/Mind 2013); Victim's Commissioner (n 15) 46.

106 Victims' Commissioner (n 15) 26.

107 Criminal Justice Joint Inspection, 'Achieving Best Evidence in Child Sexual Cases – A Joint Inspection' [1.4] and [6.7]; Ministry of Justice (2014) 'Report on Review of Ways to Reduce Distress of Victims in Trials of Sexual Violence' [49].

108 Criminal Justice Joint Inspection (n 107).

> test language and how they communicate and what kinds of questions or vocabulary, grammar might give them a problem.
>
> (E&W-2)

> It is useful because you can always read up on the nature of the person's condition beforehand. Yesterday I was in a police station with an individual who was bipolar who had drug-induced schizophrenia and who suffered from depression. Now, you could say 'Where do you begin?' but really you begin by simply saying 'look, will this person understand a question that is asked of them? Will they be able to process that and respond in a clear, logical and coherent manner?' The only way to know that is to ask them a question. Then you can add complexity to it until they reach a level where they can't cope.
>
> (NI-2)

These three intermediaries hail from different professional backgrounds (social work, occupational therapy, and speech and language therapy) and demonstrate how the approach to diagnosing individual communication issues can vary. This plurality of diagnostic techniques is not unusual per se, with Abbott recognising the 'staggering complexity' often involved with the task.[109] In echoing this, Grimen identifies the theoretical foundations of professional knowledge as heterogeneous which rarely map onto one single academic discipline.[110] That such a broad range of professional knowledge bases can be accommodated under the unifying role of 'intermediary' is, therefore, perhaps unsurprising. Indeed, the need for a heterogeneous skill set among intermediaries is understandable based on how the intermediary matching service operates. Cases are matched to Registered Intermediaries based on seven categories of 'vulnerability': i) Child without Concurrent Vulnerability, ii) Child with Mental Disorder, iii) Child with Learning Disability, iv) Child with Physical Disability, v) Adult with Mental Disorder, vi) Adult with Learning Disability, vii) Adult with Physical Disability.[111] The broad range of skill sets intermediaries possess is represented in **Figure 5.1**. Despite the spectrum of specialisms, gaps in the intermediary knowledge base still exist. In 2023, 2.2% of requests lodged with the NCA were 'unmatched' due to the unavailability of a suitably skilled intermediary.[112] E&W-11 explained how, despite her willingness to accept a broad range of cases, her theoretical knowledge of an applied behaviour

109 Abbott (n 8) 41.
110 Harald Grimen, 'Profesjon og kunnskap' in A Molander and LI Terum (eds), *Profesjonsstudier* (Oslo Universitetsforlaget 2008) 71.
111 MoJ (n 1) 18.
112 MoJ (n 1) 15.

analysis programme known as 'The Picture Exchange Communication System' or 'Pic Exchange' was insufficient:

> I was quite comfortable working with mental health, with kids who were ASD, with autism. I had a range so I said from the beginning: 'look I'm happy to take any age' [but] there would be things that I've had to pass back. There were two assessments that came through where there were children who used pics, like the 'pic exchange', and then I had to hand those cases back. That became evident before I actually did the assessment . . . I had to pass the case back for somebody else to do.

These comments reflect the multidisciplinary theoretical content that constitutes the intermediary role. In other words, the requirements of a given

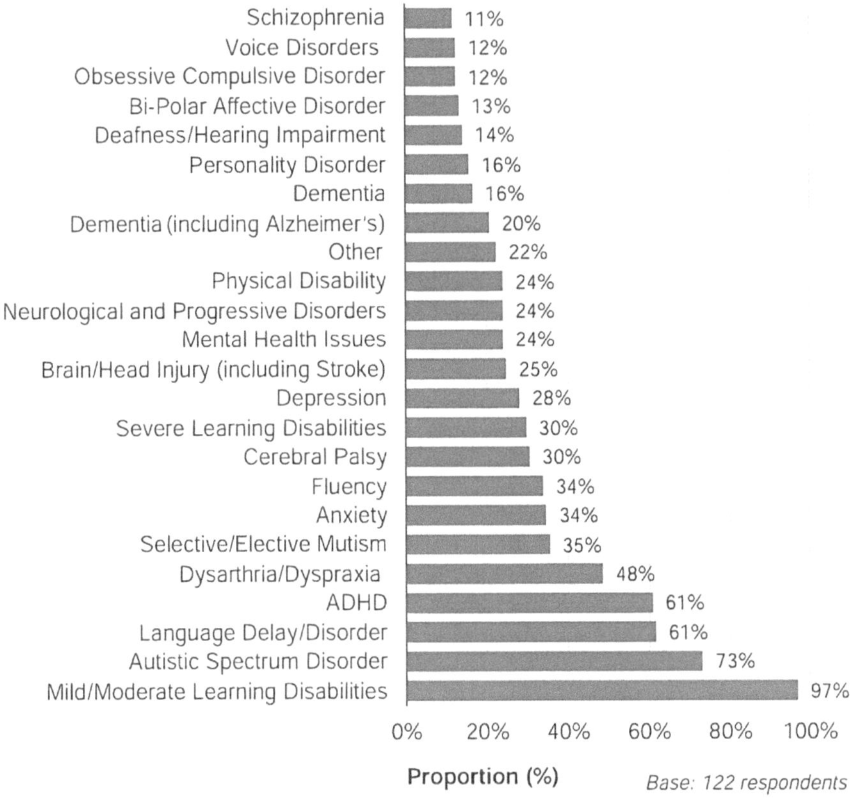

Figure 5.1 Specialisms of Registered Intermediaries (referred to as Figure 6 in original source)

Source: Victims' Commissioner, 'A Voice for the Voiceless: The Victims' Commissioner's Review into the Provision of Registered Intermediaries for Children and Vulnerable Victims and Witnesses (January 2018) 35.

referral dictate what theoretical resources are required for the intermediary to be able to initially make a diagnosis.[113]

However, there are inherent risks in the diagnostic process. How individual problems are classified may damage the professional expertise the intermediary seeks to project. This expertise is particularly vulnerable when diagnosis is performed weakly and/or not clearly conceptualised. This, in turn, creates fertile conditions for 'inter-professional poaching'[114] which occurs when intermediary work is defined by another professional using its own terms.[115] In my research interviews, intermediaries, police and judges raised concerns about a lack of diagnosis uniformity. Several intermediaries from a traditional speech and language therapy (SLT) background in particular identified issues about how non-SLT intermediaries were diagnosing and classifying the problems of vulnerable individuals:

> A speech therapist writes a report not only as a diagnostic tool but also 'what should be done to deal with this'. . . . I know a social worker who has no background in assessing communication. They would often ring some of us and they were talking about a Down syndrome boy with a learning disability. They told me what was wrong with him and they have an innate sense of how to assess someone, but they just don't know the terminology. They had that guy down to a tee, but couldn't organise it.
>
> (NI-7)

One intermediary with a background in occupational health was acutely aware that her techniques did not match up with a typical SLT assessment:

> [Speech and Language Therapists] are very language focused like '12 words in a sentence' whereas I don't really bother with any of that . . . I usually read a little story and then ask them questions about it, so I get the chance to test all the language things. I test to see if I suggest something will they go along with it, I get some people to describe a family member to see if they can generate information. . . . I've got an assessment of interaction skills which I use quite often which is an OT assessment about how people interact, focus, articulate and it's like a score out of 4.
>
> (E&W-10)

The varied skill set of intermediaries was a feature of the decision of *R(AB) v Hampshire Constabulary & Ors* in which no intermediary with the requisite skill set could initially be found for a young witness with Down syndrome,

113 MoJ (n 1) 15.
114 Abbott (n 8) 44.
115 Abbott (n 8) 190.

autism and severe learning difficulties.[116] Eventually, the child's teacher was required to substitute as the court considered that she 'understood [the child]' and was someone 'with whom [the child] was comfortable and would communicate'.[117] Despite the teacher having no professional background in communication assessment, the court was satisfied that the witness was assisted by those who 'knew him best' and could enable him to give his best evidence.[118] There is perhaps a limitation to what can be drawn from such a specific case, but when faced with the pressures of an investigation and a vulnerable witness with complex needs, it appears that courts are willing to allow some leeway regarding who performs the intermediary role.

In interview, most intermediaries expressed interest in knowing how their colleagues conducted assessments. However, the solitary nature of the role and lack of peer review, particularly for non-registered intermediaries, means that individualised practices appear common. The lack of uniformity in diagnosis technique was highlighted by the police who are the only other criminal justice actors to see different approaches first-hand. Two police officers doubted the appropriateness of intermediaries in many cases and questioned their diagnostic methods. When asked about an intermediary assessment one said:

> I could have done a better job myself. Anybody can simplify a question, can't they?
>
> (PO-1)

Another officer commented:

> Anybody with a bit of nous can simplify a question. I can ask the same question of you at one level and the same question of a kid at a different level. . . . You just have to figure out what level they are at to allow you to ask it . . . all that is important but none of it is the intermediary, that's about the interviewer doing their job properly which is why I have a problem with how intermediaries work.
>
> (PO-2)

While these comments relate to the act of 'treatment' (see later in this chapter) in terms of *how* to ask questions, they also provide an external perspective on the diagnosis component of intermediary work. There is an implication that diagnosing the extent of a communication disorder ought not be the sole domain of the intermediary. Recounting her experience of another

116 [2019] EWHC 3461.
117 [2019] EWHC 3461 [24].
118 [2019] EWHC 3461 [2013].

assessment, PO-2 explained how an intermediary pointed to parts of her own body to gauge whether a child understood the names of body parts. PO-2's explanation of the incident and demeanour implied scepticism of the intermediary's diagnostic techniques. Indicating her unhappiness with the conduct of another intermediary during assessment of a 3-year-old child, she said:

> I have raised some concerns. I used one recently that I wasn't happy with because some of the things that she did were not correct.
>
> (PO-2)

The fact that the officer then decided to conduct the interview without an intermediary suggests that the jurisdictional control which intermediaries exert over this aspect of their work is unstable and susceptible to encroachment. Put more bluntly, the police offer sought to appropriate jurisdiction from the intermediary when the objective of obtaining an 'accurate and reliable account' from the victim was not seen to be furthered by their involvement.[119] This example is redolent of professional dominance never being permanently secured and, as Timmermans explains: 'competing groups can invalidate any claim for jurisdiction'.[120] These attempts appear to be built on a process of 'boundary blurring' where one professional (police) encroaches on the domain of another.[121] What appears to facilitate the initial blurring of boundaries is the fact that there is an element of cooperation intrinsically involved between police and intermediaries during assessment. This 'simultaneous cooperation and conflict' produces the conditions where the exclusive jurisdiction may be questioned and then boundaries blurred.[122] Police see how intermediaries assess vulnerable people and identify enough commonalities of practice to deny the intermediary's jurisdiction. This blurring does not necessarily mean that the police can operate with the same expertise as the intermediary.[123] Indeed, the same police who were quick to criticise the diagnostic abilities of some intermediaries accepted that others were 'exceptional' and an asset to the police during interview. In this context at least, boundary blurring may be contained to specific incidents rather than amounting to a full-scale invasion of the intermediary's diagnostic domain.

It is worth noting that no intermediary that I interviewed had experienced solicitor interference with the communication assessment. The reasons for

119 College of Policing, 'Investigate Interviewing' Principle 1' <https://www.app.college.police.uk/app-content/investigations/investigative-interviewing/> accessed 5 November 2020.

120 Timmermans (n 82) 551.

121 Liu (n 64) 48.

122 Liu (n 64) 48.

123 Rosemary Rushmer and Gillian Pallis, 'Inter-Professional Working: The Wisdom of Integrated Working and The Disaster of Blurred Boundaries' (2003) 23(1) Public Money and Management 59.

this may be numerous, but one that was cited by several intermediaries relates to the issue of neutrality, i.e. many defence solicitors view the engagement of an intermediary as a distinct benefit 'because their client appears more vulnerable' [NI-6]. There seems to be less desire to undermine the jurisdictional claim of intermediaries over assessment when the role is viewed as an ally or an asset. Colley and Guéry found similar experiences among public service interpreters in their interactions with 'service users', such as police and prosecutors.[124] These 'service users' were often indifferent to notions of impartiality and desired allegiance from interpreters whom they viewed as 'tools' to assist their work.[125] My data suggest that being viewed instrumentally by defence solicitors in this way makes intermediaries feel that their expertise and theoretical knowledge is recognised.

Ordinarily, a non-registered intermediary will assess a suspect/defendant alone with the instructed lawyers present, and so the risk of external interference is minimised. This contrasts with other criminal justice settings, particularly the courtroom, where a 'workplace assimilation' process occurs. This involves a form of knowledge transfer where other subordinate professionals, non-professionals and members of related professionals 'learn on the job a craft version of [a] profession's knowledge systems'.[126] This concept is important for both Registered Intermediaries and non-registered intermediaries, and a key question emerges: are other criminal justice actors able to acquire aspects of intermediary work so as to undermine the role's exclusive jurisdiction? The aforementioned examples suggest, at least at the assessment stage, that intermediaries are more likely to be vulnerable to jurisdiction incursion from police than from solicitors. This conclusion reflects a broader theme throughout the book – that the roles of Registered Intermediaries and non-registered intermediaries are often experienced differently by their practitioners. However, it may also be significant for the future development of both roles. If non-registered intermediaries can retain more jurisdictional control over work tasks than Registered Intermediaries, what might this mean for the sustainability of both roles in the criminal justice system? Section 5.7 titled 'Jurisdictional settlement' probes this question further.

One final point about diagnosis deserves attention, and it is of potentially existential importance for intermediary claims to exclusive jurisdiction. It relates to the systems put in place by the MoJ to ensure that Registered Intermediaries are sufficiently trained prior to being matched in a case. A senior intermediary, who is also a registered trainer, was critical of the MoJ

124 Colley and Guéry (n 76).
125 Colley and Guéry (n 76).
126 Abbott (n 8) 67.

recruitment process for recruits, claiming that many lacked the basic assessment skills:

> as a training team we wondered why we had people on our training course who didn't seem to have some of the basics and we looked at the interviewing, why were some people being put forward for interview? So, we don't do the sifting, the MoJ do it and they don't know what they are doing and so we then went even further back and looked at the wording of the interview and that's when we spotted they have taken out the necessity of having a degree and being a professional.
>
> (E&W-7)

E&W-7 accepted that non-SLT Registered Intermediaries would be 'up in arms' about her comments. However, this view indicates a fear that many in the intermediary community share: that the credibility and legitimacy of the intermediary role would suffer should it not be recognised as a profession with consistent standards. As noted in the introduction to the chapter, many intermediaries echoed this desire to attain professional recognition. The call for training to be standardised in the way E&W-7 suggests mirrors Abbott's argument that 'the more strongly organised a profession is, the more effective its claims to jurisdiction'.[127] Inconsistency, or incompetence, in diagnostic methods not only threatens the role's relative standing, but it also damages the ability to isolate assessment/diagnosis as the intermediary's 'exclusive area of jurisdiction and expertise [and] a legitimate area of knowledge'.[128] The fact that training is organised and delivered across different commercial providers operating under the HMCTS Appointed Intermediary Service (HAIS) means that assessment technique standards are less likely to be consistent compared to the Witness Intermediary Scheme (WIS). In fact, it was a surprise when one intermediary with considerable experience working with both witnesses and defendants described the latter work as 'the Wild West':

> The 'Wild West' analogy is quite a good one. I love it, absolutely love it. Given the choice if I had to pick defendants or witnesses I would pick defendants because it suits my personality better. I don't like being told what to do and you are much more your own boss.
>
> (E&W-13)

E&W-13 was one of four intermediaries who explained that they preferred defendant work over witness work. Yet practitioner satisfaction does not necessarily equal strong jurisdictional claims over work. Based on Abbott's argument that claims to jurisdiction are more effective when a profession

127 Abbott (n 8) 82.
128 Fournier (n 66) 69.

is well-organised, non-registered intermediaries are less able to compete for legitimacy. While E&W-7 identified deficiencies in Registered Intermediary assessment capabilities, training has at least been updated to ensure basic assessment competencies are met. For non-registered intermediaries, there is no equivalent organisation to organise such training centrally. Even though the introduction of HAIS in 2022 formalised defendant intermediary appointments, intermediary provision and training remains fragmented amongst several commercial providers. Through an inability to control its members and collectively respond to threats to its jurisdiction, non-registered intermediaries seem to lack the 'cultural machinery for jurisdiction'.[129] An example of the distinction in organisation between the two groups is the 'Registered Intermediary Procedural Guidance' which is published and updated by the MoJ. While affording discretion to registered practitioners regarding assessment format, this document nonetheless acts as a reference point for the diagnostic elements of the intermediary role. The lack of similar guidance for non-registered intermediaries exacerbates the lack of confidence many feel when performing the role. As Plotnikoff and Woolfson note, the lack of regulation of non-registered intermediaries and their inability to access standardised training damages the role's standing within the criminal justice system and may lead to resistance from other criminal justice actors.[130]

As this section has revealed, intermediaries execute their diagnostic function primarily by assessing communication needs. The assessment 'assembles' these needs into a picture to ensure that any communication assistance required is appropriately categorised.[131] The next section in this sequence is 'inference'.

5.6.2 *Inference*

The second element of Abbott's tripartite professional work model is 'inference'. Abbott considers inference to be the principal component of professional work which 'takes the information from diagnosis and indicates a range of treatments with their predicted outcomes'.[132] In other words, inference links diagnosis and treatment through the application of expert, theoretical knowledge.[133] In the case of the intermediary, the overlaps between inference and treatment are obvious. During the assessment, the intermediary utilises their professional knowledge to diagnose any communication problems and decide whether the involvement of an intermediary is appropriate.[134] While

129 Abbott (n 8) 82–83.
130 Plotnikoff and Woolfson (n 15) 277.
131 Abbott (n 8) 41.
132 Abbott (n 8) 40.
133 Beverley Burris, *Technocracy at Work* (SUNY Press 1993) 119.
134 MoJ (n 14).

the presentation of the recommendations to the police or the court will follow, the professional inferences take place at the assessment stage.

The action of inference raises several issues related to the intermediary's professional jurisdiction. Unlike a doctor who is presented with a patient at a surgery or a solicitor who may meet a client at a consultation, the intermediary relies exclusively on other actors for the initial details of a vulnerable individual. In the case of a witness, the matching process pairs the Registered Intermediary with the vulnerable individual based on their experience and expertise. Contact is then made with the relevant police officer who will often provide further details and clarify that the Registered Intermediary has the necessary skill set. For suspects or defendants, intermediaries are almost exclusively contacted by the instructing solicitor. Yet, even if a defendant has received a prior diagnosis, the solicitor may not be aware of this and the opportunity to engage an intermediary at first instance may be missed. The recommendation to engage an intermediary for a defendant may often arise out of the defence commissioning a psychological report.[135] The failure of police, lawyers and others to identify vulnerability early on means that an intermediary may not become involved in a case where they are sorely needed.[136] For both witnesses and defendants, the intermediary must make a judgement call, not about the appropriate 'treatment', but whether they are sufficiently skilled individually for the task based on the initial diagnosis of another. This creates a problem for the intermediary as E&W-20 explained:

> Recently I had a case allocated to me on the basis of mental health and I made some initial enquiries of the officer and I formed the opinion that the difficulties that were going to be the barrier to communication were not the mental health issues which I thought were more suited to SLT and I recommended that the case be re-matched. I spoke to the police officer and I think this is what every intermediary should do. I spoke to the officer about my thoughts and said about the referral coming through on paper but based on my conversation with you which has added to what I knew, I am changing my mind whether I am the right person to take this case and for these reasons and I think it would be better matched to someone from a different discipline and a different skill set. So, I handed it back to the matching service.
>
> (E&W-20)

135 Plotnikoff and Woolfson (n 15) 257.

136 Gisli Gudjonsson and others, *Persons at Risk during Interviews in Police Custody: The Identification of Vulnerabilities* (Royal Commission on Criminal Procedure Research Study No. 12) (HMSO 1993); Roxanna Dehaghani, 'Vulnerability in Police Custody: Definition, Identification and Implementation in the Context of the Appropriate Adult Safeguard' (PhD thesis, University of Leicester 2017).

This example provides an insight into the intermediary role's diagnosis, inference and treatment functions. A police officer had presented a vague case of mental health problems to the intermediary who sought further information in a bid to diagnose with more certainty. Concurrently, a self-diagnosis took place, and the intermediary had to decide if she was competent to assess the individual. The intricacies of this latter process are understandably complex and rely on the subjective value judgements of individuals. Focal to this self-assessment is what E&W-20 termed 'being absolutely boundaried' as to one's competencies. As Riesch notes, the construction of boundaries amounts to professions seeking to 'communicate their subject [and] establish their own credibility to talk authoritatively about their subject'.[137] By only accepting referrals which match her skill set, E&W-20 strengthens rather than weakens her authority and credibility over her work. Further, this form of boundary work encourages intermediaries to be reflective about their own knowledge claims and resist spreading their jurisdictional net so wide to make it a target for criticism and possibly attack.

While E&W-20 commendably returned the referral, intermediaries find themselves in a veritable 'Catch 22' situation. On the one hand, those who accept complex referrals (for which they may potentially be underqualified) and make recommendations accordingly may conduct 'too little inference'.[138] This involves a seamless movement from diagnosis to treatment. The problem with this approach is that it becomes an obvious target for poaching by other professions. If there is a routine, ineluctable link between diagnosis and treatment – why do we need intermediaries at all? The task could be conducted by existing members of the criminal justice system and the activity would arguably not warrant specific professional status.[139] On the other hand, too much 'formal inference' involving intermediaries applying their professional knowledge to the presented diagnosis in more obscure cases is dangerous. This is because of the risk that the overall activity is perceived as a 'mass of personal judgements, well informed, but ultimately idiosyncratic'.[140] Abbott explains that many of the 'occult' professions, such as astrology, historically faced this very issue by adopting the position that every problem must be handled in its own special way.[141] Further, a profession that frames itself in purely abstract terms faces difficulty in demonstrating what Abbott terms 'cultural legitimacy'.[142]

137 Riesch (n 12) 454.
138 Abbott (n 8) 51.
139 Burris (n 133).
140 Abbott (n 8) 52.
141 Andrew Abbott, 'The Emergence of American Psychiatry' (PhD thesis, University of Chicago) 388–93.
142 Abbott (n 8) 54.

The mutually conflicting scenario described earlier was well understood by every professional group interviewed. There was a palpable sense of unease among many intermediaries who saw opportunities for other actors, particularly members of the court workgroup, to undermine the role's credibility and legitimacy. One particular quote encapsulates this:

> I feel that all those dichotomies going on and there is 'divide and conquer' and that is how judges and barristers are going to get you in the end.
>
> (NI-7)

This language illustrates the unease that many intermediaries have regarding their role and its susceptibility to attack. It also aligns with Abbott's conception of jurisdiction as competition with malleable jurisdictional boundaries waiting to be capitalised upon by other predatory professions. The professional activities of individual actors in any system of work cannot be unilaterally defined but are instead subject to the dynamics of interdependent relationships.[143] Yet, the preceding quotes from E&W-20 and NI-7 suggest a cognisance of this threat and a willingness to react. In particular, E&W-20 places the responsibility on intermediaries to engage in introspection, not just to ensure more appropriate matching but to protect the role's professional jurisdiction within the 'ecology' of the criminal justice system.[144] E&W-20's clarion call can be viewed as a response to the threat of workplace assimilation, which Abbott notes 'reaches its maximum in publicly funded worksites specializing in pariah clients – mental hospitals, jails, criminal courts'.[145] This assimilation may involve the police, lawyers and judges appropriating intermediary tasks based on perceptions of incompetence. Backen identifies another catalyst for this assimilation: intermediary reports that do not recommend intermediary involvement are never seen by judges or lawyers.[146] As a result, a skewed view exists of how the intermediary performs its core professional tasks and, crucially, how they recommend their involvement. Without seeing reports in which intermediaries justify their non-involvement, how can judges understand the theoretical knowledge and expertise underpinning diagnosis, inference and treatment? Many intermediaries interviewed echoed this point and felt that lawyers and judges were oblivious to their 'backstage' role during assessment. Citing previous research conducted by Communicourt, E&W-17 claimed that 24% of all intermediary assessments conclude with a recommendation of no intermediary involvement. E&W-17 also

143 Timmermans (n 82) 552.
144 Abbott (n 8) 33.
145 Abbott (n 8) 66.
146 Paula Backen, *They Just Don't Get It: Communication and the Work of an Intermediary with Vulnerable People in the Justice System* (independently published 2017) 63.

lamented the judicial perception of the intermediary as primarily self-serving and 'on the make':

> They don't want to know if we recommend [intermediary involvement] because we're 'self-serving' aren't we? We're appointing ourselves! We're 'desperately looking for work'. I could be in three other courts today. There's no shortage of work! But they think we are looking for work for ourselves!

The aforementioned analysis suggests that intermediaries are conscious of ongoing jurisdictional conflicts and are often prepared to confront them. But can jurisdictional conflicts be resolved systemically? Abbott notes that in inter-professional jurisdictional contests, 'the profession with more extensive organisation usually wins.[147] A strong, coordinated response to threats to jurisdiction requires an organised professional body or, at the very least, a figurehead. As we have seen in previous chapters, no group of intermediaries currently has such a body or lead individual.

According to Abbott, the act of inference is a 'purely professional act'.[148] As we have seen in this section, for intermediaries, the act of inference is the link between the diagnosis of communication issues and relevant treatment. It is closely tied to how jurisdictional claims are made and defended. The next act in the sequence is treatment.

5.6.3 Treatment

The third component of professional practice is 'treatment'. Abbott's conception of treatment is self-evident and refers to methods to remedy problems or complications made apparent from the diagnosis. Like diagnosis, it is organised around a 'classification and brokering process' which gives a result rather than taking information.[149] Unlike some professions, the intermediary advises the most appropriate treatment rather than administering directly. The intermediary report constitutes the 'treatment' outlined by Abbott. The treatments suggested are embodied in the reports compiled for police prior to interview (if involved at that stage) and then later for the court, if required.[150] This latter, and more substantial report, should include the witness's background, the 'diagnosis' from the assessment and ABE interview, the witness's communication abilities and specific needs, and practical suggestions about how the witness can best be questioned at court.[151] These essentially amount

147 Abbott (n 8) 83.
148 Abbott (n 8) 40.
149 Abbott (n 8) 44.
150 MoJ (n 14).
151 MoJ (n 14) 16.

to instructions, or 'practical precepts' premised on academic work and theoretical principles.[152]

Outlining recommendations in the form of 'treatment' is a potentially hazardous area for the intermediary with a risk of 'outside interloping' into its professional jurisdiction.[153] In other words, the efficacy of treatment, as judged by external actors, such as police, lawyers and judges, is critical to how the intermediary role is perceived and how it gains legitimacy. The quality of recommendations, whether given directly to the police orally or in written form to the court, was a contentious topic in my interviews. Whether from taking responsibility for another intermediary's case or being asked to provide advice on another's court report, some intermediaries were visibly concerned about the quality of recommendations. For example, when reviewing another Registered Intermediary's preliminary report, NI-7 was shocked to find '32 points for the police' to follow in a suspect interview. In her view, this was overly complicated and risked damaging the image and reputation of intermediaries in general. These fears appear well-founded, with police officers critical of intermediary recommendations that appeared to amount to 'common sense'. In the words of Officer PO-2:

> If we train police officers to ask simple questions, stay on one topic and build rapport then they don't need a speech and language therapist! . . . you need police officers with heightened training to recognise that and do something about it.
>
> (PO-2)

A similar concern, voiced by some judges in Northern Ireland, lamented the generic nature of the court reports:

> Sometimes, some of the reports I have had I have thought: 'I could have worked that out myself' and that might sound arrogant, and I don't mean that. But those are strategies that I think we already have.
>
> (MCJ-2)

> They were kind of generic, I have to say which detracts from them to some extent because you feel that it's a 'tick-box exercise'. I would like to see something a bit more individual, and I think it gives it more weight.
>
> (CCJ-1)

152 David Sciulli, *Professions in Civil Society and the State: Invariant Foundations and Consequences* (Brill 2009) 350.

153 Abbott (n 8) 45.

Another judge responded almost identically:

> The reports that I have been getting, quite often I find myself apologising as I say to the defence: 'That all seems to me to be common sense' and then I always have to apologise because I know there is expertise and all the rest of it, but most of us can see when a child is getting stressed and needs a break.
>
> (MCJ-1)

CCJ-2 conveyed a less critical judicial tone about intermediaries' recommendations but remarked that they are 'usually fairly pedestrian [and] rarely differ'. Yet, the tone of these responses signals a potentially serious credibility issue concerning the confidence that other key criminal justice actors have in the intermediary role. There were, of course, many intermediaries who had not experienced any adverse comments or attitudes from police, lawyers or judges regarding their recommendations. Further, some intermediaries were surprised when the aforementioned judicial perspective was presented, with a number becoming noticeably defensive. One wonders whether a much more serious discord exists between intermediaries, the police and judges about the appropriateness of recommendations. A practice that aggravates the situation is the failure to allow intermediaries to explain their recommendations to the court in a GRH. The requirement to hold a GRH is contained within the relevant Criminal Practice Directions (CPD),[154] Criminal Procedure Rules (CPR)[155] and in the Judicial College guidance.[156] Plotnikoff and Woolfson found that only 30% of Registered Intermediaries were almost always asked to discuss their recommendations at a GRH, whereas 95% of judges said they almost always invited intermediaries to discuss key recommendations.[157] This discrepancy is not easily explained but is nonetheless evidence of a disharmony between judges and intermediaries. Most intermediaries had at least one experience of no GRH taking place in a case, but when it did, the minimisation of their role was evident:

> You don't as an RI ever get asked for any knowledge, half of the time you don't get to open your mouth in a GRH. The longest GRH I had as an RI

154 CPD (n 103) [6.1.4].
155 Criminal Procedure Rules (October 2020) Pt 3, rules 3.9(6) and (7).
156 Judicial College 'Crown Court Compendium: Part I' (July 2024) [10–21].
157 Joyce Plotnikoff and Richard Woolfson, *Falling Short? A Snapshot of Young Witness Policy and Practice: A Report for the NSPCC, Revisiting 'Measuring Up? Evaluating Implementation of Government Commitments to Young Witnesses in Criminal Proceedings'* (NSPCC, February 2019) 81.

> was 20 minutes. The shortest was about 30 seconds and I didn't even get in the box. It varies very much from judge to judge.
>
> (E&W-13)

> An effective GRH only needs to be 15 minutes or something. But I do think I need to be given an opportunity to speak – that would make it much better. But when the judge says, 'Yes we have read your report and will follow your advice' and that's it, that leaves you no room for questioning anything because the assumption is you are going to move on to the next thing to discuss.
>
> (E&W-8)

While most intermediaries spoke of an improving judicial attitude to GRHs, E&W-2 recounted a shocking judicial response to her attempt to explain her recommendations:

> the law has changed and we have to have you here now, but I am not impressed. I have seen your report, you're trying to tie counsel's hands behind their back and if you intervene I will hold you in contempt of court.
>
> (E&W-2)

This quote encapsulates what is at the heart of much intermediary – court workgroup conflict over treatment. Lawyers and judges can view recommendations in the court report as no different to what has been practiced for years, with the intermediary role merely committing age-old techniques to paper. This differs from the experience of other therapeutic agents, such as probation officers, who have become embedded into the institutional arrangements of judicial institutions such as problem-solving courts.[158] For example, research into American drug courts found that probation officers often wielded a 'substantially superior level of power when compared to other court team members', which in turn substantially influenced case outcomes.[159]

My data suggest that the court workgroup is often reticent to acknowledge treatment recommended by the intermediary. This seems, at least partially, to be based on a lack of understanding of the theoretical basis of recommendations and a belief that the court workgroup can facilitate communication without intermediary assistance. These conclusions support the earlier

158 Young (n 25) 219; Vladimir Konecni and Ebbe Ebbesen, *The Criminal Justice System: A Social-Psychological Analysis* (W.H. Freeman 1982).

159 Danielle Rudes and Shannon Portillo, 'Roles and Powers within Federal Problem Solving Workgroups' (2012) 34(4) Law and Policy at 420; Ursula Castellano, 'Beyond the Courtroom Workgroup: Caseworkers as the New Satellite of Social Control' (2009) 31(4) Law & Policy 429.

suggestion that a discord exists between intermediaries and the court work-group in terms of how the 'treatment' function of the intermediary role is conceptualised and approached in practice.

5.7 Jurisdictional settlement

Intermediaries not only feel like outsiders but are also conscious of incursions into their jurisdiction and often struggle with how they can sustain control. What heightens their fears is that, in being part of a 'culture change' towards improved treatment of vulnerable witnesses and defendants, they may be making a rod for their own back. This notion was first suggested to me by an intermediary in Northern Ireland who argued that the profession should be 'working ourselves out of a job' (NI-2). She explained how in five- or ten-years' time lawyers and judges should have learned sufficiently from the practice of intermediaries that the role should be minimised. Many intermediaries I subsequently interviewed were appalled by this suggestion and argued that it betrayed a lack of understanding of the role.

There is, however, an alternative analysis of the preceding quote from NI-2. While ostensibly advocating a narrower, more nuanced role for the intermediary, NI-2's comments may reflect an attempt to protect the role's jurisdiction in the long-term. This implicitly involves a form of boundary work in which, rather than seeking 'expansion or authority' into a domain claimed by another professional, the intermediary goal is 'protection of autonomy'.[160] Unlike E&W-17 and E&W-7, who advocated for increased intermediary involvement at all stages, NI-2's comments suggest what Abbott terms a 'jurisdictional settlement' between intermediaries and other actors in the criminal justice system.[161] While Abbott details five distinct types of jurisdictional settlement, NI-2 suggests an 'advisory jurisdiction' for intermediaries in the long-term. This involves intermediaries accepting a 'weaker form of control', which involves other actors eventually claiming aspects of the intermediary's current jurisdiction.[162] As explored in Chapter 1 (Introduction), the case of *R v Rashid* signalled a restriction to the availability of defendant intermediaries. These developments could be viewed as evidence of an advisory jurisdiction in practice as judges are expected to 'adapt the trial process to address a defendant's communication needs'.[163] Further, the court in *Rashid* emphasised that defence advocates should be able to perform the 'basic tasks' of asking questions based on their 'training and experience'.[164]

160 Gieryn (n 11) 792.
161 Abbott (n 8) 575.
162 Abbott (n 8).
163 *R v Rashid* [2017] 1 WLR 2449 [73].
164 *R v Rashid* (n 163) [80].

Abbott notes that advisory jurisdiction involves a profession seeking a legitimate right to 'interpret, buffer or partially modify actions another takes within its own full jurisdiction'.[165] In practice, this could arguably involve intermediaries providing more general recommendations about facilitating communication without the sort of 'hands on' involvement the role often currently involves. For example, a written report about the vulnerable individual, which the court could use as it wishes, may amount to an advisory jurisdiction. The intermediary may not even be physically present at any stage save for the communication assessment at the outset. Paradoxically, NI-2 views this diminution of the intermediary's jurisdiction as inevitable but ultimately necessary for survival of the role. However, the judges interviewed were largely cautious about the idea that the intermediary's jurisdiction could be incrementally allocated to other professions as an 'advisory settlement'. While some judges acknowledged that the intermediary had forced the judiciary to be 'more alert and aware of the issues that defendants and witnesses may have' (MCJ-2), this did not mean that the role should be phased out:

> The intermediary is bespoke to that particular client's needs so whilst I, as the lay-person, think I am terribly clever and think I know a lot about autism and don't need the expert because I have a handle on this, when you get the particular individual it's how that condition manifests itself with that particular person in the particular circumstances and the stress you are going to put them under. For those reasons, you will still need the RI expertise.
>
> (MCJ-2)

> It could well be that we get to a point where, if everyone is on the same page, then there is less need for a Registered Intermediary because the questioning is appropriate and the judges are more informed about what is appropriate. . . . If we are doing it properly, their role ought to diminish and they should be self-limiting to a large degree because, as the process accommodates what they are doing better and as it becomes more familiar, you should see their role reducing. But I would be worried that we get to a point where we get to a degree of complacency where we say: 'oh that's not needed at all now, we know everything about this'.
>
> (CCJ-1)

Professional competition over jurisdiction can produce various outcomes since not every profession aiming for full jurisdiction will obtain it. If an advisory jurisdiction is the outcome of the intermediary's jurisdictional disputes, a salient question is whether this amounts to the 'leading edge of invasion [or] the

165 *R v Rashid* (n 163) [80].

trailing edge of defeat' for intermediary work.[166] At such an early stage in the role's development, this is a difficult question to answer conclusively. It will be interesting to monitor how the intermediary role develops in other international jurisdictions and how other criminal justice actors respond to the role's claim for jurisdiction. If, for example, the role is embraced and afforded control over its work tasks, understanding and responding to the perceptions of the role by lawyers and judges will be fundamental. In any event, there is ample scope for comparative research into how the role is performed across the various jurisdictions discussed in Chapter 3 (The international context).

Crucial to the future of the intermediary role will be the ability of those who perform it to communicate its exclusive authority over its workplace tasks and the acceptability of the role's professional boundaries to other criminal justice actors. This reality is reflected in the comments of judges included in this chapter. The generally sanguine judicial perception of intermediaries and their work appears a good augury for the role's future in the criminal justice system. As will be discussed further in Chapter 8 (Conclusion), the introduction of the new HAIS scheme, which provides intermediaries for vulnerable court users who are not eligible under the WIS, suggests that intermediary presence in the justice system looks set to expand rather than diminish.

However, there is a question of legitimacy surrounding the role's future and, more specifically, whether the intermediary can convince other actors of its cultural legitimacy. Drawing parallels with Abbott's work on social workers, my interview data suggest that intermediaries consistently struggle to convince police, lawyers and judges of the role's legitimacy. Just as Abbott discovered with social workers, there is a risk that the central public legitimacy of the intermediary derives not from its expertise and theoretical knowledge, but from 'altruism'.[167] In other words, the role is often framed by the caring backgrounds from which most intermediaries are sourced rather than the specialist function practitioners seek to emphasise.[168] Some of the more recent intermediary recruits felt that the older generation of intermediaries did little to dispel this image. E&W-18 talked about tension between these two factions and how projecting the role as a 'volunteer' rather than as a professional was concerning:

> They don't like the fact that there's quite a few of us who have gone full time with it and like proper do the job and have made these relationships and we don't do it as a hobby . . . we're not just retired doing it [because it's] the right thing to do. . . . There's a bit of conflict there. I think, whether

166 *R v Rashid* (n 163) 76.

167 Abbott (n 8) 561.

168 See: Eliot Freidson, *Profession of Medicine: A Study of the Sociology of Applied* (Chicago UP 1970).

> it's a profession or whether it is just being 'us kind people, and we are just trying to be kind, and are we trying to help'.
>
> (E&W-18)

Parallels can be drawn between the situation E&W-18 describes and the ultimately unsuccessful volunteer communication partner scheme in South Australia (see Chapter 3: The international context). Any jurisdiction considering the introduction of an intermediary-type role should carefully consider engaging with other criminal justice professionals to ensure its function and status in the criminal process is understood. Despite many issues surrounding the intermediary role discussed in this book, it appears that criminal justice professionals in the U.K generally know that the intermediary is a paid (i.e. not a volunteer) role.[169] This can be contrasted, for example, with the appropriate adult role which was originally designed to be performed by volunteers and mostly continues to be.[170]

Aside from such internal divisions, which do little to foster a united intermediary front, the struggle for legitimacy manifests in other ways. One intermediary (E&W-20) explained in interview that the attitude of the judge and lawyers towards her changed once she obtained her doctorate and formally introduced herself as 'Dr X' at a GRH. She explained that the recommendations contained in her court report were taken more seriously compared to previous interactions in court. This exchange illustrates the 'them and us' divide between the 'marginal or passive role of court users [and] the active, central role of the legal professionals in the courtroom'.[171] In this example, the granting of a voice to the intermediary based on a perception of elevated status fits the various theorisations of the criminal court as hierarchical and run by the elite courtroom workgroup.[172] This was, however, largely symbolic since the inner zones, or 'circles' using Rock's terminology, of the court are impermeable to an actor such as the intermediary who is not viewed as sharing the same collective goals of the legal professionals.[173] The aforementioned example is an outlier, and the daily struggles for legitimacy faced by intermediaries better reflect the reality of the role. Notwithstanding positive signals from some judges and lawyers and that many recent recruits appear to have settled on the role as a full-time

169 Samantha Fairclough and John Taggart, 'Lost in Translation? Perceptions of Defendant Intermediaries in the Legal Profession' (2023) 7 Criminal Law Review 440.

170 Harriet Pierpoint, 'Quickening the PACE? The Use of Volunteers as Appropriate Adults in England and Wales' (2008) 18(4) Policing and Society: An International Journal of Research and Policy 397; Roxanna Dehaghani, 'Defining the "Appropriate" in "Appropriate Adult": Restrictions and Opportunities for Reform' (2020) 12 Criminal Law Review 1137.

171 Jacobson and others (n 47) 96.

172 Mulcahy and Rowden (n 47) 247.

173 Rock (n 46); Paul Rock, 'Rules, Boundaries and the Courts: Some Problems in the Neo-Durkheimian Sociology of Deviance' (1998) 49(4) The British Journal of Sociology 586.

profession, the role's parameters and claims to jurisdiction have been shown to be far from settled. Questions remain about how willing the key criminal justice actors are to accommodate the 'professional work' of the intermediary and how disputes over jurisdictions and boundaries will be settled.

5.8 Conclusion

This chapter has identified how the intermediary tussles for control over its work tasks with other criminal justice actors. Through diagnosis, inference and treatment the intermediary performs professional work which is relational at its core. Interaction with other criminal justice actors shapes the role's content in several ways. It enables the intermediary to demonstrate its theoretical knowledge and expertise to persuade audiences of its jurisdictional claims. Equally, other professionals scope out the role and often question its legitimacy. My data reveal the resistance of the court workgroup to threats challenging its cultural norms and how the intermediary role often treads a thin line between gaining acceptance and seeing its jurisdiction vulnerable to encroachment. Boundaries are fundamental to understanding the nature of these interjurisdictional conflicts as they mediate inter-professional interaction and delineate the intermediary's tasks. Although the scope of the intermediary role was initially untested, individual practices have seen the construction of boundaries which are continually negotiated between actors. We have also seen how encroachment on the intermediary's tasks often appears to be preceded by the action of 'boundary blurring'. This was illustrated through intermediary cooperation with the police at the assessment stage, during which joint sharing of jurisdiction led to police dispensing altogether with the intermediary.

While this chapter has given a snapshot of the intermediary's professional work, the question of where these interjurisdictional disputes will lead remains. In other words, what will the resulting 'outcome' or 'settlement' of these jurisdictional conflicts be? This remains a live question in the U.K, although it must also be relevant in jurisdictions where the intermediary (or similar communication assistance role) has more recently been implemented. In the research interviews which underpin this book, intermediaries were acutely aware of their outsider status and that many legal professionals would welcome a reduction in their influence throughout the criminal justice system. Importantly, it is before this audience that the intermediary claims jurisdiction and seeks legitimacy. Any eventual settlement will depend on the acceptance of the claims which are staked.[174] If the objective is for the intermediary to retain its jurisdiction over its workplace tasks, then much will depend on how inter-professional disputes over jurisdictions are settled and how associated boundaries are negotiated.

174 Abbott (n 8) 191.

Chapter 6

The neutrality paradox

6.1 Introduction

So far, we have seen that the scope of the intermediary role is contested and its parameters are in need of clarification. While the relevant procedural guidance from the Ministry of Justice (MoJ) and the Department of Justice (Northern Ireland) (DoJ) puts some flesh on the 'bare bones' of the legislation, case law reveals how a standardised depiction of the role is elusive.[1] Notwithstanding the need for clarity, the intermediary is consistently represented as a normatively impartial, neutral and objective role.[2] As an 'Officer of the Court', the role shares a responsibility for the administration of justice and the proper functioning of the judicial system.[3] This chapter examines the neutrality of the intermediary role and problematises the value of neutrality as a core tenet of intermediary practice. During my interviews, it became evident that the relationship between intermediaries and the neutrality underpinning their work is complex, poorly understood and somewhat 'taboo'. O'Mahony et al. have written about the developing occupational identities of intermediaries and the challenge of reconciling the role's neutrality with different professional backgrounds.[4] This theme, however, has not been developed in the subsequent literature, and numerous questions remain. What exactly does it mean for an intermediary to be neutral? How

1 Diane Birch, 'A Better Deal for Vulnerable Witnesses?' (2000) Criminal Law Review 223, 249.

2 Department of Justice (Northern Ireland), 'The Registered Intermediaries Procedural Guidance Manual' (April 2024); Ministry of Justice, 'Registered Intermediary Procedural Guidance Manual 2024' <https://assets.publishing.service.gov.uk/media/671b819bfc28a840abc6d26d/Registered_Intermediary_Procedural_Guidance_Manual_2024__Official_.pdf> accessed 8 February 2025; Joyce Plotnikoff and Richard Woolfson, *Intermediaries in the Criminal Justice System* (Policy Press 2015) 11.

3 Joyce Plotnikoff and Richard Woolfson, 'Registered Intermediaries in Action: Messages for the CJS from the Witness Intermediary Scheme SmartSite' (NSPCC and MoJ, December 2011).

4 Brendan O'Mahony and others, 'Developing a Professional Identity in a New Work Environment: The Views of Defendant Intermediaries Working in the Criminal Courts' (2016) 18(2) Journal of Forensic Practice 155.

DOI: 10.4324/9781003461166-6

do intermediaries navigate situations that call their neutrality into question? Can the imperative of working neutrally hinder the role's objective of 'facilitating communication'? These salient questions should cause us to think critically about the contours of the intermediary role.

This chapter centres on the key finding that intermediaries are embroiled in an ongoing struggle about how the principle of neutrality is conceptualised and negotiated. Generally, there is a strong commitment to these normative principles among intermediaries. However, when their practical application is examined, it is evident that the role can transcend that of an objective conduit. I have termed the tension between these two sides of intermediary practice, 'the neutrality paradox'. Conceptualising the role as hermetically sealed from its emotionally charged work appears illusory and disconnected from the reality of actual practice.[5] More specifically, the intermediaries whom I interviewed were committed to facilitating communication, which often sees them override the official rubrics of the profession to ensure that the individual needs of vulnerable people are met. This involves prioritising their own judgement over the official stance of objectivity and reconceptualising the boundaries of their own neutrality.

This chapter explores this 'neutrality paradox' using the Bourdieusian concept of 'illusio'. Illusio relates to a collective belief among members of a 'field' in the value of participating in collective struggles.[6] Drawing on metaphors of game and game playing, the concept captures how members feel invested in the game and how they are motivated by its stakes.[7] When applied to the intermediary role, we may use illusio as an explanatory concept to examine deviations from the expected performance of neutrality. How and why intermediaries demonstrate indifference or lack of commitment to these values is instructive to understanding the role's scope in practice. Reflecting on the strength (or weakness) of the illusio generated by intermediaries helps locate the role within the social world of the criminal justice system. If the core tenet of neutrality is not considered an intrinsic value by intermediary practitioners, this may have significant implications for the role more generally. Examining the intermediary role through the prism of neutrality also reinforces a key theme emerging from my data: the roles of Registered Intermediaries and non-registered intermediaries are qualitatively different. It is axiomatic that intermediary involvement differs when working with a defendant compared to working with a witness, but this chapter examines how these differing demands impact, and are impacted by, the principle of neutrality.

5 Helen Colley and Frédérique Guéry, 'Understanding New Hybrid Professions: Bourdieu, *illusio* and the Case of Public Service Interpreters' (2015) 45 Cambridge Journal of Education 113.

6 Pierre Bourdieu, *Pascalian Meditations* (CUP 2000) 187.

7 Bourdieu, *Pascalian Meditations* (n 6).

The examination of the neutrality paradox is important for intermediaries when reflecting on and coping with the tensions and challenges involved in their work. It is also relevant for criminal justice actors such as lawyers and judges, who interact with intermediaries and seek to better understand the scope and content of the role. Finally, the issue of intermediary neutrality is relevant for policy makers in terms of how the role is organised, governed and detailed in the relevant legal rules and procedural guidance. For example, in 2022 the HMCTS awarded contracts for the provision of 'Court Appointed Intermediary Services (HAIS)' for vulnerable individuals who fall outside the remit of the MoJ's existing intermediary scheme.[8] As intermediaries are introduced into new justice settings, understanding of the role's nature and scope becomes increasingly important.

6.2 Exploring the normative basis of neutrality

Neutrality is recognised as one of several critical dimensions of procedural justice and is closely linked to the concept of legitimacy.[9] As discussed in Chapter 4 (Locating the intermediary within theories of the criminal trial), for criminal justice institutions to operate effectively they must hold legitimate authority in the eyes of those they serve.[10] The view that the criminal justice system must constantly demonstrate its legitimacy to the public reflects the imperative that decisions are seen to be taken in a 'genuinely unbiased and neutral way'.[11] Intermediaries in England and Wales and Northern Ireland must adopt and maintain a neutral position in all aspects of their work.[12] Although similar schemes established in Australia and New Zealand operate slightly differently in some areas of intermediary practice, they retain neutrality as a core tenet of the role. However, varying definitions of 'neutrality' and 'impartiality' exist. While some academic commentators view the terms as distinctive, others use them interchangeably. For example, in mediation,

8 HMCTS, 'New Contracts Awarded to Support Vulnerable Court and Tribunal Users' (26 January 2022) <https://www.gov.uk/government/news/new-contracts-awarded-to-support-vulnerable-court-and-tribunal-users> accessed 24 March 2022; For further information on the new scheme, see section 9.4 below; Also see: John Taggart 'Vulnerable Defendants and the HMCTS Court-Appointed Intermediary Services' (2022) 6 Criminal Law Review 427.

9 Tom Tyler, *Why People Obey the Law* (Yale UP 1990); Miranda Boone and Mieke Kox, 'Neutrality as an Element of Perceived Justice in Prison: Consistency versus Individualization' (2014) 10(4) Utrecht Law Review 118; Somjen Frazer, *The Impact of the Community Court Model on Defendant Perceptions of Fairness: A Case Study at the Red Hook Community Justice Center* (Center for Court Innovation 2006).

10 Anthony Bottoms and Justice Tankebe, 'Beyond Procedural Justice: A Dialogic Approach to Legitimacy in Criminal Justice' (2013) 102(1) Journal of Criminal Law and Criminology 119.

11 Lord Neuberger, 'Fairness in the Courts: The Best We Can Do' (Address to the Criminal Justice Alliance, 10 April 2015).

12 MoJ (n 2); DoJ (n 2).

impartiality often connotes a freedom from favouritism and even-handedness, with neutrality more concerned with decision makers not taking a position regarding the dispute or the parties.[13] Indeed, the updated Registered Intermediary Procedural Guidance of 2024 published by the Ministry of Justice exclusively uses the term 'impartial' whereas previous versions relied on both terms at different points.[14] In any case, significant overlap exists between the usage of the terms in the criminal justice literature.[15] Considering the variance of definitions, the term neutrality used in this chapter refers to the objective, non-biased status of the intermediary as an officer of the court.[16] This means that intermediaries act independently of the defence or prosecution.[17]

Within the criminal justice literature, the discussion of neutrality and impartiality has often been dominated by a focus on adjudication.[18] Both neutrality and impartiality are central to conceptions of judicial legitimacy and authority.[19] Even within the jurisprudential debate between legal positivism and natural law, judicial impartiality is a shared concern of any theory of legal regulation.[20] Perhaps surprisingly, the impartiality of the prosecution within the English legal system has received relatively little academic critique.[21] Most academic research has taken place within the context of the American judicial system, much of which focuses on prosecutorial discretion and the vexed issue of politicisation.[22] The English courts have, however, recognised the position of the prosecution within the adversarial system as

13 Debbie De Girolamo, 'The Mediation Process: Challenges to Neutrality and the Delivery of Procedural Justice' (2019) 39(4) Oxford Journal of Legal Studies 834, 841.
14 MoJ (n 2).
15 Stephanos Bibas, *The Machinery of Justice* (OUP 2015) 106.
16 The MoJ's 'Registered Intermediary Procedural Guidance Manual' from 2015 uses the terms 'impartial and neutral' whereas since 2020 the guidance simply uses 'impartial'. Correspondence between the author and the MoJ in May 2020 confirmed that this change was made merely for the sake of brevity.
17 DoJ, 'Registered Intermediary Schemes' <https://www.justice-ni.gov.uk/publications/registered-intermediary-schemes> accessed 26 February 2021.
18 There is a separate, albeit related, discussion of judicial independence amidst concerns that the judiciary, as an institution, is not detached from other arms of the state as traditional views of separation of powers dictate. See: Mike McConville and Luke Marsh, *The Myth of Judicial Independence* (OUP 2020).
19 Sharyn Roach Anleu and Kathy Mack, *Performing Judicial Authority in the Lower Courts* (Palgrave 2017) 8.
20 Ofer Raban, *Modern Legal Theory and Judicial Impartiality* (Routledge 2003).
21 Ellison notes how the role of the prosecution counsel has rarely been examined through the lens of impartiality: Louise Ellison, 'A Comparative Study of Rape Trials in Adversarial and Inquisitorial Criminal Justice Systems' (PhD thesis, University of Leeds 1997).
22 For example, see: Richard Uviller, 'The Neutral Prosecutor: The Obligation of Dispassion in a Passionate Pursuit' (2000) 68 Fordham Law Review 1695; Bennett Gershman, 'The Prosecutor's Duty to Truth' (2001) 14 Journal of Legal Ethics 309; Wayne LaFave, 'The Prosecutor's Discretion in the United States' (1970) 18 American Journal of Comparative Law 532; Ellen Podgor, 'The Tainted Federal Prosecutor in an Overcriminalized Justice System' (2010) 67 Washington and Lee Law Review 1569.

that of a Crown representative overarchingly concerned with the administration of justice.[23] The prosecutor does not bear the responsibility of securing a conviction at all costs; rather they aim to secure a result to which 'on his view, the evidence fairly leads; his methods and his motivation should be dispassionate'.[24] Sanders has questioned this normative depiction of the prosecution and argued that, in practice, it represents police interests as enthusiastically as defence practitioners do their clients.[25] The practices of the court workgroup, particularly in the magistrates' court where speed and efficiency are the essence of summary justice, produce legitimate questions about how achievable ideals of neutrality are.[26]

Outside of the court workgroup, the position of the court interpreter is a valuable analogue when examining the neutrality of the intermediary. Despite the differing interests of the parties within the adversarial system, court interpreters are required to adhere to the principle of neutrality at all times.[27] The traditional, positivist Anglo-American conception of the interpreter is that of a 'linguistic conduit' limiting itself to faithful, verbatim translation of what is said in court.[28] This model has received sustained criticism, much focusing on the disconnect between theory and practice. For example, Angellini questions the conceptualisation of interpreters as passive translation machines and points to their status as 'social beings who are subject to the interplay of social factors, institutional constraints and societal beliefs'.[29] This is linked to the argument that interpreters, as experts in facilitating intercultural communication, must be afforded some leeway to achieve this objective. These critiques recognise that the role is not merely providing communication, but *effective* communication, which never occurs in a social vacuum.[30] Rudvin explains how the notion of a wholly neutral interpreter is difficult to sustain:

> If the interpreter is an active protagonist in the interpreting encounter, constantly making decisions – subjective decisions and fruit of individual

23 *Banks* [1916] 2 KB 621 (Avory J); *R v Sugarman* (1936) 25 Cr App R 109; *R v Whitehorn* [1983] HCA 42; (1983) 152 CLR 657.
24 Andrew Ashworth, 'Prosecution and Procedure in Criminal Justice' [1979] Criminal Law Review 482.
25 Andrew Sanders, 'A Community Justice. Modernising the Magistracy in England and Wales' (Institute of Public Policy Research 2000) 33.
26 James Eisenstein and Herbert Jacob, *Felony Justice: An Organizational Analysis of Criminal Courts* (Little, Brown 1977); Mike McConville, Andrew Sanders and Roger Leng, *The Case for the Prosecution* (Routledge 1991) 6.
27 Roseann Gonzalez, Victoria Vasquez and Holly Mikkelson, *Fundamentals of Court Interpretation. Theory, Policy, and Practice* (Carolina Academic Press 1991).
28 Alicia Edwards, *The Practice of Court Interpreting* (John Benjamins 1995); Gonzalez, Vasquez and Mikkelson (n 27).
29 Claudia Angellini, *Revisiting the Interpreter's Role* (John Benjamins 2004) 47.
30 Christina Bratt Paulston, Scott Kiesling and Elizabeth Rangel, *The Handbook of Intercultural Communication* (Wiley 2012) 435.

> interpretation – s/he can hardly be a transparent entity through which some assumedly fixed meaning passes, crosses linguistic systems and comes out the other side 'untouched'.[31]

Despite the lack of academic attention given to the normative basis of the intermediary's neutrality, drawing parallels with the court interpreter is a useful starting point. The value attached to neutrality in both roles is broadly the same: any allegation of partiality or undue proximity to the prosecution or defence can undermine judicial proceedings. Both interpreters and intermediaries participate in interpreted events between individuals and the criminal justice system, e.g. during police interviews, consultations with lawyers or court testimony. There is concordance between the 'dynamic' view of language in the interpreting literature and my interview data which reveals intermediaries seeking to facilitate communication but often struggling with how to effect this within the constraints of their neutrality.[32] Dynamic interaction views language as a communication system in which each participant presents themselves to the exchange, and the outcome is regarded as a result of combined interaction.[33] My interview data, explored later, reveals that the formal recommendations intermediaries make, and the more informal, often unrecognised steps they take to facilitate communication, stem directly and inevitably from their interpretation of communicative situations. These interpretations can – at least in theory – never be finite or fixed but will result from a hermeneutic process.[34] From a sociological perspective, a 'thick' understanding of the intermediary's conditions of practice and social interactions is central to analysing its neutrality.[35] In short, it is contended that the role's neutrality is intrinsically relational and functions 'interactively and dynamically' based on the social norms and rules of particular criminal justice settings.[36] This is a critical point of departure for the analysis in this chapter, as neutrality is recognised as contextual and multifaceted. More broadly, this supports the argument that neutrality should be viewed as a 'process' rather than an inherent quality – a point further developed in the section titled 'Reconceptualising neutrality'.

31 Mette Rudvin, 'How Neutral is Neutral? Issues in Interaction and Participation in Community Interpreting' in Giuliana Garzone and Maurizio Viezzi (eds), *Perspectives on Interpreting* (CLUEB 2002) 4.
32 Cecilia Wadensjö, *Interpreting as Interaction* (Routledge 2013).
33 Wadensjö (n 32).
34 Rudvin (n 31) 3.
35 Wadensjö (n 32) 17.
36 John Touchie, 'On the Possibility of Impartiality in Decision-Making' (2001) 1 Macquarie Law Journal 21, 30.

The following section explores Bourdieu's conception of the social world. It introduces the ideas of 'habitus', 'field' and, most notably for this chapter, 'illusio'.

6.3 Bourdieu's social world

This chapter focuses on Bourdieu's concept of 'illusio', specifically in relation to the principle of neutrality. However, an examination of illusio must necessarily recognise two other central organising concepts of Bourdieu's work, namely 'field' and 'habitus'. Collectively, these concepts reflect the dialectic dimensions of objectivity and subjectivity in the social world and help facilitate analysis of their relational construction.[37] While the perception and classification of the social world is central to Bourdieu's reflexive sociology, he was also concerned with the existence of specific 'fields' within it. Bourdieu developed a framework to explain how power and knowledge interact in particular areas of society that are relatively autonomous 'fields'.[38] He argued that each field is a specific microcosm with its own logic, characterised by specific rules of action. Within a field, behaviours and social relations become routine and concretised over time and actors become subjugated to the predominant social order.[39] To think in terms of field is to think 'relationally', Bourdieu explained, and the limits of the field are 'always at stake'.[40] Fields and the social spaces that constitute them do not amount to an 'objective' structure, but instead form a structure subjectively constructed by individual and collective practices. It is interesting to note that Bourdieu rejected much of the standard theories of the 'professions' and instead recommended the concept of field as an alternative analytical tool.[41] This would allow, he contended, for 'the full reality it intends to capture' to be accounted for.[42]

Drawing on Bourdieu, we view social organisation as a system of relationships composed of invisible structures. The metaphor of the 'game' is used to illustrate the concept of the field and the role of habitus within the game.[43] Habitus is a 'structured system of dispositions' formed in relation to individually perceived conditions of existence.[44] In other words, habitus refers to

37 Pierre Bourdieu, *Outline of a Theory of Practice* (CUP 1977) 172–79.

38 Pierre Bourdieu, *The State Nobility: Elite Schools in the Field of Power* (Stanford UP 1998); Pierre Bourdieu, *The Field of Cultural Production* (Columbia UP 1993).

39 Pierre Bourdieu and Loïc Wacquant, *An Invitation to Reflexive Sociology* (Blackwell Publishers 1992) 101.

40 Loïc Wacquant, 'Towards a Reflexive Sociology: A Workshop with Pierre Bourdieu' (1989) 7(1) Sociological Theory 26.

41 Bourdieu and Wacquant (n 39) 242.

42 Wacquant (n 40) 38.

43 Phil Hodkinson, Andrew Sparkes and Heather Hodkinson, *Triumphs and Tears: Young People, Markets and the Transition from School to Work* (David Fulton 1996).

44 Bourdieu (n 37) 72.

an individual's set of quotidian thoughts and practices learned socially and taken for granted. Rather than being viewed as a collection of attributes or inherent characteristics, the habitus is a mediative frame of reference that imprints objective social structures and generates the observed views and practices of agents.[45] It implies that agents are socially produced in states occurring before the system of social relations. Habitus is, therefore, a framework through which the world is perceived, and which determines one's actions within it. As a cognitive map, it guides and evaluates an individual's choices, options and habitual ways of performing routine tasks.[46]

As an increasingly common feature of criminal trials and the criminal justice system, the intermediary and its work constitute a field. Viewing fields as networks of agents occupying symbolic social spaces, with each possessing unique attributes and power dynamics, enables us to locate the intermediary within the social world of the criminal justice system.[47] The physical manifestations of the field, including the courtroom, consultation room, police stations and interview suites, are all social spaces where conflict and struggle occur between the intermediary and other criminal justice actors. For example, more peripheral criminal justice actors, such as interpreters, also inhabit criminal justice settings but adhere to their own internal logic and principles of organisation.[48] Each of these 'subfields' is imbued with its own 'doxa' – an established order that engenders an unconscious, unquestionable acceptance of the status quo.[49] To participate in a field, an individual must be conscious of the 'rules' in play and have 'the minimum amount of knowledge, skill or "talent" to be accepted as a legitimate player'.[50] The 'rules of the game' that relate to the intermediary are developed later in this chapter in a discussion of illusio. It is clear that the intermediary role emerged because a knowledge/skills gap existed among traditional criminal justice actors. Having identified the intermediary's 'field', it follows that the role is strongly influenced by its habitus. This habitus is objectively structured by the role's relative position in the field but also by the subjective experiences of individual practitioners which are orientated by their perception and classification of their social world.[51] We are concerned here with how adapted the intermediary's habitus

45 Bourdieu (n 37) 72.

46 Karen Robson and Chris Sanders, *Quantifying Theory: Pierre Bourdieu* (Springer 2009).

47 Pierre Bourdieu, *In Other Words: Essays Towards a Reflexive Sociology* (Stanford UP 1990); Pierre Bourdieu, *Language & Symbolic Power* (Polity Press 1991).

48 Moira Inghilleri, 'Habitus, Field and Discourse: Interpreting as a Socially Situated Activity' (2003) 15(2) Target 243.

49 Bourdieu, *Outline of a Theory* (n 37); Damon Golsorkhi and others, 'Analysing, Accounting for and Unmasking Domination: On our Role as Scholars of Practice, Practitioners of Social Science and Public Intellectuals' (2009) 16(6) Organization 779.

50 Pierre Bourdieu, *The Field of Cultural Production* (Columbia UP 1993) 8.

51 Bourdieu, *In Other Words* (n 47).

is to the field and its 'predisposed way of thinking, acting and moving in and through the social environment'.[52] How the intermediary presents itself to other criminal justice actors, most of whom have more established roles and are familiar with criminal proceedings, is constitutive of its habitus. All criminal justice actors apprehend the social world of the criminal justice system through their own habitus, and the intermediary is no different.

Finally, the concepts of 'field' and 'habitus' are inextricably linked to 'illusio'. How the field functions and is conditioned relies on its members' collective belief, demonstrated through participation in internal struggles.[53] By demonstrating a 'visceral commitment' to their membership of the field, members take an interest in its stakes and are taken in by it. Bordieu refers to this as 'illusio', which is created through repeated action and routines and represents an unreflexive commitment to reproducing and enforcing the rules of the game.[54] In this chapter, I use illusio as a conceptual tool to explore what I have termed the 'neutrality paradox' of the intermediary role. As briefly discussed earlier, examining neutrality can be conceptually problematic, particularly when the principle is considered integral to the intermediary role.[55] The neutrality paradox centres on the internal struggles and apparent contradictions in how intermediaries practice their neutrality and justify their actions. It reflects the strong attachment intermediaries display to the ideals of neutrality on the one hand and their willingness to view these principles as malleable and open to reconceptualisation on the other. This dynamic allows us to critically examine neutrality as a core tenet of the intermediary role and to question its conceptual underpinnings. Firstly, we examine how neutrality as a 'locus of tension'[56] within intermediary practice is partly revealed through demonstrating its 'congruent illusio'.

6.4 Congruent illusio

Bourdieu contended that membership of a particular field involves a belief in its claims and compliance with the 'necessities of the field'.[57] Here, we focus on the core principle of neutrality and the extent intermediaries view it as a necessary, non-derogable component of their work. We examine whether,

52 Paul Sweetman, 'Twenty-first Century Dis-ease? Habitual Reflexivity or the Reflexive Habitus' (2003) 51(4) Sociological Review 528, 532.

53 Wacquant (n 40) 40.

54 Ioana Lupu and Laura Empson, 'Illusio and Overwork: Playing the Game in the Accounting Field' (2015) 28(8) Accounting, Auditing and Accountability 1310.

55 Vidal Claramonte recognises similar issues when the neutrality legal interpreters is examined: Maria Carmen África Vidal Claramonte, 'Re-presenting the "Real"' (2005) 11(2) The Translator 259.

56 Vidal Claramonte (n 55) 263.

57 Bourdieu, *In Other Words* (n 47) 6; Bourdieu and Wacquant (n 39) 115.

and to what extent, intermediaries adhere to their official stance of neutrality 'and do not question its underlying principles'.[58] This examination is concerned with how invested intermediaries are in maintaining and reinforcing their neutral status and whether they are engaged in reproducing the 'doxa', i.e. the presuppositions of the game through their illusio.

In almost every interview with intermediaries, the issue of neutrality arose, not through a question posed, but rather from interviewees describing their work: 'I am there as a neutral party' (E&W-3), 'Our role is neutral' (NI-3), 'You have to be very mindful that we are neutral' (E&W-16), 'You have to be a neutral person or you can't do the job properly' (NI-1). Unsurprisingly, a focal part of initial intermediary induction and training in both England and Wales and Northern Ireland emphasises the neutrality of the role and thus the value appears ingrained in recruits from an early stage. In this way, the illusio surrounding the neutrality of the intermediary is viewed as what Bourdieu called a 'precondition for successful entry into the field'.[59] In other words, the consistent mentioning of neutrality reflects the collective belief that this is a necessary part of the role. NI-7 and NI-3, both intermediaries in Northern Ireland, explained this:

> I remember from the training that we need to be there with a poker face, and we need to keep a professional hat on and sometimes it is difficult.
>
> (NI-7)

> in our training we were just told about the whole neutrality, the importance of that . . . we were given guidance as to where you are supposed to stand for Ground Rules Hearings and things, we are supposed to be at the back sort of and you try to sit maybe in between but more often than not I am called up into the witness box.
>
> (NI-3)

These comments are redolent of the illusio implicitly assumed by all who undergo intermediary training and subject themselves to the rules of the game.[60] Yet, when examining illusio, we are primarily concerned with the subjective reality of the field and how members internalise its rules. This involves examining whether intermediaries get caught up and taken in by the game to the extent they take their neutrality for granted. At this point, we can see one side of the neutrality paradox develop. My interviews reveal that

58 Pierre Bourdieu, *Practical Reason: On the Theory of Action* (Stanford UP 1998).

59 Pierre Bourdieu, *The State Nobility: Elite Schools in the Field of Power* (Stanford UP 1998) 170.

60 This is similar to the judicial commitment to impartiality which Anleu and Mack explain is deeply ingrained in both legal training and judicial work: Roach Anleu and Mack (n 19) 61.

intermediaries express compliance with the official line requiring strict adherence to the oath of neutrality. More strikingly, the individual reflections that emerged from the interviews never seemed superficial or perfunctory. On the contrary, interviewees often took the time to carefully explain and justify the rationale behind their neutral stance:

> You are there for the courts, you are there to help the barristers ask questions in a way that somebody understands, and you are there to ensure that person can give information and answer the questions in a way that is understood, so you are there for that two way process . . . and you are more like a vehicle, an instrument to support that . . . that's why we work for the court. We are not there to support that person to give their story or their version of events, you are there to make sure the court process flows. (NI-1)

It is important to be reflexive and introspective about such responses. As a researcher examining issues in the criminal justice system, I am a player in the broader field. Regardless of how interviewees perceived me, it is possible that they viewed me as someone who was actively looking for instances of their neutrality being compromised or, as Goffman termed it, a slip of the 'mask' which individuals wear during a performance.[61] When faced with questions about their neutrality, interviewees reaffirmed their belief in its virtues as if reading from an official script. The cost of their integrity being called into question appeared too high, and no interviewee spoke of the neutrality label being a burden or a hindrance.[62] This reflects the investment intermediaries make in their neutrality, as opposed to being indifferent to it. While the analysis later in this chapter questions how committed intermediaries are to performing neutrality in practice, it is apparent that an impression of attachment to the principle is viewed as crucial for the role's credibility among other actors.[63]

Intermediaries were more vocal describing situations when their neutrality was questioned. Although not a common occurrence, some occasionally receive such accusations, explicitly or implicitly, from other criminal justice actors. When this occurs, intermediaries distance themselves from the 'ataraxy' that characterises other uninvested players in their respective fields.[64]

61 Erving Goffman, *The Presentation of Self in Everyday Life* (U of Edinburgh Social Science Research Centre 1956) 73.

62 Erving Goffman, *Interaction Ritual: essays on face-to-face behaviour* (Pantheon 1967) 261.

63 Pierre Bourdieu, *The Rules of Art: Genesis and Structure of the Literary Field* (Stanford UP 1996) 227–28. This also links in with the conclusions reached in Chapter 5 (Professional work – jurisdictions and boundary work) as intermediaries strive for exclusive jurisdiction and legitimacy through the approval of other criminal justice professionals.

64 Bourdieu and Wacquant (n 39) 116.

In other words, intermediaries often appear annoyed that their stake in the game is questioned and that their attitude to neutrality may be viewed as one of 'indifference'.[65] E&W-1 expressed this position strongly:

> There was one barrister who, let's say, accused me of 'over-egging' things in my report because I had sympathy for the defendant which is really offensive. I was really, really angry because it is offensive because I am there as a neutral party and because it is calling into question the integrity of my opinion and my response was that I categorically disagreed.
>
> (E&W-1)

More common than explicit questioning of the role's neutrality was the perception that the police or defence legal representatives may seek to bring the intermediary on board or into a particular 'team' (E&W-14). This happens most frequently at court when defendant intermediaries often spend long periods with the defendant and their legal representatives. In Northern Ireland, where intermediary appointments are generally for evidence only, it is unsurprising that this is less common. Further, the DoJ explicitly prohibits intermediaries from attending consultations between the defendant and their lawyers.[66] Social encounters between intermediaries and other actors present an opportunity to reaffirm the attachment to neutrality and demonstrate a strong illusio. In this sense, intermediaries can identify and conserve the principle of neutrality as capital which is uniquely generated in their field.[67] E&W-20 explained how maintaining the illusio translates into practice:

> If you're seen to be in and out of these meetings, consultation rooms and you're seen to be going in and out of there. I have had counsel say negative things about police to me and it's those sort of things that can breach those boundaries and you've got to be very, very clear in the intermediary role about that. I am not here for that discussion; I am here to facilitate communication. It's a difficult area being a human being, being absolutely non-partisan in your role and being explicit about what you can and cannot do.
>
> (E&W-20)

Many intermediaries commented on the need to proactively 'perform' neutrality and be seen to do so. In Bourdieusian terms, this fosters a visceral commitment to the game and rationalises the participant's investment in it.[68]

65 Bourdieu and Wacquant (n 39) 116.
66 DoJ (n 2) 26; R v WP [2017] NICA 21.
67 Bourdieu, *Outline of a Theory* (n 37) 153.
68 Bourdieu, *Outline of a Theory* (n 37) 102.

The illusio helps explain why intermediaries submit unequivocally to the underlying principles of their neutrality and proceed to externalise it.[69] In some cases, this acts as a defence mechanism to protect the role from accusations or perceptions of partiality. E&W-17 explained how engaging with the so-called other side of the case is crucial:

> I make a big point of arriving in court on the first day and finding the prosecution barrister to say hello. Because if you don't do that, and they see you all the time walking around with the defendant and his team, then you look like you're part of the team. So, for instance, I always make sure that I sit halfway when I am sitting on the back of the benches, I sit halfway between the two. I don't sit behind the barrister.
>
> (E&W-17)

This deliberate positioning of oneself in a neutral space was a common theme in interview. It appeared more pronounced in Northern Ireland, where intermediaries firmly believed that the role operates independently of any side in the criminal process. All Northern Irish intermediaries showed a strong attachment to the ideal of neutrality. NI-2's comments exemplify this position:

> I am not beholden to anyone. I am an independent provider of a service and I work to my standard . . . I am not working for a lawyer, I am not working for the police. I consider myself to be an officer of the court and, as such, an officer of the criminal justice system.
>
> (NI-2)

Another Northern Irish intermediary, NI-4, discussed how the suspect interview at the police station is a good place to 'practice our neutrality'. She continued:

> I think it's very important to make it clear that either verbally or non-verbally I am neutral here. I'm not on anybody's side. . . . In terms of neutrality, I think that our non-verbal language can speak as loud as things that we do say.
>
> (NI-4)

In England and Wales, one phenomenon which encapsulates the notion of a congruent illusio relates to the preparedness of intermediaries to work on both sides of the 'two-tier' system during the same trial. In other words, as an independent communication expert, an intermediary could be appointed to

69 Bourdieu, *Outline of a Theory* (n 37) 102.

facilitate communication for several individuals rather than being appointed to one witness or defendant. There is currently no provision for such an appointment in the legislation, Criminal Procedure Rules (CPR) or Criminal Practice Directions (CPD), and it is instead a case management issue for the judge. This practice, which three interviewees had experienced, may be described as 'crossing the court'. This term was coined by E&W-7 who had been asked by the judge to assist a vulnerable defendant after the commercial organisation providing an intermediary withdrew.[70] E&W-7 admitted feeling initially unsure about the idea but rationalised that 'the job was no different, sitting next to the witness, listening to the questioning, reading questions, intervening, simplifying the language'. E&W-7 went on to explain in more detail why her decision to 'cross' the court was justifiable and, ultimately, utilitarian:

> I think I can switch from one to the other. Some intermediaries think that is unethical. If the court has agreed and I have been asked to do that, I can't see why anyone is going to object. I am just there assisting the court and if a whole case is going to collapse because of an invoice they don't want to pay!
>
> (E&W-7)

The topic of crossing the court prompted other intermediaries to reflect and evaluate their attitudes towards the role's neutrality. This often revealed a sense of ambivalence. While there was a recognition that assisting communication should transcend notions of 'sides', interviewees generally concluded that it would not be good practice and was best avoided. It was argued in Chapter 4 (Locating the intermediary within theories of the criminal trial) that intermediaries can help legitimise the criminal justice process, but the practice of crossing the court could possibly have the opposite effect. Despite intermediaries in Northern Ireland routinely working with both defendants and witnesses, one magistrate considered that an intermediary crossing the court could prove problematic 'in a sensitively charged case . . . [and would be] best avoided if possible' (MCJ-2). It was suggested that vulnerable witnesses may struggle to cope with seeing the person with whom they have developed a rapport now sitting with the accused (or witness). As E&W-15 explained, the risk of the witness (or defendant) feeling let down by such a

70 This seems to be a relatively common occurrence due to the policy of one commercial provider to provide intermediaries for full trial appointments only. For judicial comment on this policy: see *R v Biddle* [2019] EWCA Crim 86.

practice may be more than merely cosmetic and could adversely affect the ability to communicate:

> It would depend on that witness and if they would have that knowledge before giving evidence or at all because I think it could jeopardise them and the support I give to them if they saw me on the 'other side' because frequently whilst we say 'we are not on anyone's side', the witness will see us as 'theirs' and it's a fine line.
>
> (E&W-15)

It is useful to reflect on how these individual understandings and perceptions of neutrality map onto the concept of illusio. Bourdieu contends that illusio is 'removed from discussion' and that adherence to the doxa 'forbids questioning of the principles of belief'.[71] Heidegren and Lundberg echo this by noting that the unthinking commitment to the logic of the field means that 'no-one questions whether the battles in question are meaningful. . . . Illusio is thus never questioned'.[72] On one hand, these statements resonate with much of what I observed about intermediary culture. Despite the often-isolated nature of the role and high levels of autonomy, many issues within the intermediary community generate debate and internal discussion. Some of these are extremely contentious, for example, the divide between the speech and language therapy cohort of intermediaries and the 'nouveau' intermediaries who predominately hail from a social work, nursing and teaching background. However, the lack of discussion between intermediaries around the neutrality issue and its potentially blurred edges is surprising. I initially concluded that the role's neutrality must be a 'taboo' subject which is personally navigated but not externalised. While O'Mahony et al. identified the potential for conflict between individual intermediary practices and the value of neutrality, I saw little evidence of this in interview.[73]

Yet it was clear in interview that intermediaries were acutely aware of the underpinning rationale of their neutrality and its centrality to the role's work. Bourdieu wrote that adherence to the necessities of the field is unconscious and inscribed into the bodies of participants.[74] The acceptance of illusio is not depicted as a deliberate choice, since the agent who was raised in the field will not question its norms and principles.[75] How can we reconcile this with the account emerging from the interview data? Bourdieu's account of illusio is premised on the inculcation of norms, principles and beliefs through

71 Bourdieu, *Pascalian Meditations* (n 6) 102.
72 Carl-Göran Heidegren and Henrik Lundberg, 'Towards a Sociology of Philosophy' (2010) 53(1) Acta Sociologica 3.
73 O'Mahony and others (n 4) 155.
74 Bourdieu, *Pascalian Meditations* (n 6) 171.
75 Kirsten Donskov Felter, 'Breaking with Illusio' (2012) 66(1) Studia Theologia 86, 102.

action and routine. But importantly, these go unquestioned because they are perceived as immemorial and embedded. They are done 'and have always been done that way'.[76] The newness of the intermediary 'profession' must be considered as the role's habitus and logic of practice have not been examined. The role may be described as in a liminal state, inhabiting a social space which lacks clear pre-prescribed ways of doing and being.[77] Therefore, what constitutes the internal logic of the intermediary field is still embryonic, particularly compared with traditional professions. For example, Bourdieu explicates numerous types of 'conservation strategies' used by those in dominant positions in a field to preserve hierarchisation and enhance their positions.[78] The dearth of academic research into the intermediary role, its organisation and governance means that examining internal struggles for capital, power and positions is difficult. We may say that the doxa – the presuppositions that constitute the intermediary field – are not yet settled.[79] Newcomers to any field must learn and play by the unarticulated rules and conventions. However, if these are still in flux then it is unsurprising that the content of a key principle like neutrality remains unresolved.

6.5 Weak illusio

As the preceding discussion explains, intermediaries demonstrate a commitment to the principle of neutrality and have a stake in reproducing this as a rule of the game. In this regard, my data suggest a congruence between the official standards and protocols of the role and the belief intermediaries have in them. The reverse side of the neutrality paradox reveals a conflict with this congruent account, as intermediaries appear to resist the constraints imposed on them by their neutrality. Defining resistance within a discussion of illusio can be a difficult task. While some authors have focused on the inseparability of resistance and power, there has been little elaboration on how resistance actually operates.[80] Other research has conceptualised resistance as a refusal to prevailing ideas which enable people to comprehend the dominant order.[81] However, I found the patterns of resistance among intermediaries difficult to reconcile with accounts of resistance in other empirical settings. For example, the idea that individuals 'must try individually or collectively, to subvert' the

76 Bourdieu, *Pascalian Meditations* (n 6) 102.
77 Victor Turner, *The Forest of Symbols* (Cornell UP 1976).
78 Pierre Bourdieu, *Sociology in Question* (SAGE Publishing 1993); Ahu Tatli, Mustafa Ozbilgin and Mine Karatas-Ozkan, *Pierre Bourdieu, Organization and Management* (Routledge 2015) 211.
79 Pierre Bourdieu, *The Logic of Practice* (Polity Press 1992) 66.
80 Deborah Reed-Danahay, *Locating Bourdeiu* (Indiana UP 2004) 64.
81 Penny Dick, 'Resistance, Gender and Bourdieu's Notion of Field' (2008) 21(3) Management Communication 327.

rules of the game to resist did not resonate with my data.[82] The conceptualisation of resistance as associated with 'strategic manoeuvres' and premeditated strategies to undermine occupational practices may be more applicable to traditional workplace settings with bureaucratic institutions and complex professional hierarchies.[83] Instead, any resistance among intermediaries appears to be individually driven without any obvious ideological motive. The type of collective resistance that is often embodied through organisations such as trade unions was noticeably absent among intermediaries.[84] Consequently, intermediaries do not seem to experience the 'establishment of a dispositional habitus around behaviours and knowledge' arising from strong collective organisation.[85] Yet, despite not being engaged in any coordinated resistance strategy, resistance among intermediaries is evident in a subtler way. Although not vocally disavowing their neutrality, intermediaries experience an ongoing struggle between the practical demands of their emotionally demanding work, their professional backgrounds and their need to remain detached and objective.

While illusio provides that players believe in the necessity of the game, my interview data give an insight into how intermediaries view the relationship between the role's overarching function of facilitating communication and the norms and principles that constitute their illusio. In terms of neutrality, a discord is evident between the neutrality narrative that intermediaries subscribe to and reproduce, and the strategies, tactics and methods employed in facilitating communication. This may be termed a 'weak illusio', defined by the simultaneity of belief in the role's neutrality and a willingness to compromise its integrity. A sustained process of 'toggling' ensues between a desire to protect the legitimacy of the role and the need to ensure that communication is effectively facilitated.[86] My interviews are replete with examples of this tension which occurs throughout the stages of intermediary involvement in a case. In the following comments, E&W-2 gives an example of a witness contradicting themselves during ABE interview and the interviewing officer not picking up on the discrepancy. E&W-2 later raised the issue with the officer but sought to justify her actions:

> E&W-2 – . . . so they may contradict themselves or say something that doesn't quite make sense and I'll be wanting to ask something just so they

82 Dick (n 81) 337.

83 Sierk Ybema and Martha Horvers, 'Resistance Through Compliance: The Strategic and Subversive Potential of Frontstage and Backstage Resistance' (2017) 38(9) Organization Studies 1233; Senia Kalfa, Adrian Wilkinson and Paul Gollan, 'The Academic Game: Compliance and Resistance in Universities' (2019) 32(2) Work, Employment and Society 274.

84 Tatli and others (n 78) 127.

85 Tatli and others (n 78) 127.

86 Craig Calhoun and Richard Sennett, *Practicing Culture* (Routledge 2007) 165.

understand what they are telling me. I will say to the officer afterwards. So, if someone is describing something that happened at night and then they might say 'he had sunglasses on' I will think 'why has he got sunglasses on at night?'

Interviewer – But you might say to the officer afterwards?

E&W-2 – Afterwards yeh, but not on camera and not with the witness there. But that's me asking it kind of as [name] and not as the intermediary.

Similarly, E&W-13 suggested that the intermediary necessarily concerns itself with the emerging evidential picture at police interview. She staunchly defended the position that intermediaries ought to be more 'assertive' with police officers in terms of how interview questions are formulated:

> in the interview the intermediary is not just the intermediary but is also potentially looking at it at like a juror would. Because it's the first time you have heard their account and if my brain is going 'well, what about this?' and if I am doing that then a jury member is likely to do that. So, in the breaks I go with the officer . . . and I would say 'Don't know about you, but there's just one thing that's rattling in my mind' because I don't know the rest of the evidence but I am thinking 'If I am thinking it, a jury member might be thinking it'.
>
> (E&W-13)

In these two examples, the strategies and tactics adopted by the intermediaries constitute the role's habitus. These methods reflect not just how intermediaries navigate the settings of the criminal justice system, but specifically how they develop a 'feel' for the rules of the game.[87] These seemingly innocuous comments and informal chats with the interviewing officer inform what Sweetman terms the 'predisposed way of thinking, acting and moving in and through the social environment'.[88] The relationship between the habitus and illusio here is revealing. As Bourdieu notes, illusio is most potent when the habitus embodies the field.[89] Players must 'bring to the game . . . a habitus that is practically compatible . . . and above all, malleable and capable of being converted'.[90] The comments of E&W-2 and E&W-13 reflect the ability of intermediaries to view their habitus as transformative and amenable to restructuring.[91] The tension with the role's neutrality is central to this: through

87 Bourdieu, *Practical Reason* (n 58) 77.
88 Sweetman (n 52).
89 Bourdieu, *Practical Reason* (n 58).
90 Bourdieu, *Practical Reason* (n 58) 100.
91 Bourdieu, *Pascalian Meditations* (n 6) 100; Diane Reay, Gill Crozier and John Clayton, 'Strangers in Paradise: Working-class Students in Elite Universities' (2009) 43(6) Sociology 1103, 1105.

reconceptualising their own neutrality, intermediaries reconcile the principle with their primary function of facilitating communication. By viewing their oath of neutrality as complementary to, rather than a restriction on, their core functions, intermediaries remain engaged and committed to the game.

The type of social interactions which provide the setting for the earlier quotes are important to understanding the intermediary illusio and its fragility. Criminal justice sites, such as the interview suite, consultation room and courtroom, are where investment in the illusio begins and is reinforced.[92] As new entrants, intermediaries bring to the field their own dispositions, which are gradually transmuted imperceptibly without obvious crisis or conflict.[93] For example, the criminal court initially bewildered many intermediaries, who slowly became accustomed to its rituals and customs. The tendencies and practices of intermediaries when working with other criminal justice professionals become embedded in the habitus and such practices then attain a coherence and regularity. Yet, the social relations which develop in the field often challenge the intermediary role's neutrality. The working relationships which intermediaries foster often threaten to 'shatter' the illusio and the commitment and investment in the game.[94] This is essentially the other side of the 'congruent illusio' explained earlier, whereby intermediaries vehemently defend their neutrality and want to be seen as neutral. The neutrality paradox sees intermediaries sometimes drawn to sides, most notably to the police during ABE interviews and with the defence at court. As early as the police station, achieving best evidence can be viewed as a collective goal which demands a coordinated approach:

> I think [police] feel like you're working with them, and in a way you are because they want to get the best evidence from the witness and that's what you're both trying to do . . . there is a feeling that you have got to be on the same page or otherwise you couldn't really do it, you've got to be a bit of a team.
>
> (E&W-9)

E&W-6 similarly uses the analogy of working as a 'team' to describe a joint effort with police during ABE interview:

> Last year I worked with two police officers over a very significant period of time, nine months. I would say we had a very professional but very supportive relationship . . . we all had a role to play and obviously I remained

92 Bourdieu, *Pascalian Meditations* (n 6) 166.
93 Bourdieu, *Pascalian Meditations* (n 6) 165.
94 Helen Colley, 'Not Learning in the Workplace: Austerity and the Shattering of Illusio in Public Service' (2012) 24(5) Journal of Workplace Learning 317.

> objective to help the witness give evidence but it was like the boundaries became blurred almost because I would go afterwards, not in front of the witness, and go: 'you know what she said there? This doesn't mean it . . .' which I suppose in a way was stepping out of my role, kind of going: 'I don't get this, she said that then and then she said that?' but I think we formed a good team.
> (E&W-6)

This latter quote encapsulates the nature of the neutrality paradox. Although initially emphasising the objective approach to her work, E&W-6 then recognised how discussing the evidence with the police officer compromised the integrity of her role. The contrast between the enclosed, more intimate setting of the interview suite and the open, public setting of the criminal court also appears to influence the conceptualisation and performance of neutrality. When 'backstage', the intermediary seems more willing to risk their neutrality than in the 'front', public stage of the criminal courtroom.[95] The concentration and effort required to be seen as neutral by the judge, lawyers and general audience contrast with the off-camera moments when an intermediary may, for example, raise evidential issues with the interviewing officer. We may view these incidents as deviations from the 'official stance' of neutrality as 'the impression fostered by the presentation is knowingly contradicted as a matter of course'.[96] The emotional energy expended in such cases is evidenced by comments from several intermediaries in interview that they no longer accept defendant cases due to the nature of allegations involved.

The notion of intermediaries being 'pulled' into the 'defence camp' was frequently mentioned in interview, although many considered this was based more on perception than reality. Two Northern Ireland judges noted the risk of intermediaries being assimilated into the defence legal team and the collegiality associated with it. However, both stressed that they had seen no evidence of this. In England and Wales, these fears appear to have foundation. Intermediaries explained that their close involvement with defence representatives when assisting a suspect/defendant led to a sense of being closely involved. This contrasts with the experience of assisting a witness, which tends to be brief and limited to the period of their examination. Plotnikoff and Woolfson highlighted this reality and how the 'behind the scenes' work of defendant intermediaries often goes unnoticed by judges.[97] This backstage role often involves close proximity to the defence legal representatives and can lead to a lack of appreciation of the intermediary's neutrality. This places a unique strain on the neutrality of the defendant intermediary role which practitioners must be aware of to avoid 'cross[ing] the boundary into

95 Goffman (n 61) 114.
96 Goffman (n 61) 112.
97 Plotnikoff and Woolfson (n 2) 271.

a support role'.[98] O'Mahony et al. found that intermediaries felt excluded by the setting of legal consultations and were reluctantly drawn into discussing case details which they recognised threatened their neutral stance.[99]

The gravitation of intermediaries towards defence representatives, or the 'defence camp', as explained by the earlier quotes, requires closer examination. As explored in Chapter 5 (Professional work – jurisdictions and boundary work), intermediaries generally identify as outsiders in the criminal justice system. In terms of special configuration at least, this is not surprising. As Mulcahy and Rowden outline, modern court design in the U.K is engineered to separate different groups of users and intermediaries are effectively excluded from many of the 'deep' spaces inhabited by the court workgroup.[100] Intermediaries in interview spoke of the discomfort of 'hanging around' (E&W-11; E&W-7) the precincts of the courthouse, often without anywhere to sit, read or even eat. The lack of intermediary space within the court precinct is, however, more pronounced when working as a defendant intermediary. Most interviewees spoke about liaising with Victim Support (or Witness Service in Northern Ireland) when working with witnesses and becoming accustomed to the surroundings of the Witness Support Suite. When working in a defendant intermediary capacity, the same practitioners reported feeling excluded and had no similar physically separate space to occupy (unless in the cells with a defendant in custody). Instead, they mainly inhabit 'shallow' zones such as public and circulation areas.[101] E&W-3's experience reflects this difference:

> it's bloody awkward when there is nowhere to put your bag. . . . When assisting a defendant it's even more awkward because you don't even have the Witness Service to help. I have my coat and bag with me and they get shoved under the bench. Where do I go? With the defendant cases I just hang out in the corridor.
>
> (E&W-3)

E&W-10 discussed the problem of 'small talk' with witnesses but said that she is often able to 'leave that to the Witness Service'. In a defendant intermediary capacity, this is not an option, and the prolonged periods spent with the defendant and their legal representatives can understandably lead to a spirit of camaraderie. Just as the differences in intermediary provision can affect approaches to neutrality among intermediaries, so too can the built

98 Plotnikoff and Woolfson (n 2) 276.
99 O'Mahony and others (n 4) 160.
100 Linda Mulcahy and Emma Rowden, *The Democratic Courthouse* (Routledge 2020) 87.
101 Thomas Markus, *Buildings and Power: Freedom and Control in the Origin of Modern Building Types* (Routledge 1993) 167.

environment in which intermediaries operate. As Rowden notes, special configuration can dictate how individuals are expected to behave and, of relevance to the intermediary, perceive their own role and its parameters.[102]

It is instructive at this stage to return to the concept of resistance in the context of the empirical data presented. It may be misleading to examine the reconceptualisation of neutrality in terms of resistance at all.[103] Rather than 'resisting' occupational norms and directives, the process of reconceptualising neutrality reveals a hierarchy of values which guides intermediaries in their practice. This mirrors the findings of Colley and Guery who concluded that public service interpreters invest more in the stakes of what drove the role's creation in the first place than the profession's official rubrics.[104] Where broad objects of value are not deemed best served by the profession's official code, the personal judgement of interpreters supplants it. This was also evident in my data as intermediaries prioritised the facilitation of communication above all else, almost oblivious of the collateral risks to their neutrality. For example, one intermediary (NI-2) in Northern Ireland insisted on attending a legal consultation without prior approval from the DoJ because of the imperative that the defendant could 'understand the advice being given and that the barrister was getting clear instructions'. Colley and Guéry contend that public service interpreters demonstrate a 'weak illusio' by distancing themselves from official protocols through their practice. While intermediaries risk breaching their neutrality, this may not necessarily equate to a lack of investment in the role and its underpinning rationale.[105] Since the concept of illusio is imbricated with habitus, we must recognise the notion of habitus not only as malleable but also as 'transformative'.[106] This allows us to view the reconceptualisation of neutrality not as an aberration or an outlier, but as being incorporated into the intermediary habitus.[107]

Bourdieu and Wacquant describe habitus as an 'open system of dispositions that is constantly subjected to experiences'.[108] Thus, the intermediary habitus is responsive to the conditions of work. This explains intermediaries framing communication facilitation as the role's core concern and centring their practices around it. It must also be relevant that those performing the intermediary role, usually professionals in their own right, display attitudes,

102 Emma Rowden, 'Remote Participation and the Distributed Court: An Approach to Court Architecture in the Age of Video-Mediated Communication' (PhD thesis, University of Melbourne 2011).
103 For a discussion of multiple forms of resistance including 'subtle', 'ineffective' and 'counter-productive' resistance, see: Ybema and Horvers (n 83).
104 Colley and Guéry (n 5) 13.
105 Colley and Guéry (n 5).
106 Reay and others (n 91) 1105.
107 Reay and others (n 91) 1105.
108 Bourdieu and Wacquant (n 39) 133.

dispositions and expectations from different occupational fields. These are acquired in their respective social environments, where preferences and customs are equally deemed natural and obvious. Yet, when these individuals encounter an unfamiliar field, such as the criminal justice system, resulting 'disjunctures' can 'generate change and transformation'.[109] Intermediaries appear to effect this change and shape their habitus as a result. It follows that this has implications for the intermediary illusio. Intermediaries may not, in practical terms, display an unwavering commitment to the logic or value of neutrality, but they appear invested in their membership of the game more broadly, in particular in ensuring that their primary function of communication facilitation is discharged. Like habitus, illusio is constitutive of individual experiences and can be thought of in the plural, i.e. consisting of differing investments which can be distinguished from one another without abdicating illusio completely.[110]

6.6 Witness work vs defendant work

The 'two-tier' provision of intermediaries in England and Wales has been explained previously. Yet apart from O'Mahony, who has researched the identities of defendant intermediaries, relevant guidance and associated literature tend to view intermediary work as homogeneous.[111] The inability of some judges to differentiate Registered Intermediaries from non-registered intermediaries has also been highlighted with some concern.[112] My interview data suggest that intermediaries recognise the differing demands of working with witnesses on one hand and defendants on the other. Such a finding should cause us to reflect on the state of the 'two-tier' system of intermediaries in England and Wales and consider its viability and desirability. This is increasingly important as other jurisdictions internationally seek to establish intermediary-type roles. For the current chapter, we can focus on the principle of neutrality and how different approaches to intermediary work may impact its conceptualisation. If intermediaries consider that the 'two-tier' system gives rise to different working demands, how does this impact their approach to the principle of neutrality?

Several intermediaries in England and Wales explicitly recognised the aforementioned divide created by the 'two-tier' system. Beyond mere labels, these intermediaries outlined the practical differences between 'witness work' and 'defendant work' and a considerable number stated their preference for defendant work over witness work. Two reasons cited were the increased

109 Diane Reay, '"It's All Becoming a Habitus": Beyond the Habitual Use of Habitus in Educational Research' (2004) 25(4) British Journal of Sociology of Education 431, 436.
110 Reay (n 109); Raphael Dalleo, *Bourdieu and Postcolonial Studies* (Liverpool UP 2017) 206.
111 Brendan O'Mahony, 'How Do Intermediaries Experience Their Role in Facilitating Communication for Vulnerable Defendants?' (DCrimJ thesis, University of Portsmouth 2013).
112 Plotnikoff and Woolfson (n 2) 124.

autonomy of defendant work and a desire to balance out the perceived injustices that defendants face throughout the criminal justice system.[113] For example, the plight of vulnerable defendants in the dock, unable to follow proceedings, was highlighted. E&W-6 described the experience of one defendant confined to a 'glass thing, with two security guards either side of us – it didn't feel conducive to communication'. When speaking about vulnerable defendants, the emotionally charged nature of intermediary work was apparent. E&W-17 explained how sentencing can often be the most difficult stage for intermediaries to remain detached:

> What I really care about is their sentence. I really worry about vulnerable people who have done something wrong and then people don't take into account their vulnerability. That is what bothers me . . . I want them to be treated fairly. When I find out there's no presentencing report, when I find out that people take them straight to the cells, and they have no time to say goodbye to their wife of 60 years who's dying of cancer, that's when I get upset.
> (E&W-17)

The potential blurring of the boundaries between the role of neutral communication conduit and sympathetic supporter is evident in the preceding quote. This links with O'Mahony's finding that some defendant intermediaries may emotionally attach to defendants and feel a sense of loss when a trial concludes, particularly when a defendant is convicted and imprisoned.[114] In their court report, intermediaries must explain the recommended duration of their involvement in a case. However, E&W-17's quote points to the risk of intermediaries recommending their involvement for purposes not directly tied to the facilitation of communication. As mentioned, several intermediaries in England and Wales noted that vulnerable defendants have no dedicated support provision or designated space within the court building except for the cells. The lack of court familiarisation visits for vulnerable defendants was also noted as unfair, especially considering these routinely take place for witnesses.[115] Despite this, many intermediaries showed initiative and organised

113 For further discussion on equality of treatment between defendants and other witnesses, see: Diane Birch, 'Evidence: Evidence via Television Link and Video Recording of Interview with Child' [2001] Criminal Law Review 473, 477; Laura Hoyano, 'Striking a Balance between the Rights of Defendants and Vulnerable Witnesses: Will Special Measures Directions Contravene Guarantees of a Fair Trial?' [2001] Criminal Law Review 948, 968; Jessica Jacobson and Jenny Talbot, *Vulnerable Defendants in the Criminal Courts: A Review of Provision for Adults and Children* (Prison Reform Trust 2009, ISBN: 0 946209 96 0) 50.

114 O'Mahony and others (n 4) 162.

115 Criminal Practice Directions 2023 (CrimPRC(23)90(b)) note that 'An opportunity for a vulnerable defendant to visit the courtroom' should be discussed at a Ground Rules Hearing involving a 'young or otherwise vulnerable defendant' ([6.4]).

a viewing of the court for defendants despite no judicial direction or policy requiring them to do so. These reflections reveal how intermediaries negotiate their own neutrality and are prepared to act beyond their agreed scope based on perceived inequalities.

In Northern Ireland, the unitary system of intermediaries has meant that such a sharp distinction has not emerged. Intermediaries in Northern Ireland recognised the right of defendants to effective participation and how defendants have a different stake in the criminal process compared to witnesses. Procedural differences between witness work and defendant work in terms of interview format with police and the length of time physically spent in the courtroom were noted. However, there was no obvious divergence in how the core aspects of the role were approached whether it was a vulnerable witness or a suspect/defendant being assisted. Interestingly, intermediaries in both jurisdictions felt treated differently when working with defendants. E&W-3, who has extensive experience of both witness and defendant work, described this difference in treatment:

> Yeh, [the roles] are quite different. Well, I would say the role is similar but the way that it is perceived is so different, the way that you have to present the role has to be different if that makes sense? . . . There's a lot more resistance for intermediates for defendants than for witnesses . . . a lot more, so I think you have to be a lot more persuasive as a non-registered intermediary.
>
> (E&W-3)

Despite interviewees in both systems acknowledging this disparity in treatment, the notion of having to consciously perform the role differently when working with defendants was only apparent in England and Wales. When I mentioned the concepts of 'witness work' and 'defendant work' to intermediaries in Northern Ireland, they were viewed with a mixture of alarm and incredulity. Intermediaries in Northern Ireland spoke more about differences between individual courts and judges than differences in their approach to witnesses and defendants. Significantly, the judges interviewed in Northern Ireland echoed this conception of a unitary intermediary role:

> everybody is clear they are professional experts who are providing an independent role within the trial . . . I haven't noticed any difference and I have seen some intermediaries who have worked in both roles. I haven't discerned any difference.
>
> (MCJ-2)

NI-3 explained how the unitary system is firmly embedded in the role's culture:

> We were told right from the beginning, I think it was the Lord Chief Justice who said this service will be available for witnesses and has to be for defendants too. From the get-go, I haven't known anything else.
>
> (NI-3)

As a hallmark of the intermediary role, neutrality defines and shapes our understanding of its work and content. The finding that intermediaries in England and Wales conceptualise and operationalise the principle differently is significant as we begin to understand the role's complexities and the factors that affect its performance. Equally, the finding that intermediary provision in Northern Ireland has not generated this issue is important and invites comparison between the two jurisdictions.[116] The following section seeks to problematise the value of neutrality and suggests a fundamental rethink of its understanding and application within intermediary praxis.

6.7 Reconceptualising neutrality

Chapter 2 (Emergence of the intermediary role), which tracks the emergence of the intermediary role, reveals how the position of an interlocutor/intermediary has not historically been characterised by its objectivity or detachment from the vulnerable individual. The findings explored in the present chapter suggest that the normative underpinnings of the intermediary are ripe for examination. This is premised on the paradox between the commitment to the ideals of neutrality and the struggle to remain within its normative parameters. As has been explored, the approach intermediaries adopt towards their neutrality varies considerably and individual practices often reveal internal inconsistencies and contradictions. The fact that intermediaries demonstrate what I have termed 'congruent' and 'weak' illusio seamlessly, and often interchangeably, is significant. Questioning the normative basis of neutrality allows for a recognition that complete consistency among practitioners is both unrealistic and undesirable.[117] Instead, the principle of neutrality should be viewed as reflexive in a way that allows for diverse attitudes and experiences of those executing the intermediary role. This would allow for the specific demands of the intermediary role to be considered, separate from standard accounts of neutrality, which tend to focus on the complex adjudication and dispute resolution processes.[118]

Reconceptualising the neutrality of the intermediary requires a more dynamic and relational view which sees the principle not as an endpoint, but as a process. This rejects the notion of neutrality as an inherent quality in favour of viewing it as a principle realised through striving towards a normative ideal.[119] It also echoes Kramer's theorisation of neutrality as an

116 For a comparison of intermediary provision between England and Wales and Northern Ireland, see: John Taggart, '"I Am Not Beholden to Anyone . . . I Consider Myself to be an Officer of the Court": A Comparison of the Intermediary Role in England and Wales and Northern Ireland' (2021) 25(2) International Journal of Evidence and Proof 141.

117 Brian Tamanha, *Beyond the Formalist-Realist Divide: The Role of Politics in Judging* (Princeton UP 2010).

118 William Lucy, 'The Possibility of Impartiality' (2005) 25(1) Oxford Journal of Legal Studies 3.

119 Touchie (n 36); Roach Anleu and Mack (n 19) 9.

'endeavour' by which individuals reach decisions prescribed by legal norms within a liberal-democratic legal system.[120] Such a model fits the realities of intermediary work and the nature of the role as unattached, autonomous yet simultaneously involved in the emotionally loaded details of a case and the individuals involved. For example, the fallacy of intermediaries operating an evidential 'vacuum' described earlier highlights this point. Drawing on the court interpreter comparison, our conception of neutrality should allow the social skills of practitioners to be brought to the foreground during all communicative events.[121] Viewing these communicative events as co-constructed between the intermediary and the vulnerable individual (as indeed any other participating parties) allows for the complexity of communication barriers to be recognised.[122] Affording discretion to intermediaries in this way strengthens their professional jurisdictional claims through the trust and deference invested in them by fellow professionals.

The empirical data explored in this chapter reveal how intermediaries balance conflicting demands to uphold a neutral presentation. This often requires what Bergman-Blix and Wettergren describe as 'skillful inter-professional emotional attuning'.[123] The same authors use the concept of 'objectivity work' to explain the nature and content of neutrality among different courtroom actors.[124] For example, they argue that adjudication requires judges to emphasise their 'impartial demeanour' whereas prosecutors experience a 'contingent and shifting' objectivity due to their case involvement and interaction with witnesses.[125] Acknowledging that criminal justice actors experience and perform neutrality differently allows us to focus on the interactional and emotional aspects of intermediary work. As Lucy notes, impartiality is not a ubiquitous term that is easily transferable between different contexts.[126] This does not mean that intermediaries are excused from neutrality as a duty; rather the value should be seen through the lens of a role which has a unique status within the criminal process and is populated by individuals with varied occupational backgrounds.

It is perhaps unsurprising that the quotes from intermediaries that point to a 'weak illusio' relate to conduct that would be deemed non-controversial in fields such as speech and language therapy, social work or teaching. For example, while speech and language therapists and intermediaries are encouraged

120 Matthew Kramer, *Objectivity and the Rule of Law* (CUP 2009) 64.
121 Wadensjö (n 32).
122 Wadensjö (n 32).
123 Stina Bergman Blix and Åsa Wettergren, 'The Emotional Interaction of Judicial Objectivity' (2019) 9(5) Oñati Socio-Legal Series 726.
124 Bergman Blix and Wettergren (n 123) 723.
125 Stina Bergman Blix and Åsa Wettergren, *Professional Emotions in Court: A Sociological Perspective* (Routledge 2018) 161.
126 Lucy (n 118) 30.

to build rapport with a vulnerable individual, the former may achieve this through empathetic concern and emotional support.[127] Intermediaries may make recommendations based on emotional issues affecting communication, however, any emotional support must be left to the court defendant support (in Northern Ireland) or a friend or family member.[128] Similarly, Carlen and Powell noted a preference among social workers and probation officers to avoid inter-professional conflict through the use of 'courtroom lore' which involves close working relationships with lawyers and informal rule usage.[129] This resonates with the interactions described earlier between some intermediaries and police officers, arguably undermining the intermediary role's neutrality. Just as the craft of judging has deeply ingrained values that judges are rarely asked to critically examine, intermediaries are recruited from backgrounds with their own norms, values and unquestioned practices.[130] Indeed, O'Mahony et al. identified potential role conflict resulting from some intermediaries 'wearing more than one professional hat'.[131] As noted earlier, Bergman-Blix and Wetergren argue for greater understanding of the heterogeneity among court professionals in terms of their objectivity and role performance. It seems odd not to examine the intermediary's relationship with neutrality in a similar vein and we should question whether the illusion of neutrality is necessary to the role's acceptance.

6.8 Conclusion

This chapter reveals the neutrality paradox experienced by intermediaries in their work. While there is a strong commitment to the normative principle of neutrality among all intermediaries, the role often transcends that of an objective communication conduit as framed by the relevant procedural guidance and case law. The normative expectation of the role as a detached, objective communication facilitator indicates a lack of understanding of intermediary work and its content. Bourdieu's concept of illusio operates as a useful explanatory tool for investigating how intermediaries conceptualise their neutrality and how they negotiate its content. Reflecting on the strength (or weakness) of the illusio generated by intermediaries helps locate the intermediary within the social world of the criminal justice system. How and why

127 Wendy Papir-Bernstein, *The Practitioner's Path in Speech and Language Pathology* (Plural Publishing Inc 2018) 122.
128 MoJ (n 2) 13.
129 Pat Carlen and Margaret Powell, '"Professionals in the Magistrates" Courts: The Courtroom Lore of Probation Officers and Social Workers' in Howard Parker (ed), *Social Work and the Courts* (Hodder and Stoughton 1979).
130 Roach Anleu and Mack (n 19) 61.
131 O'Mahony and others (n 4) 160.

intermediaries demonstrate indifference or lack of commitment to these values is instructive to understanding the role's scope in practice.

How should these findings influence the provision and organisation of intermediaries? A starting point must be a recognition of what O'Mahony et al. term the 'intricacies of the non-partisan relationship' between intermediaries and the vulnerable individuals they assist.[132] This should be a feature of intermediary training so that practitioners know how their commitment to neutrality may be challenged at different stages. Yet, a hurdle to any discussion of intermediary neutrality is the relatively poor understanding of the role among lawyers and judges who rarely see the 'behind-the-scenes' work involved. Plotnikoff and Woolfson have already highlighted the urgent need for collaboration between judges, lawyers and intermediaries.[133] The unique challenges associated with intermediary neutrality must firstly be recognised before the viability of neutrality as an ethical standard can be seriously debated.

Finally, examining the intermediary role through the prism of neutrality reinforces a key theme emerging from the data underpinning this book: the roles of Registered Intermediaries and non-registered intermediaries in England and Wales are qualitatively different. In Northern Ireland, where a unitary system of intermediaries exists, such a distinction has not emerged, and neutrality appears a less contested aspect of the role. This finding should be instructive to the MoJ as it operates the HMCTS Court Appointed Intermediary Scheme (HAIS). This system covers intermediary provision for vulnerable defendants to replace the previously unregulated, ad-hoc system of non-registered intermediaries. At first glance, the HAIS system perpetuates the 'two-tier' intermediary provision leading to the emergence of what this book has termed 'witness work' and 'defendant work'.[134] To date, there has been no research examining how intermediary provision under HAIS compares with the Witness Intermediary Scheme operated by the MoJ. It is suggested that the MoJ must consider how the perception of intermediary neutrality could be affected by the existence of two different 'types' of intermediary work. Based on the experience in Northern Ireland, a unitary system of intermediaries covering both witnesses and defendants appears best placed to avoid such a distinction emerging.

132 O'Mahony and others (n 4) 164.
133 Plotnikoff and Woolfson (n 2) 23.
134 Emily Henderson, '"A Very Valuable Tool": Judges, Advocates and Intermediaries Discuss the Intermediary System in England and Wales' (2015) 19(3) International Journal of Evidence and Proof 154.

Chapter 7

Witness work, defendant work and participatory roles

7.1 Introduction

Damaska defines the adversarial criminal trial as 'proceedings structured as a dispute between two sides in a position of theoretical equality before a court which must decide on the outcome of the contest'.[1] Conceptualised in this way, the trial as the centrepiece of criminal proceedings is depicted as a state mechanism to resolve grievances against suspects, defendants and offenders.[2] While the adversarial nature of criminal proceedings is often framed around the state's obligations in relation to establishing the guilt of the accused, it is generally accepted that the administration of justice demands recognition of the rights and interests of other people affected by the criminal action.[3] This is one reason behind the movement towards modified adversarialism, discussed in Chapter 4 (Locating the intermediary within theories of the criminal trial). Despite this development, the primacy given to orality and cross-examination within the criminal trial leads some to question whether other parties, such as complainants and witnesses, can ever be fully integrated into the criminal justice process.[4] For example, Doak argues that these groups are 'conscripted' into a purely operational role in which their views, interests and rights are subservient to the collective interest of calling defendants to account for their actions.[5] As discussed in Chapter 4 (Locating the intermediary within theories

1 Mirjan Damaska, 'Evidentiary Barriers to Conviction and Two Models of Criminal Procedure: A Comparative Study' (1973) 121 University of Pennsylvania Law Review 506, 563.
2 Jonathan Doak and Claire McGourlay, *Evidence in Context* (3rd edn, Routledge 2012) 1.
3 Criminal Procedure Rules (CPR) (October 2020) Pt 1, rule 1.1; Also see: *Doorson v Netherlands* (1996) 22 EHRR 330 where the ECtHR noted that 'principles of fair trial also require that in appropriate cases the interests of the defence are balanced against those of witnesses or victims called upon to testify' [43].
4 Nicola Lacey and Hannah Pickard, 'A Dual-Process Approach to Criminal Law: Victims and the Clinical Model of Responsibility without Blame' (2019) 27(2) The Journal of Political Philosophy 229.
5 Doak and McGourlay (n 2) 35. For an alternative account, see: Abenaa Owusu-Bempah, *Defendant Participation in the Criminal Process* (Routledge 2016).

DOI: 10.4324/9781003461166-7

of the criminal trial), these issues go to the heart of how we conceptualise the aims and underpinning values of the trial.

This chapter focuses on participation, specifically the relationship between intermediaries and the participatory roles of witnesses and defendants. It examines how the intermediary role is inextricably tied to the different ways vulnerable individuals participate within the criminal justice process. It returns to the concepts of 'witness work' and 'defendant work', which are further developed through a focused analysis of participatory rights. The data presented here suggest that the communication difficulties experienced by defendants, the inhibiting nature of the criminal court environment (in particular the dock) and the deficiencies in defendant intermediary provision result in a form of participation which distinguishes defendants from witnesses. While the defendant's right to 'effective participation' is recognised through case law and relevant guidance, the experiences of intermediaries provide insight into how the role adapts to differing participation roles and is, in turn, shaped by them. The findings from my interviews challenge a 'balancing approach' to participation which seeks to equalise the rights of witnesses and defendants. The chapter analyses the meaning and experience of participation and how this can relate to the nature and scope of the intermediary role.[6]

7.2 Participatory 'roles' and rights

Chapter 4 (Locating the intermediary within theories of the criminal trial) introduced participation as a core aim or value of the criminal trial and the wider criminal justice process. When studying participatory roles, one difficulty is that the term participation may feasibly apply to a broad range of criminal justice participants. Edwards links participation to the broader concept of citizenship and the notion of 'being in control, having a say, being listened to, or being treated with dignity and respect'.[7] This definition could apply to all victims, witnesses, defendants and even jury members. While participation is viewed as instrumental in achieving many criminal justice objectives, there is a need to clarify how these objectives relate to different criminal justice participants.[8] For example, Kirby et al. discussed

6 John Jackson, 'Justice for All: Putting Victims at the Heart of Criminal Justice' (2003) 30(2) Journal of Law and Society 309, 317; Andrew Ashworth, *The Criminal Process: An Evaluative Study* (2nd edn, OUP 1998) 30.

7 Ian Edwards, 'An Ambiguous Participant: The Crime Victim and Criminal Justice Decision-Making' (2004) 44 British Journal of Criminology 967.

8 Neil Walker and Mark Telford, 'Designing Criminal Justice: The System in Comparative Perspective, Report 14, Review of the Criminal Justice System in Northern Ireland' (London, HMSO) 10.

the 'multifaceted' nature of participation and conceptualised the term in relation to court users rather than one group, such as witnesses or defendants.[9] Cooper et al. highlight the usefulness of a 'generic, crossjurisdictional approach to participation'.[10] Elsewhere in the same text, the authors point to the 'long established principle . . . that people should be able to participate effectively in the court and tribunal proceedings that directly concern them'.[11]

It is widely accepted that non-defendant witnesses, as autonomous participants, should be treated with respect and dignity throughout the criminal justice process. As explored in Chapter 2 (Emergence of the intermediary role), concern for witness welfare and the facilitation of best evidence led to the introduction of special measures through the Youth Justice and Criminal Evidence 1999 (YJCEA). The interests of non-defendant witnesses are now codified through the overriding objective of the Criminal Procedure Rules (CPR), which requires courts to respect 'the interests of witnesses, victims and jurors and keeping them informed of the progress of the case'.[12] Further, courts must take 'every reasonable step' to facilitate the participation of *all* individuals within proceedings, including witnesses.[13] However, reforms in England and Wales have not yet granted witnesses a set of procedural rights along the same lines as the defendant.[14] For example, neither witnesses nor complainants enjoy a right to be present during the trial, question witnesses, present evidence or have legal representation.[15] Efforts to enhance or reform the role of non-defendant witnesses as participants have, so far, largely failed. Despite increased recognition of their status within the criminal process, Doak concludes that any formal non-defendant participatory right is 'fundamentally impossible to realise in a meaningful way'.[16]

As noted, the participatory rights of defendants are more firmly established than those of non-defendants. Fundamentally, the accused enjoys the

9 Amy Kirby, Jessica Jacobson and Gillian Hunter, 'Effective Participation or Passive Acceptance: How Can Defendants Participate More Effectively in the Court Process?' (Howard League What is Justice? Working Papers 9/2014) 11.

10 Jessica Jacobson and Penny Cooper, *Participation in Courts and Tribunals: Concepts, Realities and Aspirations* (Bristol UP 2020) 4.

11 Jacobson and Cooper (n 10) 1.

12 CPR (n 3) rule 1.1.

13 CPR (n 3) rule 3.8(3); Criminal Practice Directions 2023 (CPD) (updated July 2024) [6.1.1].

14 Owusu-Bempah (n 5) 28; Ernestine Henriëtte Hoegen and Marion Eleonora Ingeborg Brienen, *Victims of Crime in 22 European Criminal Justice Systems: The Implementation of Recommendation (85) 11 of the Council of Europe on the Position of the Victim in the Framework of Criminal Law and Procedure* (Wolf Legal Productions 2000).

15 Jonathan Doak, *Victim's Rights, Human Rights and Criminal Justice: Reconceiving the Role of Third Parties* (Hart Publishing 2008) 138.

16 Doak (n 15) 158.

right to be present at their trial as well as the right of confrontation.[17] It is also a long-standing principle in criminal law that defendants must be able to understand and participate effectively in the criminal proceedings of which they are a part.[18] The right to effective participation is an 'implied' right that derives not only from the guarantees contained within Article 6 of the ECHR, but is implicit in the notion of an adversarial adjudication system.[19] The ECtHR first recognised the right to effective participation in the case of *Stanford v U.K.*[20] In *SC v U.K*, the court explained that defendants enjoy not only the 'right to be present, but also to hear and follow the proceedings'.[21] The court went further and stated that:

> 'effective participation' in this context presupposes that the accused has a broad understanding of the nature of the trial process and of what is at stake for him or her, including the significance of any penalty which may be imposed. It means that he or she, if necessary with the assistance of, for example, an interpreter, lawyer, social worker or friend, should be able to understand the general thrust of what is said in court. The defendant should be able to follow what is said by the prosecution witnesses and, if represented, to explain to his own lawyers his version of events, point out any statements with which he disagrees and make them aware of any facts which should be put forward in his defence.[22]

While subsequent case law has grappled with the concept of effective participation, the scope of the right remains relatively unclear. Although the court's explanation in *SC v U.K* remains the most instructive statement on the right to effective participation, questions about its content and reach remain. Firstly, it is unclear whether the right includes the ability to provide coherent and intelligible testimony. The special measures available to defendants (use of live-link and intermediary assistance) were introduced to facilitate the effective participation of defendants.[23] It follows that since these measures

17 The right of confrontation under Art.6 of the Convention affords the defendant the right to 'examine or have examined witnesses against him'. Also see: Elmar Widder, 'The Right to Challenge Witnesses – An Application of Strasbourg's Flexible "Sole and Decisive" Rule to other Human Rights' (2014) 3(4) Cambridge Journal of International and Comparative Law 1084.

18 Jessica Jacobson and Jenny Talbot, *Vulnerable Defendants in the Criminal Courts: A Review of Provision for Adults and Children* (Prison Reform Trust 2009, ISBN: 0 946209 96 0) 8.

19 European Court of Human Rights, 'Guide on Article 6 of the European Convention on Human Rights' (31 August 2020) 30.

20 App no 16757/90 (ECHR, 23 February 1994 [26]).

21 *SC v U.K* (2005) 40 EHRR 10 [29].

22 *SC v U.K* (n 21).

23 Samantha Fairclough, 'The Role of the Principle of Equality in the Provision of Special Measures to Vulnerable Court Users' (PhD thesis, University of Birmingham 2017).

seek to enable defendants to testify, and improve the quality of their evidence, the right to effective participation incorporates the ability to provide good quality evidence.[24]

This chapter challenges a broad and generic approach to the concept of participation. Discussion of 'participatory parity' is not particularly helpful in understanding the scope and content of the intermediary role.[25] One of the core findings of this book – that the intermediary role is plagued by confusion as to its parameters – becomes much more difficult to examine if participatory entitlements of criminal justice actors are homogenised. A more useful approach recognises that the criminal justice system is the 'scene of conflicting aims and interests' in which witnesses and defendants have different roles with correspondingly differing interests.[26] This should facilitate a more nuanced analysis rather than a preoccupation with the notion of balance. Thus, it does not necessarily follow that participation rights must be granted to complainants simply because they are granted to defendants. A rigorous critique of individual participatory roles is an effective antidote to a 'zero-sum game' which assumes that promoting defendant rights must necessarily lead to losses for complainants.[27]

Despite commonalities between witnesses and defendants, a distinction must be drawn. We can recognise the instrumental role intermediaries play in assisting the production of complete, coherent and accurate testimony of both defendant and non-defendant witnesses and acknowledge the defendant's unique participatory role within the criminal process.[28] To be clear, while intermediary involvement may contribute to efficient fact-finding, the participatory role of defendants is much broader, and the defendant intermediary role invariably mirrors this.[29] This enhanced participatory role reflects the accused's interest in criminal proceedings and the consequences of any outcome. The fundamental guarantees and protections which the defendant enjoys within the criminal process are based mainly on the public censure of conviction and state punishment which are at stake.[30] To argue otherwise risks reliance on what Jackson terms a 'dubious symmetry' between the

24 Abenaa Owusu-Bempah, 'The Interpretation and Application of the Right to Effective Participation' (2018) 22(4) International Journal of Evidence and Proof 321, 327.

25 Judith Resnik and Dennis Curtis, *Representing Justice: Invention, Controversy and Rights in City-states and Democratic Courtrooms* (Yale UP 2011) 17.

26 Ashworth (n 6) 30.

27 John Jackson, 'Justice for All: Putting Victims at the Heart of Criminal Justice' (2003) 30(2) Journal of Law and Society 309, 313.

28 YJCEA, s.16(3).

29 Owusu-Bempah (n 5) 6.

30 Abenaa Owusu-Bempah, 'Penalising Defendant Non-Cooperation in the Criminal Process and the Implications for English Criminal Procedure' (PhD thesis, University College London 2012) 27; Andrew Ashworth and Lucia Zedner, 'Justice Prevention: Preventive Rationales and the Limits of the Criminal Law' in Antony Duff and Stuart Green (eds), *Philosophical Foundations of Criminal Law* (OUP 2011) 293.

interests of witnesses on one hand, and the interests of the accused on the other.[31] Rather than pursuing a 'justice for all' policy, a rights-centred approach better addresses the rights that complainants, witnesses and defendants are afforded within criminal proceedings. This chapter takes this position as a point of departure and argues that intermediary practice reflects the differing participatory roles enjoyed by witnesses and defendants. It elaborates the concepts of 'witness work' and 'defendant work' described in Chapter 7 (Witness work, defendant work and participatory roles) and reveals how intermediaries conceptualise the differences.

7.3 'Effective participation' means 'early participation'

Although difficult to imagine today, before the Police and Criminal Evidence Act 1984 (PACE) criminal defence lawyers had very little contact with their clients before their appearance at court. Since then, increased sociolegal research into the treatment of suspects at the police station has revealed the importance of advisors as a restraint on coercive police behaviour.[32] While most attention has been given to the plight of vulnerable witnesses, it is now accepted that *any* individual who is unable to access relevant advice or support is placed at a disadvantage.[33] Although not an advisor, the presence of the intermediary to continually assess the defendant's ability to participate and intervene if necessary acts as a safeguard for his welfare and treatment.[34] Recent research has shown how suspects with mental health disorders are over-represented in custody and that many suffer heightened levels of suggestibility, compliance and acquiescence.[35] Therefore, it is difficult to explain or justify that intermediaries are rarely matched with vulnerable suspects at the police station in England and Wales (see Chapter 1: Introduction).[36]

The importance of intermediary involvement at the police station for vulnerable suspects was a prevailing theme across my interviews. A preference for earlier involvement can be linked to how intermediaries conceptualise

31 Jackson (n 27) 317.

32 Mike McConville and others, *Standing Accused: The Organization and Practices of Criminal Defence Lawyers in Britain* (Clarendon Press 1994) 101; John Walkley, *Police Interrogation* (Police Review Publishing Co. 1987); Layla Skinns, *Police Custody: Governance, Legitimacy and Reform in the Criminal Justice Process* (Routledge 2011).

33 McConville and others (n 32) 100.

34 HM Government, 'Working Together to Safeguard Children: A Guide to Inter-agency Working to Safeguard and Promote the Welfare of Children' (July 2018) 11.

35 Gisli Gudjonsson, 'Psychological Vulnerabilities during Police Interviews. Why Are They Important?' (2018) 15 Legal and Criminological Psychology 161; Björn Hofvander and others, 'Mental Health among Young Adults in Prison: The Importance of Childhood-Onset Conduct Disorder' (2017) 3 BJPsych Open 78.

36 Laura Farrugia and Fiona Gabbert, 'Vulnerable Suspects in Police Interviews: Exploring Current Practice in England and Wales' (2020) 17(1) Journal of Investigative Psychology and Offender Profiling 17.

defendant participatory rights. Consistent with Owusu-Bempah's position that the term 'effective participation' needs clarification, the reasons advanced by intermediaries were multifaceted and reveal different understandings of the right's content.[37] It was noteworthy that no intermediary resorted to the narrative of 'equal justice', i.e. suspects should be automatically entitled to the same intermediary access as vulnerable complainants.[38] Instead, most interviewees spoke separately about the position of the accused and the myriad participation challenges they face in criminal proceedings. This finding is significant because the study sample consisted of intermediaries who had experience working with both witnesses and defendants. The following analysis reveals that intermediaries conceptualise 'witness work' and 'defendant work' based not only on the differences in governance and organisation of the roles, but also because of differing participatory entitlements.

7.4 Assessment and interview

As noted earlier, the legislative basis for defendant intermediaries in England and Wales limits assistance to courtroom testimony. While judges have allowed for broader involvement at trial, defendant intermediaries become involved in proceedings much later than Registered Intermediaries for witnesses.[39] This practice, directed and overseen by the judge, seems to have led to a degree of passive acceptance among intermediaries. Most of the intermediaries I interviewed in England and Wales had no experience assessing a suspect before police interview and viewed the defendant's role as being primarily court-based. The two police officers interviewed had never encountered an intermediary assisting a suspect and regarded the role as intrinsically witness focused: 'intermediaries go with witnesses, appropriate adults with defendants' (PO-2). Despite this, when intermediaries were directly questioned in interview, there was unanimous agreement that the role *should* be involved as early as possible. It seemed counterintuitive to them that a vulnerable suspect, who later warranted intermediary assistance at court, would have had to endure a police interview without an intermediary:

> It just makes no sense whatsoever, because all the damage is done already because the interview has already taken place, so loads of stuff has gone on already and it's inherently unfair. Like my guy who I went to court with recently as a defendant, he said 'I just wait my turn and then I answer

37 Abenaa Owusu-Bempah, 'The Interpretation and Application of the Right to Effective Participation' (2018) 22(4) International Journal of Evidence and Proof 321.

38 Jackson (n 27).

39 Communicourt, 'The Changing Role of an Intermediary: Criminal Court vs Family Court' <https://www.communicourt.co.uk/news/the-changing-role-of-an-intermediary-criminal-court-vs-family-court/> accessed 27 February 2025.

when they ask and I don't really pay attention. I would like to understand' but it was just beyond him.

(E&W-10)

The picture depicted by E&W-10, of a vulnerable defendant who 'participated' in a police interview yet was seemingly oblivious to the case against him, is a regrettable consequence of the current defendant intermediary provision. It resonates with what Baldwin and McConville term the 'profound sense of non-involvement' many defendants experience, despite being legally represented.[40] When we compare such examples with the early involvement of Registered Intermediaries for witnesses, questions around the participatory roles of both groups come into focus. In interview, intermediaries explained the importance of assessing the vulnerable witness with the police officer in attendance, planning the Achieving Best Evidence (ABE) interview with the officer based on their observations in assessment and working through the questions to ensure their suitability. The evidential importance of the ABE requires 'effective planning', and intermediaries were generally positive about their suggestions and recommendations being listened to by police.[41] My interview data echo the observations of Plotnikoff and Woolfson that effective coordination of ABE interviews can involve phone calls, emails and sharing of question formats between police and intermediaries.[42] The Registered Intermediary Procedural Guidance details how interaction between Registered Intermediaries and police should be conducted.[43]

In Northern Ireland, the Department of Justice (DoJ) justifies the provision of intermediary assistance at the police station on the need to 'enable suspects to participate effectively when being interviewed by the police'.[44] One consequence of providing Registered Intermediaries for both suspects at police interview and witnesses at the ABE interview is that the concepts of 'witness work' and 'defendant work' have not emerged.[45] Police feedback

40 John Baldwin and Michael McConville, *Jury Trials* (OUP 1979) 83.

41 Criminal Justice Joint Inspectorate, 'A Joint Inspection of the Treatment of Offenders with Learning Disabilities Within the Criminal Justice System' (January 2014) [5.9].

42 Joyce Plotnikoff and Richard Woolfson, *Intermediaries in the Criminal Justice System* (Policy Press 2015) 77.

43 Ministry of Justice, 'Registered Intermediary Procedural Guidance Manual 2024' 12–13 <https://assets.publishing.service.gov.uk/media/671b819bfc28a840abc6d26d/Registered_Intermediary_Procedural_Guidance_Manual_2024__Official_.pdf> accessed 8 February 2025.

44 Department of Justice (Northern Ireland) (DoJ), 'The Registered Intermediaries Procedural Guidance Manual' (April 2024) 3.

45 The author has published an interjurisdictional comparison of intermediary provision in England and Wales and Northern Ireland in the following journal article: John Taggart, '"I Am Not Beholden to Anyone . . . I Consider Myself to be an Officer of the Court": A Comparison of the Intermediary Role in England and Wales and Northern Ireland' (2021) 25(2) The International Journal of Evidence and Proof 141.

on intermediaries has been extremely positive and there are collaborative efforts to improve vulnerability identification.[46] Despite these developments, challenges have emerged. A recurring theme among intermediary interviewees was the comparative lack of time for planning and reviewing questions before a suspect interview compared to an ABE interview. NI-4 explained that this issue, as well as the confrontational style of the suspect interview, exacerbates the risks of miscommunication and the need for intermediary intervention:

> There won't have been the same time for planning. To be honest, when I do intervene it's sometimes met with irritation. The police, going into that suspect interview, have a very specific tunnel of questions that they want to ask. They're not used to deviating off or changing language, so I can understand that it's different for them and for someone like me to come in and question their questioning and it is asking a lot of them.
>
> (NI-4)

This example suggests that even when witnesses and suspects enjoy equal intermediary access at the investigative stage, the task of facilitating communication can vary significantly. Similarly, it highlights how distinctions between 'witness work' and 'defendant work' may emerge within a unitary system of intermediaries. As NI-4 explained, many of the communication issues associated with suspect interviews arise because of external time pressures. It seems likely that if intermediaries in England and Wales were involved with suspects at the investigative stage (as they are in Northern Ireland) the distinction between 'witnesses work' and 'defendant work' would be reinforced.

The defendant's presence at the police interview also engages the Article 6 right to effective participation.[47] Arguably, without an intermediary, many vulnerable suspects cannot reach the threshold for participation as set out in *SC v U.K.* The involvement of intermediaries in assessing vulnerable witnesses pre-interview is premised on aiding participation through the facilitation of communication, yet the same reasoning has not led to similar provision for defendants.[48] Intermediaries highlighted this unsatisfactory situation, and their reflections shed light on how they conceptualise defendant participation. The thrust of their responses may be summarised as follows: while

46 DoJ, 'Northern Ireland Registered Intermediaries Schemes Pilot Project: Post-Project Review' (January 2015) 6.

47 Owusu-Bempah further argues that the case law in respect of legal advice to remain silent creates expectation of defendant participation, see: Owusu-Bempah (n 5) 110.

48 As explained earlier, intermediaries for witnesses and defendants are both engaged to help further the broad criminal justice objective of 'achieving best evidence'. Also, see: Owusu-Bempah (n 5).

witness involvement amounts to a mere snapshot of proceedings, defendants must be assessed more globally based on their need to understand and follow the whole case. E&W-3's view on this distinction explains this reasoning:

> With a defendant you have to assess, it is a different skill-set standing and answering questions to sitting in a dock for maybe days and weeks, processing all that information, listening to a lot of complex language, having to pick out all the important points, assimilate it and somehow understand which parts are relevant to your case . . . with a witness you only need to assess their ability to understand the questions and give the answer . . . whereas with a defendant you also have to be able to assess their ability to sit in a dock, so the assessments are longer with a defendant generally.
>
> (E&W-3)

Most intermediaries broadly acknowledged differences in assessment approach. As discussed earlier, intermediaries accepted that 'defendant work' is distinct and operates under different rules than 'witness work'. Yet, it was by explaining the participatory role of defendants that the distinction became most apparent:

> When it is a defendant being assessed, I am thinking more about their ability to understand things that aren't directly involving them. That is the difference really and their understanding has to be so much bigger. It is so challenging understanding what is going on in court from minute to minute. It's really hard to get your head around, and the volume of information is huge so I am thinking about that more really.
>
> (E&W-10)

These comments reflect a recognition among intermediaries that the participatory role of the accused is not only broader than that of witnesses, but also more complex and individual. At the assessment stage, the intermediary can prospectively evaluate how well the accused will navigate the communication challenges of the criminal justice system. It is, however, absurd to suggest that such challenges first emerge at court. Suspects in police interview may be at higher risk of not fully understanding the significance of questions put to them or the implications of their answers.[49] E&W-10's comment that intermediaries become involved after the 'damage' of the suspect interview is concerning but also revealing. In this context, this 'damage' may often equate to the denial of participatory rights as the vulnerable accused struggles to

49 Gisli Gudjonsson and others, 'Persons at Risk During Interviews in Police Custody: The Identification of Vulnerabilities' (Royal Commission on Criminal Procedure Research Study No 12, HMSO 1993).

understand the evidence against him and what is at stake. As Dehaghani notes, PACE Code C, which outlines the requirements for the detention, treatment and questioning of suspects, implicitly recognises that suspects are afforded additional safeguards at police investigation.[50] It follows that the 'damage' done is theoretically preventable, or at least limited, by appointing a suitable intermediary.[51]

While defendant intermediaries work predominantly in and around the trial, interviewees recognised that someone struggling to comprehend questions from a barrister in court will inevitably struggle to comprehend questions in a police interview. This supports Hodgson's contention that defence participation is *most* important at the pre-trial investigation stage.[52] Fairness requires that the accused is properly informed about critical choices and can have their voice heard – two imperatives that are clearly engaged at the investigative stage.[53] In a similar vein, McConville et al. identify the police interview as the key forum where the complex, interactive process of case construction takes place.[54] If we view access to legal advice, disclosure of evidence and authenticated interview recording as conductive to 'informed defence participation',[55] why would a vulnerable suspect's access to an intermediary not be considered as such? In addition, there is a risk of adverse inferences being drawn where a defendant relies on facts not mentioned in the police interview.[56] This increases pressure on suspects to answer police questions, despite possible communication problems. For all these reasons, there is a strong argument for the prioritisation of intermediary presence at police interview to protect the accused's participation – something which is not happening in practice.

Despite the lack of intermediary presence at the investigatory stage for suspects, reflecting on this preliminary stage is instructive when considering how defendant participation may be conceptualised. The Divisional Court

50 Roxanna Dehaghani, 'Interrogating Vulnerability: Reframing the Vulnerable Suspect in Police Custody' (2021) 30(2) Social & Legal Studies 251.

51 The appointment of an appropriate adult may be appropriate in certain situations, but the role is markedly different from that of an intermediary: see Roxanna Dehaghani, 'Defining the "appropriate" in "appropriate adult": Restrictions and Opportunities for Reform' (2020) 12 Criminal Law Review 1137.

52 Jacqueline Hodgson, 'Conceptions of the Trial in Inquisitorial and Adversarial Procedure' in Antony Duff and others (eds), *The Trial on Trial 2: Judgment and Calling to Account* (Hart Publishing 2006) 223, 241.

53 Grainne McKeever, 'Comparing Courts and Tribunals through the Lens of Participation' (2020) 38(3) Civil Justice Quarterly 217, 233.

54 Mike McConville, Andrew Sanders and Roger Leng, *The Case for the Prosecution* (Routledge 1991).

55 Owusu-Bempah (n 5) 100.

56 Jodie Blackstock and others, *Inside Police Custody: An Empirical Account of Suspects' Rights in Four Jurisdictions* (Intersentia 2014) 275.

in *OP* recognised the unique challenges vulnerable defendants face under cross-examination at court, which it noted amounts to the 'point of maximum strain'.[57] It held that when the accused submits himself to such questioning, the 'developed skills' of an intermediary would often be required. Since defendant intermediaries are appointed to ensure the defendant's right to effective participation, this invariably includes the role's involvement with the accused during court examination. As the previous paragraph outlined, the accused's participation during suspect interview ought to be relevant to the broad assessment of participation. It is ill-conceived to argue that the accused's participation, recognised during trial examination, should not extend to confrontation at the police interview.[58] The ECtHR reinforced this point in *Panovits v Cyprus* and held that effective participation is engaged from the beginning of a criminal investigation and, in particular, 'during any questioning by the police'.[59]

Roberts and Zuckerman stress the importance of 'open exchange of arguments and information at every significant stage of the litigation', which includes the nature of the prosecution case 'well in advance of trial'.[60] However, this presupposes comprehension of such information by the accused, which the empirical data reveal is patently not the case.[61] While the presence of legal representatives is beneficial to the accused at police interview, it can also act to marginalise and exclude participation.[62] Intermediaries in interview cited countless examples of being appointed to a vulnerable defendant at court who had little to no appreciation of the case against them despite having the benefit of a lawyer during suspect interview. E&W-3 summarised the plight of defendants with an analogy: 'it's like [the defendant] being asked questions about chapter 12 of a book without having read the first 11 chapters'. Such a description is realistically not applicable to vulnerable witnesses who have a 'snapshot' involvement in proceedings compared to defendants. It is argued that greater emphasis should be given to the 'effectiveness' of suspect participation at the investigative stage – reflecting the procedural rights afforded to the accused in the broader criminal process.[63]

57 *OP v Secretary of State for Justice* [2014] EWHC 1944 (Admin) [36].
58 Geoffrey Stephenson and Stephen Moston, 'Police Interrogation' (1994) 1 Psychology, Crime and Law 151.
59 [2008] 27 BHRC 464 [67].
60 Paul Roberts and Adrian Zuckerman, *Criminal Evidence* (OUP 2010) 57.
61 Directive 2012/13/EU on the right to information in criminal proceedings stipulates that information about applicable procedural rights should be given in an 'easily comprehensible manner' ([22]).
62 Hodgson (n 52) 243; Zenon Bankowski and Geoff Mungham, *Images of Law* (Routledge 1976) 86.
63 For further development of this argument, see: John Taggart, 'The Effective Participation of Suspects in Police Custody' (2024) 9 Criminal Law Review 590.

7.5 'Pragmatic and flexible' intermediary appointments

Apart from unequal intermediary provision between witnesses and defendants, no other issue has caused more contention among the intermediary community than the terms of intermediary involvement with a vulnerable defendant.[64] What have become known as 'evidence only' appointments have been criticised by commercial intermediary providers, such as Communicourt, who have historically adopted a blanket policy of refusing such requests.[65] This echoes Hoyano's argument that if a defendant cannot understand questions during his own testimony without an intermediary, it is highly probable that he will not understand the rest of the trial without one.[66] As defendant intermediary appointments are entirely ad-hoc, the terms of appointment are decided by the judge. Section 104 of the Coroners and Justice Act 2009 (CJA) provides for defendant intermediary involvement for the period of testimony only, and the early case law reinforced this. The Divisional Court in *OP* distinguished two types of assistance that a vulnerable defendant may require.[67] The first, which the court considered could be performed by an adult, such as a friend or relative, involves assisting the vulnerable individual throughout the trial by providing 'general support, reassurance and calm interpretation of unfolding events'.[68] The second, which requires the presence of an intermediary, involves assisting a defendant during his testimony and providing 'skilled support and interpretation'.[69]

In interview, intermediaries were eager to correct a misassumption that they routinely recommend their involvement at every stage of proceedings. There was palpable frustration among intermediaries in my interviews that many police, lawyers and judges view the intermediary role as 'self-serving'.[70] Fairclough and Taggart cite data from interviews with barristers which

64 This assertion is based upon my experience of interviewing intermediaries, attending different conferences where the intermediary role has been discussed and many informal conversations with other academics and lawyers working in this area.

65 Since the establishment of His Majesty's Courts and Tribunal Service (HMCTS) Appointed Intermediary Service (HAIS), Communicourt appears to have changed this policy and now also accept 'evidence only' bookings, see: Communicourt, 'Criminal Proceedings' <https://www.communicourt.co.uk/referral-booking-howto/criminal-proceedings/> accessed 10 February 2025.

66 Laura Hoyano, 'Coroners and Justice Act 2009: Special Measures Directions Take Two: Entrenching Unequal Access to Justice?' (2010) 5 Criminal Law Review 345, 360.

67 *OP v Secretary of State for Justice* (n 57).

68 *OP v Secretary of State for Justice* (n 57) [34].

69 *OP v Secretary of State for Justice* (n 57) [36].

70 Paula Backen, 'They Just Don't Get It: Communication and the Work of an Intermediary with Vulnerable People in the Justice System' (independently published 2017) 67. Precise figures on the proportion of cases in which an intermediary is recommended for evidence only are hard to obtain.

echo this suspicion with one describing the current system as a 'job creation scheme' for intermediaries.[71] The most recent data from Communicourt suggest that since HAIS launched in 2022, there has been a recommendation of 'no intermediary assistance needed' in 22% of cases.[72] The substance of intermediary recommendations is instructive to understand how defendant participation is conceptualised. Although a handful of intermediaries wanted to see broader involvement for the role as a starting point, a more representative view was that a 'pragmatic and flexible' (E&W-16) approach would better reflect the individual participatory needs of defendants. While intermediaries were broadly dissatisfied with the 'rarity' provisions of the Criminal Practice Directions (CPD),[73] this disgruntlement stemmed from the fact that it deprived them of flexibility in terms of their recommendations. E&W-16 explained the importance of intermediaries being afforded latitude when crafting their recommendations but equally being responsive to the individual needs of the vulnerable defendant:

> I think it's worth being pragmatic and it's worth being flexible rather than dogmatic. In lots of ways the role is carried and can be won through flexibility and by being responsive to the needs of the court. I don't know how anyone could advocate a position where every defendant needs an intermediary for the whole trial.
>
> (E&W-16)

This characterisation of the role in defensive terms, which can be 'won' through tactical action, mirrors the arguments made in Chapter 6 (The neutrality paradox), i.e. that intermediaries are aware of the constant pressure to reinforce their professional expertise and jurisdiction. This was also evident in Northern Ireland, with NI-7 stressing that intermediaries 'should be able to decide when an intermediary isn't needed, because that's where our demise will come'. While these quotes illustrate the protectiveness of intermediaries over their expertise, they also speak to an appreciation of defendant participation and its content. Intermediaries rejected the 'full trial' versus 'evidence only' dichotomy and explained how they often recommend their involvement at discrete stages of proceedings, such as pre-trial conferences, during the prosecution's case or even at sentencing. This information is fascinating not only because defendant intermediaries are under-researched, but also because

71 Samantha Fairclough and John Taggart, 'Lost in Translation? Perceptions of Defendant Intermediaries in the Legal Profession' (2023) 7 Criminal Law Review 440, 451.

72 Communicourt, 'Intermediary Case Law Update: Mr Justice Williams [2024] EWHC 906 (Fam)' <https://www.communicourt.co.uk/news/category/blog-post/> accessed 27 December 2024.

73 Criminal Practice Directions 2015 (October 2020 amended) 3F.14. The updated Criminal Practice Directions (n 13) contain no reference to intermediary appointments for defendants being 'rare'.

it reveals how intermediaries respond to the different participatory role of defendants compared to witnesses. While for witnesses the focus of intermediary involvement is oral testimony, interviewees recognised the unique communication challenges the criminal justice system generates for defendants and how the intermediary role must creatively adapt to confront them. As the examples in the following paragraphs illustrate, the unique participatory needs of defendants contour the scope and character of the intermediary role and support the conceptualisation of 'witness work' and 'defendant work'.

7.6 Pre-trial involvement: consultations and guilty pleas

The configuration of criminal justice spaces can impact the nature of social relations and the ability of citizens to participate.[74] The spaces in which the intermediary meets, interacts and communicates with other actors are instructive in understanding how the role operates and the potential limitations on its functions. The importance of a designated space with aural and visual privacy where a defendant can instruct his legal advisors is recognised in the Court and Tribunal Design Guide.[75] It provides that 'other associated parties' may also be in attendance, which would seem broad enough to cover an interpreter or an intermediary if either, or both, are appointed.[76] While it is common for defendant intermediaries in England and Wales to attend legal consultations, the interview data revealed how crucial this stage of proceedings is viewed in assessing the defendant's communication and, by extension, participation in proceedings. Unsurprisingly, the value of intermediary attendance at consultations where legal instructions are given is increased when the vulnerable defendant has not previously been assessed. In such circumstances, which appear worryingly common, intermediaries viewed pre-trial consultations as a crucial juncture to the defendant's prospective participation. E&W-1 explained:

> sometimes I've gone for conferences and it's the first time the defendant has fully understood the evidence against them and they have pleaded because they basically realise that they are not going to win and there is no

74 Linda Mulcahy and Emma Rowden, The *Democratic Courthouse* (Routledge 2020) 10.

75 HM Courts and Tribunal Services (HMCTS), 'Court and Tribunal Design Guide' (HMCTS 2019) 142.

76 HMCTS (n 75); in a recent virtual trial pilot study conducted by JUSTICE, provision was made for a 'virtual room' for the defendant to consult with counsel: Linda Mulcahy, Emma Rowden and Wend Teeder, 'Testing the Case for a Virtual Courtroom with a Physical Jury Hub Second Evaluation of a Virtual Trial Pilot Study Conducted by JUSTICE' (JUSTICE 2020) 4.

> point in chancing their luck because it's not going to work, but if you think about money and the time that saves in court for the sake of a conference. (E&W-1)

E&W-17 also highlighted the importance of intermediary involvement at legal consultations when the defendant is deciding how to plead:

> I might help them to plead guilty if that's what they need to do. That's when you need me there. I had a case when I've actually said: 'please appoint me on the first day because the barrister's saying there is so much overwhelming evidence'. Six years ago I went to see a defendant in a pretrial conference with his barrister. The barrister said: 'there's DNA evidence Billy'. Billy said: 'didn't do it'. They said it five times and I said: 'Billy, they found bits of your body in her knickers'. He went: 'yes I did it' and we had no trial. So, I am convinced that we have *such* a role to play meanwhile. (E&W-17)

Most intermediaries described similar experiences, whereby their involvement was viewed as an efficient way of helping to procure a sensible guilty plea. Plotnikoff and Woolfson have recognised this aspect of the intermediary role as instrumental to pre-trial processes being adapted 'so far as necessary' to facilitate the defendant's effective participation.[77] Backen remarks that many vulnerable defendants with poor reasoning stubbornly deny charges – as they believe it is their 'best way to freedom', despite overwhelming evidence to the contrary.[78] This element of participation is uniquely defendant-centred and distinguishes 'defendant work' from 'witness work'. Beyond this transactional facilitation of communication, the intermediary may play an unrecognised yet important role in legal consultations: mitigating pressure from defence counsel who seek to 'negotiate' with the prosecution, resulting in a guilty plea. E&W-17's example earlier could accurately be described as the intermediary communicating the barrister's advice more comprehensibly. However, the empirical findings of McConville and Baldwin point to a more concerning practice of defence counsel coercing defendants into pleading guilty.[79] Helm's recent empirical work identifies 'problematic incentives' to plead guilty, which, more worryingly, appear to affect vulnerable defendants disproportionately.[80] Admittedly, it is difficult to empirically gauge the

77 Plotnikoff and Woolfson (n 42) 261.

78 Backen (n 70) 40.

79 Baldwin and McConville (n 40) 39; Mike McConville and others, *Standing Accused: The organisation of criminal defence lawyers in Britain* (Clarendon 1994); Peter Nardulli, *The Courtroom Elite* (Ballinger Publishing Company 1978).

80 Rebecca Helm, 'Constrained Waiver of Trial Rights? Incentives to Plead Guilty and the Right to a Fair Trial' (2019) 46(3) Journal of Law and Society 423.

impact that intermediary presence may have on defence lawyers in terms of their advice regarding plea. There may also be questions over the blurring of lines between a) good communication facilitation that helps the defendant to understand the evidence and b) the intermediary effectively encouraging a guilty plea.

In my interviews, only one intermediary specifically addressed the issue of guilty pleas being procured. E&W-10 noted the case of one defendant who 'miraculously' pleaded guilty after his defence counsel visibly struggled to amend questions in line with the intermediary's recommendations. The intermediary was suggesting that the guilty plea was procured to save the barrister the ordeal of an uncomfortable examination-in-chief. This example resonates with the court workgroup's view of the guilty plea as an efficient method of case disposition, with little regard given to the deleterious effect on the defendant's right to challenge the prosecution case.[81] While my sample did not include legal representatives, it would be insightful to interview defence lawyers and intermediaries, *ex post facto*, about their experiences of consultations in which the defendant decided to plead guilty. The potential of the intermediary to act as a restraint on defence representatives raises a litany of questions about defendant participation and the scope of the intermediary role, in particular its neutrality and relative status within criminal proceedings.

7.7 The 'unknowns' of defendant work

The decision to plead guilty will often require the intermediary's communication expertise, yet the role is potentially much broader and more varied. Reflecting on the pre-trial position of witnesses compared to defendants, E&W-16 recognised the significance of the defendant's pre-trial discussions with counsel and remarked that 'with defendants you are more actively making sure they've understood'. Almost every interviewee recognised this enhanced defendant intermediary role at the pre-trial stage and that defendants require a broader understanding of the case and its potential ramifications. E&W-14 drew an interesting comparison:

> I think the witness has a very limited role at court. They are there to literally turn up . . . so all they are there to do is to be cross-examined. Whereas, with a defendant there are still so many unknowns . . . the intermediary needs to be there [at the consultation] so the defendant is able to give instructions and understand what is going on.
>
> (E&W-14)

81 Herbert Jacob, *Justice in America: Courts, Lawyers, and the Judicial Process* (Little Brown and Company 1965).

The 'unknowns' which E&W-14 described warrant closer examination. As well as helping to facilitate guilty pleas, these relate to the defendant's prospective role in proceedings and centre on some salient issues: a) does the defendant understand the charges and prosecution evidence? b) can the defendant identify aspects of the prosecution evidence with which he disagrees? c) is the defendant able to instruct his lawyer? This is not an exhaustive list, but it underscores how, even before trial, the defendant's participation is engaged. It is paradoxical that intermediaries assess the defendant's ability to effectively participate yet are prohibited from expressing an opinion on the issue of competence.[82] Of course, an intermediary appointed at the investigative stage will be able to assess the defendant's communication and prospective participation much earlier, as evidenced by intermediary practice in Northern Ireland.[83]

Perhaps the most significant 'unknown' at the pre-trial stage, apart from the decision as to plea, relates to whether the defendant will testify. While this chapter advocates a broad understanding of defendant participation, it is understandable that much significance is given to oral examination. Lady Justice Rafferty's remarks in *OP* that cross-examination represents the 'point of maximum strain' for the defendant reflects this view.[84] Intermediaries in interview placed importance on *all* vulnerable individuals being given the opportunity to have their voice heard in court 'to enable them to give their best evidence' (E&W-8). For example, enabling young sexual abuse complainants to give evidence brought a sense of fulfilment to intermediaries. Yet, my interview data suggest that the oral testimony of the accused, around whom the criminal trial centres, is approached differently by intermediaries. This is not to suggest that intermediaries demonstrated less commitment to ensuring the best evidence of witnesses is produced. Instead, it may stem from the perceived lack of support for defendants compared to witnesses and the belief that facilitating a defendant's 'best evidence' sometimes requires catalytic action from the intermediary. This perception of inequality is evidenced by the following comment from E&W-13:

> The defendants are at a loss at the start [and] have got as many needs, if not more, and they have got nothing. I came into the defendant work partly because I was seeing defendants not getting help which is ethically and morally wrong to me.
>
> (E&W-13)

82 In determining whether a defendant is fit to plead, a court should consider whether the use of an intermediary or other special measures would enable a defendant to be accommodated within the trial process: *R v Walls* [2011] EWCA Crim 443 [37].

83 DoJ (n 44) 3.

84 *OP v Secretary of State for Justice* (n 57) [36].

Focusing on the decision about whether to testify, my interview data suggest that intermediaries assume a more proactive role in a bid to secure defendant participation. E&W-17 revealed how intermediaries can feel compelled to 'enable' defendants to give evidence in a way that exceeds the orthodox facilitation of the communication role. Beyond tackling the perceived systemic inequalities within the criminal justice system, intermediaries can find themselves fighting the defendant's corner against the advice of legal representatives:

> Barristers don't want them to give evidence either. Barristers don't want inconsistent defendants getting in the witness box and saying the wrong thing. I was with one about six weeks ago, somebody who had just become a QC, who thought he really knew his stuff. He said twice to this defendant, in a week and a half trial – 'I'm not sure it's a good idea for you to give evidence' . . . in front of me I said: 'really? Why would that be? Because the jury really need to hear his voice. All they've got to see is him sitting in the dock, they've got no idea about who he is', and when you hear somebody's voice it completely changes. He said it to him twice, and I pushed and he gave evidence and he was acquitted. That's not my job, I'm not there to get anybody acquitted – but if he just had his barrister standing up for him I don't think they would have got the flavour of what this man was.
>
> (E&W-17)

E&W-17 was aware that by 'pushing' the defendant to give evidence she overstepped the limits of her neutral, objective role. Her actions seem to be in response to the defendant's role being minimised and the perceived failings of the defence barrister to protect his client's best interests. Just as intermediaries justify the stretching of their impartiality as part of the overriding responsibility to facilitate communication, E&W-17's eagerness for the defendant to testify may arguably be viewed through a participatory lens. This position views the accused's 'voice' as their focal instrument with a need for the jury to see 'who he is' and for him to be recognised as a rational and autonomous human being.[85] The ethical issues with this position are, however, plain to see. What did the defendant want to do, and was his decision to testify truly informed? E&W-17's actions seem veiled with concern for the accused's participation but should cause us to question the extent to which his individual autonomy was respected. It is worth briefly noting again that in Northern Ireland, where the concepts of 'witness work' and 'defendant work' were not recognised by intermediary interviewees, these ethical issues relating to neutrality were not so pronounced.

85 Hock Lai Ho, 'Liberalism and the Criminal Trial' (2010) 32 Sydney Law Review 269.

It is important to remember that the intermediary and defence representatives have different roles and duties that impact how they conceptualise and engage with the right to effective participation. Due to the primary duty which the intermediary owes to the court, the role is concerned with facilitating communication which often seems indistinguishable from, or at least instrumental to, their role in facilitating participation. Access to legal representation has been interpreted as integral to effective participation, particularly since a lawyer will often be best placed to articulate the defendant's version of events and challenge the evidence against him.[86] A barrister owes a professional obligation to act in the best interests of his client, which may not necessarily result in advice that the accused should testify.[87] Indeed, a defendant may understand the 'thrust' of what is said in court and be able to follow proceedings yet decide not to testify based on legal advice.[88] The preceding exchange between E&W-17 and the defence barrister suggests that settings such as legal conferences act as sites of conflict between these two positions.

An alternative perspective is that E&W-17's frustration was based on a misassumption that both she and the barrister were primarily concerned with effecting the same right. Lord Thomas in *Grant Murray* noted that intermediaries are 'instructed to provide advice and guidance to the judge (and to the advocates), not to dictate to anyone what is to happen [or] interfere with the functions of others'.[89] While intermediaries are concerned with ensuring the right to effective participation, the burden of ensuring the right is upheld rests with the trial judge.[90] E&W-17's actions arguably blur the boundaries between the responsibilities of criminal justice actors in protecting the right to effective participation and, in the words of Lord Thomas, suggest that she 'misunderstood her role'.[91]

Yet not all vulnerable defendants who require intermediary assistance decide to testify. At consultation stage, intermediaries must also assess the utility of their assistance throughout the 'first half' of proceedings in helping the defendant to understand the impact of his decision. These nuances of the defendant intermediary role question the participation narrative that focuses solely on the defendant's testimony. The accused who chooses not to

86 Owusu-Bempah (n 5) 332.
87 Bar Standards Board, 'The BSB Handbook- Version 4.8' <https://www.barstandardsboard.org.uk/the-bsb-handbook.html?part=E3FF76D3-9538-4B97-94C02111664E5709&audience=&csrfToken=&q=#part-C9631C45-F7A4-41F7-BF341296EC253160> accessed 10 February 2025 [CD2].
88 Kirby, Jacobson and Hunter (n 9) 9.
89 *R v Grant-Murray* [2017] EWCA Crim 1228 [199].
90 *R v Grant-Murray* (n 89). This point was also echoed by the Court of Appeal in *R v Thomas* [2020] EWCA Crim 117 [38].
91 *R v Grant-Murray* (n 89).

testify should be treated as a free, dignified and autonomous agent within his own trial.[92] Theories of the criminal trial that centre on defendant participation through oral testimony, such as those advanced by Duff et al., struggle to accommodate this position since they are undergirded by a normative expectation that the accused will testify.[93] Duff's conception of the trial as a 'communicative enterprise' is premised on engaging the accused through 'argument and justification'.[94] A non-testifying defendant who seeks to put the prosecution to proof remains worthy of a participatory role through what Ho terms as a 'dialogue' throughout the trial.[95] An intermediary assisting a non-testifying defendant may even assume a heightened responsibility since this 'dialogue' will not be reciprocal in the same way. While effective participation is broadly construed, providing testimony is an important element since the accused can demonstrate an awareness of the case against him through his answers to questions. When a defendant does not testify, the scope for defendant engagement is invariably restricted and thus, the intermediary may have to compensate for this. As Ho argues, the trial has a 'communicative purpose', but the form of the defendant participation within it varies and intermediaries are responsive to this through the facilitation of communication.[96]

7.8 Participation and the dock

So far, the chapter has focused on differentiating criminal justice participants based on their individual participatory roles. Although these roles are often discussed in abstract terms, they are reified through the criminal justice built environment and the spaces within it.[97] The ability of criminal justice spaces to encourage or inhibit participation has been the subject of sociolegal enquiry, much of which has lamented the exclusion of the laity as outsiders.[98] As the defendant is the central participant of the criminal trial, it is reasonable to assume that their needs would be prioritised within such spaces. The

92 Owusu-Bempah (n 5) 44.
93 Antony Duff and others, *The Trial on Trial 1: Truth and Due Process* (Hart Publishing 2004) 101.
94 Antony Duff, *Trials and Punishments* (CUP 1986) 133.
95 Lai Ho (n 85) 105.
96 Lai Ho (n 85) 104.
97 Emma Rowden, 'Remote Participation and the Distributed Court: An Approach to Court Architecture in the Age of Video-Mediated Communications' (PhD thesis, University of Melbourne 2011).
98 Pat Carlen, *Magistrates Justice* (Wiley-Blackwell 1976); Sharyn Roach Anleu and Kathy Mack, 'Magistrates' Everyday Work and Emotional Labour' (2005) 32(4) Journal of Law and Society 590; Pat Carlen, 'The Staging of Magistrates' Justice' (1976) 16(1) The British Journal of Criminology 48.

values of legitimacy, autonomy and participation, as discussed in Chapter 4 (Locating the intermediary within theories of the criminal trial), require the defendant to be afforded the time and space to converse properly with his lawyer throughout and follow proceedings from an appropriately located space within the courtroom. The reality of the modern criminal court is, however, starkly different. Facilities for the accused have progressively diminished over the last 50 years in ways that 'radically distinguish the material conditions of those presumed innocent from others participating in trials'.[99] The spatial configuration of the courtroom has the potential to marginalise the accused and to dehumanise him in his trial.[100] Mulcahy and Rowden conclude that no other criminal justice participant has had access to facilities diminished more than the defendant in this period.[101] Among the design changes made to defendant facilities have been the loss of a writing desk, increased distancing from his legal representative, disruption of sightlines to the public gallery and the reduced capacity of courts to provide good quality catering facilities to the cells.[102]

When intermediaries discussed defendant participation and court design, one key issue emerged: the dock. The spatial configuration of the dock itself, its relative location in the courtroom and the impact of the accused being physically separated from the other trial participants were all viewed as detrimental to communication. Most intermediaries recounted stories of defendants being exhausted, confused and resigned to their fate in this enclosed space. Rosen's description of the dock as a 'humiliating and degrading' experience was echoed by interviewees, many of whom recalled visceral memories of distraught defendants with their heads in their hands, impatient for the ordeal to end.[103]

My interviews with intermediaries raised many of the same concerns which formed the basis of the ECtHR case of *Stanford v U.K* 23 years earlier. Two recurring issues which intermediaries identified as being problematic for defendants were the poor acoustics of the courtroom and restricted visibility from the confined dock. E&W-16 and E&W-14 both explained how the sense of disconnection and isolation from proceedings is exacerbated by the physical barriers that separate the defendant from the rest of the court:

> In the dock you can hardly hear what is going on. The visibility is not good either. The defendant then goes face in hand and gives up on listening. The

99 Mulcahy and Rowden (n 74) 31.
100 Paul Rock, *The Social World of an English Crown Court* (Clarendon Press 1993) 240.
101 Mulcahy and Rowden (n 74) 31.
102 Mulcahy and Rowden (n 74).
103 Lionel Rosen, 'The Dock – Should It Be Abolished?' (1966) 29 Modern Law Review 289, 296.

> barristers are speaking forwards and you have a view of their back and they are mumbling. It makes you feel really separate.
>
> (E&W-16)

> I do think, unless there is a very good reason for being behind a screen, the Perspex glass automatically separates. If you have someone who is not very good at concentrating, they will think they don't have to listen.
>
> (E&W-14)

E&W-7 echoed these viewpoints and further explained how recent developments in terms of dock design have made conditions worse:

> You can't communicate in the dock. It's toughened glass and a tiny slit . . . it's very hard to hear, you are isolated from the court unnecessarily in a lot of cases. . . . The dock has been made worse recently because recently they have put grills at the top and some have gone solid at the top so it's hot, it's sticky, it's smelly and you can't hear anything and it's bloody uncomfortable. The architecture is crap.
>
> (E&W-7)

The special configuration of the dock impacts the relationship between the intermediary and the right to effective participation. As the previous quotes demonstrate, intermediaries were acutely aware that participatory entitlements of defendants were poorly served by the dock and its design. Some intermediaries explained how they often seek to counter these difficulties through recommendations in their court report. For example, two intermediaries, E&W-17 and E&W-13, explained how they actively recommend the defendant's removal from the dock with the judge's permission. Both described this recommendation as necessary to ensure the 'effective participation' of the defendant. When asked, E&W-17 suggested that such action was often required to ameliorate the inherent deficiencies of the defendant's position and explained that intermediaries have an 'enhanced' role to 'break through' these barriers:

> I think if we could just get the defendants on the side and not with the barristers having their backs to them, that would make a huge difference. . . . Who in their life experience ever sits in a room to people with their backs? It is just ridiculous. I think once I get them out of the dock . . . although you see once I've got them out the dock, I still have a very active role sitting at the back with them. I did a couple of weeks ago, I asked the judge [if we could] sit outside the dock.
>
> (E&W-17)

E&W-13 explained how she adopts the same practice:

> One of my recommendations is that they don't sit in the dock. It's about the person engaging and participating in their trial, so how can it be fair if they can't properly participate? You are there to ensure effective participation in trial. I ask for them to be outside. . . . Also, in the dock you have those stupid leaning bars. If I need to be creating visual aids for someone about what's happening in the court, who's who, what people are saying . . . I can't do that on my knees, I can't type on my knees. It might be that I sit outside the dock so I have a bench. In fairness, courts have always accepted that.
>
> (E&W-13)

These comments suggest that the dock inhibits the defendant's participation in proceedings and also negatively impacts the intermediary's ability to do their job. Intermediaries are more than a passive communication conduit – they can also actively manage a defendant's environment to promote participation. This echoes the 'broad' conception of communication and sees intermediaries attempting to neutralise barriers to defendant participation. While intermediaries working with witnesses are also concerned with environmental factors, particularly room layout during assessment and the spatial configuration of the live-link room, the dock presents a unique set of difficulties. For example, during the Ground Rules Hearing, intermediaries normally agree on a method of intervention so they can alert the judge when a witness has not understood a question or if it needs to be rephrased. When in the dock, however, intermediaries are often unable to get the defence lawyer's or the judge's attention to flag concerns. Miller argues that the dock interferes with the defendant-lawyer relationship by 'effectively prohibiting free and uninterrupted consultation and suggestion throughout the trial'.[104] There is also little time for the intermediary to communicate to the accused what is happening throughout a case. Another significant issue created by the enclosed dock emerges when a vulnerable accused is a co-defendant in a multi-handed case. E&W-8 was appointed to assist a defendant with severe communication difficulties in a case with nine other defendants:

> I did one multi-defendant case with about 10 people, and it was so noisy. I can't believe what happens in the dock, with the noise and the mucking around. It was phenomenal. Everyone was just talking to each other and things were being thrown . . . but the problem is that the person you are with is getting distracted, and it does have an effect on their ability to concentrate

104 Julie Miller, 'A Rights-Based Argument Against the Dock' [2011] Criminal Law Review 216, 221.

> and follow what is going on. So you need to think carefully about layout . . . I would always make sure that if we do have any control over it then we are sitting in the most sensible place . . . it's so important they can see and hear.
>
> (E&W-8)

This quote encapsulates how inhibiting the dock and its design can be for the defendant's participation. The disempowering effect of the dock is also evident as E&W-8 is constrained in terms of practical recommendations. This contrasts significantly with the freedom many intermediaries are afforded when working with witnesses. The following quote from E&W-9 provides an excellent example of this in practice:

> with a witness you can pretty much say anything, for example I had someone and it was agreed that they could take their dog into witness service with them while they were waiting . . . you would never get that for a defendant in a million years. I had a dock officer report the fact that I had given the defendant a stress ball . . . which was in my report!
>
> (E&W-9)

E&W-9's experience reflects a key theme of the findings: intermediaries feel their role is perceived differently by judges and lawyers when working with defendants compared to witnesses and that the nature of the work is often more challenging. The present section reveals that the dock's ability to prejudice and alienate extends to the intermediary as an associated party of the defendant. This leads to the situation whereby intermediaries strive to mitigate the participatory challenges of the dock yet find their ability to do so inhibited by their placement within it. The dock reinforces what Mulcahy and Rowden term the 'strict hierarchy' of court users and the reality that the participatory rights of the defendant have never been prioritised in the design of modern court buildings.[105] The incremental fortification of the dock and its 'removal' of the defendant from proceedings is incongruous with the enhanced participatory role of the defendant, which this chapter advocates.[106] As Miller has noted, the dock poses a serious risk to the presumption of innocence, right to legal assistance and, crucially, the accused's right to participate effectively in the criminal trial.[107] The experiences of intermediaries explored in this section emphasise that taking the defendant's right to effective participation seriously must necessarily include addressing current deficiencies associated with the dock.

105 Mulcahy and Rowden (n 74) 275.

106 Linda Mulcahy, 'Putting the Defendant in Their Place: Why Do We Still Use the Dock in Criminal Proceedings?' (2013) 53(6) British Journal of Criminology 1139.

107 Julie Miller, 'A Rights-Based Argument Against the Dock' [2011] Criminal Law Review 216.

7.9 Sentencing

Sentencing lies at the heart of the criminal justice system, and it is at this stage that the 'communicative nature' of the process is most apparent.[108] Sentences communicate official censure or blame, the communication being chiefly to the offender but also to the complainant and to wider society.[109] In recent years, complainants in some jurisdictions have gained the right to participate in sentencing and diversion processes. For example, the Labour government introduced the 'Victim Personal Statement Scheme' in 2001 to enable complainants to explain the impact of the crime in their own words through a personal statement made to the police. Yet complainants are granted a relatively limited participatory role at sentencing. While the right to challenge a sentence may exist because it constitutes an inadequate punishment, there is no corresponding right to participate.[110] Inter alia, this has been based on the view that granting such a procedural right may interfere with the public nature of the prosecution system.[111]

As a key juncture in the criminal trial, the question of intermediary involvement with defendants at the sentencing stage deserves attention. Any sentencing model, regardless of its underpinning ideals, must communicate the punishment to the offender even if he chooses not to listen or be persuaded by it.[112] However, while a court can deliver a sentence, there should be a concomitant understanding of its content and what it practically means for the offender. The notion of 'informed sentencing' requires a court to make reasonable adjustments and consider the individual abilities and support needs of offenders to avoid unreasonable expectations being imposed.[113] As the ECtHR held in *SC v U.K*, effective participation must involve the accused understanding the significance of any penalties imposed.[114] Domestically, the Equal Treatment Bench Book emphasises the need for sentences to be framed in an 'accessible way', noting that intermediary presence at the sentencing hearing may be required to ensure this is achieved.[115] The Sentencing Council also notes that courts may consider requesting information

108 Owusu-Bempah (n 5) 58; Julian Roberts, *Exploring Sentencing Practice in England and Wales* (Palgrave Macmillan 2015) 6.

109 Andrew Ashworth, *Sentencing and Criminal Justice* (6th edn, CUP 2015) 94.

110 Doak (n 15) 167–71; *McCourt v United Kingdom* App no 20433/92, 2 December 1992.

111 Andrew Ashworth and Mike Redmayne, *The Criminal Process* (3rd edn, OUP 2005) 50.

112 Antony Duff, *Punishment, Communication and Community* (OUP 2001) 126.

113 Prison Reform Trust, 'Prison Reform Trust Response to the Ministry of Justice Consultation, Punishment and Reform: Effective Community Sentences' (June 2012) 8.

114 *SC v U.K* (n 21) [29].

115 Judicial College, *Equal Treatment Bench Book* (July 2024) 98 <https://www.judiciary.uk/wp-content/uploads/2022/09/Equal-Treatment-Bench-Book.pdf>.

about a defendant's communication difficulties and how an intermediary may assist during sentencing.[116]

In interview, intermediaries felt strongly about the need for communication assistance at the sentencing stage. However, this has not been reflected in the literature or wider academic or policy discussions. While Kirby et al. have highlighted the connection between effective participation and the role of the judge at sentencing, the nature of intermediary involvement has received little elaboration.[117] Since Article 6 ECHR applies to the determination of a criminal charge, the right to effective participation arguably does not cover the sentencing stage (although this is certainly open to academic debate). Examining the intermediary role at sentencing is instructive in understanding different participatory roles within the criminal process. Unsurprisingly, when intermediaries were asked about their involvement at the sentencing stage, they spoke only about the defendant. The prevailing view was that the defendant's involvement in the process would be diminished if the outcome was incomprehensible to the defendant. For those who had previously worked with vulnerable individuals in the criminal justice system, seeing the defendant bypassed at the sentencing stage left a lasting impression:

> A lot of the vulnerable young people I worked with in my previous role would come out of court without having understood what had just happened to them. One observation I did with the defendant where they were getting a custodial sentence, I understood that when the judge gave it, but I watched [the defendant's] face and they didn't know that until they came out and had a debrief.
>
> (E&W-15)

As was explored in earlier chapters, different conceptions of the intermediary role and its scope have emerged between some judges and intermediaries. This tension, evidenced, for example, in the case of *R v Grant Murray*, appears to be mainly based on different views about the extent of the role's involvement throughout trial.[118] 'Pragmatic and flexible' appointments should not only involve intermediaries justifying their recommendations to the court but should also promote collaboration between the two to ensure appointments are effective. The sentencing stage offers an opportunity for judges to use intermediaries as an instrument to ensure that the verdict is understood.

116 Sentencing Council, 'Sentencing Offenders with Mental Disorders, Developmental Disorders, or Neurological Impairments' (effective from 1 October 2020).

117 Kirby, Jacobson and Hunter (n 9).

118 *R v Grant-Murray* (n 89).

E&W-13 recounted an example of such a practice from a case involving an extremely vulnerable defendant:

> The judge was absolutely amazing and kept asking if [the defendant] was understanding. . . . The judge actually requested me to come and see him in chambers to help him word the sentence. I said [the defendant] is so fixed on the sentence that she won't listen to anything before that . . . and the likelihood is that if you do the sentence first and then explain then she will listen and I will make sure she listens. And it worked really well.
>
> (E&W-13)

In Northern Ireland, NI-5 lauded one District Judge who has developed a reputation for positively including the intermediary in the Youth Court:

> Judge [X] has been excellent. He's just got it into his practice . . . he will meet with the young person and he brings lay magistrates with him. He takes you into his chambers and there's everybody there and the case is discussed and he gives the intermediary the opportunity to speak. And there's lots of discussion around that . . . [he] creates this kind of 'let's talk about this, let's do the right thing'.
>
> (NI-5)

The centrality of the judge's role in the previous examples must be recognised. The power to appoint defendant intermediaries not only rests with the court, but the judge must also adapt the trial process to address the defendant's particular communication needs.[119] As the Court of Appeal recognised in *Grant Murray*, the 'burden rests on the trial judge to ensure the effective participation of a vulnerable person, not on the intermediary'.[120] Since judges are required to approach intermediary appointments on an individual basis, consulting intermediaries about the defendant's particular communication needs is central to ensuring the right is upheld. Yet in interview, intermediaries explained that judges often failed to utilise their communication expertise. E&W-18 explained how a magistrate's bench adopted an inflexible approach and preferred to stick rigidly to their original terms of appointment:

> They paid me to be there for the 3 days . . . then the judge said: 'I haven't granted for the intermediary to be in here'. Well, do you want to pay me to just sit outside? That's ridiculous . . . I said 'well I'm here still, I'll stay for sentencing and probation and I can help him understand those processes'. And the judge was like: 'Well I haven't asked you to do that!' and It's like

119 *R v Cox* [2012] EWCA Crim 549; CPD (n 13) [6.1.1].
120 *R v Grant-Murray* (n 89) [199].

> I'm here and you're paying me, it's a lack of understanding of how you could be used I suppose.
>
> (E&W-18)

While intermediaries have the tools to facilitate communication, these can be rendered redundant if judges are unwilling to be flexible in the terms of their appointment. In the preceding example, even if E&W-18 had not originally recommended her presence at the sentencing hearing, the defendant's participation would have only been enhanced by an intermediary explaining the significance of the sentence and impact of probation. Of course, adherence to 'pragmatic and flexible' intermediary appointments does not mean automatic entitlement to communication assistance at every stage. However, the principles of pragmatism and flexibility should involve some deference to intermediary expertise regarding their involvement at discrete stages of proceedings. As the following example from E&W-17 demonstrates, intermediaries can disagree with legal professionals and recommend their involvement only when the defendant requires it:

> The defence barrister turned up to say: 'I'd like the intermediary [at the sentencing hearing]' and I stood up, put my hand up and said: 'Your Honour', – the judge's first response was: 'we do have to think about the public purse you know?' . . . and I said: 'Can I just say that in this case, this man will not have to play an active role in the sentencing hearing . . . so he doesn't actually need me here because there are other people who can help him I'm sure' . . . the judge said: 'thank you very much Ms [X]! I won't be calling on you for the sentencing'. . . . and then the judge said: 'I think Mr.' [X], the defence barrister, 'is becoming a little too dependent on his intermediary!'
>
> (E&W-17)

It is useful to conclude this section on sentencing by returning to some theoretical approaches. Owusu-Bempah argues that the defendant cannot begin to account for his criminal conduct, or be 'called to account', until the sentencing stage, when it has been proved that they are guilty of the offence.[121] She continues that at this stage of the process, 'the wrongness of the act, as well as its consequences, can be communicated to the defendant and the public'.[122] This is based less on the argument that the defendant cannot begin to account pre-sentence, but that it is not legitimate to expect him to (or call him to) account for his wrongdoing until the charge has actually been proven. Duff's account of the trial emphasises the need for 'repentance and

121 Owusu-Bempah (n 5) 58.
122 Owusu-Bempah (n 5).

atonement'[123] from the defendant and expects an acceptance of responsibility and positive evidence of redress.[124] While these accounts espouse differing normative theories of the criminal process, they both recognise a minimum requirement of defendant participation at sentencing. Both accounts value sentencing as a communicative enterprise and, at a minimum, the ability of the defendant to understand the wrongfulness of his actions and their consequences.[125] The reflections of intermediaries in interview echo the importance of these imperatives but also highlight the potential adverse outcomes when they are not prioritised.

While all stages of criminal proceedings present communication challenges for vulnerable defendants, sentencing can often be the most bewildering and disempowering.[126] Yet, despite the right to effective participation gaining more academic attention, the participatory role of the defendant at sentencing tends to be ignored. As Peay and Player lament, the little qualitative research into the importance of vulnerability at sentencing focuses on complainants and witnesses rather than defendants.[127] Theoretical accounts of sentencing generally recognise that vulnerable defendants should be proportionately punished for their wrongdoing, relative to other offenders. There is also a broad consensus that alternative dispositions should be available to sentencers when dealing with a vulnerable accused.[128] But rather than focusing on how the defendant's vulnerability affects what is done *to* him, the right to effective participation requires a reciprocal understanding of the court's disposal and its significance. Respect for the accused as an autonomous citizen requires nothing less. Traditionally, the responsibility of ensuring that defendants understand their penalty and its significance has fallen to defence legal representatives, yet the ability of lawyers to satisfactorily execute this function has been questioned.[129] As communication experts and likely the individual who best understands the unique communication challenges the

123 Antony Duff, 'Penance, Punishment and the Limits of Community' (2003) 5(3) Punishment & Society 295, 298.

124 Antony Duff, 'Penal Communities' (1999) 1(1) Punishment & Society 27.

125 Duff's account of punishment, however, focuses on a process of 'two-way communication' which seeks to demonstrate to offenders the extent to which they have done wrong and focuses their attention on their crime and its consequences. See: Marguerite Schinkel, 'Punishment as Moral Communication: The Experiences of Long-Term Prisoners' (2014) 16(5) Punishment and Society 578.

126 Jacobson and Talbot (n 18) 17; Jacobson and Cooper (n 10) 123.

127 Jill Peay and Elaine Player, 'Pleading Guilty: Why Vulnerability Matters (2018) 81(6) The Modern Law Review 929, 952.

128 Lea Johnston, 'Vulnerability and Just Desert: A Theory of Sentencing and Mental Illness (2013) 103(1) The Journal of Criminal Law and Criminology 147; Richard Frase, *Just Sentencing: Principles and Procedures for a Workable System* (OUP 2013).

129 Stephen Andrew Noguera, 'Communicative Sentencing: Exploring the Perceptions of Young Offenders in the Community' (D.Phil thesis, University of Oxford 2010) 233.

accused faces, intermediaries are central to ensuring the defendant's participatory role at sentencing is respected. More broadly, the work of intermediaries at sentencing can help generate a more nuanced discussion of effective participation and a better understanding of its multifaceted nature.

7.10 Conclusion

There is a broad consensus that, as an institution of the state, the criminal justice system must allow for at least a minimum degree of lay participation to be balanced with the input of professionals and experts.[130] Drawing on the experiences of intermediaries, it is recognised that participation is approached as a relative concept, with its content dependant on the profile of the vulnerable individual and the nature of their communication difficulties. Recognising the differing participatory roles of witnesses/complainants and defendants is important to understanding their relative positions within the criminal justice system and ensuring that respective participatory entitlements are maximised rather than diminished.[131]

This chapter also reveals that different participatory roles are central to understanding intermediary practice and how intermediaries themselves conceptualise the role's scope. The interview data suggest that intermediaries can adapt to the differing participatory challenges of the vulnerable individual. The concepts of 'witness work' and 'defendant work' are further developed through the physical environment of the criminal justice system, the attitudes and perceptions of other criminal justice actors and the relationships which intermediaries negotiate in their role. This chapter challenges judicial conceptions of the intermediary role and calls for judges to adopt a more flexible and pragmatic approach to defendant appointments. The 'unknowns' of the trial necessitate flexibility, and many defendants require communication assistance long before the trial and sometimes even after it concludes. The appellate courts have advocated an overly simplistic 'binarised' approach to defendant intermediary appointments whereby intermediary assistance is granted either for full trials or testimony only.[132] Intermediaries consistently avoided such rigid formulations of the level of support vulnerable individuals require to communicate. Collaboration between intermediaries, lawyers and judges is essential to ensure individualised assistance for vulnerable witnesses and defendants – something intermediaries recognised would likely be more cost-effective and time-efficient.

Finally, this chapter has revealed how the differing systems of intermediary provision in England and Wales and Northern Ireland impact the relationship

130 Albert Dzur, *Punishment, Participatory Democracy and the Jury* (OUP 2014).
131 Rock (n 100) 181–96.
132 *OP v Secretary of State for Justice* (n 57); *R v Rashid* [2017] 1 WLR 2449.

between the intermediary role and the criminal justice aim/value of participation. This finding should be noted by policy-makers, especially in jurisdictions where a specialist communication assistance role is being considered. In particular, policy and guidance should recognise that the participation of witnesses and defendants differs throughout the criminal process and that intermediary provision must reflect that. Registered Intermediaries working within the Registered Intermediary Scheme (RIS) in Northern Ireland can impact participation earlier at the police station than their counterparts in England and Wales. Yet the RIS does not permit intermediary assistance beyond the period of evidence-giving. As a result, the ad-hoc system of intermediaries for defendants in England and Wales is more conducive to the type of 'pragmatic and flexible' appointments which this chapter has advocated.

Chapter 8

Conclusion

8.1 Introduction

This book focuses on the role of the intermediary in the criminal justice system in England and Wales and Northern Ireland. However, the book has also considered analogous roles in other jurisdictions, such as communication partners and communication assistants in countries such as Australia and New Zealand. These roles are shaped and negotiated through a web of interactions with other criminal justice actors (e.g. lawyers and judges) which, in turn, impact how communication is facilitated between vulnerable individuals and the criminal justice system. Notwithstanding the analysis contained within the book, the intermediary remains a relative newcomer in the 'complex social world' of the criminal justice system, and much more research into its operation is required.[1]

As recognition of speech and communication problems, learning disabilities and mental health issues increases within the criminal justice system, demand for intermediary assistance rises too. Intermediary-type roles are being established in various jurisdictions internationally to promote access to justice and the participation of vulnerable individuals in legal proceedings. In its 2023 Annual Report of the Witness Intermediary Scheme (WIS) in England and Wales, the Ministry of Justice (MoJ) declared that increased intermediary capacity was a 'priority' to ensure that the most vulnerable individuals receive communication support.[2] The recently established HMCTS Court Appointed Intermediary Services (HAIS) sees an extension of intermediary services beyond the WIS (see further later). With the work of intermediaries expanding into other justice fora, such as family courts, civil courts and employment tribunals, intermediary work looks set to become increasingly important.

1 Paul Rock, *The Social World of an English Crown Court* (Clarendon Press 1993).

2 MoJ, 'The Witness Intermediary Scheme Annual Report 2023' <https://assets.publishing.service.gov.uk/media/664487d0993111924d9d3504/Witness_Intermediary_Scheme_Annual_Report_2023.pdf> accessed 10 February 2025 [7].

DOI: 10.4324/9781003461166-8

Focusing mainly on the U.K, this book expands knowledge about the role of the intermediary, including how intermediaries interact with and experience the social world of the criminal justice system. The lack of empirical research into the intermediary role has resulted in a poor (and often confused) understanding of the role's scope and content. The book has drawn on the experiences of those working at the coalface of intermediary work and contributes to a better understanding of the realities of the role. By including the experiences of intermediaries working with both witnesses and defendants in England and Wales and Northern Ireland, the 'complexities and the richness' of the intermediary world are illuminated.[3] Fundamentally, this book strives to give a voice to intermediaries, to talk about their work and the challenges faced within it. Some of the chapters relate to more practical aspects of intermediary work, while others relate to the nature of the criminal process and the role's relative status within it. Reflecting on the book as a whole, several key themes which thread throughout the chapters can be identified. These themes will be discussed in turn.

8.2 The parameters of the intermediary role

Over 20 years on from the rollout of the first intermediary pilot study in England and Wales, the role's formal parameters are contained within the Criminal Practice Directions,[4] Criminal Procedure Rules[5] and relevant procedural guidance from the MoJ.[6] A relatively stable picture of the intermediary role emerges from these sources: an objective communication conduit, primarily focused on facilitating communication and owing its primary duty to the court. As explained in Chapter 1 (Introduction) and noted throughout the book, the judicial depiction of the intermediary role has been somewhat less consistent. This book has problematised the normative description of the intermediary role and has generated a rich understanding of how those performing it view their work, its scope and content. The parameters of the intermediary role have been shown to be adaptable to the circumstances of a case, the extent of the communication issues and the nature of interactions with other criminal justice agents.

The issue of the intermediary's professional status, and whether the role is perceived as a criminal justice professional, was an unexpected finding from the field. However, the issue of professional status consistently arose in early

3 Lisa Given, *The SAGE Encyclopaedia of Qualitative Research Methods* (SAGE publishing 2008) 794.

4 Criminal Practice Directions 2023 (CrimPRC(23)90(b)) [6.2].

5 Criminal Procedure Rules (October 2020) (CPR) Pt 3, rules 3.8–3.9.

6 MoJ, 'Registered Intermediary Procedural Guidance Manual 2024' <https://assets.publishing.service.gov.uk/media/671b819bfc28a840abc6d26d/Registered_Intermediary_Procedural_Guidance_Manual_2024__Official_.pdf> accessed 4 February 2025.

interviews, and I decided to pursue this line of enquiry in later interviews. One moment stands out as particularly instructive when reflecting on the impact of professional identity/status on the parameters of the intermediary role. After one interview, when walking with an interviewee to the tube station, she mentioned that only recently did she feel that she was being genuinely listened to at Ground Rules Hearings (GRH). She explained that since obtaining her doctorate and could therefore officially be referred to as 'Dr X', judges and lawyers were more responsive to her court report recommendations. She felt that she could make recommendations more confidently and suggest strategies and adjustments that she previously may not have done. This vignette caused me to reflect on the intermediary's relative status within the professional world of the court – a line of analysis developed in Chapter 5 (Professional work – jurisdictions and boundary work). It illustrates how and why the professional status of the intermediary and the perception of 'professional work' are relevant to understanding the parameters of the role. It also provides a snapshot of the 'tussle' for control over work tasks in which court professionals engage. This, in turn, has the potential to impact the legitimacy of their work.

Chapter 6 (The neutrality paradox) reveals that although the scope of the intermediary role was initially untested, individual practices have seen the construction of boundaries which are continually negotiated between actors. Intermediaries thus engage in 'boundary work' to protect their professional jurisdiction and to carve out their own area of expertise. As the intermediary role continues to develop and expand, further questions around the professionalisation of the role are likely to emerge and shape its scope and content. Looking ahead, how the introduction of the HAIS scheme (see further later) impacts the intermediary's control over its work and its professional jurisdiction will deserve attention. Research into the operation of HAIS will be needed to assess whether a 'jurisdictional settlement' is reached between intermediaries and other criminal justice actors and, consequently, what impact this may have on the nature and scope of the intermediary role.

One of the most obvious ways in which the parameters of the intermediary role are fluid and context-dependent relates to the issue of neutrality. As explained in Chapter 7 (Witness work, defendant work and participatory roles), O'Mahony et al. have previously written about the developing occupational identities of intermediaries and the challenge of reconciling the role's neutrality with different professional backgrounds.[7] This included issues about emotional attachment to defendants and potential role conflict resulting from

7 Brendan O'Mahony and others, 'Developing a Professional Identity in a New Work Environment: The Views of Defendant Intermediaries Working in the Criminal Courts' (2016) 18(2) Journal of Forensic Practice 155.

some intermediaries 'wearing more than one professional hat'.[8] My findings further develop these concepts and explicate the tension some intermediaries face between the commitment to neutrality on one hand and the struggle to remain within its normative parameters on the other. By developing the concept of the 'neutrality paradox', I explored how intermediaries conceptualise their role, its demands and relative position within the criminal justice system. Bourdieu's concept of 'illusio' was used as an instructive explanatory concept to examine deviations from the expected performance of neutrality. Illusio also allows us to view the role's parameters as contoured by intermediaries themselves through their iterative work practices. Just as intermediaries negotiate their own professional boundaries and identity through their social interactions, they similarly co-construct their neutrality with other actors. As Chapter 6 (The neutrality paradox) concludes, the content of the role's neutrality remains unsettled and is ripe for collaborative discussion between judges, advocates and intermediaries. Any attempt to demarcate the intermediary role's parameters must necessarily address the vexed issue of neutrality. My findings suggest that the unique challenges associated with intermediary neutrality must first be recognised before the viability of neutrality as an ethical standard can be seriously debated.

This book has explored how the parameters of the intermediary role are coloured and shaped by the conceptualisation of the criminal justice value of participation. Chapter 4 (Locating the intermediary within theories of the criminal trial) set the scene for later discussion about how the different participatory roles of witnesses and defendants qualitatively impact intermediary work. Chapter 7 (Witness work, defendant work and participatory roles) explored how these different participatory roles are central to understanding intermediary practice and how intermediaries conceptualise the role's scope. As discussed further later, this often centres around whether intermediaries work with vulnerable witnesses or defendants. It has been shown that effective communication is a prerequisite to effective participation, notwithstanding that witnesses and defendants occupy different positions in the criminal process. My findings suggest that intermediaries respond to the different participatory roles of vulnerable court users which, in turn, impacts the nature of the intermediary role. It remains to be seen whether the newly introduced HAIS scheme will recognise such variations in intermediary work. More broadly, these findings support the view that intermediaries are not an occupational monolith or mere conduits conducting a passive communication role. This echoes the conclusion in Chapter 6 (The neutrality paradox) that any reconceptualisation of the intermediary role requires a more dynamic, relational view of the nature of its work and its challenges.

8 O'Mahony and others (n 7) 160.

8.3 Conceptualisation of the role by key stakeholders

One of the key points emphasised in Chapter 4 (Locating the intermediary within theories of the criminal trial) was the overlapping nature of the functions that can be ascribed to the intermediary and how the role is inherently relational and multifaceted. To this extent, the parameters of the intermediary role appear heavily dependent on the practices of the established court workgroup, particularly the judge. Chapter 5 (Professional work – jurisdictions and boundary work) developed this further by arguing that intermediaries are involved in a process of negotiation, conflict and exchange with other criminal justice actors over jurisdictional claims. I conclude this chapter by arguing that these processes are fundamental to understanding the complexity of the intermediary role and how its parameters are to be understood. The 'complex social world' of the criminal court, as vividly described by Rock, remains highly resonant and influenced how I analysed my interview data.[9]

How, then, do key stakeholders conceptualise the intermediary role? It was noted in Chapter 1 (Introduction) that the judicial conception of the intermediary role has been inconsistent and, at times, confused or misunderstood. One example of this was highlighted by Plotnikoff and Woolfson who found that many judges were unable to distinguish between Registered Intermediaries for witnesses and defendant intermediaries.[10] In my own interviews, several intermediaries explained how they had been mistaken as interpreters and had to explain their function to the Court. E&W-7 explained how she had to explain numerous times to a defence solicitor that she was not, in fact, an appropriate adult. Understanding how the judiciary interacts with the role is particularly important since intermediaries cannot be expected to operate effectively without the confidence of the judiciary.[11] My interview data reinforce the importance of the relationship between the bench and intermediaries. Judges decide the terms of intermediary involvement in a criminal case and intermediaries understood that their role is heavily dependent on direction from the bench. The power dynamics of this relationship must be understood. As discussed in Chapter 4 (Locating the intermediary within theories of the criminal trial), advocates have less incentive to collaborate with intermediaries and adhere to the agreed ground rules without judicial oversight. In this regard, intermediaries rely on coercive judicial power to enforce their recommendations and legitimise their position. This was illustrated by E&W-17 who remarked: 'You've got a report to write to go to the court, to convince the court that you should be appointed'. Such comments demonstrate how intermediaries are aware of the power imbalances within the

9 Rock (n 1) 2.

10 Rock (n 1).

11 Joyce Plotnikoff and Richard Woolfson, *Intermediaries in the Criminal Justice System* (Policy Press 2015) 17.

court's implicit hierarchical structures which can serve to exclude them. As intermediary-type roles emerge internationally, it is encouraging that in some jurisdictions, such as New Zealand, the senior judiciary is increasingly recognising the vital role intermediaries can play in securing access to justice.[12]

As explored in Chapter 5 (Professional work – jurisdictions and boundary work), the tools of diagnosis, inference and treatment may be viewed as an attempt to gain exclusive jurisdiction over work tasks and permeate the established, legitimised inner groups of the court. However, the interview data revealed that intermediaries consistently struggle to convince police, lawyers and judges of the role's 'cultural legitimacy'. This seems, at least partially, to be based on a lack of understanding of the theoretical basis of intermediary recommendations and a belief that the court workgroup can facilitate communication without intermediary assistance. While many lawyers and judges are increasingly accepting of the intermediary role, it is not obvious that there is a broad understanding of the rationale for its introduction or the need for its continued existence. It is important that intermediary work is accepted and that other court actors understand its role and function.

As developed in Chapter 6 (The neutrality paradox), how the role's neutrality is approached is significant in terms of how the role is conceptualised more broadly. In the highly partisan world of the criminal court, an objective, neutral role, such as the intermediary, is understandably viewed with interest and, perhaps at times, suspicion. Chapter 5 (Professional work – jurisdictions and boundary work) highlights the lack of serious debate around the nature of intermediary work and the challenges involved in its performance. The 'neutrality paradox' is a concept mainly based on the struggles intermediaries experience adhering to the official rubrics of the role. However, a more nuanced understanding of this concept would require further judicial insight and the experiences of legal professionals. As Bourdieu explains, the concept of habitus is objectively structured by the role's relative position in the field and by the subjective experiences of individual practitioners which are orientated by their perception and classification of their social world.[13] This is true for intermediaries as it is for judges, lawyers and other criminal justice actors. This research underpinning this book lays some of the groundwork for understanding how the intermediary role is conceptualised. Further research with a more diverse sample of participants could explore these issues further. In particular, how the neutrality issue is navigated in the various international intermediary schemes discussed in Chapter 3 (The international context) deserves further research.

More generally, the notion of the intermediary as an 'outsider' significantly impacts how the role is conceptualised by those executing it. Firstly, almost

12 *Mylesha Port Tihema v R* [2024] NZSC 112 [49].
13 Pierre Bourdieu, *In Other Words: Essays Towards a Reflexive Sociology* (Stanford UP 1990).

every intermediary who was interviewed as part of this research talked about feeling excluded by the archaic world of the criminal justice system. Rock's description of the criminal court as 'ceremonial, disciplined and staged' resonated with intermediary interviewees who spoke of the demands of the transition into the legal world from their other occupational backgrounds.[14] The role's relative placement outside the inner circles of the court has been explored earlier. Yet the role's status as an outsider was less pronounced in the more 'backstage' areas of the criminal justice system, such as the police station. It was clear that intermediaries felt able to develop working relationships with police officers more easily than courtroom actors. As explained in Chapter 6 (The neutrality paradox), increased informality seems to provide fertile conditions for the role's neutrality to be tested. This distinction between intermediary work in or around the court compared to the earlier, investigative stage seems significant in terms of the role's conceptualisation. Firstly, intermediaries who attend the police station to assist with ABE interviews are there on request. In many cases, they develop relationships with police officers who know their skill set, have their contact details and often genuinely seek their communication expertise. The deference shown to some of the more senior intermediaries by police officers was evident in my interviews. This contrasts with the court environment where no members of the court workgroup (i.e. the lawyers and judge) are in a position to witness an intermediary assessment or develop a rapport with the vulnerable individual. Instead, the intermediary presents as an outsider, their expertise and recommendations reduced to a court report, which is often discussed in a perfunctory manner at the GRH.

Based on the aforementioned, there is scope for further research to investigate the nature of the working relationships between intermediaries and police officers both in ABE and at police interview. There is also scope for research into judicial attitudes towards intermediary practice and how this may have changed over the years. This book provides judicial insight from Northern Ireland and emphasises the importance of the working relationships between intermediaries and the bench. It highlights how lawyers and judges, as members of the court workgroup, play an essential role in shaping how the intermediary functions day-to-day. Indications from Australia and New Zealand suggest strong judicial support for the role. The fact that judges in Chile are actually *performing* the intermediary role raises critical questions about the nature of intermediary work and the role's relationship with established legal professionals. In any event, there is much to be gained from comparative research between different jurisdictions with intermediary-type roles to better understand how judicial support can be harnessed and maximised.

14 Rock (n 1).

8.4 Distinction between the roles of 'registered' and 'non-registered' intermediaries

It may be contended that since the establishment of the HAIS scheme in 2022, the term 'non-registered' intermediary is unnecessary. While such intermediaries are not technically 'registered', they now work under a formal arrangement with the MoJ. However, there is also an argument that the establishment of HAIS as an ostensible antidote to the 'two-tier' intermediary provision requires particular scrutiny. Unlike the Department of Justice (Northern Ireland) (DoJ), the MoJ decided not to extend the WIS to cover vulnerable defendants and suspects.[15] The rationale for establishing HAIS was based more on the MoJ's compliance requirements than on promoting access to justice.[16] As such, whether there are differences in the work of intermediaries assisting witnesses on one hand and defendants on the other is extremely important.

When courts first began to allow applications for defendant intermediaries, there was initial confusion about whether an intermediary registered with the WIS could be appointed. In the case of *OP*, the magistrates' court initially directed that '[a]n intermediary shall be appointed to assist the defendant, subject to availability this should be a registered intermediary'.[17] The MoJ then refused the defendant access to an intermediary on their official register. As explained, courts subsequently developed the practice of allowing 'non-registered' intermediaries who fall outside the scope of the WIS for eligible defendants.

While witnesses and defendants are entitled to different 'types' of intermediaries, I wanted to find out what this distinction means in practice. The sample cohort for this research project was chosen because I wanted to speak to intermediaries with experience of working in both roles. These individuals were best placed to explain what it meant to be a 'witness intermediary' in one case and a 'defendant intermediary' in another. As has been explored, the significance of this distinction in how the intermediary role is performed has been largely overlooked. The fact that several judges interviewed by Plotnikoff and Woolfson were unable to differentiate between the two types of intermediaries is indicative of this problem.[18] This caused me to reflect on the normative function of the intermediary role and whether the profile of the vulnerable individual being assisted may change the role's scope and content.

15 For further discussion on the establishment of HAIS, see; John Taggart, 'Vulnerable Defendants and the HMCTS Court Appointed Intermediary Services' (2022) 6 Criminal Law Review 432.

16 Further discussed below in section 8.5.

17 *OP v Secretary of State for Justice* [2014] EWHC 1944 (Admin) [1].

18 Joyce Plotnikoff and Richard Woolfson, 'Falling Short? A Snapshot of Young Witness Policy and Practice: A Report for the NSPCC, Revisiting "Measuring up? Evaluating Implementation of Government Commitments to Young Witnesses in Criminal Proceedings"' (February 2019. London: NSPCC) 17.

This theme centres on the conceptualisation of 'witness work' and 'defendant work', which threads throughout the book. Put simply, intermediaries view the demands of working with defendants and witnesses differently and perform a qualitatively different function with each. This echoes Plotnikoff and Woolfson's view that intermediaries for defendants 'require a broader and more in-depth understanding of the legal process and terminology'.[19] Evidence of this distinction in my data was apparent in all aspects of intermediary work, from working with police at the investigative stage to interactions with vulnerable individuals at court. Several intermediaries not only identified differences in how the two roles operate but expressed a clear preference for working with defendants. Although likely hyperbolic, E&W-13 described non-registered intermediary work as 'the Wild West' compared to working as a witness intermediary under the WIS.

The emergence of the concepts of 'witness work' and 'defendant work' was perhaps not surprising considering Henderson's early recognition of the 'two-tier' intermediary provision.[20] However, I wanted to investigate further and better understand the factors that contribute to the distinction. Viewing the different roles through the lens of participation was instructive in understanding how the communication needs of the vulnerable individual shape intermediary practice. It became clear that defendants do not merely receive a unique form of communication assistance during proceedings – the nature of their participatory role *demands* it. Although intermediaries rarely used the term 'participation' in describing their function, time and time again in interview they explained the unique communication challenges faced by defendants compared to witnesses. The challenges of the confrontational police interview, the use of arcane language in legal consultations, poor acoustics in the dock and complex sentencing remarks were all cited as uniquely defendant experiences. I found that defendant intermediaries often moulded their communication facilitation role in response to these conditions.

As explained in Chapter 6 (The neutrality paradox), defendant work can conflict with the role's impartiality. Indeed, elaboration of the 'witness work/defendant work' concept acts as a heuristic for understanding the conflicts intermediaries experience between their impartiality and facilitating communication. It has been explored how close relationships can potentially develop with the defence and that sympathy can be generated for the defendant. These findings are perhaps better understood when compared with the shorter, often less developed relationships which intermediaries develop with witnesses. Recognising the witness work/defendant work distinction is

19 Plotnikoff and Woolfson (n 18) 275.

20 Emily Henderson, '"A Very Valuable Tool": Judges, Advocates and Intermediaries Discuss the Intermediary System in England and Wales' (2015) 19(3) International Journal of Evidence and Proof 154.

a prerequisite for any serious discussion about how the intermediary role's neutrality may be reconceptualised. As noted at the end of Chapter 6 (The neutrality paradox), conceptualising the role as 'hermetically sealed' from the emotionally charged cases in which intermediaries are involved ignores the realities of intermediary work.[21] It would be futile to question the role's impartiality without appreciating that intermediaries experience differing demands depending on the profile of the vulnerable individual being assisted.

Finally, the book uses Northern Ireland as a useful comparator based on its unitary system of intermediaries. The fact that intermediaries registered with the DoJ are equally likely to be matched with a witness or a suspect/defendant has meant that no apparent distinction between witness work and defendant work has emerged. Intermediaries in Northern Ireland recognised the right of defendants to effective participation and how defendants have a different stake in the criminal process compared to witnesses. Procedural differences between witness work and defendant work in terms of interview format and the length of time physically spent in the courtroom were noted. However, there was no obvious divergence in how the essential elements of the role were approached whether it was a vulnerable witness, or a suspect/defendant being assisted. Tellingly, many Northern Irish intermediaries in interview were puzzled at the suggestion that such a distinction between witness work and defendant work could even exist. This is strong evidence of the impact a unitary system of intermediaries can have, not just on the organisation of intermediary provision, but on the conceptualisation of the role by those who execute it.

8.5 Defendant intermediaries – a formalised role in sight?

As noted earlier, a key motivation for conducting this research project was an interest in the differing provision of intermediaries for defendants compared to witnesses. The 'two-tier' system raises questions about access to justice, fair trial rights and equality of arms.[22] It is also worth noting that the most recent research into the intermediary scheme in Ireland, which formally launched in mid-2024, has identified 'equality of access' as a priority area for developing the role.[23] Further, as explored in Chapter 3 (The international context), a prevailing issue of concern in many Australian states and territories centres

21 Helen Colley and Frédérique Guéry, 'Understanding New Hybrid Professions: Bourdieu, *illusio* and the Case of Public Service Interpreters' (2015) 45 Cambridge Journal of Education 113.

22 Henderson (n 20).

23 Aoife Gallagher and others, 'Establishing Stakeholder Priorities for Advancing the Role of the Intermediary in the Justice System: Findings from a Consensus Study' (2024) The International Journal of Evidence & Proof (online first, 27 December 2024).

on how eligibility for intermediary assistance can be broadened to include other vulnerable groups, including defendants.

In July 2020, the MoJ in England and Wales announced that it was 'seeking to engage with the market for the provision of HMCTS Court Appointed Intermediary Services (HAIS)'.[24] In January 2022, contracts were awarded to a selection of suppliers for the provision of new intermediary services and the HAIS scheme has been operational from April 2022.[25] The MoJ explained that these services would be provided in the courts and tribunals in England and Wales, with a specific focus on the appointment of intermediaries to provide an assessment of a person's communication needs. These intermediaries would also provide recommendations on measures to support vulnerable people, young people and children and other individuals who may need assistance during court proceedings.[26] The HAIS scheme relates only to intermediary services that fall outside the remit of the MoJ WIS.

In its 'Invitation to Tender' documentation, the MoJ outlined a list of objectives underpinning the introduction of the HAIS system. These objectives were as follows: i) achieving compliance with Public Contracts Regulations, ii) ensuring visible and accessible routes for intermediary applications/appointments, iii) improving management of intermediary services, iv) facilitating oversight of intermediary services, v) providing protection for the MoJ and service providers, vi) enabling effective financial controls and vii) facilitating market participation.[27] Notably, none of these objectives specifically relate to achieving parity in intermediary provision or ensuring 'equality of arms' between defendants and witnesses. It is encouraging that the Invitation to Tender notes the need to 'increase . . . knowledge of the work intermediaries do' and to 'more clearly communicate what intermediaries are, how they can be commissioned and who can provide the required services'.[28] However, there is a failure in the documentation to recognise the myriad problems associated with the 'two-tier' system of intermediary provision as context for the introduction of HAIS.

The HAIS scheme does not formally implement s.104 of the Coroners and Justice Act 2009. As such, there will continue to be no statutory basis for defendant intermediaries and the inherent jurisdiction route will continue to be used by judges. The MoJ has outlined that several 'commissioning bodies'

24 MoJ, 'Court Appointed Intermediary Services: A Pre-Procurement Notice' (20 July 2020).

25 HMCTS, 'New Contracts Awarded to Support Vulnerable Court and Tribunal Users' (26 January 2022) <https://www.gov.uk/government/news/new-contracts-awarded-to-support-vulnerable-court-and-tribunal-users> accessed 10 February 2025.

26 HMCTS (n 25).

27 MoJ, 'Court Appointed Intermediary Services (Also referred to as HMCTS Appointed Intermediary Services (HAIS)): Invitation to Tender' (ITT2 ITT Reference: 8598).

28 MoJ (n 27).

will be responsible for directly booking an intermediary.[29] These commissioners choose an intermediary from one of two frameworks: MASP (Managed & Approved Service Providers) and ASP (Approved Service Providers). The MoJ differentiates between the two frameworks based on 'organisational capacity and capability'.[30] MASPs are expected to be larger groupings of intermediaries who deliver appropriate training for their own intermediaries, either provided in-house or via a third party. The MASP framework is likely to be more complex and contain more obligations than the ASP framework.[31] The ASP framework applies to smaller groupings of intermediaries or independent intermediaries who are unlikely to have the same capacity as MASPs to accept bookings.[32] Intermediaries working for an ASP must demonstrate at least two years' experience or have experience of court hearings from another role, or experience of supporting vulnerable people.[33] There is no equivalent requirement for MASP intermediaries. Further, ASPs will not be expected to offer the same in-house training and recruitment opportunities and will need to be assessed as part of a competency-based assessment process.[34] Unlike the WIS, no centralised work allocation/booking system exists within HAIS. As such, HAIS has no 'matching service' equivalent to that operated by the National Crime Agency for Registered Intermediaries.[35]

The HAIS scheme is a potentially significant development in terms of the intermediary role and the provision of communication assistance for defendants. It represents an effort to bring a degree of formality to defendant intermediary provision and end the informal system of ad-hoc appointments. Yet the scheme perpetuates the 'two-tier' system of intermediaries by continuing to exclude eligible defendants from the WIS. As the charity Intermediaries for Justice (IFJ) has argued, there will continue to be a 'lack of parity for vulnerable people across all aspects of the Justice system'.[36] Other concerns include a lack of regulation or quality control and increased fragmentation of services across geographical regions and court services.[37] Unsurprisingly, the majority of international intermediary schemes discussed in Chapter 3 (The international context) have eschewed an approach that provides a statutory

29 MoJ, 'Court Appointed Intermediary Services Market Engagement: Questions and Answers' (2 June 2021) 2.
30 MoJ (n 29) 16.
31 MoJ, 'Court Appointed Intermediary Services Market Engagement: Questions and Answers' (17 June 2021) 5.
32 MoJ (n 31) 2.
33 MoJ (n 31) 39.
34 MoJ (n 31).
35 MoJ (n 31) 24.
36 IFJ, 'Letter from Intermediaries for Justice (IFJ) to MoJ Procurement' (28 August 2020) <https://www.intermediaries-for-justice.org/sites/default/files/legal_union_sectors_workers_to_moj.pdf> accessed 14 June 2021.
37 IFJ (n 36).

entitlement for witnesses and relies on ad-hoc appointments for defendants.[38] The 'two-tier' model that continues to characterise intermediary provision in England and Wales would surely have never been conceived as such if the intermediary special measure were introduced today.

While the HAIS scheme is relevant to the present study, the data underpinning the book's analysis cannot speak to the scheme's prospective operation. Intermediaries in my interviews talked about their experiences working within the ad-hoc non-registered intermediary role. However, the introduction of the HAIS arguably affirms the importance of the findings in the book. One of the main arguments advanced throughout is that intermediaries conceptualise 'witness work' and 'defendant work' differently. In other words, intermediaries approach aspects of their role differently when working with a vulnerable witness or defendant. It is possible that the organisation and structure of intermediary provision within HAIS will recognise this. It may make sense that intermediaries working within HAIS are given defendant-specific training to reflect qualitative differences in the roles. However, formal segregation of intermediaries into 'registered' and 'HAIS/defendant' roles may have unintended consequences. Differences in quality control, oversight and organisation may create at least the perception of an inequality of arms. Perhaps the most worrying aspect of the HAIS scheme is the lack of provision of intermediaries for vulnerable suspects at the police station. I argue in Chapter 7 (Witness work, defendant work and participatory roles) that the lack of such provision for suspects is indefensible given the accused's participatory rights. These findings provide a powerful argument for the MoJ to take the defendant's rights seriously and extend intermediary provision to the investigatory stage. Northern Ireland provides an example of how this can be done successfully through the operation of a 'unitary' model.[39]

8.6 Future directions

It is hoped that this book can harness change in policy relating to intermediary practice and in terms of how the role is theorised. Firstly, by demonstrating the utility of intermediary assistance at all stages of the criminal process, the findings explored in this book should cause policy makers to think more globally about intermediary provision. The notion of the intermediary as a solely court-based role is misconceived and contributes to a lack of understanding of the role's purpose. The objective must be to involve

38 As noted in Chapter 3, Western Australia currently operates a 'communication partner' scheme that only covers the accused. However, legislation to introduce an intermediary scheme for witnesses is expected to be introduced soon.

39 John Taggart, '"I Am Not Beholden to Anyone . . . I Consider Myself to be an Officer of the Court": A Comparison of the Intermediary Role in England and Wales and Northern Ireland' (2021) 25(2) The International Journal of Evidence & Proof 141.

intermediaries (both for suspects and witnesses) at an earlier stage to assess potential communication issues. The biggest concern in this regard relates to suspects at the police station who have historically been denied such assistance. Unfortunately, this situation looks set to continue with the operation of the new HAIS scheme. The MoJ must reconsider this policy or, at the very least, clearly justify its decision to deny suspects access to specialist communication assistance at the investigative stage. It seems likely that the exclusion of intermediary assistance for suspects at the police station is resource related. However, this does not change the uncomfortable reality that many suspects who will later be appointed an intermediary at court will have already completed a police interview without specialist communication assistance. This position is untenable and must be addressed urgently.

Of course, intermediary appointments at an earlier stage are dependent on vulnerability being identified and responded to. This is a significant issue, with police identification of vulnerability at the police station inconsistent. This appears due, at least partially, to various definitions of vulnerability used across different police forces.[40] There is an urgent need for standardised police training on how vulnerability can be identified and how officers should act upon it. Such training must reference the intermediary role, its scope and content. As noted earlier, a triage system, whereby intermediaries provide telephone advice to police when screening, has previously been suggested but has not been adopted by the MoJ.[41] More research on such a proposal is needed, and intermediaries must be consulted about the viability of such a scheme in practice. More generally, increased collaboration between police, appropriate adults and intermediaries would help with understanding the different roles and responsibilities. Now that the MoJ has formalised defendant intermediary provision through HAIS, intermediaries working with defendants should be easier to organise and coordinate as a collective group. It is incumbent on the MoJ to seek constructive feedback from intermediaries as to how their services can best be utilised, particularly at the pre-court stage.

This book has highlighted further work that needs to be done to secure the legitimacy of the intermediary as an independent, communication specialist and better integrate the role into the criminal justice system. How can this be achieved? Judicial training should continue to highlight the utility of intermediary work and underline the responsibility to have due regard to the intermediary court report as per the Criminal Procedure Rules.[42] Further, ensuring that the vocational training of lawyers includes reference to the intermediary

40 Emily Critchfield, Hannah Kennedy and Andy Myhill, 'Recognising and Responding to Vulnerability-Related Risks Guideline: Evidence Review Part Two Frontline Policing Vulnerability Risk Assessment Tools' (College of Policing, November 2021).

41 Bridget Pettitt and others, 'At Risk, Yet Dismissed: The Criminal Victimisation of People with Mental Health Problems' (Victim Support/Mind 2013).

42 CPR (n 5) rule 18.23(2)(a)-(b).

role is important. Prospective criminal lawyers entering the profession must understand what the intermediary role involves and the scope of its function. In terms of criminal justice design, the lack of dedicated space for the intermediary at court and the police station should be addressed. If the intermediary role is to be recognised and accepted as a legitimate criminal justice actor, then more thought must be given to the spaces it inhabits. The work of Mulcahy and Rowden is instructive as they highlight the need for court design to reflect the needs of those who work there.[43] Regard should be given to what location is available for intermediaries to assess vulnerable individuals, what spaces exist in the court building to meet with lawyers to review questions and the suitability of spatial configuration within the court itself. Further, building on the work of Mulcahy, Rowden and Rossner,[44] academic critique of the dock in the criminal court should incorporate the voices of intermediaries who have experienced the challenges of the dock when working with vulnerable defendants.

Finally, this book can also influence theoretical work examining more nuanced aspects of the criminal process and the criminal trial. As explored in Chapter 4 (Locating the intermediary within theories of the criminal trial), most work in this area has overlooked or sidelined the significance of intermediary work. What we understand the purpose of the criminal process (with the trial at its centre) to be is enriched by a deeper understanding of the intermediary role. Recent developments in criminal justice only augment the need for more theoretical work into the intermediary role. For example, in light of the establishment of remote courts due to the Covid-19 pandemic, important questions emerge about the treatment of vulnerable suspects and defendants and the collection of best evidence. How the intermediary role operates in such an environment and how intermediary work impacts the aims and values of the overall criminal process deserve further attention. While this book has not focused on these specific questions, my findings relating to the intermediary role, its scope and its content are instructive. Further, the ongoing funding crisis in the criminal justice system has focused minds on how resources are allocated. It would be regrettable if intermediaries were treated as low-hanging fruit in any future budget cuts. This book has drawn attention to the possibility of intermediaries accepting a reduced 'advisory jurisdiction' (see Chapter 5: Professional work – jurisdictions and boundary work) which would likely be less costly financially for government departments. However, any policy decisions relating to the scope of the intermediary role must recognise the impact the role has had on the nature of the criminal process. Further theoretical work on intermediaries is important to

43 Linda Mulcahy and Emma Rowden, *The Democratic Courthouse* (Routledge 2020).

44 Linda Mulcahy, Meredith Rossner and Emma Rowden, 'What if the Dock was Abolished in Criminal Courts?' (Howard League for Penal Reform 2020).

better understand how the role relates to the underpinnings, aims and values of the criminal process.

8.7 Conclusion

This book set out to better understand the role of the intermediary in the criminal justice system, including the role's scope and the content of its work. The result of this investigation is that we can better appreciate not only what intermediary work involves but also the impact of that work on vulnerable individuals within the criminal justice system. This book draws particular attention to the intermediary's development of a professional status, complications associated with the role's neutrality and the role's contribution to ensuring the participation of vulnerable court users. Of course, these three aspects of the intermediary role's function are not exhaustive. However, the examination of the role's scope and function in Chapters 5–7 provides a relatively comprehensive insight into its operation and broader impact on criminal proceedings.

This research has set the intermediary role in the context of the social world of the criminal justice system. This should have several implications for those who perform the role and criminal justice professionals. I hope both prosecution and defence lawyers can view the intermediary as a useful tool for facilitating communication, rather than a hindrance to their work. While the adversarial nature of the trial system inevitably poses challenges to realising this objective, there is scope for improved engagement with intermediaries. Reflecting on the discussion in Chapter 4 (Locating the intermediary within theories of the criminal trial), it should be recognised that intermediaries can further the aims and values of the criminal process. The legitimacy of the criminal trial as an institution, and indeed the criminal justice system more broadly, is strengthened if individuals within it are treated with dignity, as autonomous agents. The evidence collected in this research demonstrates that intermediaries seek *earlier* and *better* engagement with the lawyers involved in a case. Similarly, intermediaries view better judicial understanding of their role and its content as critical for its effective performance. The work of intermediaries must form part of police training, barrister training and judicial training. For example, recent developments in Northern Ireland have seen intermediaries engaged in the training of barristers at the Institute of Professional Legal Studies (IPLS) as well as the training of the judiciary of Northern Ireland. All discussions about the future of the intermediary role must be underpinned by collaboration between police, lawyers, judges and intermediaries themselves. This book has revealed the importance of better understanding the complex relationships between these actors and the intermediary.

This book has developed the notion of 'two-tier' intermediary provision by elaborating upon the concepts of 'witness work' and 'defendant work'. It has been explored how this distinction impacts the practical demands of the intermediary role, how intermediaries approach their work and how other criminal justice actors perceive the role. The new HAIS scheme formalises this distinction in intermediary work since vulnerable suspects/defendants will continue to be excluded from the WIS. Whatever the reason for the establishment of the HAIS scheme, it is not apparent at this point that it will protect the participatory rights of the defendant better than the current ad-hoc system of judicial appointments. Therefore, it is incumbent on the MoJ to monitor and review the operation of the HAIS scheme and ensure that access to intermediaries for vulnerable accused persons is maximised. How might these developments impact the operation of the WIS and the work of Registered Intermediaries assisting complainants and witnesses? The significance of the distinction between 'witness work' and 'defendant work' will need to be revisited once more information/data from the operation of HAIS are available.

The importance of this book goes beyond understanding the day-to-day work of intermediaries, and many of the findings are indicative of broader issues within the criminal justice system. For example, doubts remain over the suitability of the criminal trial to accommodate the needs of vulnerable court users adequately. It is helpful to reflect on the fact that the intermediary was initially introduced as one of a range of special measures aimed at improving the experience of vulnerable witnesses in criminal courts. As a result of s.29 of the Youth Justice and Criminal Evidence Act 1999 (YJCEA), communication facilitation expertise was outsourced to the intermediary as a neutral, independent actor. However, it is unrealistic to expect the intermediary to unilaterally 'fix' communication issues in the criminal justice system. The structure of the adversarial process limits the extent to which the trial may be reformed.[45] Nevertheless, the work of intermediaries is changing how lawyers and judges approach the treatment of vulnerable court users, particularly how witnesses are orally examined. While there is undoubtedly still work to do, Cooper and Wurtzel are correct that the intermediary role has initiated a 'culture change' in how the most vulnerable are accommodated in criminal proceedings.

There is a serious debate to be had about whether intermediaries should become a permanent fixture in criminal courts or whether their primary role is to 'skill up' other court actors when dealing with vulnerable court users.[46] This question is fundamental to whether the intermediary will be integrated further into the criminal process or will have its functions absorbed by the

45 Tyrone Kirchengast, *The Criminal Trial in Law and Discourse* (Palgrave Macmillan 2010) 119.

46 This was a phrase used by E&W-4 when reflecting on the how the role may develop in the future.

court workgroup. Indeed, many of the issues discussed in this book relating to the intermediary's status and legitimacy are linked to the perceived future of the role. It is, however, premature to consider how the intermediary role may be 'phased out' in this way. Growing recognition of the complex communication difficulties faced by vulnerable individuals means that communication expertise is still sorely needed. I saw no evidence in my research that police, lawyers and judges are currently better placed to perform the bespoke communication facilitation role of the intermediary. Indeed, the most recent empirical data collected in Northern Ireland suggest that police in the custody environment often rely on intermediary assistance to help facilitate communication with some of the most vulnerable suspects.[47] A key challenge, however, relates to how vulnerability is detected in the first place. As such, there needs to be a better understanding of how criminal justice professionals conceptualise the purpose of the intermediary role and, crucially, the circumstances in which a communication assessment is viewed as necessary.

Finally, while this book has traced the emergence of the intermediary role and examined its current practice in the U.K, there is scope for further research to question how intermediary work can and should develop. As argued earlier, it is appropriate that a wide range of stakeholders such as lawyers, judges, police and, of course, intermediaries are involved in such a project. As intermediary schemes continue to develop internationally, there is ample scope for further research into the normative function of the role and how its performance may differ depending on different legal systems and legal cultures.

47 Early findings from ongoing empirical work carried out by the author in police custody in Northern Ireland have found increasing awareness of the intermediary role among custody sergeants and broadly positive views of the intermediary role among police interviewing officers.

Bibliography

Abbott A, 'Boundaries of Social Work or Social Work of Boundaries?' (1995) 69 (4) Social Service Review 545

Abbott A, 'Jurisdictional Conflicts: A New Approach to the Development of the Legal Professions' (1986) 11(2) American Bar Foundation Research Journal 187

Abbott A, 'The Emergence of American Psychiatry, 1880–1930' (PhD thesis, University of Chicago 1982)

Abbott A, *The System of Professions: An Essay on the Division of Expert Labor* (Chicago UP 1988)

Abbott A, 'Things of Boundaries' (1995) 62(4) Social Research 857

Access to Justice Knowledge Hub for Fair Participation, 'Report on Intermediaries for Justice Around the Globe' (November 2020) <https://justiceintermediary.org/wp-content/uploads/report-on-intermediaries-for-justice.pdf>

Ackroyd S, 'Sociological and Organisational Theories of Professions and Professionalism' in M Dent and others (eds), *The Routledge Companion to the Professions and Professionalism* (Routledge 2016)

ACT Human Rights Commission, 'ACT Intermediary Program' <https://www.hrc.act.gov.au/intermediaries#:~:text=Intermediaries%20are%20officers%20of%20the,during%20the%20criminal%20trial%20process>

ACT Human Rights Commission, 'Australian First as ACT Intermediary Program Expands to Support Communication Needs of Vulnerable Accused' (13 March 2024) <https://www.hrc.act.gov.au/news-and-events/news/australian-first-as-act-intermediary-program-expands,-supporting-communication-needs-of-vulnerable-accused>

Alfonso Fuentes Maureira C, 'Vulnerable Witnesses in Chilean Criminal Proceedings: New Developments' (2024) 28(1) International Journal of Evidence and Proof 65

Angellini A, *Revisiting the Interpreter's Role* (John Benjamins 2004)

Angouri J, M Marra and J Holmes, 'Introduction: Negotiating Boundaries at Work' in J Angouri, M Marra and J Holmes (eds), *Negotiating Boundaries at Work: Talking and Transitions* (Edinburgh UP 2017)

Antolak-Saper N and H MacPherson, 'Vulnerable Witnesses and Victoria's Intermediary Pilot Program' (2019) 43 Criminal Law Journal 325

Arthur R, 'Giving Effect to Young People's Right to Effectively Participate in Criminal Proceedings' (2016) 28(3) Child and Family Law Quarterly 223

Arthur R, 'The Use of Intermediaries for Young Defendants: Overcoming Barriers to Young People's Participation in Criminal Proceedings' (2022) 34(2) Child and Family Law Quarterly 149

Ashworth A, 'Prosecution and Procedure in Criminal Justice' [1979] Criminal Law Review 482

Ashworth A, *Sentencing and Criminal Justice* (5th edn, CUP 2010)

Ashworth A, *Sentencing and Criminal Justice* (6th edn, CUP 2015)

Ashworth A, *The Criminal Process: An Evaluative Study* (2nd edn, OUP 1998)

Ashworth A, L Campbell and M Redmayne, *The Criminal Process* (5th edn, OUP 2019)

Ashworth A and M Redmayne, *The Criminal Process* (3rd edn, OUP 2005)

Ashworth A and M Redmayne, *The Criminal Process* (4th edn, OUP 2010)

Ashworth A and L Zedner, 'Justice Prevention: Preventive Rationales and the Limits of the Criminal Law' in A Duff and S Green (eds), *Philosophical Foundations of Criminal Law* (OUP 2011)

Ashworth A and L Zedner, *Preventative Justice* (OUP 2014)

Attorney-General (South Australia), Disability Justice Plan 2014–2017 (June 2014)

Australian Human Rights Commission, 'Access to Justice in the Criminal Justice System for People with Disability' (Issues Paper: April 2013, ABN 47 996 232 602)

Australian Law Reform Commission, 'Chapter 7: Access to Justice' <https://www.alrc.gov.au/wp-content/uploads/2019/08/fr124._chapter_7_access_to_justice.pdf>

Australian Law Reform Commission, 'Review of the Adversarial System of Litigation: Rethinking the Federal Civil Litigation System (Issues Paper No 20, Canberra, Australia Government Publishing Service 1997)

Backen P, 'They Just Don't Get It: Communication and the Work of an Intermediary with Vulnerable People in the Justice System' (independently published 2017)

Baldwin J and M McConville, *Jury Trials* (OUP 1979)

Banaker R and M Travers, *Law and Social Theory* (Hart Publishing 2013)

Bankowski Z and G Mungham, *Images of Law* (Routledge 1976)

Bantekas I, M Stein and D Anastasiou, *The UN Convention on the Rights of Persons with Disabilities: A Commentary* (OUP 2018)

Bar Standards Board, 'The BSB Handbook- Version 4.8'
<https://www.barstandardsboard.org.uk/the-bsb-handbook.html?part=E3FF76D3-9538-4B97-94C02111664E5709&audience=&csrfToken=&q=#part-C9631C45-F7A4-41F7-BF341296EC253160>

Barber M, 'The Youth Justice and Criminal Evidence Bill [HL]' (HOC Research Paper 99/40, Bill 74 of 1998–1999)

Beatriz Hale S, *The Discourse of Court Interpreting: Discourse Practices of the Law, the Witness and the Interpreter* (John Benjamins 2004)

Becker H, *Whose Side Are We On?* (1967) 14(3) Social Problems 239

Beckett A, *Citizenship and Vulnerability: Disability and Issues of Social and Political Engagement* (Springer 2006)

Beech A and G Davies, *Forensic Psychology: Crime, Justice, Law Interventions* (Wiley-Blackwell 2017)

Belloni F and J Hodgson, *Criminal Injustice: An Evaluation of the Criminal Justice Process in Britain* (Palgrave MacMillan 2000)

Beqiraj J, L McNamara and V Wicks, 'Access to Justice for Persons with Disabilities: From International Principles to Practice' (International Bar Association, October 2017)

Bergman Blix S and A Wettergren, *Professional Emotions in Court: A Sociological Perspective* (Routledge 2018)

Bergman Blix S and A Wettergren, 'The Emotional Interaction of Judicial Objectivity' (2019) 9(5) Oñati Socio-Legal Series 726

Bibas S, *The Machinery of Justice* (OUP 2015)

Bibas S, 'Transparency and Participation in Criminal Procedure' (2006) 81(3) New York University Law Review 911

Birch D, 'A Better Deal for Vulnerable Witnesses?' (2000) Criminal Law Review 223

Birch D, 'Evidence: Evidence via Television Link and Video Recording of Interview with Child' [2001] Criminal Law Review 473

Blackstock J and others, *Inside Police Custody: An Empirical Account of Suspects' Rights in Four Jurisdictions* (Intersentia 2014)

Blanco R, R Hutt and H Rojas, 'Reform to the Criminal Justice System in Chile: Evaluation and Challenges' (2004) 2(2) Loyola University Chicago International Law Review 253

Blok A and others, 'Ecologies of Boundaries: Modes of Boundary Work in Professional Work Boundaries' (2019) 42(4) Symbolic Interaction 588

Boone M and M Kox, 'Neutrality as an Element of Perceived Justice in Prison: Consistency versus Individualization' (2014) 10(4) Utrecht Law Review 118

Bottoms A and J Tankebe, 'Beyond Procedural Justice: A Dialogic Approach to Legitimacy in Criminal Justice' (2013) 102(1) Journal of Criminal Law and Criminology 119

Bourdieu P, *In Other Words: Essays Towards a Reflexive Sociology* (Stanford UP 1990)

Bourdieu P, *Language & Symbolic Power* (Polity Press 1991)

Bourdieu P, *Outline of a Theory of Practice* (CUP 1977)

Bourdieu P, *Pascalian Meditations* (CUP 2000)

Bourdieu P, *Practical Reason: On the Theory of Action* (Stanford UP 1998)

Bourdieu P, *Sociology in Question* (SAGE Publishing 1993)

Bourdieu P, *The Field of Cultural Production* (Columbia UP 1993)

Bourdieu P, *The Logic of Practice* (Polity Press 1992)

Bourdieu P, *The Rules of Art: Genesis and Structure of the Literary Field* (Stanford UP 1996)

Bourdieu P, *The State Nobility: Elite Schools in the Field of Power* (Stanford UP 1998)

Bourdieu P and L Wacquant, *An Invitation to Reflexive Sociology* (Blackwell Publishers 1992)

Bowcott O, 'Two Year-Old Girl Gives Evidence in UK Abuse Case' *The Guardian* (Tuesday, 10 October 2017)

Bowden P, T Henning and D Plater, 'Balancing Fairness to Victims, Society and Defendants in the Cross-Examination of Vulnerable Witnesses: An Impossible Triangulation' (2014) 37 Melbourne University Law Review 539

Bratt Paulston C, S Kiesling and E Rangel, *The Handbook of Intercultural Communication* (Wiley 2012)

Breckenbridge J and others, 'Choosing a Methodological Path: Reflections on the Constructivist Turn' (2012) 11(1) Grounded Theory Review 64

Brinkman S and S Kvale, *Interviews: Learning the Craft of Qualitative Research Interviewing* (3rd edn, SAGE Publishing 2015)

Broderick A and A Ferri, *European Disability Law and Policy: Text, Cases and Materials* (CUP 2019)

Brooks C, *Lawyers, Litigation and English Society since 1450* (The Hambledon Press 1998)

Brough P, Brown J and Biggs A, *Improving Criminal Justice Workspaces: Translating Theory and Research into Evidence-Based Practice* (Routledge 2016)

Brown D, JI Turner and B Weisser, *The Oxford Handbook of Criminal Process* (OUP 2019)

Brown K, *Vulnerability and Young People: Care and Social Control in Policy and Practice* (Policy Press 2015)

Burris B, *Technocracy at Work* (SUNY Press 1993)

Burton M, R Evans and A Sanders, 'Are Special Measures for Vulnerable and Intimidated Witnesses Working?: Evidence from the Criminal Justice Agencies' (Home Office Online Report 01/06)

Cabinet Social Policy Committee, 'Amendment to the Evidence Act 2006' (Obtained under Official Information Act 1982: Request to the Ministry of Justice, Wellington, New Zealand 2013)
Calhoun C and R Sennett, *Practicing Culture* (Routledge 2007)
Callus A and R Farrugia, *The Disabled Child's Participation Rights* (Routledge 2016)
Cappelletti M and B Garth, 'Access to Justice: The Newest Wave in the Worldwide Movement to Make Rights Effective' (1978) 27(2) Buffalo Law Review 181
Carlen P, *Magistrates Justice* (Wiley-Blackwell 1976)
Carlen P, 'The Staging of Magistrates' Justice' (1976) 16(1) The British Journal of Criminology 48
Carlen P and M Powell, 'Professionals in the Magistrates' Courts: The Courtroom Lore of Probation Officers And Social Workers' in H Parker (ed), *Social Work and the Courts* (Hodder and Stoughton 1979)
Cashmore J and R Shackel, 'Evaluation of the Child Sexual Offence Evidence Pilot Final Outcome Evaluation Report, Prepared for: Victims Services, NSW Department of Justice' (August 2018)
Cashmore J and others, 'Evaluation of the Child Sexual Offence Evidence Pilot: Process Evaluation Report' (NSW Government Department of Justice Report No SPRC Report 16/17, October 2017)
Castellano U, 'Beyond the Courtroom Workgroup: Caseworkers as the New Satellite of Social Control' (2009) 31(4) Law & Policy 429
Charmaz K, *Constructing Grounded Theory. A Practical Guide Through Qualitative Analysis* (SAGE Publishing 2006)
Charmaz K, 'Grounded Theory' in J Smith, R Harré and L Langenhove (eds), *Rethinking Methods in Psychology* (SAGE Publishing 1995)
Christman J and J Anderson, *Autonomy and the Challenges to Liberalism* (CUP 2009)
Civil Justice Council, 'Vulnerable Witnesses and Parties Within Civil Proceedings: Current Position and Recommendations for Change' (August 2019)
Coicaud J, 'Crime, Justice and Legitimacy: A Brief Theoretical Inquiry' in J Tankebe and A Liebling (eds), *Legitimacy and Criminal Justice: An International Exploration* (OUP 2013)
College of Policing, 'Investigate Interviewing Principle 1' <https://www.app.college.police.uk/app-content/investigations/investigative-interviewing/>
Colley C and F Guéry, 'Understanding New Hybrid Professions: Bourdieu, *Illusio* and the Case of Public Service Interpreters' (2015) 45 Cambridge Journal of Education 113
Colley H, 'Not Learning in the Workplace: Austerity and the Shattering of Illusio in Public Service' (2012) 24(5) Journal of Workplace Learning 317
Collins K, N Harker and G Antonopoulos, 'The Impact of Registered Intermediary Presence on Adults' Perceptions of Child Witnesses: Evidence from a Mock Cross Examination' (2016) 23 European Journal on Criminal Policy and Research 211
Commission of Inquiry into the Tasmanian Government's Responses to Child Sexual Abuse in Institutional Settings, *Who Was Looking after Me? Prioritising the Safety of Tasmanian Children, Volume 1: Summary, Recommendations and Findings* (2023)
Communicourt, 'Criminal Proceedings' <https://www.communicourt.co.uk/referral-booking-howto/criminal-proceedings/>
Communicourt, 'Intermediary Case Law Update: Mr Justice Williams [2024] EWHC 906 (Fam)' <https://www.communicourt.co.uk/news/category/blog-post/> accessed 27 December 2024
Cooper P, *Highs and Lows: The 4th Intermediary Survey* (Kingston University London, 13 October 2014) <http://eprints.kingston.ac.uk/28868/1/Cooper-P–28868.pdf>

Cooper P, 'Joint Enterprise: R. v Grant-Murray (Janhelle); R. v McGill (Joseph) Court of Appeal (Criminal Division): Lord Thomas of Cwmgiedd CJ, Hallett LJ (VP CACD) and Goss J: 11 August 2017; [2017] EWCA Crim 1228' (2018) 1 Criminal Law Review 71

Cooper P, 'Like Ducks to Water? Intermediaries for Vulnerable Witnesses and Parties' (2016) Family Law 374

Cooper P, 'Ticketing Talk Gets Serious' *Counsel Magazine* (November 2014) 11–12

Cooper P, P Backen and R Marchant, 'Getting to Grips with Ground Rules Hearings – A Checklist For Judges, Advocates and Intermediaries' (2015) 6 Criminal Law Review 420

Cooper P and L Farrugia, 'Ground Rules Hearings' in P Cooper and H Norton (eds), *Vulnerable People and the Criminal Justice System – A Guide to Law and Practice* (OUP 2017)

Cooper P and L Hunting, *Access to Justice for Vulnerable People* (Wildy, Simmonds and Hill Publishing 2018)

Cooper P and M Mattison, 'Intermediaries, Vulnerable People and the Quality of Evidence: An International Comparison of Three Versions of the English Intermediary Model' (2017) 21(4) International Journal of Evidence and Proof 351

Cooper P, M Mattison and H Norton, 'Looking Ahead' in P Cooper and H Norton (eds), *Vulnerable People and the Criminal Justice System – A Guide to Law and Practice* (OUP 2017)

Cooper P and D Wurtzel, 'A Day Late and a Dollar Short: In Search of an Intermediary Scheme for Vulnerable Defendants in England and Wales' (2013) 1 Criminal Law Review 4

Cooper P and D Wurtzel, 'Better the Second Time Around? Department of Justice Registered Intermediaries Schemes and Lessons from England and Wales' (2014) 65(1) Northern Ireland Legal Quarterly 39

Cooper P and D Wurtzel, 'Intermediaries' in P Cooper and H Norton (eds), *Vulnerable People and the Criminal Justice System – A Guide to Law and Practice* (OUP 2017)

County Court of Victoria, 'Multi-jurisdictional Court Guide for Ground Rules and the Intermediary Program' (28 July 2023)

Crawford A and A Hucklesby, *Legitimacy and Compliance in Criminal Justice* (Routledge 2013)

CRC Committee, General Comment No 12, The Right of the Child to be Heard (CRC/C/GC/12, 2009)

CRC Committee, General Comment No 10, Children's Rights in Juvenile Justice (CRC/C/GC/10, 2007)

CRC Committee, General Comment No 14, The Right of the Child to Have His or Her Best Interests Taken as a Primary Consideration (CRC/C/GC/14, 2013)

CRC Committee, General Comment No 24, Children's Rights in Juvenile Justice (CRC/C/GC/24, 2019)

CRC Committee, General Guidelines Regarding the Form and Contents of Periodic Reports to Be Submitted by States Parties Under Article 44, Paragraph 1(b) of the Convention (UN Doc No CRC/C/58, 1996)

Creswell J, *Qualitative Inquiry and Research Design: Choosing Among Five Approaches* (SAGE Publishing 2012)

CRPD Committee, General Comment No 1, Article 12: Equal Recognition before the Law (CRPD/C/GC/1, 2014)

CRPD Committee, General Comment No 4, Article 24 – the Right to Inclusive Education (CRPD/C/GC/4, 2016)

Criminal Justice Joint Inspection, 'Achieving Best Evidence in Child Sexual Cases – A Joint Inspection' (2014)

Criminal Justice Joint Inspectorate, 'A Joint Inspection of the Treatment of Offenders with Learning Disabilities Within the Criminal Justice System' (January 2014)

Crown Prosecution Service (CPS), 'Special Measures | The Crown Prosecution Service' <https://www.cps.gov.uk/legal-guidance/special-measures>

Dalleo R, *Bourdieu and Postcolonial Studies* (Liverpool UP 2017)

Daly A, 'Assessing Children's Capacity: Reconceptualising our Understanding through the UN Convention on the Rights of the Child' (2020) 28(3) International Journal of Children's Rights 471

Damaska M, 'Evidentiary Barriers to Conviction and Two Models of Criminal Procedure: A Comparative Study' (1973) 121 University of Pennsylvania Law Review 506

Damaska M, *The Faces of Justice and State Authority: A Comparative Approach to the Legal Process* (Yale UP 1986)

Darbyshire P, 'Judicial Case Management in Ten Crown Courts' [2014] 1 Criminal Law Review 30

De Girolamo D, 'The Mediation Process: Challenges to Neutrality and the Delivery of Procedural Justice' (2019) 39(4) Oxford Journal of Legal Studies 834

Dehaghani R, 'Defining the "Appropriate" in "Appropriate Adult": Restrictions and Opportunities for Reform' (2020) 12 Criminal Law Review 1137

Dehaghani R, 'Interrogating Vulnerability: Reframing the Vulnerable Suspect in Police Custody' (2021) 30(2) Social & Legal Studies 251

Dehaghani R, 'Vulnerability in Police Custody: Definition, Identification and Implementation in the Context of the Appropriate Adult Safeguard' (PhD thesis, University of Leicester 2017)

Dehaghani R, *Vulnerability in Police Custody: Police Decision Making and the Appropriate Adult Safeguard* (Routledge 2019)

Dennis I, 'Reconstructing the Law of Criminal Evidence' (1989) 42(1) Current Legal Problems 21

Dennis I, *The Law of Evidence* (5th edn, Sweet & Maxwell 2013)

Department of Justice (Northern Ireland), 'Northern Ireland Registered Intermediaries Schemes Pilot Project: Post-Project Review' (January 2015)

Department of Justice (Northern Ireland) (DoJ), 'The Registered Intermediaries Procedural Guidance Manual' (April 2024)

Dick P, 'Resistance, Gender and Bourdieu's notion of field' (2008) 21(3) Management Communication 327

Doak J, *Victim's Rights, Human Rights and Criminal Justice: Reconceiving the Role of Third Parties* (Hart Publishing 2008)

Doak J and L Doak, 'Non-verbal Victims in the Adversarial Criminal Process: Communication, Competency, and Credibility' (2017) 68(4) Northern Ireland Legal Quarterly 451

Doak J and C McGourlay, *Evidence in Context* (3rd edn, Routledge 2012)

DoJ, 'Application Information Pack' (August 2012)

DoJ, 'Northern Ireland Registered Intermediaries Schemes Pilot Project: Post-Project Review' (January 2015)

DoJ, 'Registered Intermediary Schemes' <https://www.justice-ni.gov.uk/publications/registered-intermediary-schemes>

DoJ, 'The Registered Intermediaries Procedural Guidance Manual' (Northern Ireland) (April 2024)

Donskov Felter K, 'Breaking with Illusio' (2012) 66(1) Studia Theologia 86

Dubber M, 'The Criminal Trial and the Legitimation of Punishment' in A Duff and others (eds), *The Trial on Trial 1: Truth and Due Process* (Hart Publishing 2004)

Duff A, 'Penance, Punishment and the Limits of Community' (2003) 5(3) Punishment & Society 295
Duff A, 'Penal Communities' (1999) 1(1) Punishment & Society 27
Duff A, *Punishment, Communication and Community* (OUP 2001)
Duff A, *The Realm of Criminal Law* (OUP 2018)
Duff A, *Trials and Punishments* (CUP 1986)
Duff A and others, 'Introduction: Towards a Normative Theory of the Criminal Trial' in A Duff and others (eds), *The Trial on Trial 1: Truth and Due Process* (Hart Publishing 2004)
Duff A and others, *The Trial on Trial 1: Truth and Due Process* (Hart Publishing 2004)
Duff A and others, *The Trial on Trial 3: Towards a Normative Theory of the Criminal Trial* (Hart Publishing 2007)
Duff A, 'Theories of Criminal Law' (The Stanford Encyclopedia of Philosophy, Summer 2013 Edition) <https://plato.stanford.edu/archives/sum2013/entries/criminal-law/>
Duff P, 'Changing Conceptions of the Scottish Criminal Trial: The Duty to Agree Uncontroversial Evidence' in A Duff and others (eds), *The Trial on Trial 1: Truth and Due Process* (Hart Publishing 2004)
Dzur A, *Punishment, Participatory Democracy and the Jury* (OUP 2014)
Eaglestin S and Y Karniel, 'The Youth Examiner: An Israeli Socio-legal Experiment' (1991) 5(4) Children and Society 317
Eberle E, 'The Methodology of Comparative Law' (2011) 16(1) Roger Williams University Law Review 51, 52
Edwards A, *The Practice of Court Interpreting* (John Benjamins 1995)
Edwards I, 'An Ambiguous Participant: The Crime Victim and Criminal Justice Decision-Making' (2004) 44 British Journal of Criminology 967
Eisenstein J and H Jacob, *Felony Justice: An Organizational Analysis of Criminal Courts* (Little, Brown 1977)
Ellison L, 'A Comparative Study of Rape Trials in Adversarial and Inquisitorial Criminal Justice Systems' (PhD thesis, University of Leeds 1997)
Ellison L, 'Responding to the Needs of Victims with Psychosocial Disabilities: Challenges to Equality of Access to Justice' (2015) 1 Criminal Law Review 28
Ellison L, *The Adversarial Process and the Vulnerable Witness* (OUP 2002)
Ellison L, 'The Mosaic Art?: Cross-Examination and the Vulnerable Witness' (2001) 21(3) Legal Studies 353
Ellison L, 'The Protection of Vulnerable Witnesses in Court: An Anglo-Dutch Comparison' (1999) 3(1) The International Journal of Evidence of Proof 29
Endress Gómez S, 'Update: Essential Issues of the Chilean Legal System' (Hauser Global Law School Program, February 2019) <www.nyulawglobal.org/globalex/Chile1.html#_Regarding_the_Criminal_Procedure%20Re>
European Court of Human Rights, 'Guide on Article 6 of the European Convention on Human Rights' (31 August 2020)
Evans W, 'On the Law of Evidence' in R Pothier (ed), *A Treatise on the Law of Obligations* (WD Evans tr, London 1806)
Evetts J, 'Short Note: The Sociology of Professional Groups' (2006) 54(1) Current Sociology 133
Fairclough S, 'The Lost Leg of the Youth Justice and Criminal Evidence Act (1999): Special Measures and Humane Treatment' (2021) 41(4) Oxford Journal of Legal Studies 1066
Fairclough S, 'The Role of Equality in the Provision of Special Measures to Vulnerable and/or Intimidated Court Users Giving Evidence in Crown Court Trials' (PhD thesis, University of Birmingham 2017)

Fairclough S and J Taggart, 'Lost in Translation? Perceptions of Defendant Intermediaries in the Legal Profession' (2023) 7 Criminal Law Review 440
Farrugia L and F Gabbert, 'Vulnerable Suspects in Police Interviews: Exploring Current Practice in England and Wales' (2020) 17(1) Journal of Investigative Psychology and Offender Profiling 17
Fedorova M, *The Principle of Equality of Arms in International Criminal Proceedings* (Intersentia 2012)
Flick U, E Von Kardoff and I Steinke, *A Companion to Qualitative Research* (SAGE Publishing 2004)
Flynn E, 'Art.13 Access to Justice' in I Bantekas, M Ashley Stein and D Anastasiou (eds), *Oxford Public International Law* (OUP 2018)
Fournier V, 'Boundary Work and the (Un)making of the Professions' in N Malin (ed), *Professionalism, Boundaries and the Workplace* (Routledge 2000)
Frase R, *Just Sentencing: Principles and Procedures for a Workable System* (OUP 2013)
Frazer S, *The Impact of the Community Court Model on Defendant Perceptions of Fairness: A Case Study at the Red Hook Community Justice Center* (Center for Court Innovation 2006)
Freidson E, *Profession of Medicine: A Study of the Sociology of Applied* (Chicago UP 1970)
Gallagher A and others, 'Establishing Stakeholder Priorities for Advancing the Role of the Intermediary in the Justice System: Findings from a Consensus Study' (2024) The International Journal of Evidence & Proof (online first, 27 December 2024)
Gershman B, 'The Prosecutor's Duty to Truth' (2001) 14 Journal of Legal Ethics 309
Gieryn A, 'Boundary-Work and the Demarcation of Science from Non-Science: Strains and Interests in Professional Ideologies of Scientists' (1983) 48 American Sociological Review 781
Giuffrida J and A Mackay, 'Extending Witness Intermediary Schemes to Vulnerable Defendants' (2021) 33(4) Current Issues in Criminal Justice 49
Glaser B and A Strauss, *The Discovery of Grounded Theory: Strategies for Qualitative Research* (Aldine 1967)
Goffman E, *Interaction Ritual: Essays on Face-to-Face Behaviour* (Pantheon 1967)
Goffman E, *The Presentation of Self in Everyday Life* (U of Edinburgh Social Science Research Centre 1956)
Golsorkhi D and others, 'Analysing, Accounting for and Unmasking Domination: On our Role as Scholars of Practice, Practitioners of Social Science and Public Intellectuals' (2009) 16(6) Organization 779
Gonzalez R, V Vasquez and H Mikkelson, *Fundamentals of Court Interpretation. Theory, Policy, and Practice* (Carolina Academic Press 1991)
Goodey J, *Victims and Victimology: Research, Policy and Practice* (Longman 2004)
Government of South Australia, 'A Guide for Communication Partners' (2020) <https://www.sa.gov.au/__data/assets/pdf_file/0009/599337/Guide-for-communication-partners.pdf>
Green J and N Thorogood, *Qualitative Methods for Health Research* (2nd edn, SAGE Publishing 2009)
Green T and A Gates, 'Understanding the Process of Professionalisation in the Police Organisation' (2014) 87(2) The Police Journal: Theory, Practice and Principles 75
Grimen H, 'Profesjon og kunnskap' in A Molander and LI Terum (eds), *Profesjonsstudier* (Oslo Universitetsforlaget 2008)
Gudjonsson G, 'Psychological Vulnerabilities during Police Interviews. Why Are They Important?' (2018) Legal and Criminological Psychology 161
Gudjonsson G and others, 'Persons at Risk During Interviews in Police Custody: The Identification of Vulnerabilities' (Royal Commission on Criminal Procedure Research Study No 12, HMSO 1993)

Guest G, Namey E and Mitchell M, 'In-depth Interviews' in G Guest, E Namey and M Mitchell (eds), *Collecting Qualitative Data: A Field Manual for Applied Research* (SAGE Publishing 2013)
Hale S, 'Interpreter Policies, Practices and Protocols in Australian Courts and Tribunals: A National Survey' (Australasian Institute of Judicial Administration 2011)
Hanna K and E Henderson, 'Child Witnesses in the Criminal Courts' in A Deckert and R Sarr (eds), *The Palgrave Handbook of Australian and New Zealand Criminology, Crime and Justice* (Palgrave Macmillan 2017)
Hashimoto E, 'Resurrecting Autonomy: The Criminal Defendant's Right to Control the Case' (2010) 90 Boston University Law Review 1147
Hawkins K, 'Prologue: Donald Harris and the Early Years of the Oxford Centre' in K Hawkins (ed), *The Human Face of Law: Essays in Honour of Donald Harris* (Clarendon Press 1997)
Heidegren C and H Lundberg, 'Towards a Sociology of Philosophy' (2010) 53(1) Acta Sociologica 3
Heilbron R, 'Report of the Advisory Group on the Law of Rape' (HMSO, London 1975)
Helm R, 'Constrained Waiver of Trial Rights? Incentives to Plead Guilty and the Right to a Fair Trial' (2019) 46(3) Journal of Law and Society 423
Henderson E, '"A Very Valuable Tool": Judges, Advocates and Intermediaries Discuss the Intermediary System in England and Wales' (2015) 19(3) International Journal of Evidence and Proof 154
Henderson E, 'All the Proper Protections – The Court of Appeal Rewrites the Rules for the Cross-Examination of Vulnerable Witnesses' (2014) Criminal Law Review 93
Henderson E, 'Best Evidence or Best Interests? What Does the Case Law Say about the Function of Criminal Cross-Examination' (2016) 20(3) Journal of International Evidence and Proof 183
Henderson E, 'Theoretically Speaking: English Judges and Advocates Discuss the Changing Theory of Cross-Examination' (2015) 12 Criminal Law Review 927
Henegan M, 'Final Appeal Courts and Article 3 of the UN CRC: What Do the Best Interests of the Particular Child Have to Do with It?' in E Sutherland and L Macfarlane (eds), *Implementing Article 3 of the United Nations CRC* (CUP 2016)
Henriëtte Hoegen E and E Marion Brienen, *Victims of Crime in 22 European Criminal Justice Systems: The Implementation of Recommendation (85) 11 of the Council of Europe on the Position of the Victim in the Framework of Criminal Law and Procedure* (Wolf Legal Productions 2000)
Herring J, *Vulnerable Adults and the Law* (OUP 2015)
Hildebrandt M, 'Trial and "Fair Trial": From Peer to Subject to Citizen' in A Duff and others (eds), *The Trial on Trial 2: Truth and Due Process* (Hart Publishing 2006)
Himma K, *Coercion and the Nature of Law* (OUP 2020)
Hirschkorn K, 'Exclusive versus Everyday Forms of Professional Knowledge: Legitimacy Claims in Conventional and Alternative Medicine' (2006) 28 Sociology of Health and Illness 533
HM Courts and Tribunal Services (HMCTS), 'Court and Tribunal Design Guide' (HMCTS 2019)
HMCTS, 'New Contracts Awarded to Support Vulnerable Court and Tribunal Users' (26 January 2022) <https://www.gov.uk/government/news/new-contracts-awarded-to-support-vulnerable-court-and-tribunal-users>
HM Government, 'Working Together to Safeguard Children: A Guide to Inter-agency Working to Safeguard and Promote the Welfare of Children' (July 2018)
Hodgson J, 'Conceptions of the Trial in Inquisitorial and Adversarial Procedure' in A Duff and others (eds), *The Trial on Trial 2: Judgment and Calling to Account* (Hart Publishing 2006)

Hodgson J, *French Criminal Justice* (Hart Publishing 2005)
Hodgson J, *The Metamorphosis of Criminal Justice* (OUP 2020)
Hodkinson P, A Sparkes and H Hodkinson, *Triumphs and Tears: Young People, Markets and the Transition from School to Work* (David Fulton 1996)
Hoegen E and M Brienen, *Victims of Crime in 22 European Criminal Justice Systems: The Implementation of Recommendation (85) 11 of the Council of Europe on the Position of the Victim in the Framework of Criminal Law and Procedure* (Wolf Legal Productions 2000)
Hoff S, M Powell and D Plater, 'When Good Intentions Are Not Enough: Professionals' Perceptions of the South Australian Communication Partner Scheme' (2022) 57(4) Australian Journal of Social Sciences 970
Hofvander B and others, 'Mental Health Among Young Adults in Prison: The Importance of Childhood-Onset Conduct Disorder' (2017) 3 BJPsych Open 78
Hollingsworth K, 'Theorising Children's Rights in Youth Justice: The Significance of Autonomy and Foundational Rights' (2013) 76(6) Modern Law Review 1046
Home Office, 'Action for Justice: Achieving Best Evidence in Criminal Proceedings: Guidance for Vulnerable or Intimidated Witnesses, Including Children: Implementing the Speaking up for Justice Report' (Home Office 2000)
Home Office, 'Code C: Revised Code of Practice for the Detention, Treatment and Questioning of Persons by Police Officers' (Police and Criminal Evidence Act (PACE) 1984)
Home Office, 'Guidance for Appropriate Adults' (London, 19 April 2011)
Home Office, 'Measures to Assist Vulnerable or Intimidated Witnesses in the Criminal Justice System: Implementing the Speaking up for Justice Report' (Home Office Communication Directorate 2002)
Home Office, 'Rebalancing the Criminal Justice System in Favour of the Law Abiding Majority' (2006)
Home Office, 'Report of the Advisory Group on Video Evidence' (London December 1989)
Home Office, 'Speaking up for Justice: Report of the Interdepartmental Working Group on the Treatment of Vulnerable or Intimidated Witnesses in the Criminal Justice System' (London 1998)
Hough M, J Jackson and B Bradford, 'Trust in Justice and the Legitimacy of Legal Authorities: Topline Findings from a European Comparative Study' in S Body-Gendrot and others (eds), *The Routledge Handbook of European Criminology* (Routledge 2013)
Hough M and others, 'Procedural Justice, Trust and Institutional Legitimacy' (2010) 4(3) Policing: A Journal of Policy and Practice 203
House of Commons Library, 'Rights of Children in Police Custody (Number CDP 2022/0122)' (21 June 2022)
Howard K, C McCann and M Dudley, '"It's Really Good . . . Why Hasn't it Happened Earlier?" Professionals' Perspectives on the Benefits of communication Assistance in the New Zealand Youth Justice System' (2020) 53(2) Journal of Criminology 265
Howard K, C McCann and M Dudley, 'What is Communication Assistance? Describing a New and Emerging Profession in the New Zealand Youth Justice System' (2020) 27(2) Psychiatry, Psychology and Law 300
Hoyano L, 'Commentary on *R (on the application of OP) v Secretary of State for* Justice' (2015) 1 Criminal Law Review 79
Hoyano L, 'Coroners and Justice Act 2009: Special Measures Directions Take Two: Entrenching Unequal Access to Justice?' (2010) 5 Criminal Law Review 345
Hoyano L, 'Striking a Balance between the Rights of Defendants and Vulnerable Witnesses: Will Special Measures Directions Contravene Guarantees of a Fair Trial?' [2001] Criminal Law Review 948

Hoyano L, 'Variations on a Theme by Pigot: Special Measures Directions for Child Witnesses' (2000) Criminal Law Review 250

Hoyano L and A Rafferty, 'Rationing Defence Intermediaries under the April 2016 Criminal Practice Direction' (2017) Criminal Law Review 90

Hoyle C and L Zedner, 'Victims, Victimisation and Criminal Justice' in M Maguire, R Morgan and R Reiner (eds), *Oxford Handbook of Criminology* (4th edn, OUP 2007)

Independent Police Complaints Commission, 'IPCC Guidelines for Handling Allegations of Discrimination' (2015) <https://www.policeconduct.gov.uk/sites/default/files/documents/guidelines_for_handling_allegations_of_discrimination_updated.pdf>

Inghilleri M, 'Habitus, Field and Discourse: Interpreting as a Socially Situated Activity' (2003) 15(2) Target 243

Intermediaries for Justice, 'About IFJ' <https://www.intermediaries-for-justice.org/vision-and-aims>

International Commission of Jurists, 'Groundbreaking New UN Guidance on Access to Justice for Persons with Disabilities' (28 August 2020) <https://www.icj.org/a2jpwd/>

Jackson H, 'Children's Evidence in Legal Proceedings – The Position in Western Australia' in J Spencer and M Lamb (eds), *Children and Cross-Examination: Time to Change the Rules?* (Hart Publishing 2012)

Jackson J, 'Autonomy and Accuracy in the Development of Fair Trial Rights' (2009) University College Dublin Law Research Paper (No 09/2009) <http://papers.ssrn.com/sol3/papers.cfm?abstract_id=1407968>

Jackson J, 'Justice for All: Putting Victims at the Heart of Criminal Justice' (2003) 30(2) Journal of Law and Society 309

Jackson J, 'The Effect of Legal Culture and Proof in Decisions to Prosecute' (2004) 3 Law, Probability and Risk 109

Jackson J and S Summers, *The Internationalisation of Criminal Evidence: Beyond the Common Law and Civil Law Traditions* (CUP 2012)

Jacob H, *Justice in America: Courts, Lawyers, and the Judicial Process* (Little Brown and Company 1965)

Jacobs J, 'Communication Partner Service Final Report: 1 July 2016–29 February 2020' (Uniting Communities 2020). A new 'fee-for-service' model of intermediary provision has now replaced the volunteer model but there has been no focused research on its operation to date

Jacobson J and P Cooper, *Participation in Courts and Tribunals: Concepts, Realities and Aspirations* (Bristol UP 2020)

Jacobson J, G Hunter and A Kirby, *Inside Crown Court: Personal Experiences and Questions of Legitimacy* (Policy Press 2016)

Jacobson J and J Talbot, *Vulnerable Defendants in the Criminal Courts: A Review of Provision for Adults and Children* (Prison Reform Trust 2009, ISBN: 0 946209 96 0)

Johnston L, 'Vulnerability and Just Desert: A Theory of Sentencing and Mental Illness' (2013) 103(1) The Journal of Criminal Law and Criminology 147

Joint Select Committee on Sentencing of Child Sexual Assault Offenders (NSW), 'Every Sentence Tells a Story: Report on Sentencing of Child Sexual Assault Offenders' (Report No 1/55, October 2014)

Judicial College, 'Crown Court Compendium: Part I' (July 2024)

Judicial College, 'Equal Treatment Bench Book February 2024 Edition' (July 2024)

Justice Intermediary, 'Access to Justice Knowledge Hub' <https://justiceintermediary.org/>

Kalfa S, A Wilkinson and P Gollan, 'The Academic Game: Compliance and Resistance in Universities' (2019) 32(2) Work, Employment and Society 274

Kant I, *Groundwork of the Metaphysics of Morals* (CUP 1996)
Kanter A, *The Development of Disability Rights Under International Law: From Charity to Human Rights* (Routledge 2014)
Kedge S, 'Language and Communication Difficulties: Children and Young People Involved with the Legal System' (2024) 66 The Youth Court of New Zealand 7
Kirby A, J Jacobson and G Hunter, 'Effective Participation or Passive Acceptance: How Can Defendants Participate More Effectively in the Court Process?' (Howard League What is Justice? Working Papers 9/2014)
Konecni V and E Ebbesen, *The Criminal Justice System: A Social-Psychological Analysis* (W.H. Freeman 1982)
Kraatz M and E Block, 'Organizational Implications of Institutional Pluralism' in R Greenwood and others (eds), *Sage Handbook of Organizational Institutionalism* (SAGE Publishing 2008)
Kramer M, *Objectivity and the Rule of Law* (CUP 2009)
Lacey N, 'Punishment, Communication and Community' (2002) 111(442) Mind: A Quarterly Review of Philosophy 392
Lacey N and H Pickard, 'A Dual-Process Approach to Criminal Law: Victims and the Clinical Model of Responsibility without Blame' (2019) 27(2) The Journal of Political Philosophy 229
LaFave W, 'The Prosecutor's Discretion in the United States' (1970) 18 American Journal of Comparative Law 532
Lai Ho H, 'Liberalism and the Criminal Trial' (2010) 32 Sydney Law Review 269
Lamont M and Molnar V, 'The Study of Boundaries in the Social Sciences' (2002) 28 Annual Review of Sociology 167
Landsman S, *Readings on Adversarial Justice: The American Approach to Adjudication* (West Publishing 1988)
Langbein J, *The Origins of the Adversary Criminal Trial* (OUP 2003)
Lauden L, *Truth, Error and Criminal Law: An Essay in Legal Epistemology* (CUP 2006)
Law Commission, 'Evidence in Criminal Proceedings: Previous Misconduct of a Defendant' (Law Com No 141, 1996)
Law Commission, 'Unfitness to Plead, Volume 1: Report Law' (Com No 364, 2016) 117–18
Lawson A, 'Disabled People and Access to Justice: From Disablement to Enablement?' in E Flynn (ed), *Routledge Handbook of Disability Law and Human Rights* (Routledge 2016)
Lawson A, 'People with Psychosocial Impairments or Conditions, Reasonable Accommodation and the Disabilities Convention' (2008) 26 Law in Context 62
Lawson A and A Beckett, 'The Social and Human Rights Models of Disability: Towards a Complementarity Thesis' (2021) 25 The International Journal of Human Rights 348
Leader K, 'The Trial's the Thing: Performance and Legitimacy in International Criminal Trials' (2020) 24(2) Theoretical Criminology 241 (2020)
Lexicon, 'Every Reasonable Step': A More Flexible Approach to Vulnerable Witnesses and Defendants Consolidated List of Intermediary Examples (November 2017) <https://www.intermediaries-for-justice.org/sites/default/files/consolidated-list-of-a-more-flexible-approach-november–2017.pdf>
Lipetz M, *Routine Justice: Processing Cases in Women's Court* (Transaction Publishers 1984)
Liu S, 'Boundaries and Professions: Toward a Processual Theory of Action' (2018) 5(1) Journal of Professions and Organization 45

Lowndes S, 'Comprehension and Misapprehension in Courtroom Discourse (2007) 14(2) International Journal of Speech Language and the Law 305

Lucy W, 'The Possibility of Impartiality' (2005) 25(1) Oxford Journal of Legal Studies 3

Lundy L, '"Voice" Is Not Enough: Conceptualising Article 12 of the United Nations Convention on the Child' (2007) 33 (6) British Educational Research Journal 927

Lundy L and L McEvoy, 'Children's Rights and Research Processes: Assisting Children to (in)Formed Views' (2012) 19 Childhood 129

Lundy L, J Tobin and A Parkes, 'Article 12: The Right to Respect for the Views of the Child' in J Tobin (ed), *The UN Convention on the Rights of the Child: A Commentary* (OUP 2019)

Lupu I and L Empson, 'Illusio and Overwork: Playing the Game in the Accounting Field' (2015) 28(8) Accounting, Auditing and Accountability 1310

Mackay A and J Giuffrida, 'Ensuing the Right to a Fair Criminal Trial using Communication Assistance' (2022) 10(1) Griffith Journal of Law and Human Dignity 1

MacPherson C, 'The Youth Justice and Criminal Evidence Act 1999: Achieving Best Evidence?' (2001) 41(3) Medicine, Science and the Law 230

Magistrates' Court of Victoria, 'Multi-Jurisdictional Court Guide for the Intermediary Pilot Program: Intermediaries and Ground Rules' <https://www.mcv.vic.gov.au/sites/default/files/2023-08/multi-jurisdictional%20court%20guide%20intermediary%20pilot%20program%20intermediaries%20ground%20rules%20hearings.pdf>

Magistrates' Court of Victoria, 'Practice Direction, No 6 of 2018: Intermediary Pilot Program at Melbourne Magistrates' Court' (20 July 2018)

Makker L, S Clendon and E Doell, 'Speech-Language Pathologists' Perspectives of Communication Strategies for Young People in the New Zealand Youth Justice System' (2022) 24 International Journal of Speech-Language Pathology 585

Malin N, *Professionalism, Boundaries and the Workplace* (Routledge 1999)

Marchant R and M Page, 'The Memorandum and Disabled Children' in H Westcott and J Jones (eds), *Perspectives on the Memorandum* (Arena 1997)

Mark R, *Policing a Perplex Society* (George, Allen and Unwin 1977)

Markus T, *Buildings and Power: Freedom and Control in the Origin of Modern Building Types* (Routledge 1993)

McBarnet D, *Conviction: Law, the State and the Construction of Justice* (Macmillan 1981)

McConville M and L Marsh, *The Myth of Judicial Independence* (OUP 2020)

McConville M, A Sanders and R Leng, *The Case for the Prosecution* (Routledge 1991)

McConville M and others, *Standing Accused: The Organisation of Criminal Defence Lawyers in Britain* (Clarendon 1994)

McEwan J, 'From Adversarialism to Managerialism: Criminal Justice in Transition' (2011) 31(4) Legal Studies 519, 527

McEwan J, 'In Defence of Vulnerable Witnesses: The Youth Justice and Criminal Evidence Act 1999' (2000) International Journal of Evidence and Proof 1, 11

McKeever G, 'Comparing Courts and Tribunals through the Lens of Legal Participation' (2020) 39 Civil Justice Quarterly 217

McKenna C, 'The System of Professions: An Essay on the Division of Expert Labor' (Book Review) (2006) 80(1) Business History Review 141

McKinnon I, J Thorp and D Grubin, 'Improving the Detection of Detainees with Suspected Intellectual Disability in Police Custody' (2015) 9(4) Advances in Mental Health and Intellectual Disabilities 174

Miller L, 'A Rights-Based Argument Against the Dock' [2011] Criminal Law Review 216

Ministry of Justice, 'Achieving Best Evidence in Criminal Proceedings: Guidance on Interviewing Victims and Witnesses, and Guidance on Using Special Measures' (January 2022)

Ministry of Justice, 'Registered Intermediary Procedural Guidance Manual 2024' <https://assets.publishing.service.gov.uk/media/671b819bfc28a840abc6d26d/Registered_Intermediary_Procedural_Guidance_Manual_2024__Official_.pdf>

Ministry of Justice, 'Report on Review of Ways to Reduce Distress of Victims in Trials of Sexual Violence' (2014)

Ministry of Justice, 'The Witness Intermediary Scheme: Annual Report 2023' <https://assets.publishing.service.gov.uk/media/664487d0993111924d9d3504/Witness_Intermediary_Scheme_Annual_Report_2023.pdf>

Ministry of Justice (New Zealand), 'Communication Assistance Quality Framework' (July 2021) <https://www.justice.govt.nz/about/lawyers-and-service-providers/service-providers/communication-assistance/communication-assistance-quality-framework>

Morris R, 'The Gum Syndrome: Predicaments in Court Interpreting' [1999] Forensic Linguistics 6

Mulcahy L, 'Putting the Defendant in their Place: Why Do We Still Use the Dock in Criminal Proceedings?' (2013) 53(6) British Journal of Criminology 1139

Mulcahy L and E Rowden, *The Democratic Courthouse* (Routledge 2020)

Mulcahy L, E Rowden and W Teeder, 'Testing the Case for a Virtual Courtroom with a Physical Jury Hub Second Evaluation of a Virtual Trial Pilot Study Conducted by JUSTICE' (JUSTICE 2020)

Musson A, 'Lay Participation: The Paradox of the Jury' (2015) 3(2) Comparative Legal History 245

Nardulli P, *The Courtroom Elite* (Ballinger Publishing Company 1978)

National Appropriate Adult Network, 'About Appropriate Adults' (NAAN 2018) <https://www.appropriateadult.org.uk/information/what-is-an-appropriate-adult#act>

National Register of Public Service Interpreters (NRPSI), 'Code of Professional Conduct' <https://www.nrpsi.org.uk/for-clients-of-interpreters/code-of-professional-conduct.html>

Neuberger L, 'Fairness in the Courts: The Best We Can Do' (Address to the Criminal Justice Alliance, 10 April 2015)

New Zealand Law Commission, 'Evidence: Reform of the Law' (NZLV 1999, Report 55, vol 1)

New Zealand Law Commission, 'The Evidence of Children and Other Vulnerable Witnesses' (NZLC PP26, 1996)

Noguera S, 'Communicative Sentencing: Exploring the Perceptions of Young Offenders in the Community' (D.Phil thesis, University of Oxford 2010)

Northern Territory Government Department of Justice, 'Review of Vulnerable Witness Legislation' (Northern Territory Legal Policy Division, June 2011)

NSW Department of Communities and Justice, 'Witness Intermediary Handbook' (updated July 2024)

NSW Government, 'Expansion of Child Sexual Evidence Program Statewide to Reduce Trauma for Children' (12 October 2023) <https://www.nsw.gov.au/media-releases/child-sexual-evidence-program-reduce-trauma>

O'Grady C, 'Child Witnesses and Jury Trials: An Evaluation of the Use of Closed Circuit Television and Removable Screens in Western Australia' (Ministry of Justice 1996)

O'Hear M, 'Dispute Resolution in Criminal Law' (2007) 91(1) Marquette Law Review 1

O'Mahony B, 'How Do Intermediaries Experience their Role in Facilitating Communication for Vulnerable Defendants?' (DCrimJ thesis, University of Portsmouth 2013)
O'Mahony B and others, 'Developing a Professional Identity in a New Work Environment: The Views of Defendant Intermediaries Working in the Criminal Courts' (2016) 18(2) Journal of Forensic Practice 155
OHCHR, 'Article 13: List of Illustrative Indicators on Access to Justice' (UN 2020)
Oktay J, *Grounded Theory* (OUP 2012) 5
Ortoleva S, 'Inaccessible Justice: Human Rights, Persons with Disabilities and the Legal System' (2011) 17(2) ILSA Journal of International and Comparative Law 281
Owusu-Bempah A, *Defendant Participation in the Criminal Process* (Routledge 2016)
Owusu-Bempah A, 'Penalising Defendant Non-Cooperation in the Criminal Process and the Implications for English Criminal Procedure' (PhD thesis, University College London 2012)
Owusu-Bempah A, 'The Interpretation and Application of the Right to Effective Participation' (2018) 22(4) International Journal of Evidence and Proof 321
Owusu-Bempah A, 'Understanding the Barriers to Defendant Participation in Criminal Proceedings in England and Wales' (2020) 40(4) Legal Studies 69
Packer H, 'Two Models of the Criminal Process' (1964) 113(1) University of Pennsylvania Law Review 1
Padfield N and J Bild, *Text and Materials on the Criminal Process* (5th edn, Routledge 2016)
Papir-Bernstein W, *The Practitioner's Path in Speech and Language Pathology* (Plural Publishing Inc 2018)
Pearse J, 'Police Interviewing: The Identification of Vulnerabilities' (1995) 5(3) Journal of Community and Applied Social Psychology)
Peay J and E Player, 'Pleading Guilty: Why Vulnerability Matters (2018) 81(6) The Modern Law Review 929
Peršak N, 'Procedural Justice Elements of Judicial Legitimacy and their Contemporary Challenges' (2016) 6(3) Oñati Socio-legal Series 749
Pettitt B and others, 'At Risk, Yet Dismissed: The Criminal Victimisation of People with Mental Health Problems' (Victim Support/Mind 2013)
Pierpoint H, 'Quickening the PACE? The Use of Volunteers as Appropriate Adults in England and Wales' (2008) 18(4) Policing and Society: An International Journal of Research and Policy 397
Plater D and others, 'Providing a Voice to the Vulnerable: A Study of Communication Assistance in South Australia' (SALRI Report 16, September 2021)
Plotnikoff J and R Woolfson, 'Falling Short? A Snapshot of Young Witness Policy and Practice: A Report for the NSPCC, Revisiting "Measuring up? Evaluating Implementation of Government Commitments to Young Witnesses in Criminal Proceedings"' (NSPCC, February 2019)
Plotnikoff J and R Woolfson, *Intermediaries in the Criminal Justice System* (Policy Press 2015)
Plotnikoff J and R Woolfson, 'Registered Intermediaries in Action: Messages for the CJS from the Witness Intermediary Scheme SmartSite' (NSPCC and MoJ, December 2011)
Plotnikoff J and R Woolfson, *The Go-Between: Evaluation of Intermediary Pathfinder Projects* (Lexicon 2007)
Podgor E, 'The Tainted Federal Prosecutor in an Overcriminalized Justice System' (2010) 67 Washington and Lee Law Review 1569
Pound P, 'Law in Books and Law in Action' (1910) 44 American Law Review 12
Practice Direction No 2/2019, Case Management in the Crown Court Including Protocols for Vulnerable Witnesses and Defendants

Prison Reform Trust, 'Prison Reform Trust Response to the Ministry of Justice Consultation, Punishment and Reform: Effective Community Sentences' (June 2012)

Pritchard J, *Good Practice in the Law and Safeguarding Adults* (Jessica Kingsley Publishing 2008)

QIS, 'Procedural Manual' (Version 6: September 2024)

Queensland Courts, 'Queensland Intermediary Scheme' (18 November 2024) <https://www.courts.qld.gov.au/services/queensland-intermediary-scheme>

Queensland Courts, 'Queensland Intermediary Scheme: Information for Lawyers' (Version 4.00, September 2023) <https://www.courts.qld.gov.au/__data/assets/pdf_file/0011/679574/factsheet-info-for-lawyers.pdf>

Queensland Government, 'Intermediaries to Assist Vulnerable Witnesses to Give their Best Evidence' (December 2020) <https://www.justice.qld.gov.au/community-engagement/news/2020/intermediaries-to-assist-vulnerable-witnesses-to-give-their-best-evidence>

Queensland Government, 'Witness Intermediary Scheme for Qualified Communication Specialists' (QTenders, 27 November 2020) <https://qtenders.epw.qld.gov.au//qtenders/tender/display/tender-details.do?action=display-tender-details&id=31852&CSRFNONCE=A04926D4A19509364C0B447CBBF7735C>

Raban O, *Modern Legal Theory and Judicial Impartiality* (Routledge 2003)

Reay D, '"It's All Becoming a Habitus": Beyond the Habitual Use of Habitus in Educational Research' (2004) 25(4) British Journal of Sociology of Education 431

Reay D, G Crozier and J Clayton, 'Strangers in Paradise: Working-class Students in Elite Universities' (2009) 43(6) Sociology 1103

Redmayne M, 'Theorizing the Criminal Trial' (2009) 12(2) New Criminal Law Review 287

Reed-Danahay D, *Locating Bourdeiu* (Indiana UP 2004)

Resnik J and D Curtis, *Representing Justice: Invention, Controversy and Rights in City-states and Democratic Courtrooms* (Yale UP 2011)

Riesch A, 'Theorizing Boundary Work as Representation and Identity' (2010) 40(4) Journal for the Theory of Social Behaviour 452

Roach Anleu S and K Mack, 'Magistrates' Everyday Work and Emotional Labour' (2005) 32(4) Journal of Law and Society 590

Roach Anleu S and K Mack, *Performing Judicial Authority in the Lower Courts* (Palgrave 2017)

Roberts J, *Exploring Sentencing Practice in England and Wales* (Palgrave Macmillan 2015)

Roberts J and M Plesničar, 'Sentencing, Legitimacy, and Public Opinion' in J Tankebe and G Meško (eds), *Trust and Legitimacy in Criminal Justice: European Perspectives* (Springer 2015)

Roberts P and A Zuckerman, *Criminal Evidence* (OUP 2010)

Robson K and C Sanders, *Quantifying Theory: Pierre Bourdieu* (Springer 2009)

Rock P, *Constructing Victims' Rights: The Home Office, New Labour and Victims* (OUP 2004)

Rock P, 'Rules, Boundaries and the Courts: Some Problems in the Neo-Durkheimian Sociology of Deviance' (1998) 49(4) The British Journal of Sociology 586

Rock P, *The Social World of an English Crown Court* (Clarendon Press 1993)

Rosatti N and C Iturra, *Ley de entrevistas videograbadas. Un cambio procesal y sistémico* (Monografías 2011)

Rosen L, 'The Dock – Should It Be Abolished?' (1966) 29 Modern Law Review 289

Rowden E, 'Remote Participation and the Distributed Court: An Approach to Court Architecture in the Age of Video-Mediated Communications' (PhD thesis, University of Melbourne 2011)

Royal Commission into Institutional Responses to Child Sex Abuse, 'Final Report Recommendations' (Commonwealth of Australia 2017)

Rudes D and S Portillo, 'Roles and Powers within Federal Problem-Solving Workgroups' (2012) 34(4) Law and Policy at 420
Rudvin M, 'How Neutral is Neutral? Issues in Interaction and Participation in Community Interpreting' in G Garzone and M Viezzi (eds), *Perspectives on Interpreting* (CLUEB 2002)
Rushmer R and G Pallis, 'Inter-Professional Working: The Wisdom of Integrated Working and The Disaster of Blurred Boundaries' (2003) 23(1) Public Money and Management 59
SALRI, 'Review of the Use of Communication Partners in South Australia' (University of Adelaide, 9 March 2021)
Sanders A, 'A Community Justice. Modernising the Magistracy in England and Wales' (Institute of Public Policy Research 2000)
Sanders A, 'Core Values, the Magistracy, and the Auld Report' (2002) 29(2) Journal of Law and Society 324
Sanders A and others, 'Witnesses with Learning Disabilities: Research Findings No 44 (Home Office Research and Statistics Directorate, December 1996)
Schinkel M, 'Punishment as Moral Communication: The Experiences of Long-Term Prisoners' (2014) 16(5) Punishment and Society 578
Sciulli D, *Professions in Civil Society and the State: Invariant Foundations and Consequences* (Brill 2009)
Sentencing Council, 'Sentencing Offenders with Mental Disorders, Developmental Disorders, or Neurological Impairments' (effective from 1 October 2020)
Series L and A Nilsson, 'Article 12 CRPD: Equal Recognition before the Law' in I Bantekas, MA Stein and D Anastasiou (eds), *The UN Convention on the Rights of Persons with Disabilities: A Commentary* (OUP 2018)
Skinns L, *Police Custody: Governance, Legitimacy and Reform in the Criminal Justice Process* (Routledge 2011)
South Australian Law Reform Institute (SALRI), 'Review of the Use of Communication Partners in South Australia' (University of Adelaide, 9 March 2021)
Special Envoy of the Secretary-General on Disability and Accessibility, 'UN Experts Launch Ground-Breaking Guidance on Access to Justice for People with Disabilities' (28 August 2020) <https://www.ohchr.org/en/press-releases/2020/08/un-experts-launch-ground-breaking-guidance-access-justice-people>
Spencer J and M Lamb, *Children and Cross-Examination: Time to Change the Rules?* (Bloomsbury 2012)
Stein R and J Goodman-Delahunty, 'Bridging the Justice Gap: Inequity in Provision of Intermediary Assistance for Adults with Disabilities' (2024) Alternative Law Journal (online first, 22 December 2024)
Stephenson G and S Moston, 'Police Interrogation' (1994) 1 Psychology, Crime and Law 151
Strauss A and J Corbin, *Basics of Qualitative Research* (SAGE Publishing 1990)
Suddaby R and D Muzio, 'Theoretical Perspectives on The Professions' in L Empson and others (eds), *The Oxford Handbook of Professional Service Firms* (OUP 2015)
Sweetman P, 'Twenty-First Century Dis-ease? Habitual Reflexivity or the Reflexive Habitus' (2003) 51(4) Sociological Review 528
Taggart J, '"I Am Not Beholden to Anyone . . . I Consider Myself to be an Officer of the Court": A Comparison of the Intermediary Role in England and Wales and Northern Ireland' (2021) 25(2) The International Journal of Evidence and Proof 141
Taggart J, 'The Effective Participation of Suspects in Police Custody' (2024) 9 Criminal Law Review 590
Taggart J, 'Vulnerable Defendants and the HMCTS Court-Appointed Intermediary Services' (2022) 6 Criminal Law Review 427

Tamanha B, *Beyond the Formalist-Realist Divide: The Role of Politics in Judging* (Princeton UP 2010)

Tasmania Law Reform Institute, 'Facilitating Equal Access to Justice: An Intermediary/Communication Assistant Scheme for Tasmania?' (Final Report No 23, 2018)

Tatli A, M Ozbilgin and M Karatas-Ozkan, *Pierre Bourdieu, Organization and Management* (Routledge 2015)

The Access to Justice Knowledge Hub, 'Research on Good Practices to Ensure Effective Access to Justice for Persons with Disabilities' (15 August 2009) <https://www.ohchr.org/sites/default/files/Documents/Issues/Disability/SR_Disability/GoodPractices/Access_to_Justice_Knowledge_Hub.docx.>

The Advocate's Gateway, 'Cases' <https://www.theadvocatesgateway.org/cases>

The Advocate's Gateway, 'Ground Rules Hearings and the Fair Treatment of Vulnerable People in Court: Toolkit 1' (1 December 2016) <https://www.theadvocatesgateway.org/news/toolkit-1%3A-ground-rules-hearings>

The Advocate's Gateway, 'Intermediaries' <www.theadvocatesgateway.org/intermediaries>

The Advocate's Gateway, 'Intermediaries: Step by Step: Toolkit 16' (2 September 2019) <https://www.theadvocatesgateway.org/images/toolkits/16-intermediaries-step-by-step–2019.pdf>; <https://www.theadvocatesgateway.org/_files/ugd/1074f0_5ceb5d236c6b488e97d2cbbfbdd3cf06.pdf>

The Bach Commission, 'The Right to Justice: The Final Report of the Bach Commission' (Fabian Policy Report, September 2017)

The Danish Institute of Human Rights, 'Human Rights Indicators at Programme and Project Level' (2006, ISBN: 87-91836-06-9)

The Law Reform Commission of Western Australia, 'Project No 87: The Evidence of Children and Other Vulnerable Witnesses – Discussion Paper' (April 1990)

The Rt. Hon, The Lord Judge, Lord Chief Justice of England and Wales, 7 September 2012, at the 17th Australian Institute of Judicial Administration Conference in 'Vulnerable Witnesses in the Administration of Criminal Justice

The Special Rapporteur on the Rights of Persons with Disabilities, 'International Principles and Guidelines on Access to Justice for Persons with Disabilities' (August 2020)

Thompson Klein J, *Crossing Boundaries: Knowledge, Disciplinarities, and Interdisciplinarities* (UV Press 1996)

Tickle L, '"Justice Must Be for All": Why Court Intermediaries Are Vital for Vulnerable' *The Guardian* (London, 28 October 2020) <https://www.theguardian.com/society/2020/oct/28/justice-for-all-court-intermediaries-vulnerable-people-england-wales>

Timmermans S, 'The Cause of death vs. the Gift of Life: Boundary Maintenance and the Politics of Expertise in Death Investigation' (2002) 25(5) Sociology of Health & Illness 550

Tobin J, *The UN Convention on the Rights of the Child: A Commentary* (OUP 2019)

Tolbert P, 'Review of the Book: The System of Professions: An Essay on the Division of Labor' (1990) 35(2) Administrative Science Quarterly 410

Toone R, 'The Incoherence of Defendant Autonomy' (2005) 83(3) North Carolina Law Review 621

Touchie J, 'On the Possibility of Impartiality in Decision-Making' (2001) 1 Macquarie Law Journal 21

Turner V, *The Forest of Symbols* (Cornell UP 1976)

Tyler T, *Why People Obey the Law* (Yale UP 1990)

Tyler T and others, 'Legitimacy and Criminal Justice: International Perspective' in *Legitimacy and Criminal Justice: International Perspectives* (Russell Sage Foundation)

Ulloa V and R Acosta, 'Taking Oral Evidence in Chile from Child Victims in Priority Groups: Challenges for the Practice and Training of Justice Professionals' (2023) 27 Journal of Police and Criminal Psychology 1

Ulloa V, N Pietrasanta and R Acosta, 'Intermediaries in Chile: Facilitating the Right of Child Victims and Witnesses to Participate and Be Heard in Criminal Trials' (2022) 26(3) The International Journal of Evidence & Proof 223

UN High Commissioner for Human Rights, 'Access to Justice for Children' (A/HRC/25/35, 16 December 2013)

UN High Commissioner on Human Rights, 'Right to Access to Justice Under Article 13 of the Convention on the Rights of Persons with Disabilities: Report of the Office of the United Nations High Commissioner for Human Rights' (A/HRC/37/25, 27 December 2017)

Uviller R, 'The Neutral Prosecutor: The Obligation of Dispassion in a Passionate Pursuit' (2000) Fordham Law Review 1695

Vandenberg M, 'Process Evaluation of the Witness Intermediary Scheme Pilot' (Sprout Labs, December 2022)

Vandenhole W, G Türkelli and S Lembrecht, *Children's Rights: A Commentary on the Convention on the Rights of the Child and Its Protocols* (Edward Elgar 2019)

Victims' Commissioner, 'A Voice for the Voiceless: The Victims' Commissioner's Review into the Provision of Registered Intermediaries for Children and Vulnerable Victims and Witnesses' (January 2018)

Victims' Commissioner, 'Next Steps for Special Measures: A Review of the Provision of Special Measures to Vulnerable and Intimidated Witnesses' (May 2021)

Victoria Government, 'Intermediary Programme: About the Programme' <https://www.justice.vic.gov.au/node/3/courts-and-tribunals/intermediary-program/about-the-intermediary-program#about-intermediaries>

Victorian Law Reform Commission (VLRC), 'The Role of Victims of Crime in the Criminal Trial Process' (August 2016, IBN: 9780994372369)

Vidal Claramonte M, 'Re-presenting the "Real"' (2005) 11(2) The Translator 259

Vienna Declaration and Programme of Action, UN Doc A/CONF 157/23 (25 June 1993)

Wacquant L, 'Towards a Reflexive Sociology: A Workshop with Pierre Bourdieu' (1989) 7(1) Sociological Theory 26

Wadensjö C, *Interpreting as Interaction* (Routledge 2013)

Walker N and M Telford, 'Designing Criminal Justice: The System in Comparative Perspective, Report 14, Review of the Criminal Justice System in Northern Ireland' (London, HMSO 2000)

Walkley J, *Police Interrogation* (Police Review Publishing Co. 1987)

Ward J, *Transforming Summary Justice: Modernisation in the Lower Criminal Courts* (Routledge 2017)

Warner K, 'Child Witnesses: Evidentiary Reforms' in J Vernon (ed), *Children as Witnesses* (Proceedings of a Conference held 3–5 May 1988)

Webster E and others, '"Court Can Happen Anywhere": Courtroom Workgroup Members' Perceptions of the Challenges and Opportunities of a Transformed Workplace' (2023) 50(11) Criminal Justice and Behavior 1737

Wells W, *An Introduction to the Law of Evidence* (AB Caudell Adelaide 1991)

Westcott H, 'The Memorandum of Good Practice and Children with Disabilities' (1994) 3(2) Journal of Law and Practice 21

Western Australia Department of Justice, 'Communication Partners: Procedural Guidance Manual' (Version 1, September 2024)

Wheatcroft J, 'Witness Assistance and Familiarisation in England and Wales: The Right to Challenge' (2017) 21(1/2) International Journal of Evidence and Proof 158

Widder E, 'The Right to Challenge Witnesses – an Application of Strasbourg's Flexible 'Sole and Decisive' Rule to Other Human Rights' (2014) 3(4) Cambridge Journal of International and Comparative Law 1084

Williams G, 'Videotaping Children's Evidence' (1987) New Law Journal 108

Yates C, 'The Pigot Committee Report: Children, Evidence and Video-tape' (1990) 2 Journal of Child Law 96

Ybema S and M Horvers, 'Resistance Through Compliance: The Strategic and Subversive Potential of Frontstage and Backstage Resistance' (2017) 38(9) Organization Studies 1233

Young R, 'Exploring the Boundaries of the Criminal Courtroom Workgroup' (2013) 42 Common Law World Review 203

Index

Note: page numbers in *italics* indicate a figure and page numbers in **bold** indicate a table on the corresponding page.

FSC
www.fsc.org
MIX
Papier | Fördert gute Waldnutzung
FSC® C083411

Kolibri 360 GmbH
Ferdinand-Jühlke-Straße 7
99095 Erfurt, Deutschland
produktsicherheit@kolibri360.de